The Euro Crisis and International Liquidity Problems

The Euro Crisis and International Liquidity Problems

Dr. Debesh Bhowmik

SYNERGY

SYNERGY BOOKS INDIA

(An imprint of Bookwell Publications)

New Delhi

The Euro Crisis and International Liquidity Problems

First Edition 2014

ISBN: 978-93-82059-18-9

Synergy Books India
(An imprint of Bookwell Publications)
24/4800 Ansari Road, Darya Ganj
New Delhi-110002
Phone: 011-23268786, 23257264
Fax: 011-23281315
E-Mail: synergybooksindia@gmail.com
bookwell@vsnl.net

Printed at: Mudrak, 30A Patparganj, Delhi-110091

CONTENTS

	Preface	v
	Acknowledgement	vii
	Foreword	ix
	List of Tables and Figures	xv
1.	Euro Crisis: An introduction	1
2.	History of European Economic Community	7
3.	The Maastricht Treaty	29
4.	Euro Crisis: Macro fundamentals of Euro Area	45
5.	Euro Crisis: Impact on the developing countries	72
6.	Euro Crisis: Impact on money market	90
7.	Diagnostic Test Through Econometric Models	107
	[A] A short note on the behavior of US$/Euro exchange rate during 1999-2012	107
	[B] Euro crisis : Co-integration of fiscal deficit of euro area	117
	[C] Euro Crisis : The Nexus between growth and employment in EU	124

8.	Policies relating to Euro crisis	152
9.	Euro Crisis : Implications on International Monetary System	178
10.	Euro crisis: The concept of political economy	193
11.	Impact of Euro Crisis on Indian Economy	214
12.	International role of Euro	237
13.	The Euro as International Money	264
14.	From Recession to Recovery in EU: Problems and Prospects	275
15.	Conclusion	298
	Bibliography	302

PREFACE

Euro crisis is the hottest topic in the world economic affairs or rather in international liquidity problem because debt crisis of Euro Area particularly in some countries created the financial crisis in EU from which the existence of Euro becomes questionable, although it was originated from US financial crisis during 2008.Existence of currency area and single currency depend on the suitable and realistic policies to revive Euro to its original path of progress towards monetary and economic integration because the Euro has been playing a great role in maintaining the stability of international monetary system.

In this context, the book " The Euro Crisis and International Liquidity Problems "is very relevant in the area of international monetary issues that govern the international money. The problem of Euro crisis is not an independent issue rather it is deeply correlated with the currency hegemony in the world payment mechanism. Therefore, the book studied the historical perspective of EU and the convergence criteria, causes of Euro crisis-its various impacts, including developing countries and the implications of Euro crisis on the international monetary system , political economy concept of the crisis are of special importance. The impact on Indian Economy is added for an extra study area . The macro fundamentals and issues in money market of Euro crisis could not be avoided with sound reasons of the genesis of the problem. The international role of Euro may throw light on the genesis of international liquidity problems, as well as the euro as international money will justify the issue of international money game. The diagnostic test of the econometric analysis of the Euro crisis could not be considered as an insignificant part of the book.

The Euro Crisis brought about recession in EU from which the economy enters into recovery path. Therefore, what are the barriers and problems of recovery were sometimed efficiently through the policies taken by the union. Leaders and Policy makers are optimistic about the possible prospects of recovery from the crisis this idea is elderly explained.

Lastly, the Euro crisis has been discussed from every corner of the economic aspect of the problem relating to international liquidity issues and its root causes. The book would be able to attract researchers, professionals and policy makers as well as general readers.

Dr.Debesh Bhowmik
debeshbhowmik.weebly.com
dbhowmik.blog.com
debeshbhowmik@rediffmail.com
P.O.Pritinagar,Dist-
Nadia,WB,741247
07602072569(M)

ACKNOWLEDGEMENT

I should thank to Prof. Raj Kumar Sen (Prof. of Economics, Rabindra Bharati University, Kolkata and Ex. President, Indian Economic Association and President, International Institute for Development Studies, Kolkata), and Prof. Debendra Kumar Das (Ex.Vice President, Indian Economic Association) to encourage me constantly in writing this book. Also, I should thank to some of my friends of Bengal Economic Association and Indian Economic Association for their inspiration.

I should note that I must remember BBC, London from where the inspiration in writing the problem had been started initially.

I am very grateful to Prof. Tisdell for his nice foreword of the book.

Lastly, I must thank to Mr. Surjeet S. Khurana of the Bookwell Publishing Company, New Delhi to publish my work within a very short period.

Dr. Debesh Bhowmik

THE UNIVERSITY OF QUEENSLAND

FOREWORD

This book, *The Euro Crisis and International Liquidity Problems,* is a timely publication given the serious international financial and economic repercussions of the Euro Crisis and the economic suffering which it is causing within the EU itself. Furthermore, it is a crisis that has not yet been solved and consequently, its impacts and likely to be felt for several years to come. Dr Debesh Bhowmik, an experienced and perspective scholar, examines in depth the international liquidity and financial problems created by this crisis and considers its possible long-run consequences, such as the potential collapse of the EU and the serious weakening of the international monetary system. Also he is able to show that since the crisis, the international role of the euro has weakened whereas that of China's yuan has strengthened. Therefore, a tri-polar international monetary system is emerging dominated by the yuan, the US dollar and the euro. However, this significant book covers much more than this.

It places the development of the EU in its historical content, it examines the Maastricht Treaty and concludes that it has been a failure, and it analyses selected macroeconomic indicators in the EU to identify factors causing (or associated with) the onset of the crisis. The latter involves some comparison with the macro-situation of Japan and the United States.

Given that the world is, to a large extent, globalised economically and financially, one would expect the Euro crisis to have negative economic and financial impacts on countries outside the Euro-zone. Paying particular attention to India, Dr Bhowmik shows that the Euro crisis has had a negative impact on developing countries. It has, for example, been a drag on the economic growth of India and China. It has adversely affected the trade of developing countries, their access to finance and the level of foreign direct investment in them, and so on. Given this adverse situation, it is rather remarkable that the economies of many developing countries (such as those of India, China and Indonesia) have continued to exhibit strong growth, albeit at a lower rate than might have been expected in the absence of the Euro crisis, However, there is much more in this book.

It includes a comprehensive coverage of the consequences of the Euro crisis for the money market and for the international monetary system. It critically examines the policies that have been adopted in the EU to address the Euro crisis and shows how these policies have been influenced by the different political interests of member states and by special interest groups. The book employs both econometric methods and political economy arguments to reach its major conclusions. The global financial crisis first becomes evident in the United States. However, the Government of the United States stabilised the financial and economic situation in the United States relatively quickly by adopting interventionist policies. Nevertheless, the large public debt of the United States is a continuing issue, particularly given the stance taken by the Republican Party in demanding its substantial reduction. Nevertheless, there is hope for a political compromise which would enable the avoidance of policies designed to reduce this debt suddenly and by a large amount. Policies designed to reduce the US public debt quickly and by a large amount would result in considerable economic contraction of the American economy and would have serious negative global economic consequences.

On the other hand, less optimism exists about policies adopted in the Euro-zone to deal with its crisis. There seems little prospect of countries (such as Greece, Spain and Portugal) which have been subjected to strict fiscal discipline returning to economic prosperity in the foreseeable future. As Dr Bhowmik points out, there are continuing problems for the effective functioning of the Euro-zone.

It is important to read his book in order to gain in-depth insights into these problems and their global consequences.

Clement Tisdell, BCom (Econ), PhD, FASSA,
Professor Emeritus in Economics,
The University of Queensland
Brisbane 4072 QLD
Australia

LIST OF TABLES

Table-3.1:	The Structure : The 7 Titles of the Treaty on European Union (TEU)	32
Table-3.2:	EEC at a glance	38
Table-3.3:	Treaty chronologically	43
Table-4.1:	GDP at current prices	46
Table-4.1a:	Real GDP Growth	47
Table-4.2:	Credit Rating	48
Table-4.3:	Gross value added at basic prices: % of total	50
Table-4.4:	Inflation rate (%)	51
Table-4.5:	Current Account Balance(Euro 1000 million)	53
Table-4.6 :	Current Account Balance % of GDP	55
Table-4.7:	Exchange rate against Euro	56
Table-4.8:	Unemployment rate (%)	57
Table-4.9:	Unemployment by gender and by age(%)	59
Table-4.10:	Labour productivity (based on PPS)	60

Table-4.11:	Fiscal deficit % of GDP	61
Table-4.12:	Annual Growth rates for industry(%)	62
Table-4.13:	EU-27 trade by main partner(Euro 1000 million)	64
Table -4.14:	Debt % of GDP in EU	65
Table-4.15:	Expenditure on Social Protection (% of GDP).	66
Table-5.1:	Trade Weighs for the EER-40	77
Table-5.2:	Export and import of EU and Euro zone (value in million US$)	80
Table-5.3:	Intra trade of EU(% of regional total)	81
Table-5.4:	EU Trade with developing countries(% of total regional shares)	82
Table- 5.5:	FDI flows of EU Area	85
Table-5.6:	Indo-EU Trade	86
Table-7.A.1:	AC, PAC and Q Stat	111
Table-7. A.2:	ACF and PACF of ΔUS$/Euro	112
Table-7. A.3:	AR(1) and AR(2)	114
Table-7. A.4:	AR(1) and AR(2) in log	114
Table-7. C.1:	Cross Country Analysis of all EU countries (1988-1998)	125
Table-7. C.2:	Time series analysis-growth, employment, unemployment rate in EU	126
Table-7. C.3:	GDP and Employment annual change in EU-15 and US(1995-2003)	127
Table-7. C.4 :	Trace Statistic	137
Table-7. C.5:	Max-Eigen Statistic	137
Table-8.1:	IMF policy recommendations	171

Table-9.1:	Currency shares of foreign exchange reserves holding by % ,1923-2010	187
Table-9.2:	Currency composition of world foreign exchange reserves%	188
Table-9.3:	Selected indicators of the international use of key currencies in respect of world totals.	189
Table-11.1:	The transmission of European crisis to the Indian Economy	215
Table-11.2:	Indo-EU Trade	216
Table-11.3:	India's exports to EU	216
Table-11.4:	Exchange rate of Rupee per foreign currency and RBI's sale and purchase of US$ in the exchange market during 2010-11 and 2011-12	220
Table-11.5:	India's External debt stock	222
Table-11.6:	Composition of external debt(% of total external debt)	223
Table-11.7:	Currency composition of India's external debt and sovereign external debt	223
Table-11.8:	India's Key external debt indicators(%)	225
Table 11.9:	Key rates/ratios	230
Table-11.10:	Balance of Payments summary(USmillion dollar)	231
Table-11.11:	Foreign exchange Reserves on BOP(US$ billion)	232
Table-11.12:	EU FDI flows to India and China	233
Table-11.13:	Which countries have imposed the most harm?	235
Table-12.1:	Key data in the international role of the Euro	239
Table-12.2:	Primary market participation by foreign and official investors in EFSF bond issuance	243

Table-12.3:	Alternative measure of the supply of debt securities and the shares of major currencies.	243
Table-13.1:	Currency distribution of global foreign exchange Marke Turnover (%)	270
Table-13.2:	Share of SDR: 1981-2015	271

LIST OF FIGURES

Fig-3.1:	Inflation convergence of EU-11	39
Fig-3.2 :	Net lending to GDP ratio during Maastricht and SGP	40
Fig- 3.3:	Debt convergence(Debt / GDP during 1991-2007)	40
Fig-3.4 :	Long run Interest rate convergence of EU-11	41
Fig-4.1:	Euro Area Inflation Forecast	52
Fig-4.2:	Euro Area :Simulated Inflation Differentials	52
Fig-4.3:	Current account deficit % of GDP of Euro Area.	54
Fig- 4.4:	Current Account Balance % of GDP	55
Fig-4.5:	Bilateral Exchange Rate,1999=100	56
Fig-4.6:	The unemployment rates of Euro Area	58
Fig-4.7:	Industrial Production Index excluding construction, 2006=100	63
Fig-4.8:	Debt and FD of EU	65
Fig-4.9:	Saving Balance as a share of GDP.	67
Fig-5.1:	Euro Area export;2008=100	74
Fig-5.2:	Real Exchange rate,CPI deflated,Q1,1999=100	76
Fig- 5.3:	Sovereign CDS spread	78
Fig- 5.4:	Growth rate of S-5	79
Fig- 5.5:	Total LIC export	83
Fig- 5.6:	FDI flows from advanced countries	83

Fig-5.7:	World Trade in major global crises(Pre crisis level=100)	88
Fig-5.8:	Proportion of the world economy in recession, 1901-2008(in %)	88
Fig-6.1:	Implied volatility on 3-month EURIBOR rate and Evolution of 3 month EURIBOR rate	91
Fig-6.2:	Market liquidity in the option market with respect to last year.	91
Fig-6.3:	Gross issuance of Euro-denominated short term securities by issuing sector since August-2005	92
Fig-6.4:	Growth in STEP and ECP outstanding amount	93
Fig-6.5:	Sovereign Credit Default Swap Spreads (five year tenor,in basis points)	95
Fig-6.6:	Swap spreads of EU	96
Fig-6.7:	Euro Area: Corporate Bond Market	96
Fig-6.8:	Sovereign Credit Default Swaps,2007 Dec-2012Jan.	97
Fig-6.9:	10 Year Government Bond Yields (% per annum), 1990Oct-2011Dec.	98
Fig-6.10:	Credit default	100
Fig-6.11:	Net Balance with Euro system	100
Fig-6.12:	Econia volume and ECB deposit facility and interest rate	101
Fig- 7.A.1:	Linear trend line of US$/Euro	108
Fig-7.A.2 :	US$/Euro exchange rate	108
Fig-7.A.3:	US$/Euro exchange rate on quarterly data	109
Fig-7.A.4:	Nominal Effective Exchange Rate of Euro	109
Fig-7.A.5:	REER of Euro	110
Fig-7.A.6:	ACF and PACF of US$/Euro	112
Fig-7.A.7:	ACF and PACF of first difference series of US$/ Euro	113
Fig-7.B.1:	The path of fiscal deficit of Euro area	117
Fig-7.B.2 :	Trend line of Fiscal deficit of Euro area.	118
Fig-7.B.3:	The equilibrium of co-integration	120
Fig-7.B.4:	Equilibrium error of logarithmic model	121

Fig- 7.B.5: Equilibrium of ECM model. 122
Fig-7.C.1: The correlation between GDP growth and employment change:EU-15 127
Fig-7.C.2: The correlation between GDP growth and employment change: USA 128
Fig- 7.C.3: Trend of unemployment of EU 129
Fig-7.C.4: Scatter Diagram of U and G 133
Fig-7.C.5: Loess Fit 133
Fig-7.C.6: Kernel Fit 134
Fig-7.C.7: Fitted Curves of U and G 135
Fig-7.C.8: Equilibrium of U and G 136
Fig-7.C.9: Impulse response function of ÄG and ÄU 140
Fig-7C.10: Impulse Response Function in two graph and variance decomposition 141
Fig-7.C.11: Impulse Response Function in multiple graph 142
Fig-7.C.12: IRF in two graph 142
Fig-8.1: Stock market and swap spread 163
Fig-8.2: Hell holes 164
Fig-8.3: Debts in European Redemption Fund 175
Fig-9.1: Share of trade and GDP 182
Fig-9.2: Percentage shares of selected countries and areas in world GDP ,1870-2050(at 2005PPP exchange rate) 182
Fig-9.3: Currency composition and foreign claims 183
Fig- 9.4: Nominal exchange rate of currencies against dollar, 2005-2011 188
Fig-11.1: India's earnings from IT sectors 217
Fig-11.2: India's monthly exports to EU, Japan and US 218
Fig-11.3: India's monthly trade openness 218
Fig-11.4: Impact on GDP growth during EU crisis 228
Fig-11.5: Indian Fiscal deficit % of GDP
Fig-12.1: Currency composition of global foreign exchange reserves 241

Fig -12.2: Stock of international debt securities (narrow measure):outstanding amounts and currency shares 244

Fig -12.3: Settlement volumes and currency breakdown in the CLS system 246

Fig-12.4: Net shipments of euro banknotes to destinations outside the euroarea 247

Fig -12.5: Foreign currency brought into and taken out of the Russia by authorized banks 248

Fig -12.6: Euro area profile liabilities 250

Fig -12.7: External liabilities:government bonds and notes 251

Fig -12.8: External portfolio liabilities 252

Fig -12.9: Global foreign public debt selected currency shares 256

Fig -12.10: Estimated contributions to changes in the shares of the US dollar and the pound sterling in global foreign public debt between 1918 to 1932 257

Fig-13.1: Global importance of the US Dollar (%)(as on November,2010) 265

Fig-13.2: Global distribution of foreign exchange reserves. 270

Fig-14.1: On Track 277

Fig-14.2: Two-speed rebound 277

Fig-14.3: Trade Return 278

Fig-14.4: GDP Growth Contribution,2012 279

Fig-14.5: Annual Change in EA17 Structural Balance (% of GDP) 280

Fig-14.6: Returning to Pre-Crisis Unemployment Rates 281

Fig-14.7: Euro Area :Headline Inflation(%) 282

Fig-14.8: Private Consumption and Consumer Confidence, Euro Area 283

Fig-14.9: Purchasing Managers' Indices for UK,Germany, France,Italy and Spain 284

Fig-14.10: Government deficit(% of GDP),2011 289

Fig -14.11: Structural Balance(%GDP),2011 290

APPENDIX

Table- 4.A-1:	Euro Area:Main Economic Indicators, 2007-2014(%)	69
Table-4.A-2:	Euro Area:Balance of Payments	70
Table -4A-3:	Euro Area:Main Economic Indicators(% change)	71
Table -7.CA.1:	Growth rates of Euro Area	151
Table -7.CA.2:	Unemployment rate of EU-16 during 2001-2001	151
Table-12A.1:	Currency composition of foreign exchange reserves for selected countries	261
Table-12A.2:	Outstanding international debt securities by currency	262
Table-12A.3:	International dimensions of euro denominated debt securities	263
Table-14A.1:	Standard and Poor's European Economic Forecast	295
Table-14A.2:	Impact of final measures 2012-16,deviations from baseline.	296
Table-14A.3:	Euro Area Debt Dynamics	296

Figures

Fig-6A.1:	Bank lending to corporations and private households for selected countries in the Euro Area	106
Fig-7.AA-1:	Cycles of Dollar-Euro and Dollar-Yen rate	116
Fig-8A.1:	TARGET2	177

Fig-8A.2: EU Redemption Fund 177

Fig-12.2: Stock of international debt securities (narrow measure):outstanding amounts and currency shares 244

Fig-12.3: Settlement volumes and currency breakdown in the CLS system 246

Fig-12.4: Net shipments of euro banknotes to destinations outside the euroarea 247

Fig-12.5: Foreign currency brought into and taken out of the Russian Federation by authorized banks 248

Fig-12.6: Euro area profile liabilities 250

Fig-12.7: External liabilities:government bonds and notes 251

Fig-12.8: External portfolio liabilities 252

Fig-12.9: Global foreign public debt selected currency shares 256

Fig-12.10: Estimated contributions to changes in the shares of the US dollar and the pound sterling in global foreign public debt between 1918 to 1932 257

CHAPTER-1

EURO CRISIS : AN INTRODUCTION

The financial and economic crisis that started as a private (sub-prime) debt crisis spilling from the USA to Europe in 2007 reached new dimensions in 2011. In 2011, the crisis became more complex as concerns about the sustainability and potential restructuring of public finances created new tensions in financial markets. The problems that appeared already in Greece and Ireland in 2010 spilled over to other countries in 2011, putting a halt to and in some cases reversing capital flows and financial integration and threatening the foundations of European monetary integration. As the crisis evolved, it has become increasingly complex, and different feedback mechanisms created a vicious circle linking public sector finances with the banking sector and financial markets, with adverse consequences also spilling over to the real economy. Given the significant sovereign debt exposures of EU banks, the sovereign debt troubles multiplied the concerns about banks' liquidity and solvency. Concerns about the financial position of banks, as well as a lack of market transparency on their actual position, made funding more expensive and harder to obtain in the second half of the year. The interbank market dried up even further. Increased risks in the banking sector reinforced the stress in the sovereign debt markets, creating a dangerous vicious circle. The complex intertwined relationship between financial and sovereign debt markets, as well as adverse feedback effects to the real economy, complicated the solution to the crisis and called for policy action on different fronts. The financial integration process in Europe has, as a result of the crisis, partly been halted or indeed reversed in some segments of the market. Cross-border capital flows have fallen sharply.

US financial crisis and Euro crisis have tremendous unfavourable impact on the ongoing process of the international trade and finance which had an implication on the international monetary system too. To add more addressing to Euro crisis which is almost creating monetary chaos in Europe as well as in the world disrupting financial system too and had weakened the role of euro in euro area as well as in international trade and finance.

The international role of the euro was relatively resilient in 2011when compared with other major international currencies, despite the impact of the euro area sovereign debt crisis on some financial market segments and foreign investors' reduced appetite for the securities issued by a number of euro area Member States. We can simply clarify the role of Euro and its strength of crisis in international arena in trade and finance.

Let us have a quick overlook on the statistical evidences on euro. The global holding of foreign exchange reserves as percent of currency shares in foreign exchange reserves of Euro declined from 27.2% in 2002 to 25.5% in 2009 and further declined to 25.0% in 2011 as against of 62.1% of US$ in 2002 which stepped up to 66.1% in 2007 and stayed at 62.1% in 2011 but holdings of Yen was 6.2% in 2002 which fell down to 4.4% in 2007 and again declined to 3.7% in 2011.To note that the currency shares of holding of Euro by UK was 64.4% in 2007 which continually decreased to 59.1% in 2011.On the contrary, the USA holds the Euro of 37.9% in 2007 which increased to 53.5% in 2011.

The outstanding debt securities of Euro has stepped down from 26.2% in 2009 to 25.7% in 2011 where as it was 24.7% in 2000.On the other hand, the outstanding debt securities of US$ was 40.8% in 2000 which steadily declined to 38.6% in 2011 with the similar trends of Yen from 22.1% in 2000 to 16.0% in 2011 which was a significant impact of Euro crisis.

During 2009-2011,North America's outstanding international bonds and notes in terms of Euro was highest but decreasing from

23.0% to 19.1%, followed by International Organisations holding increasing trends from 7.7% to 12.2% ,followed by Offshore centres and Asia Pacific countries. But, the outstanding international bonds and notes in terms of US$ by Offshore centres ranked one and held 22.7% in 2009 to 20.3% in 2011,followed by Asia Pacific countries holding 10.7% in 2009 and 11.2% in 2011 and by Latin America holding 6.1% in 2009 and 7.2% in 2011 and then by International Organisations and North America. Again, the outstanding international bonds and notes in terms of Yen was 26.7% held by Euro Area in 2009 which stepped down to 24.0% in 2011, followed by Offshore centres from 18.9% to 18.45% and by North America from 17.6% to 14.1% during the specified period.

The Euro Area is holding the total outstanding international bonds and notes amounting to 2120 billion US$ at the end of 2011 in which 57.7% was in terms of US$. On the contrary, USA held 779 billion US$ outstanding international bonds where 60.6% was in terms of Euro. Japan's outstanding international bonds consists of 78 billion US$ in which only 13.2% is in terms of Euro and 73.6% is in terms of US $.As a whole 10619 billion US$ was the outstanding international bonds and notes at the end of 2011 in which 50% was in terms of US$ and 25.1% was in terms of Euro and 6.2% was in terms of Yen.

The external impact of Euro crisis is nearly little because 69% international Euro denominated debt securities is held by resident which was issued by the resident and the rest is held by non-resident and this figure was just one percent less in 2010.

The outstanding international loans by Euro as percent of outstanding amount at constant exchange rate was 21.4% in 2008 ,20.2% in 2010,21.8% in 2011 respectively in comparison to US$ as 56.1% in 2008,58.1% in 2010, 56.6% in 2011 and to Yen as 18.9% in 2008,19.2% in 2010 and 19.0% in 2011 respectively.

On the other hand, the outstanding international deposits by Euro as percent of outstanding amount was 20.3% in 2008,21.2% in 2010, 22.4% in 2011 in comparison to US$ as 59.9% in 2008,60.4% in 2010 , 61.1% in 2011 and to Yen as 2.3% in 2008,1.3% in 2010 and 1.4% in 2011 respectively. In spite of the crisis, Euro's share of international exports and imports had increased too from 63.8% exports in 2008 to 66.7% in 2011 and 47.5% imports in 2008 to 50.2% in 2011 respectively including the export and import shares of services.

Analysing the above bubble in international financial market after a setback of international role of euro, how much the Euro crisis can disrupt international integration and monetary system can be judged in the following salvation process.

In this context, somebody may ask, is there any contradiction in the economic integration towards the process of economic development whether it is capitalistic or socialistic?

I have a general view, the economic integration consists of three stages,namely,[i] trade integration,[ii] monetary integration,[iii] political integration.

In the 1990s,the socialist economic integration was observed in CMEA countries in USSR and in East Europe but the process of economic integration was immature containing mismatch of economic criteria including delink of stages of economic integration, so that system collapsed within a short period of time.

Hence the question arises, has economic integration a wrong signal to the capitalistic integration process too as had been observed in the Euro Area since the European debt crisis turned to financial crisis and created the possibility of break down of single currency Euro and as well as break down of Euro Area. If so, what wrong with the single currency in the economic bloc? Should we introduce more convergence criteria and classify more economic fields of integration?(like banking union as proposed by EC).If there is added into the economic system, then how long economic integration process sustain in Euro Area which can adjust with the international monetary system.?Obviously, it is a billion dollar question. Because, the currency unions in the world economic blocs are not fully sustainable in the WTO process towards trade integration and became an odd man out in the international monetary system. Reforming international monetary system through inclusion of currency areas led de facto rules of the game of international monetary system and breaking the minimum laws of optimum principles of economic integration of currency areas. So, will the multilateral trading and monetary framework will sustain through the model of economic integration or not or will the developed currency areas adjust with weak currency areas harmoniously in maintaining the stability of international monetary system?

In this context, would political supremacy or leadership through bloc or economic areas or currency areas emerge and would political integration fail even in the road map of forming an international money? So, contradiction prevails within the system. Thus why, economic integration is a myth towards a world monetary system for a single international currency whether it is in the form of socialistic or in the form of capitalistic process of development.

If Euro abolishes through break down of Euro Area as an effect of policy failures, then a new currency basket in SDR in international monetary system should be reconstituted and the hegemony of leading international currency must be reborn through calculating new weights of the selected currencies in the SDR and bi-lateral exchange rates in the flexible manner might appear in the international currency market.

In this context, European Commission of EU faces clearly two distinct policies, namely,[i] economic and monetary policies for Euro Area and non-Euro Area.,[ii] a separate policies for EU-27.EU parliament could not match two types of policies simultaneously for economic integration process in the bloc. No general consensus is achieved for Euro and non-Euro Areas in preventing from Euro debt crisis on the debt ridden countries.

On the other hand, the role of EU in the IMF as well as in stabilizing international monetary system, is diverging with USA and other EU member states on formulating policies relating to solution of Euro-debt crisis or on any bail-out programme so far.

If the revival of Euro fails and the reform of new SDR became certain and the hegemony or leadership is unchallenged in the international monetary system, then the initiative of 'dollar as the lender of the last resort' function in the IMF might be succeed through political hegemony of USA and US-led economies and blocs.

Since the US Dollar occupies the largest share in SDR and in Quota in IMF, then the domination of Dollar would revive and in unilateralism would prevalent under the super structure of multilateralism in international trade and payment system. With obvious reason, the real currency competitor would become Chinese Yuan, German DM and UK's Pound Sterling followed by Yen. The revival of Bretton Woods in international monetary system in stead of Bretton Wood-III might be greater possibility. We did not forget that the USSR had collapsed and likewise EU would break down if the crisis was not solved through the policy formation of European Commission and European Parliament by reforming the Maastricht Treaty.

In spite of flexible exchange rate system ,the fixation of bilateral exchange rate manipulation through currency dictatorship and through domination in money market would prevail .Then world trade share in terms of US Dollar would go up in favour of USA.

Of course, then, the question would arise towards the formation of anchor currency's (unit of account) standard whether it would be in terms of gold or any other numeraire. This debate is quite unsolved uptill now since the inception of the international monetary system. Will this problem be solved through the formation of European Monetary Fund?

References

Bhowmik, Debesh., 2003, *Essays on International Money*, Deep and Deep, NewDelhi

ECB, 2012, *International Role of Euro*, Eurostat.

European Commission, 2012, *European Financial Stability and Integration Report-2011*, April, 2012, Brussels.

CHAPTER-2

HISTORY OF EUROPEAN ECONOMIC COMMUNITY

An Introduction to European cooperation

After the end of the Second World War, the desire for economic and political union grew stronger in Western Europe. As early as September 1946, the British statesman Winston Churchill (1874-1965) referred in a speech to his vision of a 'United States of Europe'. In 1950, the French Foreign Minister, Robert Schuman (1886-1963) set out his ideas for a united Europe. In response to this initiative, the governments of the Benelux States and of France, Italy and the Federal Republic of Germany signed a treaty establishing the European Coal and Steel Community (ECSC) in Paris on 18 April 1951. The idea of founding the ECSC came from the Commissioner-General of the French National Planning Board, Jean Monnet (1888-1979), who also became the first President of the High Authority of the ECSC in 1952. After a projected European Defence Community had been thwarted by the opposition of the French National Assembly in 1954, efforts were focused on the creation of a Common Market. On 25 March 1957, the ECSC Member States signed the Treaties of Rome, the aim of which was the establishment of a common European market without customs duties or quantitative restrictions in the framework of a European Economic Community (EEC), combined with a European Atomic Energy Community (Euratom). The key objectives set out in the Treaties of Rome – a common market, freedom of movement and common agricultural, trade and competitive policies. In 1963, Charles de Gaulle (1890-1970), President of the French Republic, and Konrad Adenauer (1876-1967), Chancellor of the Federal Republic of Germany, signed the Franco-German Treaty of Friendship, which was to become the political engine of the European integration process.

In 1972, the United Kingdom, Ireland and Denmark acceded to the Communities.In 1970, the Member States of the EEC agreed on closer coordination of their foreign policies in the framework of a system of European political cooperation (EPC). In addition, a Franco-German initiative led to the creation of a European monetary system (EMS) with a common exchange-rate mechanism, which entered into force on 1 January 1979, and with the declared aim of establishing economic and monetary union.

In the 1980s and 1990s, the European integration process experienced a powerful upsurge, which is primarily associated with the names of France's President François Mitterrand (1916-1996), and the German Chancellor Helmut Kohl (born 1930). In the European Parliament, they played a key role in decisions taken in December 1985 to complete the internal market by 1992, to extend the principle of majority voting within the Council and to integrate European political cooperation into the legal framework of the EEC. Further important milestones were the accession of Spain and Portugal to the European Communities on 1 January 1986 and the drafting of the Single European Act, which supplemented and amended the Treaties of Rome and entered into force in 1986. At the beginning of 1995, the accession of Austria, Finland and Sweden brought the number of Member States of the European Union to 15.

The fall of the Berlin Wall on 9 November 1989 and the collapse of Communist rule in Central and Eastern Europe opened a new chapter in the process of European unification. In order to support the reform process, the EU concluded association agreements, known as Europe Agreements, with countries of Central and Eastern Europe in the early 1990s.

In February 1992, the Maastricht Treaty established a European Union as a "new stage in the process of creating an ever closer union among the peoples of Europe". In Maastricht finally, on 1 January

2002, the euro was introduced as a single European currency. The driving force behind this project was Jacques Delors' (born 1925), who presided over the Commission for many years. In view of the forthcoming eastward enlargement of the Union, the Treaties required further reform. In December 2000, the European Council agreed in the Treaty of Nice that voting by qualified majority would henceforth be the norm for Council decisions and that the composition and working methods of the Commission would be adapted to take account of the new situation after enlargement.

The chronological history of the European Union

1950: French Foreign Minister Robert Schuman proposes integrating the coal and steel industries of Western Europe. This leads to the Treaty of Paris, creating the European Coal and Steel Community (ECSC),in 1951, with six members: Belgium, France, Italy, Luxembourg, the Netherlands and West Germany.

1957: The same six countries sign the Treaties of Rome, creating the European Economic Community (EEC) and the European Atomic Energy Community(EURATOM). They begin removing trade barriers between them and move towards creating a 'common market'.

1967: The institutions of the EEC, ECSC and EURATOM are merged to form a single set of institutions: the European Commission, European Council and European Parliament (with members selected initially by national parliaments).

1973: Denmark, Ireland and the United Kingdom join the European Community.

1979: The first direct elections to the European Parliament take place, with voters in each EU Member State electing the members.

1981: Greece joins the European Community (EC).

1986: Portugal and Spain join the European Community.

The Single European Act is signed by EU governments, providing for the creation of a single market in which people, goods, capital and services can move freely around the EC.

1992: The Treaty of Maastricht is signed, creating the European Union and introducing new forms of cooperation between Member

State governments –for example, on defence and justice and home affairs issues.EU leaders also agree to create an Economic and Monetary Union, with a single currency managed by a European Central Bank, within a decade.

The Single Market is formally completed, but much work remains to be done to make the promise of free movement of people, goods, capital and services a reality.

1995: Austria, Finland and Sweden join the European Union (EU).

1999: Europe's single currency - the euro - is officially launched and 11 EU Member States adopt it as their official currency, forming what is known as the euro zone.

2001: Greece joins the euro zone. The Treaty of Nice is signed, introducing reforms to the EU's institutions to prepare for the expansion of the Union with the admission of ten new Member States in 2004.

2002: The euro becomes a reality on 1 January, when euro notes and coins replace national currencies in 12 of the 15 countries which are members of the EU: Austria, Belgium, Finland, France, Germany, Greece, Ireland, Italy, Luxembourg, the Netherlands, Portugal and Spain.

A 'convention on the future of Europe' is launched, with 105 members representing national governments and parliaments in the Member States and countries waiting to join the EU, the European Commission and the European Parliament.

2003: The convention ends and submits its draft 'Treaty establishing a Constitution for the European Union' to EU leaders. Member State governments begin negotiations on the proposals.

2004: Ten new countries join the EU, including eight from eastern and central Europe. They are: Cyprus, the Czech Republic, Estonia, Hungary, Latvia, Lithuania, Malta, Poland, Slovakia and Slovenia.EU leaders reach agreement on the Constitutional Treaty, which brings all the previous EU Treaties together in one document and introduces changes to the way the Union works. EU leaders argue these changes are needed to ensure that the Union can continue to operate effectively as it grows. Member States are given two years to ratify the Constitutional Treaty. As with all EU Treaties, it can only come into force if it is approved by all 25 Member States.

2005: Referenda are held on the Constitutional Treaty in four countries: Luxembourg and Spain vote in favour, but France and the Netherlands vote against. EU leaders launch a 'period of reflection' to consider how best to proceed in the light of the No votes.

2006: By June 2006, 15 of the EU's 25 Member States have ratified the Treaty. The European Council agrees a timetable for deciding what to do next. It calls for:

- EU leaders to adopt a political declaration setting out Europe's values and ambitions and confirming their shared commitment to deliver them, at a ceremony to commemorate the 50th anniversary of the founding of the EU on25 March 2007.
- Germany, which holds the Presidency of the Union in the first half of 2007, presented a report to EU leaders at the June European Council assessing the state of the discussions on the Constitutional Treaty and exploring possible options for the future.

A final decision was taken by the end of 2008 to prevent future violent conflicts in Europe after World War-II to tie countries together by forging closer industrial and economic co-operation. Since then, the EU's responsibilities have grown in response to new challenges and many more countries have joined. In 2009,Lisbon treaty was signed where the institutional reform were more qualified majority voting closer economic coordination between EMU member states. In 2010,EU crisis started and EMU countries agreed on support programmes for Greece and other EMU countries under EFSM and EFSF. Lastly, in 2011,the ESM treaty was signed.

How the EU works

Three main institutions are responsible for the day-to-day running of the European Union: the European Commission, the Council of the European Union and the European Parliament. Two other bodies - the European Court of Justice and the European Court of Auditors - play key roles in, respectively, ensuring that EU laws are upheld and that the EU budget is spent properly. The European Central Bank is responsible for managing the Euro.

European Commission

This is the EU's executive or 'civil service'. It has four main roles:

- To propose new EU laws;
- To manage and implement EU policies and the budget;
- To enforce European law (with the European Court of Justice);

To represent the EU on the international stage, negotiate international agreements on behalf of the EU as a whole in some policy areas. Every five years, a new President and members of the Commission (currently one from each of the EU's 27 Member States) are nominated by EU governments and approved by the European Parliament. Each Commissioner is responsible for a specific area of EU policy, and has a small private office and a department staffed by permanent EU officials based in Brussels.

The Commission is politically answerable to the European Parliament, which has the power to dismiss the President and members by adopting a motion of censure. Under the Lisbon Treaty, the number of European Commissioners would be reduced to two-thirds of the number of EU Member States, serving on a rotational basis.

Council of the European Union

The Council, in its various formations, has six main responsibilities:

- To pass EU laws .
- To coordinate the broad economic policies of the EU's Member States;
- To conclude international agreements between the EU and other countries or international organisations;
- To approve the EU's budget, jointly with the European Parliament;
- To develop the EU's Common Foreign and Security Policy;

- To coordinate cooperation between national courts and police forces in criminal matters.

Most of these responsibilities relate to areas where EU Member States have agreed to share their sovereignty and delegate decision-making powers to the EU. However, in the last two, Member States have only delegated very limited powers to the Union, but have agreed to work together on a range of issues (a process known as 'intergovernmental cooperation').

These powers would be increased under the Lisbon Treaty. A new post of High Representative of the Union for Foreign Affairs and Security Policy would also be created, plus the EU's own diplomatic service, in a move designed to enhance its influence on the international stage.

In many policy areas, the Council takes decisions by 'Qualified Majority Vote', a system under which each country has a number of votes roughly proportionate to the size of its population. Under the Lisbon Treaty, the EU would switch to a 'double majority' voting system, with proposals requiring the support of at least 55% of the EU's Member States representing at least 65% of the Union's population to become law. But the most sensitive issues, including changes to the EU Treaties and decisions on admitting new countries to the EU , are decided by a unanimous vote, giving each country the right to veto proposals single-handedly. The Lisbon Treaty would reduce the number of issues decided by unanimity, extending majority voting to around 50 new legislative areas.

The Council is chaired by each Member State in turn, for six months at a time, under a system known as the rotating Presidency. Under the Lisbon Treaty, the new President of the European Council would chair EU summits and the EU's foreign policy chief would chair foreign ministers' meetings, but the rotating Presidency would be retained for all other Council meetings.

European Parliament

The European Parliament represents the EU's citizens and its members (MEPs) are directly elected by them every five years. Every EU citizen who is registered to vote is entitled to do so.

The present Parliament, which was elected in June 2004, has 785 members from all 27 EU Member States.

MEPs represent all the different views on the EU, from those strongly in favour of closer European integration to those who want their countries to leave the EU.

The Parliament has four main roles:

- To pass EU laws, jointly with the Council, in many policy areas;
- To exercise democratic supervision over the other EU institutions;
- To approve or reject the budget proposed by the Council.
- To agree, with the Council, on the admission of new countries to the EU.

The Parliament is the only EU institution which is fully open to public scrutiny: it meets in public and its debates, opinions and resolutions are published.

Under the Lisbon Treaty, the number of MEPS would be reduced to 750, plus the Parliament's President. The Parliament's role would also be boosted by giving it joint decision-making powers in more policy areas.

Who decides?

Although the European Commission proposes new laws, it is the Council of the European Union and the European Parliament that decide to adopt them or not. In areas where these two institutions have joint decision-making powers, proposals go through a process of negotiation designed to produce agreement on the final shape of the legislation. This can be a lengthy process lasting many months or years.

European Court of Justice

This Luxembourg-based court is made up of judges from each Member State and is responsible for ensuring that Member States abide by the laws they agreed to in Brussels and that EU law is interpreted and applied in the same way in each Member State.

European Court of Auditors

This Luxembourg-based court is made up of representatives from each Member State and monitors the way the EU budget is spent. It is responsible for ensuring that EU funds are properly collected and are spent legally, economically and for their intended purpose.

The European Union budget

The EU's policies, programmes and activities are funded by a budget to which the 27 Member States contribute. The higher a country's national wealth, the more money its Government puts towards the EU's running costs every year.

The road toward the European Union

The Single European Act modified the EEC Treaties in 1987 by increasing the powers and the role of the European Parliament. The president of the Commission, French socialist Jacques Delors was the leading figure. Presumably, he had the full support of the then French President François Mitterrand who is believed to have been one of the most decisive actors in European policies during the 1980s. François Mitterrand proposed to other partners of the EEC the creation of 'European social Space' motivated by 'the idea that Europe will be socialist or nothing'. By 1993 the single market came into effect establishing mostly free movement of goods, services, capital, and people within the EC.

The Treaty of the European Union (known as the Maastricht Treaty) came into effect on 1 November 1993, giving more power to the European institutions and establishing the European Community (EC) now European Union (EU). The EU's structure is based on three pillars. The first pillar consist an expanded European Community. The second pillar is Common Foreign and Security Policy (CFSP) and the third pillar of the EU is Justice and Home Affairs. After a successful establishment, the EU sought further enlargement. On 1 January 1995 Austria, Finland and Sweden joined the EU taking the membership to fifteen. The peaceful reunification of Germany and the violent dismembering of the Soviet Union effected EU's enlargement. By this time, the eastern European countries previously under the Soviet domination were seeking to join the Union. Following the 1995 enlargement the Treaty of Amsterdam (1997) and the Treaty of Nice (2001) were signed giving more power to the EU institutions and paving the way for further enlargements.

On 1 May 2004 eight countries of central and eastern Europe joined the EU – the Czech Republic, Estonia, Latvia, Lithuania, Hungary, Poland, Slovenia and Slovakia. In contrast with the 1995 enlargement which seems to have been a fairly smooth process considering that Austria, Finland and Sweden had already advanced economies the 2004 enlargement was a difficult process. Although the 2004 expansion was seen as problematic and the EU constitution was rejected by French and Dutch voters in May and June 2005, respectively the enlargement process did not stop. Indeed, in December 2004, the EU concluded accession negotiations with Bulgaria and Romania, and on 1 January 2007, they both formally joined the EU, increasing the Union to 27 member states and completing the fifth enlargement since 1957. This enlargement stretched the borders of the EU to the Black Sea and increased the population of the Union to over 470 million.

Following of yet another successful enlargement the Treaty of Lisbon (also known as the Reform Treaty) was signed. The Treaty was signed on 13 December 2007 and is expected to be ratified by the end of 2008. The Reform Treaty amends the current treaties by giving more powers to EU institutions. Yet, the EU's parliament is 'often dismissed as weak'. Moreover, although the EU integration has been regarded as a political process from the very start, 'for most of the past fifty years the economic giant has often looked like a political dwarf'.

The dual source of European monetary unification

The European Economic Community (EEC), the predecessor of today's European Union (EU) was created in 1957. At its core was the establishment of a common market. The EEC focused on the establishment of four freedoms within it, namely the free movement of goods, capital, services and people. Monetary fluctuations were quite obviously potentially harmful, as they could provoke severe trade distortions among the different members of the zone. In the late 1960s and early 1970s – the EEC's internal customs union was still very young: it had only been achieved in 1967. Besides the customs union, the EEC of the 1960s had a flagship policy: the common agricultural policy (CAP). This system of agricultural protection and subsidy, entered into force in 1962, had one important feature: the establishment of common price levels for agricultural products. It is again easy to foresee how complex life would become with such a common price in the event of monetary fluctuations.

And here indeed was the key: all these early developments of European integration happened in a monetary co-operation, that of a stable Bretton Woods system. The common market and the CAP were not endangered by the theoretical risk of monetary fluctuations since it was yet still largely inexistent - or at the very least under control. Conversely this meant that once the international monetary system entered into crisis, the entire EEC system threatened to collapse. Hence, if increased monetary cooperation was perhaps desirable in itself, and if some dreamed of a future European single currency, the need to protect the achievements of the EEC - the common market and the CAP in particular - constituted the decisive trigger for action. On various occasions in the 1960s, 1970s and 1980s, ingenious plans were thus devised in order to improve European economic and monetary cooperation: the Barre memoranda in the 1960s; the Werner plan in the early 1970s calling for the creation of an Economic and Monetary Union in three stages, and contributing to the inception of the so-called 'snake' (a mechanism whereby currencies were allowed to fluctuate within limited margins), the European monetary system (EMS) from 1979 onwards; as well as various plans suggesting the inception of a parallel currency (the 1975 All Saints' Day Manifesto of *The Economist* for instance). They all shared a similar concern: that of stabilising monetary relations in Europe, and thereby stabilising the EEC itself. But why did monetary cooperation, from the late 1970s onwards, manage to become one of the lagship endeavours of the EEC/EU, if not of European integration as such? The answer lies in the political impetus associated with European monetary integration.

The second major source of European monetary unification in the second half of the twentieth century was the affirmation of the EEC on the international scene. In the late 1960s and early 1970s, the decision to prioritise EMU partly came from the perceived need for a new bold step in European integration. The EEC heads of government, on the occasion of The Hague summit in December 1969, thus decided to set up the Werner Committee in order to discuss EMU plans further. Similarly, the creation of the EMS had a lot to do with the affirmation of Europe as an international actor. Confronted with perceived US economic and monetary mismanagement, the EEC decided to respond at the regional level. Facing the fall of the dollar, Helmut Schmidt, the then West German Chancellor, thus declared that it was "urgently necessary that the Europeans say to the Americans, that's not going to carry on." The West German Chancellor managed to convince his European partners that the creation of a European monetary bloc would contribute to improving monetary stability in spite of transatlantic tensions. Finally, all the debates linked to currencies in the EEC, from the obscure units of accounting used for CAP purposes to the ECU and the euro, were all strongly related to questions of European identity. A distinct organisation such as the EEC/ EU, it was often purported, needed to assert its identity by having its own currency.

But the affirmation of Europe as an international actor was not only a voluntary move. Quite often, external crises spurred European (re-)action. As mentioned above, West German perception of US economic and monetary mismanagement in the late 1970s convinced Helmut Schmidt that a move at the European regional level was necessary, yet prior to this external trigger for action, the West German Chancellor was little interested in taking a step further in European monetary cooperation. Even earlier, the collapse of the Bretton Woods system in the early 1970s both condemned the implementation of the Werner plan and rendered even more salient the need to stabilise monetary relations in Europe. A near-fixed exchange rate system such as the snake, the economic development of which members often differed greatly over, could not work amidst strong international monetary fluctuations; but these strong fluctuations further stressed the need to have a zone of monetary stability in Europe, so as to protect, among others, its trade and its agricultural policy. These two dimensions were well summarised by Valéry Giscard d'Estaing, then French Finance Minister, in January 1974:

> "If the international monetary system was itself based on fixed exchange rates and on currency convertibility the problem would

have been much less acute. You know that there has been a historical co-incidence between the progressive organisation of economic and monetary union in Europe and the progressive dislocation of the international monetary system."

European monetary unification had thus two clear incentives: the consolidation of the EEC and the affirmation of Europe as an international actor. But as in any plan for monetary union, the crux of the problem rests on the question of the economic convergence of its members. How did the EEC plan to cope with this?

Well before the creation of the euro, an important academic debate developed concerning monetary unions, that of the so-called Optimum Currency Areas (OCAs). The start of the OCA debate is usually associated with the publication of Robert Mundell's eponymous article in the early 1960s. As its name suggests, the OCA debate is about determining in what areas would the use of a common currency be optimum. Put differently: in what group of countries would the use of a common currency produce no decline in well-being? Robert Mundell identified two factors helping to identify such an area: the mobility of the factors of production (labour and capital) and the symmetry of external shocks (i.e. the entire group of countries must receive identical shocks). Subsequently, other authors added new factors to this list. To name but a few, Ronald McKinnon stressed the openness of the economy, Peter Kenen the diversification of production, James Ingram the financial dimension, Gottfried Haberler and Marcus Fleming the convergence of inflation rates.

The extent to which Europe forms such an OCA, then and now, gave birth to endless and passionate debates. Whatever the conclusion one may draw while examining these criteria, the OCA debate highlights the profound implications of a full monetary union, in particular in fiscal and budgetary terms. And it is not certain that European policy-makers - then and now - while talking about the desirability of EMU or the future of the euro, had and have ever realised its full implications.

UK and EEC

Prime Minister Winston Churchill who provided the theoretical basis for the modern European community, ironically Britain has consistently represented a difficult issue in European integration. This state is one of the greatest Euro sceptics since it, more than other states, finds it particularly difficult to link domestic and European policies together. The reason for this can be attributed to Britain's historical, traditional, institutional and strategic background.

Every country has a certain idea of its role in the world, which shapes its identity and the way it sees itself in relation to other countries. The historical epoch of the British Empire has significantly influenced the way the British political elite sees the position of the country in Europe. At the end of the 16th and the beginning of the 17th centuries, the first colonies of the British Empire were established. Later, Britain expanded considerably to become the greatest world empire in history. It had colonies on every continent and in all the oceans. In the 20th century the empire saw a rapid decline and finally returned Hong Kong to China, and all former colonies became independent. In the first half of the 20th century the British Commonwealth was created. It is a voluntary intergovernmental association mostly composed of the former colonies of the Empire. All of the subordinate territories are now independent states with sovereign governments, but they all more or less remain symbolically loyal to the British Crown. Thus, Britain shaped the history of the world for over three centuries, and it comes as no surprise that many British politicians and a large part of its population still feel somewhat superior to the other European countries.

In the process of establishing the EU, Britain had a couple of opportunities to participate, but it decided not to take advantage of them. The first practical step towards creating a federal Europe was made approximately in the period of the 1950s, when negotiations over the creation of the European Coal and Steel Community began. The Labour Government of Clement Attlee was invited to take part but officially declined the offer. Later, when the ECSC was put in place, the six founding countries wanted to extend the common market for coal and steel into a general common market. In 1957the Treaty of the European Community (also known as the Treaty of Rome) was signed, which led to the creation of the European Economic Community and the European Atomic Energy Community. This was a very important event in the formation of the modern European Community, but the Conservative Government of Anthony Eden did not recognise its importance and refused to sign the treaty. According to Professor Stephen George, at the beginning the Conservative Government did discuss the possibility of joining with the six founding countries but eventually chose to back out as they saw the Community's plans as too ambitious. In the aftermath of the treaty, the six EEC members flourished economically whereas Britain suffered continuous economic decline. It was only after this most successful period of the Community, that Britain entered the EEC. In the meantime, the six states had actively shaped the community to their advantage, which offered them many more benefits than for the late comer Britain.

In 1961, this historical antagonism led the French President Charles de Gaulleto veto the British application to join the EEC. He argued that their strong link to the USA as well as the British Commonwealth could hinder the British in their dedication to the EEC. In 1967 the Labour Government, led by Harold Wilson filed another application but the French rejected it once again. Two years later the new French President Georges Pompidou removed the veto and finally in 1973 the UK, led by the Europe oriented Conservative Prime Minister Edward Heath, joined the EEC.As soon as the European Communities Act of 1972 was introduced in Britain, after only a small majority voted in favour of it, it became clear that the country's integration would encounter the so-called sovereignty barrier.

At the end of the 1950s and during the 1960s the economic decline of the UK on the one hand and the economic prosperity of the Six on the other largely influenced British politicians, who radically changed their mind about the closer links with Europe. It was the economic motivation that urged Britain into applying for membership. The UK does not strive for political integration, it is reluctant to transfer its sovereignty and it opts for the inter governmental cooperation structure instead. In order to become a member of the EEC, Britain had to accept the Communities Act as a legal basis of its membership. However, the UK continues to define its cooperation with Europe as intergovernmental and not as a constant process of political integration in which supranational institutions take precedence over all Domestic governments. In all European countries nearly all surveys of public opinion demonstrated widespread disillusionment with the European integration.

Namely, when Britain joined the EEC under Edward Heath's Conservative Government, there was no economic upturn and with the Oil Crisis in 1973,economic progress was obstructed everywhere. At the time the Labour party was opposed to the EEC and they promised to hold a referendum on withdrawal if they came into power. In 1975 the Labour Government, led by Harold Wilson, kept its word and held a referendum. However, the outcome was that the majority voted for staying in and consequently Labour change edits mind. Labour became even more interested in Europe when some social issues were raised by European law. For example, some parts of the British Employment Protection Act of 1978 were declared unfair according to European law because part-time workers received less social protection. Since most part-time workers were women, the Act even amounted to sexual discrimination. On the other hand, the Conservative Party gradually started turning against the idea of integration, which only accelerated with their new leader from 1975, Margaret Thatcher.

Margaret Thatcher, who became Prime Minister in 1979, openly expressed her very negative attitude towards the EEC. The period of her service was marked by an increasing political isolation of Britain from Europe. She was ardently against complete economic, political and social integration. Her Chancellor of the Exchequer, Sir Geoffrey however, argued that Britain contributed much more to the European budget than the other countries and he thought that something had to be done about it. In response, in 1984 Margaret Thatcher's government negotiated a rebate on the British contribution, and thus received some of its money back. The main reason for this was the fact that a great share of the European budget is spent on the Common Agricultural Policy and since farming does not represent a major sector in the UK economy, Britain felt that it benefited much less than other countries. Also, for Margaret Thatcher, Britain was losing its independence and sovereignty by transferring the power of decision-making to Brussels. In her "Bruges Speech" in 1988 she stated that:" To try to suppress nationhood and concentrate power at the centre of a European conglomerate would be highly damaging and would jeopardize the objectives we seek to achieve. Working more closely together does not require power to be centralised in Brussels or decisions to be taken by an appointed bureaucracy." Throughout the 1980s Margaret Thatcher was not ready to let the UK join the European Monetary System and adopt a common social policy because she regarded them as steps towards the formation of a closer political union. For Britain, the united Europe project is seen merely as something made out for economic reasons, a union supposed to create a common European market, not a political community.Turning back to Thatcher, she was particularly reluctant to adapt to revolutionary changes, such as the collapse of communism in Europe and the fall of the Berlin Wall, that took place on the world political scene in 1989 and 1990, and this was the main reason for her downfall. She was replaced by John Major, whose government ratified the Maastricht Treaty in 1992, which led to the formation of the EU in 1993. However, John Major opted out of the section of the treaty dealing with social policy, as well as of joining the monetary and economic union. In this way the awkward position of Britain was once again reinforced.

In 1997 the Labour Party, led by Tony Blair, ensured an outright victory with their pro-Europe manifesto. The new Prime Minister was very enthusiastic about the Union and one of the first things he did when he came into power was to sign the Social Chapter. In his election campaign, Tony Blair also announced the referendum on adopting the euro; nevertheless, it did not take place during his service. Generally observing, Labour under both Tony Blair and Gordon Brown, achieved a much more favourable image of Britain as an EU member state than it used to have. However, during this period one more issue became apparent in the UK's relationship with the EU- the "special" connection with America. Many European countries see the Union as a kind of counterweight to the USA. However, Britain is not in favour of this notion since it would jeopardise its specific relationship and hamper Britain's foreign policy options. That there is an alliance between the UK and the USA was demonstrated directly after the terrorist attacks in September 2001. Tony Blair immediately announced that Britain will support the USA and stay with them no matter what, and to back this up, he sent large numbers of British troops to Afghanistan and Iraq. In spite of the widespread unpopularity of these decisions both in Europe and at home, Tony Blair has not changed his opinion that the British interests are best guarded by remaining "shoulder to shoulder" with the American government.

To sum up, there is no doubt that the relationship between Britain and the EU is a difficult one. There are numerous reasons which render British membership in the Union problematic. As a former imperial power, the UK finds it particularly difficult to adjust and narrow its political interest only to Europe. Being a latecomer in the Community, Britain had to accommodate itself to the already established policies and rules, some of which directly conflicted with the basic principles upon which the British Constitution is based. Antagonism with France and affiliation with America are additional issues. Furthermore, the fact that the UK joined the Community only for economic reasons at an economically difficult time resulted in popular discontent. However, not only is the population dissatisfied but also this disillusionment and division is mirrored by the political elite. From 1979 until1997 Conservative Governments contributed to a high level of British isolation in the Community. Blair's Government demonstrated keen interest for and close links to the USA, which at some points seemed to exceed those with the EU. However, Labour Governments have generally showed much more interest in Europe and British membership. This could be read as a possible sign of better cooperation in the future, but bearing in mind the British background, it becomes clear that this is going to be an uphill struggle.

EU as "Mega Project Cycles"

If one analyses the history of the EU, some big mega projects can be seen, like Single Market, Monetary Union, etc., and within these mega projects an acceleration within the last years – after many years where no decision could be undertaken, for example in the 1970s (except the introduction of direct popular election of the European Parliament).

Some of these mega project cycles can be defined – for the past, present and future:

1985-1993 EU Single Market

This project started for the EU already some years before 1985 (the dates indicated have to be seen as flexible; they represent only a rough frame). Although the Single Market has been finished by 1.1.1993, there were some fields in the Single Market, which had to be made perfect or brought up-to-date.

1985-2002 European Monetary Union

The European Monetary Union has started in the middle of the 80s (even temporarily before, as concerns the plan of the former Luxembourg Prime Minister Pierre Werner from the early 70s), when a group of European Parliament members (across all political groups) founded a working group on European currency questions. Later followed the elaboration of a concept under the presidency of the President of the EU Commission, Jacques Delors (former French Minister for Economy and Finance), which ended with the Maastricht Treaty. In the Maastricht Treaty there is an exact timing for the introduction of the Euro. For companies and citizens the essential steps came after 1994, when the European Monetary Institute (predecessor of the European Central Bank, which opened in 1999) had been founded in Frankfurt.

1989-2012 Company Cooperation

After the Single Market, from 1994, there was a not very visible start date of an unorganised wave of company cooperation. It became clear to every small and medium sized enterprise, around 15 million in the EU, that cooperation is a survival factor. This is particularly important for research- intensive companies, but also research institutions like universities. As there is no administrative drive for company cooperation and every company does what it deems as necessary, any quantification is impossible. Although there will be an open end, until 2015 most of all companies will be aware that there is an objective pressure towards cooperation, also in the new Member States.

1993-2015 EU Enlargement

Since 1993 and the criteria set up at a Copenhague (Denmark) summit for enlargement candidate countries, this subject had momentum until 1.5.2004, the date of the big enlargement for 10 countries. The finishing date 2015 defines itself as possible finishing date for some other enlargements, which might still come (Romania, Bulgaria, Croatia, the other Balkan countries, Turkey, but also some Western CIS countries like Ukraine or Moldova; this is at least the possibility).

2000-2015 E-Business and International Competitivity

This new subject - also unexpected by many economic agents - culminates in initiatives like „eEurope", and mainly business is concerned (although the state is called to go into eGovernment). The Commission has proclaimed the objective that by 2010 the EU is the most dynamic economic area in the world. The EU is not bad placed, in an international comparison, with electronic networks per company or capita. Like for company cooperation this subject is not very visible, as its acceptance is due to many uncoordinated and coordinated activities in business.

2000-2015 EU Constitution

With the Charter on Fundamental Rights, a discussion on the basic values of the EU has emerged, and with the Constitutional Convent there has been, since about 2000, a new quality of constitutional discussion in the EU. The Constitution being adopted by the European Council (EU Summit) on 18th June 2004, there will be an ongoing discussion on constitutional values in the EU. As ratifications in the Member States are ongoing now, the finality of this discussion is uncertain, as well as its duration. This "open end", as it is estimated now, could last until 2015.

2002-2015 Common Foreign and Security Policy

The discussion became more and more intensive after events like the Yugoslavia conflicts in the 90s, the 11th September 2001 and the general antiterrorism activities on world level. But it is pending since decades in the EU ("economic giant - political dwarf"). Since the EU Constitution was to be taken serious, it became clear that a common foreign and defence policy should play, in the future, a more prominent part in the EU. But it will take a longer time to implement a real foreign and security policy.

2003-2015 : Sustainability, Environment and Energy Policies, Hi Tech - Hi Touch Tendency - and a Partly Revival of the *Small is Beautiful Principle*?

Sustainability is a priority since some years ago within the EU, but also the United Nations. Business will still have to jump on this train. This catchword includes mainly environment and energy aspects, but has also relevance in EU relations with the Third World. In this context, some sociologic tendencies may be discussed: the growing need for an untouched environment, if people work in context with hi-tech, and maybe also a partly revival of the small is beautiful principle, which has been discussed in Europe in the context of "post-material society". Although this is no EU policy, the EU will have to react to other voices in the dialogues it holds, and will have to cope with certain demands in this direction, which are also due to the information society. In this context, Europe might revise the topical shareholder value doctrines for public joint stock companies.

2003-2010 Industrial and Social Policy

In context with demographic pressure, the stability policy around the European currency Euro, relatively high unemployment figures in some parts of the EU and other social problems, industrial policy - under market economy aspects - and social policy seem to become one of the core subjects for the future, in particular as now there are several demands for social policy in the new EU Constitution.

2004-2010 EU Internal Security

Due to the general terrorist threat, internal security of the EU is emerging as an important subject. In 2004, a "Mr. Terrorism", a former Minister of Justice of the Netherlands, has been installed by the EU, still with small competences, but there is no doubt that these will increase. Already, police forces are cooperating in a larger deal. Until all weaknesses in this context will be deleted, and this in the new Member States too, it may take the years until 2010.

References

Bojana Perisic, Bojana., 2010, *Britain and Europe: a History of Difficult Relations*, Institute for Cultural Diplomacy, Berlin, March.

Ellison, James R V., 1995, "Explaining British Policy Towards European Integration in the 1950s" Paper presented to the European Integration and Domestic Policy-making Research Group, *Centre for European Studies*, Harvard University, 9 May 1995, and to the Fourth Biennial International Conference of the European Community Studies Association, Charleston, South Carolina, 11 May 1995.

Emmanuel Mourlon-Druol, Emmanuel., 2011, *The Euro Crisis: A Historical Perspectives,* London School of Economics, June.

European Citizens' Consultations, 2011, *The History of European Union.*

Gomez, Ricardo., Martin Burch, Simon Bulmer (University of Manchester), Patricia Hogwood (University of Glasgow), Caitriona Carter and Andrew Scott (University of Edinburgh), 2003, European Union Policy Making in the UK: A Brief History, Paper No. 5, *Devolution and European Union Policy Making Series,* May 14 , 2003.

Harold James, Harold., 2011, The Potential of a Caterpillar: or The Origins of European Monetary Integration .*Princeton Paper for Yale Economic History Seminar,* March 28, 2011.

Institute of European Studies University of California., 2002, EU and Democracy in Southern Europe: Portugal, Spain and Greece, Berkeley, November 1-2, 2002.

Laursen, Finn., 2010, The Merger Treaty 1965: The First Reform of the Founding European Community Treaties, Paper prepared for First Jean Monnet Conference, "From Paris to Lisbon: EU Treaties and their Reforms", Dalhousie University, Halifax, NS, Canada, 22-23 March 2010.

Mayer, Thomas., 2011, The Political economics of the Euro.*EU Monitor82,* July 1.

Moravcsik, Andrew., 1998, Degaulle and European Integration: Historical Revision and Social Science Theory, DE GAULLE AND EUROPEAN *Center for European Studies Working Paper Series,* Program for the Study of Germany and Europe, Working Paper Series 8.5, May.

Pinto, Antonio Costa., 2002, Portugal and European integration- An introduction, Conference.

Rempe, Martin., 2011, Decolonisation by Europeanisation: The early EEC and Transformation of French-African relation. *KFG WPNo-27,* May 2011, Berlin.

CHAPTER-3

THE MAASTRICHT TREATY

The Treaty

The Maastricht Treaty (formally, the Treaty on European Union or TEU) was signed on 7 February 1992 by the members of the European Community in Maastricht, Netherlands.[1] On 9–10 December 1991, the same city hosted the European Council which drafted the treaty.[2] Upon its entry into force on 1 November 1993 during the Delors Commission, it created the European Union and led to the creation of the single European currency, the euro. The Maastricht Treaty has been amended to a degree by later treaties.

Background

The Maastricht Treaty is a part of an evolutionary economic process that began in Europe following the devastation of World War II. Under the prodding of Jean Monnet (1888-1979) and Robert Schuman (1886-1963) of France, and Paul-Henri Spaak (1899-1972) of Belgium, many European leaders came to the conclusion that if economic growth and social and political stability were to be realized then there must be a formal plan for political and economic cooperation between the various nations of western Europe. This plan would also serve as a nonmilitary bulwark against the expansionist threats of the Soviet Union and its Eastern European communist allies.

The first step towards inter-nation cooperation was the formation of the European Coal and Steel Community (ECSC). Established by the Treaty of Paris in 1951, the ECSC united Belgium, France, Italy, Luxembourg, the Netherlands, and West Germany into a single common market that did away with trade barriers relating to coal, steel, scrap metal, and iron ore. The ECSC also allowed the free movement of labor between its signers respective to these industries. The success of the ECSC led to the 1957 signing of the Treaty of Rome and the subsequent establishment of the European Atomic Energy Community and the European Economic Community. In 1967 the executive agencies of these three institutions were combined to form the European Community (EC), which was also known as the European Common Market. Shortly thereafter tariffs relating to trade between member nations were eliminated and a common tariff on goods from nonmember nations was instituted. In 1973 Denmark, Ireland, and the United Kingdom became full members of the EC, as did Portugal and Spain in 1986 and a united Germany in 1990.

The European Economic Community began as a common market whose purpose was to eliminate trade barriers between member countries. As the institution matured over the decades, however, it began moving towards not just economic but also social, political, and monetary integration. This evolution is reflected in the name changes from European Economic Community, to European Community, and finally to European Union. In negotiating the Maastricht Treaty, EC members agreed to a number of key provisions. A common currency was to be established by the end of the 1990s, to be overseen by an Economic and Monetary Union (EMU). The EMU would be responsible for instituting the common currency and establishing a central bank which would supervise the EU's monetary policy. An important part of this plan is the exchange rate mechanism (ERM) which supervises and seeks to stabilize currency exchange rates between member countries.

Other provisions of the Maastricht Treaty called for moving towards a common defense and foreign policy as well as a shared social policy. The treaty gives the EU the right to "support and complement" the activities of member countries in areas of worker health, safety, and sexual equality. There was, however, much dissension and subsequent compromise over parts of the treaty. The

United Kingdom, for instance, felt these provisions would compromise existing British law. As with the common currency provision, Great Britain retained the option of unilateral decision making in these regards. The Maastricht accord also authorized EU activities to include: environmental and consumer protection; energy conservation; and education, health, and cultural issues.

Under the treaty, greater aid and assistance was granted to Greece, Ireland, Portugal, and Spain, the so-called poorest nations of the EU. The powers of the European Parliament, an advisory agency of the EC, were expanded in the EU to include the establishment of various "watchdog" committees, input in the appointments of European commissioners, and greater control over legislation passed by the Council of Ministers. The treaty also created an advisory Community of the Regions that represents local and regional governing units.

Ratification of the Maastricht Treaty took two years and numerous compromises and national legislative debates before the 12 EC members voted approval amidst an economic downturn in Europe and growing public disenchantment. The United Kingdom was concerned over loss of sovereignty especially over the issues of common social policies and a single unit of currency. The French National Assembly had to amend the country's constitution because of treaty provisions dealing with transnational voting rights, visa policies, and the common currency. The German parliament also had concerns over the currency issue as well as discomfort with the ambiguous powers of the European Union and the relative powers of the European Parliament. Ireland's referendum became tied to a controversy over abortion strictures and travel rights. In spite of these roadblocks, Germany in October 1993 became the 12th and final EC member to ratify the Maastricht Treaty, which became effective on November I of that year. The Economic and Monetary Union, the most far-reaching provision of the Maastricht accord, will begin formal operations in January 1999.

OBJECTIVES

The Treaty of Maastricht responds to five key goals:

- strengthen the democratic legitimacy of the institutions;

- improve the effectiveness of the institutions;
- establish economic and monetary union;
- develop the Community social dimension;
- establish a common foreign and security policy.

POLICIES

The Treaty establishes Community policies in six new areas:

- trans-European networks;
- industrial policy;
- consumer protection;
- education and vocational training;
- youth;
- culture.

The provision and significance of the Treaty are shown in Table 3.1 clearly.

Table-3.1 : The Structure :The 7 Titles of the Treaty on European Union (TEU)

Number	Name	Significance
I	Common Provisions	
II	Provisions amending the Treaty establishing the European Economic Community (the 1957 Treaty of Rome, or EEC Treaty) with a view to establishing the European Community (Treaty of the European Community, TEC, or EC Treaty)	Formally renamed the EEC the European Community, which becomes the 1st pillar of the EU
III	Provisions amending the Treaty establishing the European Coal and Steel Community (ECSC) (the 1951 Treaty of Paris)	Concerned with updating the ECSC
IV	Provisions amending the Treaty establishing the European Atomic Energy Community (Euratom, also signed in Rome in 1957)	Concerned with updating Euratom
V	Provisions on a Common Foreign and Security Policy (CFSP)	Established the, inter-governmental, 2nd pillar of the EU
VI	Provisions on cooperation in the fields of Justice and Home Affairs (JHA)	Established the, inter-governmental, 3rd pillar of the EU
VII	Final Provisions	

The Protocols included:

- On Economic and Monetary Union:
  - On the Statute of the European System of Central Banks and of the European Central Bank (ECB).
  - On the Statute of the European Monetary Institute (EMI).
  - On the Excessive Deficit Procedure.
  - On the Convergence Criteria Referred to in Article 109j of the Treaty Establishing the European Community.
  - On the Transition to the Third Stage of Economic and Monetary Union (EMU).
  - On Certain Provisions Relating to the United Kingdom (the UK "opt-out" of EMU).
- On the Social Chapter:
  - On Social Policy for 11 of the 12 member states excluding the UK.
  - On Social Policy Concluded Between the Member States of the European Community With the Exception of the UK.
- The timetable for EMU was:
  - Stage 1: cooperation and coordination in economic and monetary fields, which had already begun in July 1990, as agreed at the Madrid summit (in 1989).
  - Stage 2: laying down the basic institutional and operational rules necessary for the realisation of EMU - to start in January 1994.
  - Stage 3: the move towards irrevocably locked together exchange rates, leading to a single currency - to start in January 1999, at the latest.
- Under EMU a "cohesion fund" was to be provided for the 4 poorer members - Spain, Portugal, Ireland and Greece.

- Further extension of EC competence: to consumer protection, public health, education and vocational training, culture and "trans-European networks" (TENs).
- There was also the extension of existing powers in environmental policy, industrial policy & R&D.
- Agreement by 11 member states (excluding the UK) on the Social Chapter. The Protocol on Social Policy and an Agreement on Social Policy (The Social Chapter) was appended to the Maastricht Treaty.
- Further extension of powers of European Parliament (EP): to extend the legislative powers of the EP in EC decision-making, the appointment of the Commission & in external relations policy. Co-decision was introduced.
- The European Council was identified as responsible for providing the EU with the impetus for development and for defining the EU's general political guidelines.
- The use of QMV in the Council of Ministers was extended.
- The Committee of the Regions was created.
- The Court of Auditors was upgraded to a full Community institution.
- Other institutional changes: included the increase in the commission's term of office from 4 to 5 years, and granting to the European Court of Justice (ECJ) of the right to impose fines on member states for failing to implement its judgments.
- The new intergovernmental Common Foreign & Security Policy (CFSP) had a limited provision for QMV & a statement of intent to build a common defence policy. The Maastricht Treaty, therefore, formally initiated the development of common foreign & defence policies, with the defence issues initially subcontracted to the WEU.
- The new intergovernmental Justice & Home Affairs (JHA) pillar was concerned with police and judicial cooperation in civil and criminal matters on matters such as asylum policy and immigration & policing.

- It established the principle of subsidiarity - the principle that decisions should be taken at the lowest level consistent with effective action within a political system.

Contents of the treaty

The treaty led to the creation of the euro, and created what was commonly referred to as the pillar structure of the European Union. The treaty established the three pillars of the European Union – the European Community (EC) pillar, the Common Foreign and Security Policy (CFSP) pillar, and the Justice and Home Affairs (JHA) pillar. The first pillar was where the EU's supra-national institutions – the Commission, the European Parliament and the European Court of Justice – had the most power and influence. The other two pillars were essentially more intergovernmental in nature with decisions being made by committees composed of member states' politicians and officials.

All three pillars were the extensions of pre-existing policy structures. The European Community pillar was the continuation of the European Economic Community with the "Economic" being dropped from the name to represent the wider policy base given by the Maastricht Treaty. Co-ordination in foreign policy had taken place since the beginning of the 1970s under the name of European Political Cooperation (EPC), which had been first written into the treaties by the Single European Act but not as a part of the EEC. While the Justice and Home Affairs pillar extended cooperation in law enforcement, criminal justice, asylum, and immigration and judicial cooperation in civil matters, some of these areas had already been subject to intergovernmental cooperation under the Schengen Implementation Convention of 1990.

The creation of the pillar system was the result of the desire by many member states to extend the European Economic Community to the areas of foreign policy, military, criminal justice, judicial cooperation, and the misgiving of other member states, notably the United Kingdom, over adding areas which they considered to be too sensitive to be managed by the supra-national mechanisms of the European Economic Community. The compromise was that instead of renaming the European Economic Community as the European Union, the treaty would establish a legally separate European Union comprising the renamed European Economic Community, and the inter-governmental policy areas of foreign policy, military, criminal justice, judicial cooperation. The structure greatly limited the powers of the European Commission, the European Parliament and the European Court of Justice to influence the new intergovernmental policy areas, which were to be contained with the second and third pillars: foreign policy and military matters (the CFSP pillar) and criminal justice and cooperation in civil matters (the JHA pillar).

Euro convergence criteria

The Maastricht Treaty established the Maastricht criteria and the EU single market which ensures the free movement of goods, capital, people and services. (2003 German stamp commemorating the tenth anniversary of the enforcement of the Maastricht Treaty in 1993)

The Maastricht criteria (also known as the convergence criteria) are the criteria for European Union member states to enter the third stage of European Economic and Monetary Union (EMU) and adopt the euro as their currency. The 4 main criteria are based on Article 121(1) of the European Community Treaty.

1]. Inflation rates: No more than 1.5 percentage points higher than the average of the three best performing (lowest inflation) member states of the EU.

2]. **Government finance**

(i). Annual government deficit

The ratio of the annual government deficit to gross domestic product (GDP) must not exceed 3% at the end of the preceding fiscal year. If not, it is at least required to reach a level close to 3%. Only exceptional and temporary excesses would be granted for exceptional cases.

(ii) Government debt

The ratio of gross government debt to GDP must not exceed 60% at the end of the preceding fiscal year. Even if the target cannot be achieved due to the specific conditions, the ratio must have sufficiently diminished and must be approaching the reference value at a satisfactory pace. As of the end of 2010, only two EU member states, Poland and the Czech Republic, still meet this target.

3] Exchange rate: Applicant countries should have joined the exchange-rate mechanism (ERM II) under the European Monetary System (EMS) for two consecutive years and should not have devalued its currency during the period.

4] Long-term interest rates: The nominal long-term interest rate must not be more than 2 percentage points higher than in the three lowest inflation member states.

The purpose of setting the criteria is to maintain the price stability within the Eurozone even with the inclusion of new member states.

The process of ratifying the treaty was fraught with difficulties in three states. In Denmark, the first Danish Maastricht Treaty referendum was held on 2 June 1992 but a shortfall of fewer than 50,000 votes resulted in the treaty not being ratified. After the failure, alterations were made to the treaty through the addition of the Edinburgh Agreement which lists four Danish exceptions. The treaty was eventually ratified the following year on 18 May 1993 after a second referendum was held in Denmark.

In September 1992, a referendum in France only narrowly supported the ratification of the treaty, with 51.05% in favour. Uncertainty over the Danish and French referendums was one of the causes of the turmoil on the currency markets in September 1992, which led to the UK pound's expulsion from the Exchange Rate Mechanism.

In the United Kingdom, an opt-out from the treaty's social provisions was opposed in Parliament by the opposition Labour and Liberal Democrat MPs and the treaty itself by the Maastricht Rebels within the governing Conservative Party. The number of rebels exceeded the Conservative majority in the House of Commons, and thus the government of John Major came close to losing the confidence of the House. The Table 3.2 showed the treaty behind the Maastricht and their signing period and implementation. The structure and pillars of EU were also shown.

Table 3.2: EEC at a glance

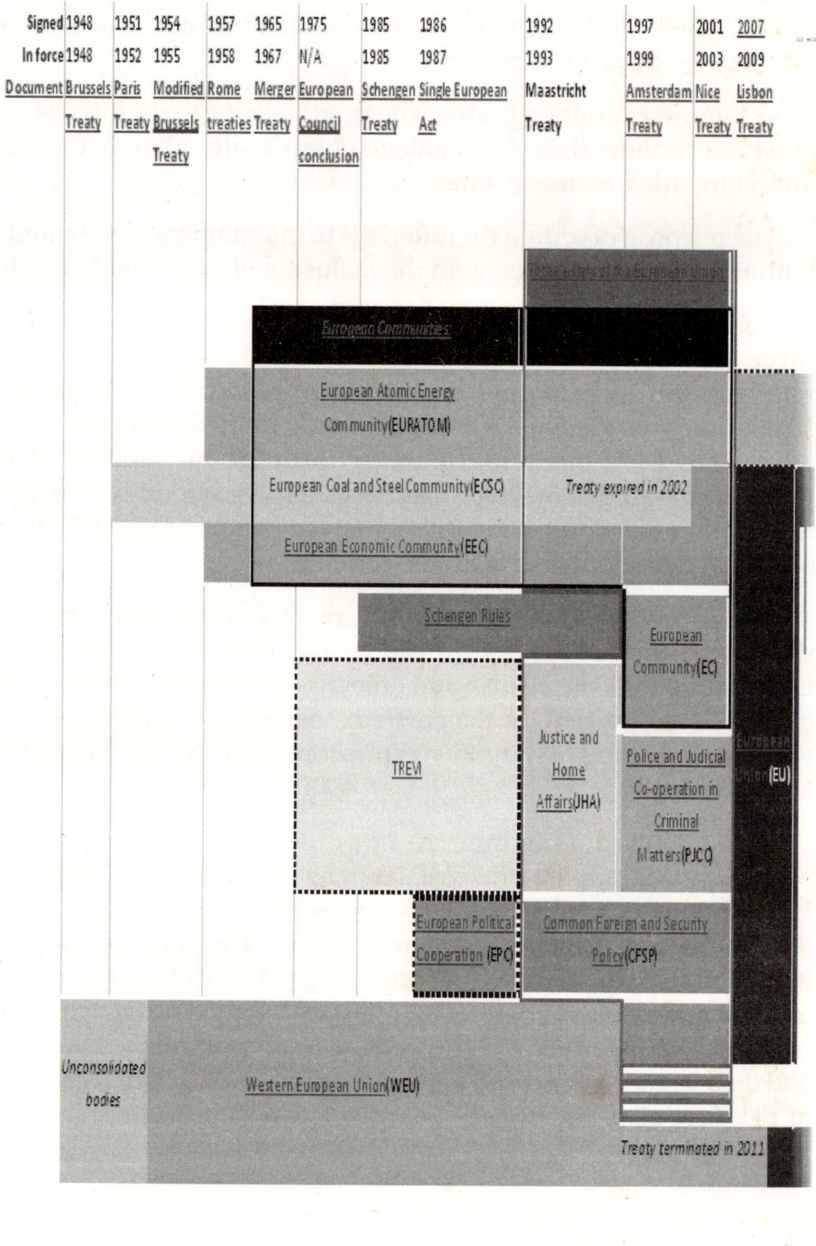

Source: Maastricht, 1992

We should have a quick look over the four convergences of EU in the figures,where we can found how the countries achieve the convergence criteria. In Fig- 3.1, the convergence of inflation of EU-11 during 1971-2007 was drawn clearly.Before the Maastricht Treaty,the inflation rates of EU-11 were more volatile but after 2000,the rates came closer to the criteria towards 2010.

Fig-3.1 : Inflation converence of EU-11

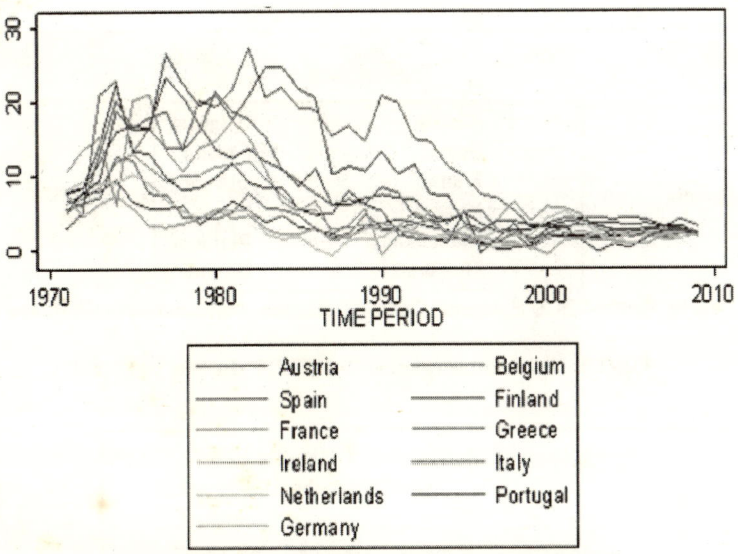

Source: SourceOECD Economic Outlook Database - GDP deflator

The convergence was not seen in Fig-3.2 for the net lending to GDP ratio during 1990-2010 but they were below4%.Before the Maastricht, the rates of most of the EU-11 countries were negative which crossed the threshold line since 2005.

In the Fig- 3.3 , the debt GDP ratio of EU-11 during 1991-2007 was drawn where convergence was not found in many countries.

Fig-3.2: Net lending to GDP ratio during Maastricht and SGP

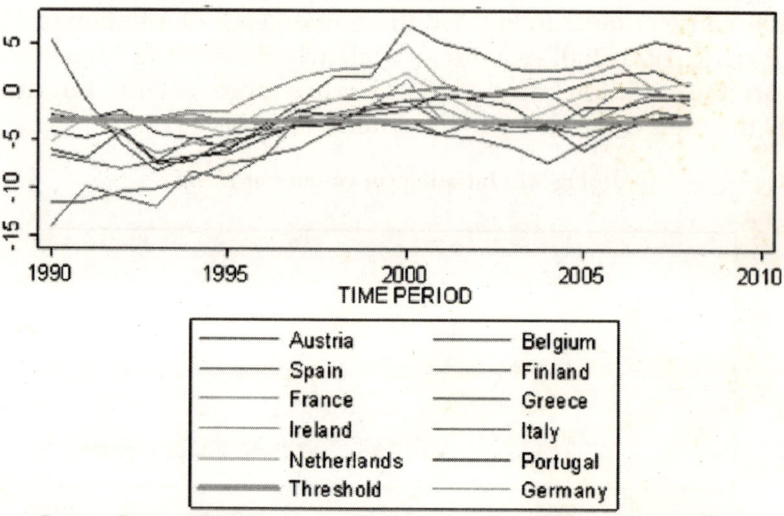

Source: SourceOECD Economic Outlook Database - Net Lending to GDP ratio

Fig-3.3: Debt convergence(Debt/GDP during 1991-2007)

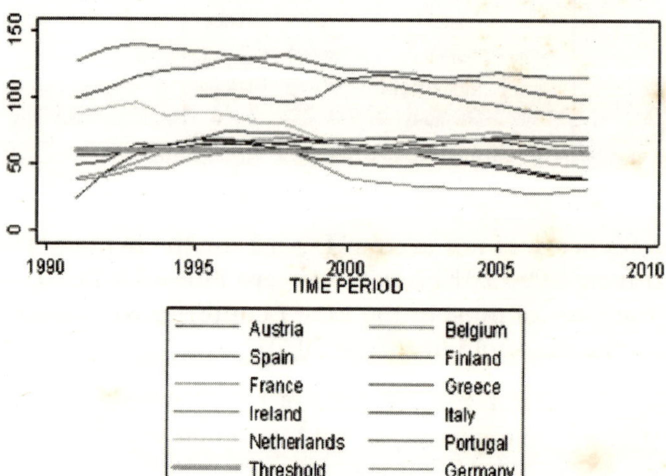

Source: SourceOECD Economic Outlook Database -General Government Gross Financial Liablities

But , there was clear convergence of long run interest rate in EU-11 that was shown in Fig- 3.4 where the rates converged to the criteria since the inception of the Maastricht Treaty.

Fig-3.4 Long run Interest rate convergence of EU-11

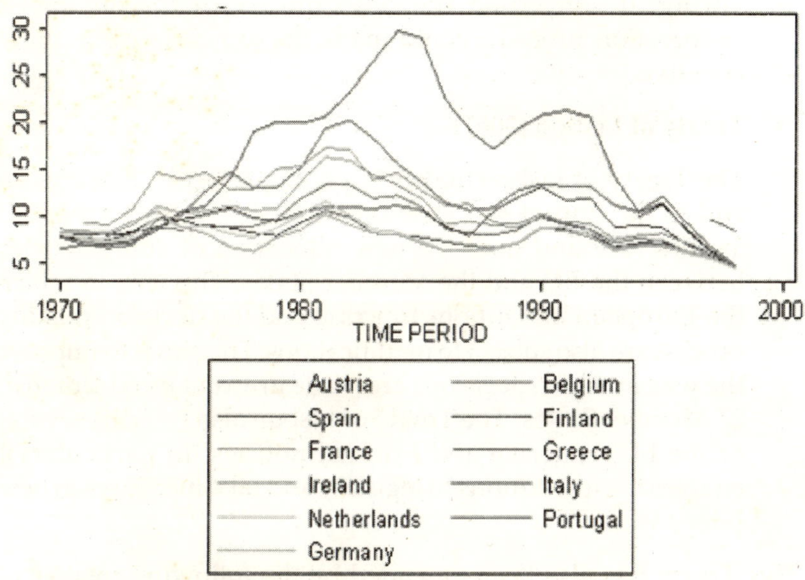

Source: SourceOECD Economic Outlook Database

AMENDMENTS MADE TO THE TREATY

- **Treaty of Amsterdam (1997)**

  The Treaty of Amsterdam increased the powers of the Union by creating a Community employment policy, transferring to the Communities some of the areas which were previously subject to intergovernmental cooperation in the fields of justice and home affairs, introducing measures aimed at bringing the Union closer to its citizens and enabling closer cooperation between certain Member States (enhanced cooperation). It also extended the co-decision procedure and qualified majority voting and simplified and renumbered the articles of the Treaties.

- **Treaty of Nice (2001)**

  The Treaty of Nice was essentially devoted to the "leftovers" of Amsterdam, i.e. the institutional problems linked to enlargement which were not resolved in 1997. It dealt with the make-up of the Commission, the weighting of votes in the Council and the extension of the areas of qualified majority voting. It simplified the rules on use of the enhanced cooperation procedure and made the judicial system more effective.

- **Treaty of Lisbon (2007)**

  The Treaty of Lisbon makes sweeping reforms. It brings an end to the European Community, abolishes the former EU architecture and makes a new allocation of competencies between the EU and the Member States. The way in which the European institutions function and the decision-making process are also subject to modifications. The aim is to improve the way in which decisions are made in an enlarged Union of 27 Member States. The Treaty of Lisbon also reforms several of the EU's internal and external policies. In particular, it enables the institutions to legislate and take measures in new policy areas

This Treaty has also been amended by the following treaties of accession:

- **Treaty of Accession of Austria, Finland and Sweden (1994)**, which increased the number of Member States of the European Community to fifteen.

- **Treaty of Accession of Cyprus, Estonia, Hungary, Latvia, Lithuania, Malta, Poland, the Czech Republic, Slovakia and Slovenia (2003)**

This Treaty increased the number of Member States of the European Community from 15 to 25.

- **Treaty of Accession of Bulgaria and Romania (2005).** This Treaty increased the number of Member States of the European Community from 25 to 27.

All the treaties have been arranged chronologically in the Table-3.3 below.

Table-3.3: Treaty chronologically

Treaties of Accession	*Date of signature*	*Entry into force*	*Official Journal*
Treaty on European Union (Treaty on Maastricht)	7.2.1992	1.11.1993	OJ C 191 of 29.7.1992
Treaty of Amsterdam	2.10.1997	1.5.1999	OJ C 340 of 10.11.1997
Treaty of Nice	26.2.2001	1.2.2003	OJ C 80 of 10.3.2001
Treaty of Lisbon	13.12.2007	1.12.2009	OJ C 306 of 17.12.2007
Treaty of Accession	*Date of signature*	*Entry into force*	*Official Journal*
Treaty of Accession of Austria, Finland and Sweden	24.6.1994	1.1.1995	OJ C 241 of 29.8.1994
Treaty of Accession of the ten new Member States	16.4.2003	1.5.2004	OJ L 236 of 23.9.2003
Treaty of Accession of Bulgaria and Romania	25.4.2005	1.1.2007	OJ L 157 of 21.6.2005

Source: Maastricht, 1992

These fact sheets are not legally binding on the European Commission. They do not claim to be exhaustive and do not represent an official interpretation of the text of the Treaty.

Conclusion

How Maastricht Treaty was formed and how does it work in the EMU though out the channels of treaties and the how the crisis emerges when the criteria fail. Thus, we can understand present consequence of the debt crisis in the structure of the Maastricht Treaty. After the enlargement of EU and the exit of UK, the new criteria were formed by the new Euro Area,ie,EU-17 and a new Treaty will be set up for smooth functioning of the single currency Euro in the EMU.

References

Delors,Jacques.,2012,The Maastricht Treaty:20 years later., Key note speech, *European Policy Centre*,February 7, Reneissance Hotel, Brussels.

Eichengreen,Barry.,1992,Should the Maastricht Treaty be saved? *Princeton Studies in International Finance no-74*,December, Princeton University, NewJersey.

Feldstein, Martin., 2005, The Euro and Stability Pact. *NBER*, March 30.

Grauwe, Paul De.,2006, What have we learnt about Monetary Integration since the Maastricht Treaty?*JCMS,Oxford, 2006*,Vol-44, No-4,711-30.

Jones, Erik., 2005, European Economic Governance forcing an integrated agenda, *International Economic Programme, BP05/02.*

Joseph,Mathew.,2009,Global Financial Crisis: How was India Impacted? InwEnt-DIE Conference on Global Financial Governance-*Challenges and Regional Responses,3-4 September*, 2009, Berlin.

Klau,Thomas., Fracois Godement and J.I.Torreblanca., 2010, Beyond Maastricht :A New Deal for the Eurozone, European Council on Foreign Relation, EU, *Policy Papers 26*, December.

Maastricht, 1992, The Maastricht Treaty provisions amending the treaty establishing the European Economic Community with a view to establishing the European community, 2 Feb.

Moltke, Konrad Von., 1995,*The Maastricht treaty and the Winnipeg principles on trade and sustainable development*, International Institute for Sustainable Development (IISD).

CHAPTER 4

EURO CRISIS : MACRO FUNDAMENTALS OF EURO AREA

Introduction

Macro economic indicators are the main pillars of the economy as well as the determinants of stability. Of them, the growth of GDP, inflation rate, interest rate, fiscal deficit, trade balance, BOP deficit, reserves of foreign exchanges, exchange rates, growth of M3 or M2 , saving and investment as percent of GDP, yields of equities and portfolios, inflows and outflows of FDI, employment or unemployment rates, public debts, index of production and so on are of very much important and indicative. The projections of such target variables are crucially vital for planning and the basis of the economy. Therefore, macro economic indicators of EU should be studied to single out the genesis of the problem of euro crisis.

The Selected Observations:

In Table -4.1,the GDP and per capita GDP are shown for EU and the individual countries in comparison to USA and Japan .It is clear that Germany, France, Italy, Spain, Netherlands, Poland and Belgium are the great pillars of EU excluding UK but all are less wealthier than Japan and USA.

In Table-4.1a,the GDP growth rate of EU-27 and Euro Area including Japan and USA were given from 2000 to 2009 and also

Table-4.1: GDP at current market price

	GDP						GDP per capita			
	(EUR 1 000 million)			(PPS 1 000 million)			(PPS, EU-27=100)			(EUR)
	1999	2008	2009	1999	2008	2009	1999	2008	2009	2009 (1)
EU-27	8 589	12 495	11 791	8 589	12 495	11 791	100	100	100	23 600
Euro area (EA-16)	6 445	9 252	8 963	6 283	8 906	8 396	113	108	108	27 200
Belgium	239	345	339	224	309	294	123	115	116	31 400
Bulgaria	12	35	35	40	82	76	27	43	:	4 700
Czech Republic	56	148	137	127	210	199	69	80	81	13 100
Denmark	163	233	223	124	165	153	131	120	118	40 400
Germany	2 012	2 481	2 397	1 786	2 366	2 233	122	115	116	29 300
Estonia	5	16	14	10	23	20	42	68	63	10 300
Ireland	90	180	160	84	149	135	126	134	128	35 700
Greece	132	236	233	160	262	247	83	93	93	20 700
Spain	580	1 088	1 054	685	1 173	1 127	96	103	104	22 900
France	1 368	1 949	1 907	1 233	1 734	1 633	115	108	107	29 600
Italy	1 127	1 568	1 521	1 192	1 527	1 445	117	102	102	25 200
Cyprus	9	17	17	11	19	18	87	96	98	21 200
Latvia	7	23	19	15	32	26	36	57	49	8 200
Lithuania	10	32	27	24	52	42	39	62	53	8 000
Luxembourg	20	39	38	18	34	31	237	277	267	75 700
Hungary	46	106	93	100	162	149	55	64	63	9 300
Malta	4	6	6	6	8	8	81	77	78	13 900
Netherlands	386	596	572	368	552	508	131	134	130	34 600
Austria	198	283	274	187	259	241	131	124	122	32 800
Poland	157	362	310	331	539	547	49	56	61	8 100
Portugal	118	172	168	147	209	196	81	79	78	15 800
Romania	34	140	116	105	259	229	26	42	:	5 800
Slovenia	21	37	35	28	46	42	81	91	87	17 300
Slovakia	19	65	63	49	98	91	50	72	72	11 700
Finland	122	185	171	105	156	139	115	117	111	32 100
Sweden	243	334	293	199	284	265	126	122	120	31 300
United Kingdom	1 410	1 815	1 563	1 231	1 785	1 693	118	116	116	25 300
Iceland	8	10	9	7	10	9	139	121	120	27 200
Liechtenstein	2	3	3	:	:	:	:	:	:	:
Norway	149	306	273	115	226	200	145	189	176	56 500
Switzerland	252	343	354	186	271	262	146	141	144	45 800
Croatia	22	47	45	39	69	66	49	63	:	10 800
FYR of Macedonia	3	7	:	10	17	:	27	34	:	3 300
Turkey	234	499	440	448	811	781	40	46	:	7 000
Japan	4 102	3 313	3 639	2 657	3 369	3 112	118	109	:	25 000
United States	8 776	9 770	10 123	8 093	11 216	10 614	163	147	146	32 900

Source-Eurostat.

Table-4.1a: Real GDP growth
(% change compared with the previous year; average 2000-2009)

	2000	2001	2002	2003	2004	2005	2006	2007	2008	2009	2000-09
EU-27	3.9	2.0	1.2	1.3	2.5	2.0	3.2	3.0	0.5	-4.2	1.5
Euro area (EA-16)	3.9	1.9	0.9	0.8	2.2	1.7	3.0	2.8	0.5	-4.1	1.4
Belgium	3.7	0.8	1.4	0.8	3.2	1.7	2.7	2.9	1.0	-2.8	1.5
Bulgaria	5.7	4.2	4.7	5.5	6.7	6.4	6.5	6.4	6.2	-4.9	4.7
Czech Republic	3.6	2.5	1.9	3.6	4.5	6.3	6.8	6.1	2.5	-4.1	3.4
Denmark	3.5	0.7	0.5	0.4	2.3	2.4	3.4	1.7	-0.9	-4.7	0.9
Germany	3.2	1.2	0.0	-0.2	1.2	0.8	3.4	2.7	1.0	-4.7	0.9
Estonia	10.0	7.5	7.9	7.6	7.2	9.4	10.6	6.9	-5.1	-13.9	4.8
Ireland	9.7	5.7	6.5	4.4	4.6	6.0	5.3	5.6	-3.5	-7.6	3.7
Greece	4.5	4.2	3.4	5.9	4.4	2.3	4.5	4.3	1.3	-2.3	3.3
Spain	5.0	3.6	2.7	3.1	3.3	3.6	4.0	3.6	0.9	-3.7	2.6
France	3.9	1.9	1.0	1.1	2.5	1.9	2.2	2.4	0.2	-2.6	1.5
Italy	3.7	1.8	0.5	0.0	1.5	0.7	2.0	1.5	-1.3	-5.0	0.5
Cyprus	5.0	4.0	2.1	1.9	4.2	3.9	4.1	5.1	3.6	-1.7	3.2
Latvia	6.9	8.0	6.5	7.2	8.7	10.6	12.2	10.0	-4.2	-18.0	4.8
Lithuania	3.3	6.7	6.9	10.2	7.4	7.8	7.8	9.8	2.9	-14.7	4.8
Luxembourg	8.4	2.5	4.1	1.5	4.4	5.4	5.0	6.6	1.4	-3.7	3.6
Hungary	4.9	3.8	4.1	4.0	4.5	3.2	3.6	0.8	0.8	-6.7	2.3
Malta ([1])	:	-1.6	2.6	-0.3	0.9	4.0	3.6	3.7	2.6	-2.1	1.5
Netherlands	3.9	1.9	0.1	0.3	2.2	2.0	3.4	3.9	1.9	-3.9	1.6
Austria	3.7	0.5	1.6	0.8	2.5	2.5	3.6	3.7	2.2	-3.9	1.7
Poland	4.3	1.2	1.4	3.9	5.3	3.6	6.2	6.8	5.1	1.7	4.0
Portugal	3.9	2.0	0.7	-0.9	1.6	0.8	1.4	2.4	0.0	-2.6	0.9
Romania	2.4	5.7	5.1	5.2	8.5	4.2	7.9	6.3	7.3	-7.1	4.6
Slovenia	4.4	2.8	4.0	2.8	4.3	4.5	5.9	6.9	3.7	-8.1	3.1
Slovakia	1.4	3.5	4.6	4.8	5.0	6.7	8.5	10.6	6.2	-4.7	4.7
Finland	5.3	2.3	1.8	2.0	4.1	2.9	4.4	5.3	0.9	-8.0	2.1
Sweden	4.5	1.3	2.5	2.3	4.2	3.2	4.3	3.3	-0.4	-5.1	2.0
United Kingdom	3.9	2.5	2.1	2.8	3.0	2.2	2.8	2.7	-0.1	-5.0	1.7
Iceland	4.3	3.9	0.1	2.4	7.7	7.5	4.6	6.0	1.0	-6.8	3.1
Norway	3.3	2.0	1.5	1.0	3.9	2.7	2.3	2.7	0.8	-1.4	1.9
Switzerland	3.6	1.2	0.4	-0.2	2.5	2.6	3.6	3.6	1.9	-1.9	1.7
Croatia	3.0	3.8	5.4	5.0	4.2	4.2	4.7	5.5	2.4	-5.8	3.2
FYR of Macedonia	4.5	-4.5	0.9	2.8	4.1	4.1	4.0	5.9	4.9	-0.7	2.6
Turkey	6.8	-5.7	6.6	4.9	9.4	8.4	6.9	4.7	0.4	-4.5	3.8
Japan	2.9	0.2	0.3	1.4	2.7	1.9	2.0	2.4	-1.2	-5.2	0.7
United States	4.1	1.1	1.8	2.5	3.6	3.1	2.7	1.9	0.0	-2.6	1.8

Source: Eurostate

average GDP growth rates were given. There is no sharp difference of average GDP growth rate of EU-27 and Euro Area since both of them attained 1.5 and 1.4 percent per annum. The rate ranges from 4-5 percent in Bulgaria, Estonia, Latvia, Lithuania, Poland, Romania, Slovakia, and countries ranged from 3-4 percent belong to Czech, Ireland, Greece, Cyprus, Slovenia, Iceland, Croatia and Turkey.GDP growth of Japan is below the EU but USA grew marginally higher than EU .In spite of facing negative growth rate in 2008 and 2009 due to financial crisis, most of the countries could reach positive growth rates in 2010 and 2011.

Fiscal convergence in EU-17 has been disrupted since before crisis began and high fiscal deficit and unsustainable debt were clouded over the economies. Some important economies like Germany, Spain, France, Greece, became highly indebted.EU-27 and EU-17 were indebted more than 80% of GDP which were above the Maastricht treaty level. Debt GDP ratio surpassed 100 in Ireland, Greece, Italy, Portugal, and even Belgium, Germany, France, Hungary, etc. approached toward 100%. Therefore, uncovered debt burden produced economies in debt crisis with depression followed by low growth rate and ultimately banking crisis and contagion broke out. Moreover, fiscal convergence in most of the giant economies like Belgium, Czech, Denmark, Ireland, Greece, Spain,Hungary, Netherlands, Portugal,Rumania, Slovenia, and UK were out of the Maastricht treaty and far above the treaty level.EU failed to sustain fiscal federalism and were fallen into increasing debt. The debt crisis of EU-17 had lowered the credit rating of the highly indebted countries as measured by S&P and others in which Germany scored AAA, followed by Italy BBB+, Spain BBB+, Ireland BBB+, Portugal BB, and Greece CCC respectively.(Table-4.2)

Table-4.2: Credit Rating

	S&P	*MOODY'S*	*FITCH*	*SyrCDS*
Greece	CCC	C	CCC	NA
Portugal	BB	Ba3	BB+	1.118
Ireland	BBB+	Ba1	BBB+	7000
Spain	BBB+	A3	BBB	591
Italy	BBB+	A3	A	548
Germany	AAA	AAA	AAA	105

Source: Economist.com

Unless the credit rating of the debt ridden countries is improved, the restructuring of the debt policy along with bad loans and banking crisis would not be minimized. Recently, EU in consultation with ECB and IMF sanctioned bailout package to PIGS amounting to €78 billion,€67.5billion,€345billion and€100billion respectively to solve the debt crisis.IMF will monitor Spain's banking sector and EU as a whole would follow Basel-III rules. Italy, being a lower deficit nation and wealthier nation is demanding a bail out sanction as like Spain ,is holding more than €2 trillion debt and is selling as much as €6.5billion of treasury bills on June13,followed by a bond auction the next day. However, Italy's debt load had traditionally led the country to be perceived as a bigger credit risk than Spain.

In the gross value added in GDP in EU, the share of agriculture is very poor limited to 2-3 percent, only five countries, namely, Bulgaria , Lithuania, Iceland ,Croatia, Turkey crossed 4%.The industrial share of the countries of EU ranged from 17 to 25 percent and the rest of the shares go to service sector which dominate the nation's output in which trade and finance covered 20-25 percent of the GDP share. Therefore, there is no significant role of agriculture in contributing to GDP.

We have derived Euro Area's Beta and Sigma convergence hypothesis where we find that convergence was satisfied. In Table-4.4 , we have inflation rates of Euro Area vis-à-vis EU where Euro area inflation rate converges along with EU. But, it is not clear about the convergence in the individual countries like Bulgaria, Estonia, Spain, Latvia, Lithuania, Hungary, Poland, Romania, Slovenia, Iceland, Turkey, etc . As we analysed earlier that new East European Countries have disrupted the convergence scenario of the EU-16 or EU-12(Euro Area), that the Table-4.4 proved the same. The inflation convergence of EU and Euro Area were compared with USA and Japan where inflation convergence was not satisfied in USA and deflationary trend was observed in Japan.

In Fig-4.1, IMF global projection model of Euro area inflation was shown on the base year 2012 where the inflation rate would reach at 4% in 2014 within 90% confidence interval or it can reach at below 2% at 70% confidence interval and then the convergence of Euro area inflation rate would be satisfied. In spite of that, IMF Staff Simulation model of inflation differentials of Euro Area closes towards the 2% between north and south as shown in Fig-4.2.

Table-4.3: Gross value added at basic prices: % of total

	Agriculture, hunting, forestry & fishing		Industry		Construction		Trade, transport & communication services		Business activities & financial services		Other services	
	1999	2009	1999	2009	1999	2009	1999	2009	1999	2009	1999	2009
EU-27	2.5	1.7	22.5	17.9	5.6	6.3	21.6	20.9	25.7	29.2	22.3	24.0
Euro area (EA-16)	2.6	1.6	22.3	17.8	5.7	6.3	21.1	20.7	25.9	29.3	22.4	24.2
Belgium	1.3	0.7	22.1	16.3	5.0	5.4	21.7	21.7	27.1	30.5	22.8	25.4
Bulgaria	15.9	5.6	20.1	21.4	5.0	8.9	22.2	25.4	19.8	23.0	17.0	15.7
Czech Republic	3.9	2.2	31.8	30.3	7.0	7.4	24.6	24.2	16.4	18.3	16.4	17.5
Denmark	2.4	1.1	20.4	17.4	5.6	4.9	22.3	19.5	21.8	27.4	27.5	29.8
Germany	1.2	0.8	24.8	22.2	5.5	4.3	17.8	17.5	28.0	31.1	22.7	24.1
Estonia	4.4	2.6	21.3	19.5	5.6	7.0	28.1	25.4	22.5	24.8	18.0	20.8
Ireland	3.6	1.4	35.8	23.9	6.6	8.5	17.8	17.5	20.0	28.7	16.2	20.0
Greece (¹)	6.6	3.2	13.9	*13.3*	7.0	*4.6*	30.1	*33.1*	20.6	*20.1*	21.7	*25.7*
Spain	4.5	2.6	21.3	15.3	7.9	10.8	26.6	24.6	18.8	23.6	21.0	23.0
France	3.0	1.7	18.0	12.4	5.1	6.4	19.2	19.0	29.5	33.7	25.2	26.7
Italy	3.0	1.8	23.8	18.8	4.9	6.3	23.9	22.2	24.1	28.8	20.3	22.1
Cyprus	4.0	2.1	12.4	9.6	7.2	9.0	30.5	25.9	23.8	28.1	22.1	25.3
Latvia	3.9	3.1	18.3	14.0	6.4	6.6	31.4	28.0	17.9	26.1	22.0	22.2
Lithuania	7.3	4.2	22.5	20.4	7.6	6.3	27.6	32.0	12.1	16.3	23.0	20.8
Luxembourg	0.8	0.3	12.9	8.2	6.1	5.8	22.0	19.9	41.6	49.0	16.6	16.9
Hungary	5.8	3.0	26.7	24.9	4.6	4.8	21.3	21.2	19.5	23.6	22.2	22.5
Malta	2.7	1.8	22.4	16.0	3.8	3.4	32.9	23.3	16.9	24.3	21.3	31.2
Netherlands	2.7	1.7	19.0	17.9	5.5	6.0	23.2	20.3	27.4	28.2	22.3	25.9
Austria	2.1	1.5	23.0	21.8	7.8	7.3	24.4	23.5	21.1	23.7	21.5	22.1
Poland	5.2	3.6	24.6	23.0	8.2	7.5	27.0	27.1	16.9	20.2	18.1	18.6
Portugal	3.9	2.3	21.4	16.8	7.4	6.1	25.2	25.7	20.5	23.6	21.7	25.5
Romania	14.4	7.0	27.9	26.4	5.4	10.9	24.6	23.6	15.4	16.8	12.3	15.4
Slovenia	3.4	2.4	29.0	23.2	7.2	7.9	20.6	22.0	20.0	23.3	19.8	21.2
Slovakia	4.8	2.6	29.7	25.5	5.6	8.8	27.1	24.3	16.4	21.9	16.4	16.9
Finland	3.5	2.7	28.0	21.2	6.1	7.0	20.9	19.5	20.1	25.0	21.5	24.7
Sweden	2.3	1.7	24.5	19.7	4.3	5.4	19.1	20.0	24.6	25.0	25.2	28.2
United Kingdom	1.1	0.8	22.3	14.9	5.1	5.9	22.9	20.4	27.0	34.1	21.5	23.9
Iceland (²)	9.7	6.3	17.9	17.7	8.0	9.3	22.1	18.4	18.5	25.5	23.8	22.8
Norway	2.4	1.2	30.0	35.2	4.7	5.3	21.3	16.3	18.4	19.5	23.2	22.5
Switzerland	1.6	1.2	22.5	21.2	5.4	5.6	21.8	22.0	23.0	23.5	25.7	26.5
Croatia (²)	9.1	6.4	23.1	20.2	5.3	8.3	22.9	25.2	18.2	22.9	21.4	16.9
FYR of Macedonia (²)	12.9	11.6	26.5	24.1	6.1	5.7	24.3	25.0	9.7	16.0	20.5	17.7
Turkey	10.7	9.1	25.4	20.9	5.6	4.2	26.8	29.4	20.6	23.9	10.9	12.4
Japan	1.4	:	24.5	:	7.2	:	:	:	18.4	:	28.5	:
United States	1.2	:	19.6	:	4.7	:	20.0	:	31.2	:	23.2	:

Source: Eurosat

Table-4.4: Inflation rate (%)

	1999	2000	2001	2002	2003	2004	2005	2006	2007	2008	2009
EU	1.2	1.9	2.2	2.1	2.0	2.0	2.2	2.2	2.3	3.7	1.0
Euro area	1.1	2.1	2.3	2.2	2.1	2.1	2.2	2.2	2.1	3.3	0.3
Belgium	1.1	2.7	2.4	1.6	1.5	1.9	2.5	2.3	1.8	4.5	0.0
Bulgaria	2.6	10.3	7.4	5.8	2.3	6.1	6.0	7.4	7.6	12.0	2.5
Czech Republic	1.8	3.9	4.5	1.4	-0.1	2.6	1.6	2.1	3.0	6.3	0.6
Denmark	2.1	2.7	2.3	2.4	2.0	0.9	1.7	1.9	1.7	3.6	1.1
Germany	0.6	1.4	1.9	1.4	1.0	1.8	1.9	1.8	2.3	2.8	0.2
Estonia	3.1	3.9	5.6	3.6	1.4	3.0	4.1	4.4	6.7	10.6	0.2
Ireland	2.5	5.3	4.0	4.7	4.0	2.3	2.2	2.7	2.9	3.1	-1.7
Greece	2.1	2.9	3.7	3.9	3.4	3.0	3.5	3.3	3.0	4.2	1.3
Spain	2.2	3.5	2.8	3.6	3.1	3.1	3.4	3.6	2.8	4.1	-0.2
France	0.6	1.8	1.8	1.9	2.2	2.3	1.9	1.9	1.6	3.2	0.1
Italy	1.7	2.6	2.3	2.6	2.8	2.3	2.2	2.2	2.0	3.5	0.8
Cyprus	1.1	4.9	2.0	2.8	4.0	1.9	2.0	2.2	2.2	4.4	0.2
Latvia	2.1	2.6	2.5	2.0	2.9	6.2	6.9	6.6	10.1	15.3	3.3
Lithuania	1.5	1.1	1.6	0.3	-1.1	1.2	2.7	3.8	5.8	11.1	4.2
Luxembourg	1.0	3.8	2.4	2.1	2.5	3.2	3.8	3.0	2.7	4.1	0.0
Hungary	10.0	10.0	9.1	5.2	4.7	6.8	3.5	4.0	7.9	6.0	4.0
Malta	2.3	3.0	2.5	2.6	1.9	2.7	2.5	2.6	0.7	4.7	1.8
Netherlands	2.0	2.3	5.1	3.9	2.2	1.4	1.5	1.7	1.6	2.2	1.0
Austria	0.5	2.0	2.3	1.7	1.3	2.0	2.1	1.7	2.2	3.2	0.4
Poland	7.2	10.1	5.3	1.9	0.7	3.6	2.2	1.3	2.6	4.2	4.0
Portugal	2.2	2.8	4.4	3.7	3.3	2.5	2.1	3.0	2.4	2.7	-0.9
Romania	45.8	45.7	34.5	22.5	15.3	11.9	9.1	6.6	4.9	7.9	5.6
Slovenia	6.1	8.9	8.6	7.5	5.7	3.7	2.5	2.5	3.8	5.5	0.9
Slovakia	10.4	12.2	7.2	3.5	8.4	7.5	2.8	4.3	1.9	3.9	0.9
Finland	1.3	2.9	2.7	2.0	1.3	0.1	0.8	1.3	1.6	3.9	1.6
Sweden	0.5	1.3	2.7	1.9	2.3	1.0	0.8	1.5	1.7	3.3	1.9
United Kingdom	1.3	0.8	1.2	1.3	1.4	1.3	2.1	2.3	2.3	3.6	2.2
Iceland	2.1	4.4	6.6	5.3	1.4	2.3	1.4	4.6	3.6	12.8	16.3
Norway	2.1	3.0	2.7	0.8	2.0	0.6	1.5	2.5	0.7	3.4	2.3
Switzerland	:	:	:	:	:	:	:	1.0	0.8	2.3	-0.7
Croatia	3.7	4.5	4.3	2.5	2.4	2.1	3.0	3.3	2.7	5.8	2.2
Turkey	61.4	53.2	56.8	47.0	25.3	10.1	8.1	9.3	8.8	10.4	6.3
Japan	-0.3	-0.7	-0.7	-0.9	-0.3	0.0	-0.3	0.3	0.0	1.4	-1.4
United States	2.2	3.4	2.8	1.6	2.3	2.7	3.4	3.2	2.8	3.8	-0.4

Source: Eurosat

Fig-4.1: Euro Area Inflation Forecast

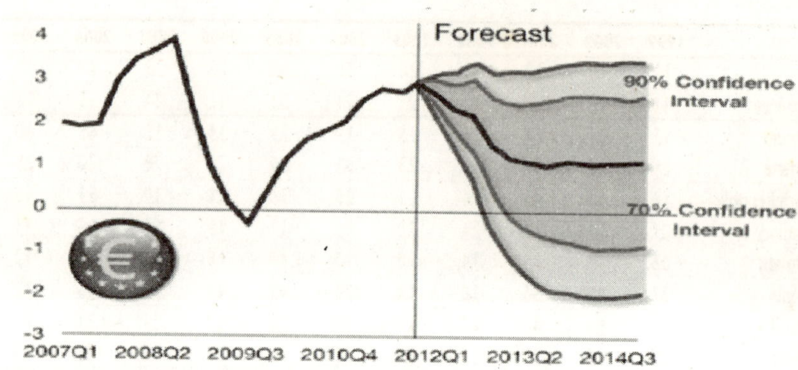

Sources: IMF; and Global Projection Model

Fig-4.2: Euro Area :Simulated Inflation Differentials

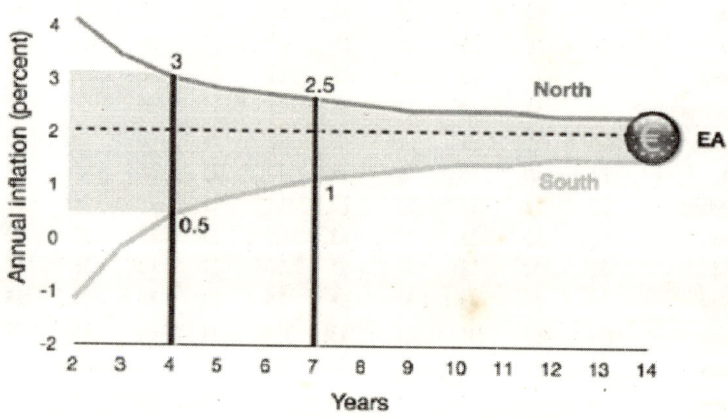

Source: IMF staff simulations

Current account deficit in Euro Area jumped to maximum level in 2008 due to financial crisis and started to decline there off but current account of the area were positive since 1999.On the other hand, EU-27 confronted with increasing current account deficit, where Greece, Spain, Italy, Portugal, UK, Turkey and Croatia are most important, although the current account deficit of EU-27 is less harmful than the current account deficit in USA. The remarkable feature is that Belgium, Denmark, Germany, Luxembourg, Netherland, Austria, Finland, Sweden, Norway have been facing with positive current account balance where Germany's huge current account surplus dominates EU.(Table-4.5)

Table-4.5: Current Account Balance(Euro 1000 million)

	2004	2005	2006	2007	2008	2009
EU-27 (¹)	-36.0	-82.9	-146.2	-127.2	-243.3	-131.8
Euro area (EA-16) (²)	61.7	11.7	-10.2	13.5	-153.8	-55.9
Belgium	19.1	7.9	6.3	7.3	-10.1	1.0
Bulgaria	-1.3	-2.7	-4.6	-7.8	-8.2	-3.2
Czech Republic	-4.7	-1.3	-2.7	-4.1	-1.0	-1.5
Denmark	5.9	9.0	6.5	3.4	5.1	9.0
Germany	102.8	114.6	150.1	185.1	167.0	119.1
Estonia	-1.1	-1.1	-2.2	-2.8	-1.5	0.6
Ireland	-0.9	-5.7	-6.3	-10.1	-10.2	-4.9
Greece	-10.7	-14.7	-23.7	-32.6	-34.8	-26.6
Spain	-44.2	-66.9	-88.3	-105.3	-106.0	-58.3
France	10.0	-10.9	-9.2	-18.9	-37.1	-36.8
Italy	-13.0	-23.6	-38.3	-37.7	-53.6	-48.2
Cyprus	-0.6	-0.8	-1.0	-1.9	-3.0	-1.4
Latvia	-1.4	-1.6	-3.6	-4.7	-3.0	1.8
Lithuania	-1.4	-1.5	-2.6	-4.1	-3.8	1.0
Luxembourg	3.3	3.3	3.5	3.6	2.1	2.1
Hungary	-6.8	-6.4	-6.5	-6.6	-7.4	0.2
Malta	-0.3	-0.4	-0.5	-0.3	-0.3	-0.2
Netherlands	36.9	37.3	50.4	49.3	28.5	28.9
Austria	4.8	4.9	7.1	9.6	:	:
Poland	-8.2	-3.0	-7.4	-14.7	-18.3	-5.0
Portugal	-12.4	-15.9	-17.2	-17.1	-21.7	-17.3
Romania	-5.1	-6.9	-10.2	-16.8	-16.2	-5.2
Slovenia	-0.7	-0.5	-0.8	-1.6	-2.5	-0.5
Slovakia	-1.2	-3.2	-3.6	-2.9	-4.3	-2.0
Finland	10.0	5.7	7.6	7.6	5.8	2.3
Sweden	21.1	20.4	26.5	27.8	31.3	21.6
United Kingdom	-36.9	-48.0	-64.4	-55.3	-27.2	-17.6
Iceland	-1.1	-2.2	-3.3	-2.4	-2.3	-0.3
Norway	28.3	39.7	46.2	40.1	57.3	38.2
Croatia	-1.5	-2.0	-2.7	-3.2	-4.4	-2.5
Turkey	-11.5	-17.8	-25.6	-27.9	-28.1	-9.9
Japan	138.5	133.3	136.0	154.0	105.1	:
United States	-507.5	-604.6	-639.5	-531.5	-479.6	:

Source: Eurosat

In Fig-4.3, the current account deficit as percent of GDP in Euro Area was shown as partially cyclical in the sense that it improved from deficit to surplus then turned into negative since 2005 and even then improved but within negative range and after 2010, it became more worse.

Fig-4.3: Current account deficit % of GDP of Euro Area.

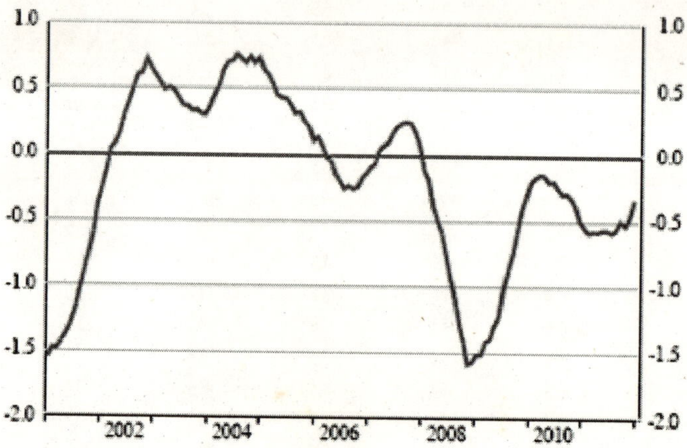

Source: ECB

The current account balance as percent of GDP of Euro zone and some important countries as compared with developed countries are given below in the Table-4.6, where we found that the positive current account balance turned into negative up till revival of the bloc after the crisis in 2010 but Italy, Spain, Greece, Portugal and Ireland went out of limited current account deficit. However, the projection for 2016 is improving.

In Fig-4.4, the current account deficit as percent of GDP of Germany, France, Greece, Italy, Spain, Portugal and Ireland have been shown taking the period from 1999 to 2010. These are asymmetric in patterns.

Table-4.6: Current Account balance % of GDP

	2003	2004	2005	2006	2007	2008	2009	2010	Projections 2011	2012	2016
Advanced Economies	**-0.7**	**-0.7**	**-1.2**	**-1.2**	**-0.9**	**-1.1**	**-0.3**	**-0.2**	**-0.3**	**-0.2**	**-0.6**
United States	-4.7	-5.3	-5.9	-6.0	-5.1	-4.7	-2.7	-3.2	-3.2	-2.8	-3.4
Euro Area	0.4	1.2	0.4	0.4	0.2	-0.6	-0.2	0.1	0.0	0.0	0.1
Germany	1.9	4.7	5.1	6.5	7.6	6.7	5.0	5.3	5.1	4.6	3.6
France	0.7	0.5	-0.5	-0.6	-1.0	-1.9	-1.9	-2.1	-2.8	-2.7	-2.2
Italy	-1.3	-0.9	-1.7	-2.6	-2.4	-2.9	-2.1	-3.5	-3.4	-3.0	-2.4
Spain	-3.5	-5.3	-7.4	-9.0	-10.0	-9.7	-5.5	-4.5	-4.8	-4.5	-3.5
Netherlands	5.6	7.6	7.4	9.3	6.7	4.3	4.6	7.1	7.9	8.2	6.0
Belgium	3.4	3.2	2.0	1.9	1.6	-1.9	0.8	1.2	1.0	1.2	2.4
Austria	1.7	2.2	2.2	2.8	3.5	4.9	2.9	3.2	3.1	3.1	3.2
Greece	-6.6	-5.9	-7.4	-11.2	-14.4	-14.7	-11.0	-10.4	-8.2	-7.1	-3.8
Portugal	-6.5	-8.4	-10.4	-10.7	-10.1	-12.6	-10.9	-9.9	-8.7	-8.5	-5.7
Finland	4.8	6.2	3.4	4.2	4.3	2.9	2.3	3.1	2.8	2.6	2.8
Ireland	-0.0	-0.6	-3.5	-3.6	-5.3	-5.6	-3.0	-0.7	0.2	0.6	0.1

Source: IMF World Economic Outlook, April 2011

Fig-4.4: Current Account Deficit % of GDP

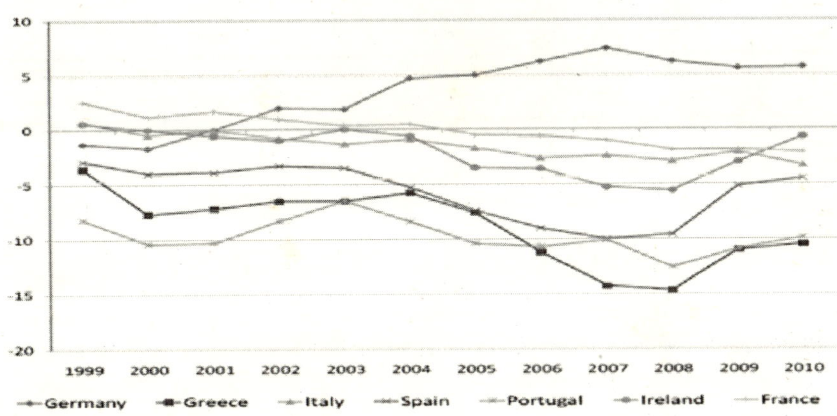

Source: Eurostat.

The national currencies of Latvia, Hungary, Romania, Sweden, UK, Ireland, Turkey and Japan with respect to Euro have been devalued, so, there is clearly a gain to Euro from those countries from international and intra-regional trade. Thus, the current account deficits have been improved by those countries from Euro trade except Japan and Sweden. (Table-4.7)

Table-4.7: Exchange rate against Euro

	2000	2001	2002	2003	2004	2005	2006	2007	2008	2009	2010 ([2])
Bulgaria	1.9522	1.9482	1.9492	1.9490	1.9533	1.9558	1.9558	1.9558	1.9558	1.9558	1.9558
Czech Republic	35.599	34.068	30.804	31.846	31.891	29.782	28.342	27.766	24.946	26.435	25.262
Denmark	7.4538	7.4521	7.4305	7.4307	7.4399	7.4518	7.4591	7.4506	7.4560	7.4462	7.4454
Estonia	15.647	15.647	15.647	15.647	15.647	15.647	15.647	15.647	15.647	15.647	15.647
Latvia	0.5592	0.5601	0.5810	0.6407	0.6652	0.6962	0.6962	0.7001	0.7027	0.7057	0.7086
Lithuania	3.6952	3.5823	3.4594	3.4527	3.4529	3.4528	3.4528	3.4528	3.4528	3.4528	3.4528
Hungary	260.04	256.59	242.96	253.62	251.66	248.05	264.26	251.35	251.51	280.33	276.95
Poland	4.0082	3.6721	3.8574	4.3996	4.5268	4.0230	3.8959	3.7837	3.5121	4.3276	3.9922
Romania	1.9922	2.6004	3.1270	3.7551	4.0510	3.6209	3.5258	3.3353	3.6826	4.2399	4.2048
Sweden	8.4452	9.2551	9.1611	9.1242	9.1243	9.2822	9.2544	9.2501	9.6152	10.6191	9.5486
United Kingdom	0.60948	0.62187	0.62883	0.69199	0.67866	0.68380	0.68173	0.68434	0.79628	0.89094	0.85324
Iceland	72.58	87.42	86.18	86.65	87.14	78.23	87.76	87.63	143.83	172.67	161.82
Norway	8.1129	8.0484	7.5086	8.0033	8.3697	8.0092	8.0472	8.0165	8.2237	8.7278	7.9717
Switzerland	1.5579	1.5105	1.4670	1.5212	1.5438	1.5483	1.5729	1.6427	1.5874	1.5100	1.3786
Croatia	7.6432	7.4820	7.4130	7.5688	7.4967	7.4008	7.3247	7.3376	7.2239	7.3400	7.2688
Turkey	0.5748	1.1024	1.4397	1.6949	1.7771	1.6771	1.8090	1.7865	1.9064	2.1631	1.9882
Japan	99.47	108.68	118.06	130.97	134.44	136.85	146.02	161.25	152.45	130.34	115.98
United States	0.9236	0.8956	0.9456	1.1312	1.2439	1.2441	1.2556	1.3705	1.4708	1.3948	1.3137

Source: Eurosat

Fig-4.5: Bilateral Exchange Rate,1999=100

Source: WEO-2012.

In Fig-4.5, the bilateral exchange rates of Euro with respect to US Dollar,Yen and Pound Sterling were shown where the rates drastically had fallen as an effect of debt crisis followed by financial crisis in Euro since 2008.Although on the inception of Euro, all the rates had been fallen marginally.

EU unemployment rate is worse than US and Japan since 1999 in which EU zone is more worse than EU-27.The unemployment rate is alarming in the macro stability scenario. It is greater than 10.0% in Estonia, Ireland, Spain, Latvia, Lithuania, Hungary, Slovakia, and Turkey. On the other hand, the rates are manageable and harmless in Netherland, Austria, Norway, and Denmark. (Table-4.8)

Table-4.8: Unemployment rate (%)

	1999	2000	2001	2002	2003	2004	2005	2006	2007	2008	2009
EU-27	:	8.7	8.5	8.9	9.0	9.1	8.9	8.2	7.1	7.0	8.9
Euro area (EA-16)	9.3	8.4	8.0	8.4	8.8	9.0	9.0	8.3	7.5	7.5	9.4
Belgium	8.5	6.9	6.6	7.5	8.2	8.4	8.5	8.3	7.5	7.0	7.9
Bulgaria	:	16.4	19.5	18.2	13.7	12.1	10.1	9.0	6.9	5.6	6.8
Czech Republic	8.6	8.7	8.0	7.3	7.8	8.3	7.9	7.2	5.3	4.4	6.7
Denmark	5.2	4.3	4.5	4.6	5.4	5.5	4.8	3.9	3.8	3.3	6.0
Germany	8.2	7.5	7.6	8.4	9.3	9.8	10.7	9.8	8.4	7.3	7.5
Estonia	:	13.6	12.6	10.3	10.0	9.7	7.9	5.9	4.7	5.5	13.8
Ireland	5.6	4.2	3.9	4.5	4.6	4.5	4.4	4.5	4.6	6.3	11.9
Greece	12.0	11.2	10.7	10.3	9.7	10.5	9.9	8.9	8.3	7.7	9.5
Spain	12.5	11.1	10.3	11.1	11.1	10.6	9.2	8.5	8.3	11.3	18.0
France	10.4	9.0	8.3	8.6	9.0	9.3	9.3	9.2	8.4	7.8	9.5
Italy	10.9	10.1	9.1	8.6	8.4	8.0	7.7	6.8	6.1	6.7	7.8
Cyprus	:	4.9	3.8	3.6	4.1	4.7	5.3	4.6	4.0	3.6	5.3
Latvia	14.0	13.7	12.9	12.2	10.5	10.4	8.9	6.8	6.0	7.5	17.1
Lithuania	13.7	16.4	16.5	13.5	12.5	11.4	8.3	5.6	4.3	5.8	13.7
Luxembourg	2.4	2.2	1.9	2.6	3.8	5.0	4.6	4.6	4.2	4.9	5.2
Hungary	6.9	6.4	5.7	5.8	5.9	6.1	7.2	7.5	7.4	7.8	10.0
Malta	:	6.7	7.6	7.5	7.6	7.4	7.2	7.1	6.4	5.9	7.0
Netherlands	3.2	2.8	2.2	2.8	3.7	4.6	4.7	3.9	3.2	2.8	3.4
Austria	3.9	3.6	3.6	4.2	4.3	4.9	5.2	4.8	4.4	3.8	4.8
Poland	13.4	16.1	18.3	20.0	19.7	19.0	17.8	13.9	9.6	7.1	8.2
Portugal	4.5	4.0	4.1	5.1	6.4	6.7	7.7	7.8	8.1	7.7	9.6
Romania	7.1	7.3	6.8	8.6	7.0	8.1	7.2	7.3	6.4	5.8	6.9
Slovenia	7.3	6.7	6.2	6.3	6.7	6.3	6.5	6.0	4.9	4.4	5.9
Slovakia	16.4	18.8	19.3	18.7	17.6	18.2	16.3	13.4	11.1	9.5	12.0
Finland	10.2	9.8	9.1	9.1	9.0	8.8	8.4	7.7	6.9	6.4	8.2
Sweden (¹)	6.7	5.6	5.8	6.0	6.6	7.4	7.6	7.0	6.1	6.2	8.3
United Kingdom	5.9	5.4	5.0	5.1	5.0	4.7	4.8	5.4	5.3	5.6	7.6
Norway	3.0	3.2	3.4	3.7	4.2	4.3	4.5	3.4	2.5	2.5	3.1
Croatia	:	:	:	14.8	14.2	13.7	12.7	11.2	9.6	8.4	9.1
Turkey	:	:	:	:	:	:	9.2	8.7	8.8	9.7	12.5
Japan	4.7	4.7	5.0	5.4	5.3	4.7	4.4	4.1	3.9	4.0	5.1
United States	4.2	4.0	4.8	5.8	6.0	5.5	5.1	4.6	4.6	5.8	9.3

Source: Eurostat

In Fig-4.6, the unemployment rates of Euro area as well as Germany, France, Italy and Spain were shown from 2006 January to 2012 January where unemployment of Euro Area had increased marginally from 2010 and high unemployment crisis observed in Spain which reached at more than 20%, but the rates of unemployment of Germany reduced from 2009, on the contrary, the rates increased and crossed 10% in Italy and France towards 2012 from 2008.

Fig-4.6: The unemployment rates of Euro Area

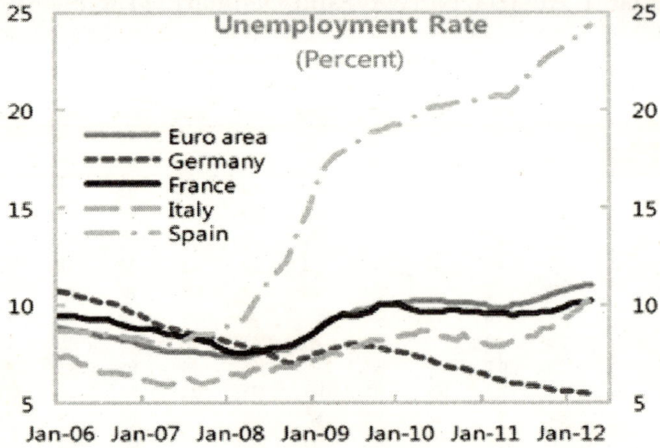

In EU-27, the unemployment rate is higher in male than the female but in Euro area, the unemployment rate in female is higher than male. The female unemployment rate is higher than male in 2009 in Belgium , Czech, Greece, Spain, France, Italy, Cyprus, Luxembourg, Malta, Poland, Portugal, Slovakia ,Croatia, respectively. In Japan and USA, the converse is true which were the same in the other EU-27 countries.(Table-4.9).This means that the gender development indices of EU-16 are more healthy.

In connection with unemployment, it is noted that the labour productivities of the most of the EU countries are falling viz,Belgium,Denmark,Germany,France,Italy,Luxembourg,Finland,Sweden etc and other countries are showing marginal increment in the labour productivity indices subject to the base EU-27=100.(Table-4.10)

Table-4.9 Unemployment by gender and by age(%)

	Male		Female		< 25 years	25-74 years
	2004	2009	2004	2009	2009	2009
EU-27	8.5	9.0	9.8	8.8	19.6	7.6
Euro area (EA-16)	8.1	9.3	10.1	9.6	19.4	8.2
Belgium	7.5	7.8	9.5	8.1	21.9	6.6
Bulgaria	12.6	7.0	11.5	6.6	16.2	6.0
Czech Republic	7.1	5.9	9.9	7.7	16.6	5.8
Denmark	5.1	6.5	6.0	5.4	11.2	5.0
Germany	10.3	8.0	9.1	6.9	10.4	7.1
Estonia	10.4	16.9	8.9	10.6	27.5	12.0
Ireland	4.8	14.9	4.0	8.0	24.4	10.1
Greece	6.6	6.9	16.2	13.2	25.8	8.3
Spain	8.0	17.7	14.3	18.4	37.8	15.9
France	8.4	9.2	10.3	9.8	23.3	7.8
Italy	6.4	6.8	10.5	9.3	25.3	6.4
Cyprus	3.6	5.2	6.0	5.5	14.0	4.4
Latvia	10.6	20.3	10.2	13.9	33.6	14.9
Lithuania	11.0	17.1	11.8	10.4	29.2	12.1
Luxembourg	3.6	4.6	6.8	6.0	16.9	4.2
Hungary	6.1	10.3	6.1	9.7	26.5	8.7
Malta	6.6	6.7	9.0	7.6	14.3	5.4
Netherlands	4.3	3.4	4.8	3.5	6.6	2.8
Austria	4.5	5.0	5.4	4.6	10.0	3.9
Poland	18.2	7.8	20.0	8.7	20.6	6.8
Portugal	5.9	9.0	7.7	10.3	20.0	8.7
Romania	9.1	7.7	6.9	5.8	20.8	5.4
Slovenia	5.9	5.9	6.9	5.8	13.6	5.1
Slovakia	17.4	11.4	19.2	12.8	27.3	10.4
Finland	8.7	8.9	8.9	7.6	21.5	6.4
Sweden	7.6	8.6	7.1	8.0	25.0	5.9
United Kingdom	5.1	8.6	4.2	6.4	19.1	5.5
Norway	4.6	3.6	3.9	2.6	8.9	2.2
Croatia	12.1	8.0	15.7	10.3	25.0	7.3
Turkey	:	12.5	:	12.6	22.7	10.3
Japan	4.9	5.3	4.4	4.8	9.1	4.7
United States	5.6	10.3	5.4	8.1	17.6	7.9

Source: Eurostat

Table-4.10:Labour productivity (based on PPS)

	Per person employed (EU-27=100)						Per hour worked (EU-15=100)					
	1999	2001	2003	2005	2007	2009	1999	2001	2003	2005	2007	2009
EU-27	100	100	100	100	100	100	:	86	87	87	87	88
Euro area (EA-16)	114	112	111	110	110	109	:	100	99	99	100	100
Belgium	134	134	135	130	127	125	*124*	*124*	*125*	*121*	*119*	*117*
Bulgaria	29	32	35	36	37	39	26	28	31	32	33	34
Czech Republic	62	63	67	69	71	72	44	47	50	51	54	55
Denmark	109	108	106	107	103	101	104	101	100	100	97	96
Germany	112	107	109	109	108	105	110	107	110	112	111	109
Estonia	43	48	55	61	66	65	:	36	40	44	48	51
Ireland	125	128	136	134	137	132	94	97	105	104	108	106
Greece	*91*	*97*	101	98	98	98	:	67	70	*69*	*68*	*74*
Spain	106	103	104	101	103	111	89	87	89	89	93	98
France	125	125	122	122	121	121	113	116	116	115	114	:
Italy	128	125	115	111	110	110	100	100	92	89	89	90
Cyprus	83	87	82	83	86	89	64	65	63	66	68	70
Latvia	38	42	44	48	51	50	:	28	30	33	36	37
Lithuania	40	47	52	54	59	56	34	38	42	43	46	44
Luxembourg	176	162	167	169	179	168	:	:	154	159	168	:
Hungary	57	62	66	68	68	70	41	45	49	50	50	52
Malta	:	90	90	91	89	88	*70*	*80*	*72*	*70*	*69*	*70*
Netherlands	112	113	111	114	114	111	114	116	115	120	121	117
Austria	120	115	118	115	114	112	103	98	100	99	100	99
Poland (¹)	54	56	60	61	62	65	:	39	42	43	44	:
Portugal	72	70	71	72	73	74	:	53	53	55	55	56
Romania	23	26	31	36	43	47	19	20	25	28	34	37
Slovenia	77	76	79	84	84	82	:	:	:	72	74	:
Slovakia	57	61	63	69	76	79	46	49	55	57	63	68
Finland	113	112	109	111	113	107	94	95	93	94	97	93
Sweden	114	109	111	111	114	112	101	98	103	102	104	101
United Kingdom	109	112	113	112	110	110	*93*	*95*	*98*	*98*	*97*	*97*
Iceland	108	104	101	105	*97*	*101*	:	:	:	:	:	:
Norway	120	137	135	153	150	145	120	140	141	157	155	150
Switzerland	111	107	105	104	*109*	*109*	96	95	94	91	97	:
Croatia	63	67	69	70	*74*	*78*	:	:	:	:	:	:
FYR of Macedonia	47	46	48	54	58	*58*	:	:	:	:	:	:
Turkey	49	*49*	*50*	*58*	*62*	*63*	:	:	:	:	:	:
Japan	97	98	99	99	98	93	:	:	:	:	:	:
United States	143	140	142	144	139	*141*	*113*	*113*	*116*	*119*	*116*	*118*

Source: Eurostat

In the Table-4.11, below, fiscal convergence of Euro Area(FD%GDP) have been shown where FD%GDP of the EU Area as a whole followed the criteria except in last year after the crisis had started and this is true in most of the countries in Euro Area, but the fiscal surplus were found in Finland, Sweden, Denmark and partially in Ireland in which deficit became out of control after the crisis. Yet, the convergence criteria in terms of Sigma and Beta convergence hypothesis were found statistically significant in the Euro Area. These convergences disrupted in 2009-2011 due to Euro-crisis.

Table-4.11: Fiscal deficit % of GDP

	EU-15	Ger	Fr	ITA	Sp	Neth	Bel	Gre	Aus	Por	Fin	Ire	Lux	Swe	Den	UK
99	-1.5	-1.6	-1.8	-1.9	-1.2	0.4	-0.6	-	-2.3	-2.7	1.7	27	3.4	0.9	13	0.9
00	-0.1	1.1	-1.5	-0.8	-0.9	2.0	0	-3.7	-1.7	-2.9	6.9	4.7	6.0	3.6	23	3.6
01	-1.9	-3.1	-1.5	-3.1	-0.5	-0.2	0.4	-4.5	0	-4.3	5.1	0.9	6.1	1.5	1.5	0.5
02	-2.6	-3.8	-3.1	-3.1	-0.2	-2.1	-0.1	-4.8	-0.7	-2.9	4.1	-0.4	21	-1.3	0.4	-2.1
03	-3.1	-4.2	-4.1	-3.6	-0.3	-3.1	-0.1	-5.6	-1.5	-3.0	26	0.4	0.5	-1.0	0.1	-3.4
04	-2.9	-3.8	-3.6	-3.5	-0.1	-1.7	-0.3	-7.5	-4.4	-3.4	25	1.4	-1.1	0.6	21	-3.5
05	-2.5	-3.3	-2.9	-4.4	13	-0.3	-2.7	-5.2	-1.7	-5.9	28	1.7	0	22	52	-3.4
06	-1.4	-1.6	-2.3	-3.4	24	0.5	0.1	-5.7	-1.5	-4.1	4.1	29	1.4	23	52	-2.7
07	-0.7	0.2	-2.7	-1.6	1.9	0.2	-0.3	-6.5	-0.9	-3.1	53	0.1	3.7	3.6	4.8	-2.7
08	-2.1	-0.1	-3.3	-2.7	-4.5	0.5	-1.3	-9.8	-0.9	-3.6	4.3	-7.3	3.0	22	32	-5.0
09	-6.4	-3.2	-7.5	-5.4	-11.2	-5.6	-5.8	-15.8	-4.1	-10.1	-2.5	-14.2	-0.9	-0.7	-2.7	-11.5
10	-6.3	-4.3	-7.1	-4.6	-9.3	-5.1	-4.1	-10.6	−4.1	-9.8	-2.5	-31.3	-1.1	0.2	-2.6	-10.3

Source: Eurostat

During the financial crisis, the index of production in most of European countries fell down steadily in 2008 and 2009 respectively. In EU-27 and Euro area-16, the indices decreased by more than 13% in 2009 which almost revitalized the present Euro crisis. (Table-4.12):

Table-4.12:Annual Growth rates for industry(%)

	Index of production (1)					Domestic output price index (2)				
	2005	2006	2007	2008	2009	2005	2006	2007	2008	2009
EU-27	1.3	4.2	3.6	-1.8	-13.8	5.1	5.6	2.7	7.6	-4.4
Euro area (EA-16)	1.4	4.3	3.7	-1.8	-14.9	4.1	5.1	2.7	6.1	-5.1
Belgium	-0.9	5.0	2.9	-0.6	-13.9	5.7	5.8	2.1	9.3	-7.2
Bulgaria	7.2	6.2	9.5	0.4	-18.2	7.3	8.7	8.0	13.2	-4.3
Czech Republic	4.3	8.7	10.6	-2.4	-13.1	3.1	1.5	4.1	4.5	-3.2
Denmark	2.7	4.1	-2.1	-1.1	-15.1	9.2	7.9	1.6	13.2	-6.7
Germany	3.5	5.7	6.0	-0.0	-16.3	4.4	5.4	1.3	5.4	-4.1
Estonia	11.1	10.2	6.4	-4.8	-25.9	1.7	4.3	9.6	9.6	-0.3
Ireland	3.9	3.2	5.2	-2.2	-4.5	2.3	3.6	2.4	6.1	-3.6
Greece	-1.6	0.8	2.3	-4.2	-9.2	5.9	7.3	4.1	10.0	-5.8
Spain	0.8	3.9	2.0	-7.3	-15.8	4.7	5.4	3.6	6.6	-3.4
France	0.3	1.3	1.3	-2.8	-12.3	3.1	3.8	2.8	5.6	-6.4
Italy	-0.7	3.6	1.8	-3.5	-18.4	4.0	5.2	3.3	5.8	-5.4
Cyprus	1.0	0.6	4.3	3.9	-8.7	4.9	5.3	3.6	11.7	-1.8
Latvia	7.4	6.5	0.9	-3.9	-15.8	7.1	9.6	18.6	15.7	-1.8
Lithuania	7.1	6.5	2.4	5.5	-14.6	5.9	6.9	9.4	15.8	-6.7
Luxembourg	2.8	2.4	-0.6	-5.3	-15.8	3.6	12.8	4.4	15.1	-9.2
Hungary	7.3	10.6	8.0	-1.0	-17.4	6.1	8.4	6.5	11.6	1.2
Malta	:	:	:	:	:	:	17.9	-3.7	14.8	9.3
Netherlands	0.5	1.5	2.3	1.4	-7.6	7.0	8.6	5.3	8.9	-9.8
Austria	4.3	7.4	5.9	1.1	-11.9	3.4	2.1	4.1	4.8	-1.8
Poland	4.4	12.2	9.5	2.0	-3.6	2.5	3.4	4.0	5.4	2.4
Portugal	-3.5	3.2	0.1	-4.1	-8.6	:	4.4	2.9	5.2	-3.8
Romania	-2.7	9.8	10.1	2.6	-5.9	10.8	10.3	8.4	12.8	2.1
Slovenia	4.6	6.3	7.4	1.6	-17.6	2.8	2.4	5.5	5.6	-0.4
Slovakia	1.0	15.7	16.9	3.1	-13.7	3.7	6.3	1.8	6.2	-2.7
Finland	-0.6	10.1	4.8	1.0	-21.1	4.3	6.3	3.9	8.6	-6.3
Sweden	2.2	3.6	3.9	-2.9	-17.9	3.9	6.1	3.6	6.1	-0.3
United Kingdom	-1.1	0.5	0.3	-3.1	-10.0	11.1	8.6	1.7	16.0	-2.9
Norway	-0.4	-2.1	-1.3	0.3	-3.6	6.1	8.6	-0.6	15.2	-1.8
Switzerland	2.7	7.8	9.5	1.2	-7.7	1.6	2.7	2.5	4.2	-2.4
Croatia	5.0	4.3	5.0	0.7	-8.9	2.7	2.7	3.4	8.3	-0.5
Turkey	5.7	7.3	6.9	-0.6	-9.8	7.1	9.8	6.0	13.0	1.0
Japan	1.4	4.4	2.8	-3.3	-21.7	:	:	:	:	:
United States	3.3	2.3	1.5	-2.3	-9.8	:	:	:	:	:

Source: Eurostat

In Fig-4.7,the industrial production of Euro area as well as Germany, France, Italy and Spain-the crisis prone countries were shown clearly from Jan 2006 to Jan 2012 where the indices started to fall since 2008,then revived up to 2011 and then again began to decline due to crisis.

Fig-4.7: Industrial Production Index excluding construction, 2006=100

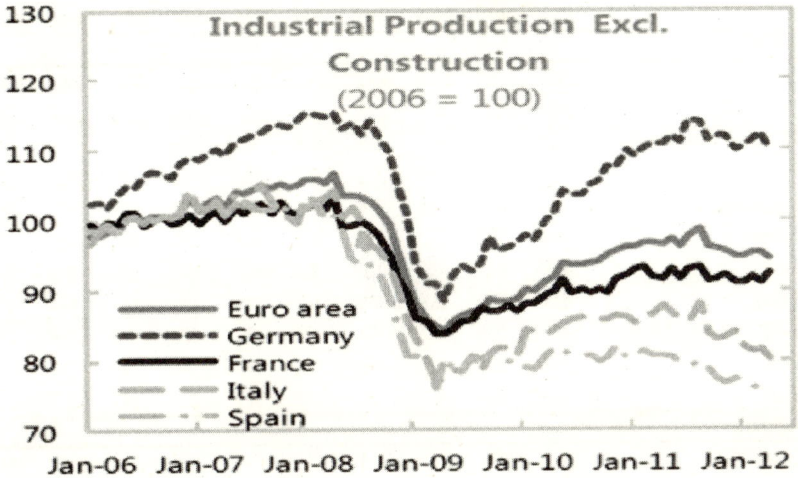

Source: WEO-2012

The chief destination of exports of EU is declining only to USA and Japan but it is stepping up to China, India, EU, Russia, Brazil etc. although its main partner is USA. On the other hand , the principal destination of imports of EU went to USA, Japan, EU, Russia, India, Brazil where the imports to USA and Japan have been dwindling since long period. The trade balances of EU with their partners became negative with China, Norway, Japan, South Korea and Brazil where negative trade balance are increasing with China and Russia.Basically,EU-27 is a deficit country in trade balance and it is upward . (Table-4.13)

In Table-4.14, Debt% of GDP of Euro Area during 1999-2011 was shown. Most of the countries of EU were out of the Maastricht Treaty and crossed the danger level of debt GDP ratio. There is no possibility of convergence of debt GDP ratio. Neither the Sigma nor the Beta convergence hypothesis was maintained by the EU. So, the debt crisis broke out with obvious reasons and it became grave in 2010 and 2011.No bailout package was fitted by the new EU members and new treaty of Brussels and Lisbon. Of late Greece, Spain , Portugal and Ireland were granted more than 112 billion Euro for bailout package by the European Commission.

	2000	2001	2002	2003	2004	2005	2006	2007	2008	2009
EXPORTS										
Extra EU-27	849.7	884.7	891.9	869.2	953.0	1 052.7	1 160.1	1 240.5	1 309.8	1 094.4
United States	238.2	245.6	247.9	227.3	235.5	252.7	269.1	261.5	250.1	204.7
China (excl. Hong Kong)	25.9	30.7	35.1	41.5	48.4	51.8	63.8	71.9	78.4	81.6
Russia	22.7	31.6	34.4	37.2	46.0	56.7	72.3	89.1	105.0	65.5
Switzerland	72.5	76.5	72.8	71.4	75.2	82.6	87.8	92.8	98.0	88.3
Norway	26.4	27.2	28.2	27.7	30.8	33.8	38.5	43.6	43.8	37.5
Japan	45.5	45.5	43.5	41.0	43.4	43.7	44.8	43.7	42.3	35.9
Turkey	31.9	21.9	26.6	30.9	40.1	44.6	50.0	52.7	54.1	43.7
South Korea (Republic of)	16.7	15.8	17.7	16.4	17.9	20.2	22.9	24.8	25.6	21.5
India	13.7	13.0	14.3	14.6	17.2	21.3	24.4	29.5	31.6	27.5
Brazil	16.9	18.6	15.7	12.4	14.2	16.1	17.7	21.3	26.3	21.6
IMPORTS										
Extra EU-27	992.7	979.1	937.0	935.3	1 027.5	1 179.6	1 352.8	1 433.4	1 564.9	1 199.2
United States	206.3	203.3	182.6	158.1	159.4	163.5	175.5	181.7	186.8	159.5
China (excl. Hong Kong)	74.6	82.0	90.1	106.2	128.7	160.3	194.9	232.7	247.9	214.8
Russia	63.8	65.9	64.5	70.7	84.0	112.6	140.9	144.5	177.8	115.3
Switzerland	62.6	63.6	61.7	59.1	62.0	66.6	71.6	77.0	80.3	73.8
Norway	47.2	46.4	48.0	51.0	55.3	67.2	79.2	76.7	95.9	68.6
Japan	92.1	81.1	73.7	72.4	74.7	74.1	77.5	78.4	75.1	55.8
Turkey	18.7	22.1	24.6	27.3	32.7	36.1	41.7	47.0	46.0	36.1
South Korea (Republic of)	27.0	23.3	24.6	26.0	30.7	34.5	40.8	41.4	39.6	32.1
India	12.8	13.5	13.7	14.1	16.4	19.1	22.6	26.6	29.5	25.4
Brazil	18.7	19.6	18.4	19.1	21.7	24.1	27.2	32.8	35.9	25.7
TRADE BALANCE										
Extra EU-27	-143.0	-94.4	-45.1	-66.0	-74.6	-126.8	-192.7	-192.9	-255.1	-104.8
United States	31.9	42.3	65.3	69.2	76.1	89.2	93.6	79.7	63.4	45.2
China (excl. Hong Kong)	-48.8	-51.3	-55.1	-64.7	-80.3	-108.5	-131.1	-160.7	-169.5	-133.1
Russia	-41.0	-34.3	-30.1	-33.5	-37.9	-55.9	-68.6	-55.3	-72.7	-49.8
Switzerland	10.0	12.9	11.1	12.3	13.2	16.0	16.1	15.9	17.7	14.5
Norway	-20.8	-19.2	-19.9	-23.4	-24.5	-33.4	-40.7	-33.1	-52.2	-31.1
Japan	-46.6	-35.6	-30.2	-31.4	-31.3	-30.3	-32.7	-34.7	-32.8	-19.9
Turkey	13.2	-0.2	2.0	3.6	7.4	8.5	8.3	5.7	8.1	7.7
South Korea (Republic of)	-10.2	-7.4	-6.9	-9.6	-12.7	-14.2	-18.0	-16.6	-14.0	-10.6
India	0.8	-0.5	0.6	0.5	0.8	2.2	1.8	2.9	2.1	2.1
Brazil	-1.8	-1.0	-2.6	-6.7	-7.6	-8.1	-9.5	-11.5	-9.5	-4.1

Table-4.14 : Debt % of GDP in EU.

	1999	2000	01	02	03	04	05	06	07	08	09	10
EU-15	71.6	69.2	68.1	67.9	69.1	69.5	70.1	68.5	66.3	70.1	79.8	85.3
Bel	113.6	107.8	106.5	103.4	98.4	94	92	88	84.1	89.3	95.9	96.2
Ger	61.3	60.2	59.1	60.7	64.4	66.3	68.6	68.1	65.2	66.7	74.4	83.2
Gre	94	103.4	103.7	101.7	97.4	98.6	100	106	107.4	113	129.3	144.9
Fra	58.9	57.3	56.9	58.8	62.9	64.9	66.4	63.7	64.2	68.2	79	82.3
Ita	113	108.5	108.2	105.1	103.9	103.4	105.4	106.1	103.1	105.8	115.5	118.4
Hun	60.8	56.1	52.7	55.9	58.6	59.5	61.7	65.9	67	72.9	79.7	81.3
Neth	61.1	53.8	50.7	50.5	52.0	52.4	51.8	47.4	45.3	58.5	60.8	62.9
Aus	66.9	66.2	66.8	66.2	65.3	64.7	64.2	62.3	60.2	63.8	69.5	71.8
Por	49.6	48.5	51.2	53.8	55.9	57.6	62.8	63.9	68.3	71.6	83	93.3
UK	43.7	41	37.7	37.5	39	40.9	42.5	43.4	44.4	54.8	69.6	79.9
Sp	62.4	59.4	55.6	52.6	48.8	46.3	43.1	39.6	36.2	40.1	53.8	61

Source: Eurostat.

In Fig-4.8, the countries whose debt GDP ratios are limited within the range of 60% and within the range of more than 60% have been identified and the vertical blackline showed the range of 3% of GDP as fiscal deficit where the countries lie would be identified clearly from this figure which could differentiate the degree of debt crisis from its originated countries so that policy formulations could be easily done.

Fig-4.8: Debt and FD of EU

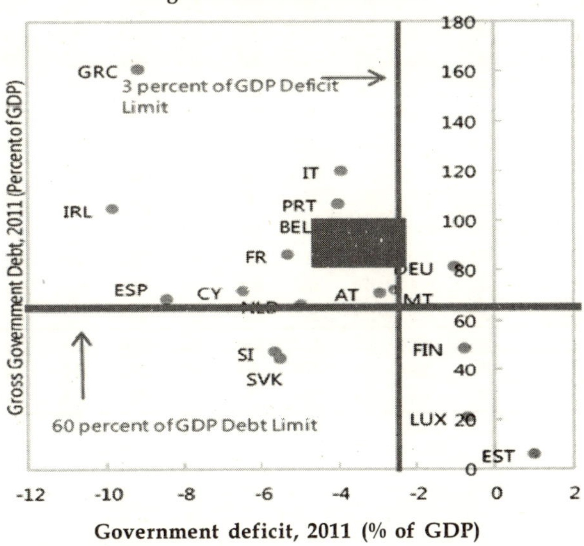

Source: Higgins & Klitgaard, 2012

On the social sector,the expenditure on the social protection are more or lass stagnant or decreasing in most of the countries except some marginal increases in Ireland,Greece,Spain,Italy, Cyprus, Hungary, Malta,Portugal etc.Therefore,EU must not ignore the greater social security for its people.(Table-4.15)

Table-4.15:Expenditure on Social Protection (% of GDP).

	1997	1998	1999	2000	2001	2002	2003	2004	2005	2006	2007
EU (¹)	27.4	27.0	26.9	26.5	26.7	27.0	27.4	27.2	27.1	26.7	26.2
Euro area (EA-16)	:	:	:	26.7	26.8	27.4	27.8	27.7	27.7	27.4	27.0
Belgium	27.4	27.1	27.0	26.5	27.3	28.0	29.0	29.2	29.6	30.2	29.5
Bulgaria	:	:	:	:	:	:	:	:	16.0	14.9	15.1
Czech Republic	18.6	18.5	19.2	19.5	19.4	20.2	20.2	19.3	19.2	18.7	18.6
Denmark	30.1	30.0	29.8	28.9	29.2	29.7	30.9	30.7	30.2	29.3	28.9
Germany	29.0	28.9	29.2	29.3	29.4	30.1	30.4	29.8	29.7	28.7	*27.7*
Estonia	:	:	:	13.9	13.0	12.7	12.5	13.0	12.6	12.3	12.5
Ireland	16.4	15.2	14.6	13.9	14.9	17.5	17.9	18.1	18.2	18.3	18.9
Greece	20.8	21.7	22.7	23.5	24.3	24.0	23.5	23.5	24.6	24.5	24.4
Spain	20.8	20.2	19.8	20.3	20.0	20.4	20.6	20.7	20.9	*20.9*	*21.0*
France	30.4	30.1	29.9	29.5	29.6	30.4	30.9	31.3	31.4	30.7	*30.5*
Italy	24.9	24.6	24.8	24.7	24.9	25.3	25.8	26.0	26.4	*26.6*	*26.7*
Cyprus	:	:	:	14.8	14.9	16.3	18.4	18.1	18.4	18.4	*18.5*
Latvia	15.3	16.1	17.2	15.3	14.3	13.9	13.8	12.9	12.4	12.3	*11.0*
Lithuania	13.7	15.1	16.3	15.8	14.7	14.0	13.5	13.3	13.1	13.2	*14.3*
Luxembourg	21.5	21.2	20.5	19.6	20.9	21.6	22.1	22.3	21.7	20.3	19.3
Hungary	:	:	20.3	19.6	19.2	20.3	21.2	20.6	21.9	22.4	22.3
Malta	18.0	17.9	17.8	16.9	17.8	17.8	18.3	18.8	18.6	18.2	18.1
Netherlands	28.7	27.8	27.1	26.4	26.5	27.6	28.3	28.3	27.9	28.8	*28.4*
Austria	28.8	28.4	29.0	28.4	28.8	29.2	29.6	29.3	28.9	28.5	28.0
Poland	:	:	:	19.7	21.0	21.1	21.0	20.1	19.7	19.4	18.1
Portugal	20.3	20.9	21.4	21.7	22.7	23.7	24.1	24.7	25.3	25.4	24.8
Romania	:	:	:	13.0	12.8	13.6	13.0	12.7	13.2	12.5	12.8
Slovenia	23.9	24.1	24.1	24.2	24.5	24.4	23.7	23.4	23.0	22.7	*21.4*
Slovakia	19.8	20.0	20.2	19.4	19.0	19.1	18.2	17.2	16.5	16.3	*16.0*
Finland	29.1	27.0	26.3	25.1	24.9	25.7	26.6	26.7	26.8	26.2	25.4
Sweden	32.2	31.4	31.0	30.1	30.8	31.6	32.6	32.0	31.5	30.7	*29.7*
United Kingdom	26.9	26.3	25.7	26.4	26.8	25.7	25.7	25.9	26.3	26.1	*25.3*
Iceland	18.5	18.3	18.8	19.2	19.4	21.2	23.0	22.6	21.6	21.2	21.5
Norway	25.1	26.9	26.9	24.4	25.4	26.0	27.2	25.9	23.8	22.6	22.8
Switzerland	27.3	27.4	27.4	27.0	27.7	28.5	29.2	29.3	29.3	28.0	27.3

Source: Eurostat (tps00098)

Thecrucial macro-economic indicator is the saving imbalance of the highly debt ridden countries in Euro area for which imbalance were created. Saving imbalances in the euro area have recently been quite large. In the 2007 run-up to the global financial crisis, Greece, Portugal, and Spain had saving deficits of 10 to 15 percent of GDP, the largest in the euro area (Fig-4.9). Ireland had a much smaller but still substantial deficit of around 5 percent of GDP. Germany, in contrast, had a surplus of roughly 8 percent of GDP. The seeds of these imbalances were planted by the creation of a history of relatively high inflation, especially compared with Germany. *Saving balance* is equal to its *current account balance*, that is, the trade balance broadly constructed: *current account balance = domestic saving – domestic investment spend.*

More detailed national accounts data from the OECD show that Greece's decline in saving is mostly attributable to lower private saving but also to larger government budget deficits. The decline in Portugal is entirely attributable to lower private saving. Spain shows a modest decline in its saving rate up to 2007, with lower private saving outweighing the impact of improved government fiscal balances leading up to the recession. Ireland displays a relatively stable saving rate through 2007, with little change on either the private or the government side. Germany, in contrast, saw a marked increase in its saving rate, from 20 percent of GDP in 1999 to 26 percent by 2007, mostly driven by higher private saving.(www.newyorkfed.org)

Fig-4.9: Saving Balance as a share of GDP.

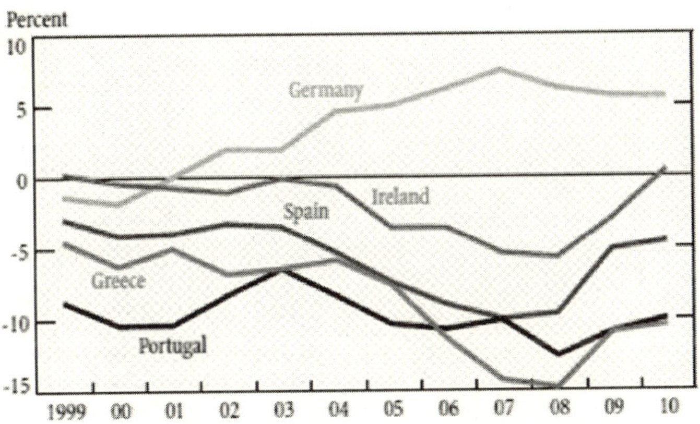

Source: Eurostat: Haver Analytics

Conclusion

We have learnt a lesson about the insufficient and weak macroeconomic indicators of Euro Area along with the social sectors from which debt crisis had been accelerated so that the common fiscal and monetary policy could not solve the crisis efficiently and completely which ultimately tuned into financial crisis. Therefore, Euro Area needs to secure high macro fundamentals with fulfillment of convergence criteria to stabilize Euro.

References

Higgins, Matthew and Thomas Klitgaard, 2012, Saving Imbalances and the Euro Area. Sovereign Debt Crisis, Federal Reserve Bank of New York in Economics and Finance *Volume 17, Number 5* &' www. newyorkfed. org/research/current_issues.

Eurostat-www.ecb.net.in.

www.economist.com.

IMF-Financial Stability Report-*2012,WEO-2012.*

APPENDIX

Table-4A-1: Euro Area-Main Economic Indicators,2007-2014(%)

	2007	2008	2009	2010	2011	2012	2013	2014
						staff projection		
Demand and Supply								
Real GDP	3.0	0.4	-4.3	1.9	1.5	-0.3	0.7	1.3
Private consumption	1.7	0.4	-1.2	0.9	0.2	-0.5	0.5	1.0
Public consumption	2.2	2.3	2.5	0.5	0.0	-0.7	-0.4	0.2
Gross fixed investment	4.7	-1.1	-12.1	-0.5	1.3	-2.4	1.1	1.8
Final domestic demand	2.4	0.5	-2.8	0.5	0.4	-0.9	0.4	1.0
Stockbuilding 1/	0.4	-0.1	-1.0	0.7	0.1	-0.5	-0.1	0.0
Domestic Demand	2.8	0.3	-3.7	1.2	0.4	-1.3	0.4	1.0
Foreign balance 1/	0.2	0.1	-0.6	0.7	1.1	1.0	0.3	0.3
Exports 2/	6.6	1.0	-12.7	11.2	6.2	2.1	3.1	3.8
Imports 2/	6.2	0.9	-11.7	9.6	3.8	-0.2	2.7	3.3
Resource Utilization								
Potential GDP	1.7	1.4	0.8	0.7	0.6	0.5	0.7	0.8
Output gap	2.7	1.6	-3.6	-2.4	-1.5	-2.3	-2.3	-1.9
Employment	1.8	0.7	-1.8	-0.5	0.1	-0.7	0.1	0.6
Unemployment rate 3/	7.6	7.7	9.6	10.1	10.2	11.1	11.3	11.1
Prices								
GDP deflator	2.4	2.0	0.9	0.7	1.3	1.9	1.4	1.5
Consumer prices	2.1	3.3	0.3	1.6	2.7	2.2	1.6	1.5
Public Finance 4/								
General government balance	-0.7	-2.1	-6.4	-6.2	-4.1	-3.2	-2.5	-2.0
General government structural balance	-2.3	-2.9	-4.4	-4.2	-3.1	-1.7	-1.1	-0.9
General government gross debt	66.4	70.2	80.0	85.8	88.1	91.4	92.4	92.2
Interest Rates 3/ 5/								
EURIBOR 3-month offered rate	4.3	4.6	1.2	0.8	1.4	0.7	...	...
10-year government benchmark bond yield	4.3	4.4	4.0	3.8	4.3	3.5	...	...
Exchange Rates 5/								
U.S. dollar per euro	1.37	1.47	1.39	1.33	1.39	1.28	...	...
Nominal effective rate (2000=100)	103.7	108.7	110.9	103.2	104.2	99.3	...	...
Real effective rate (2000=100) 6/	100.9	103.4	104.0	95.3	95.0	89.8	...	...
External Sector 4/ 7/								
Current account balance	0.1	-1.6	-0.2	-0.1	0.0	0.9	1.0	1.1

Sources: IMF, *World Economic Outlook;* Global Data Source; DataStream; and Eurostat.

APPENDIX

Table-4.A-2:Euro Area:Balance of Payments

	2003	2004	2005	2006	2007	2008	2009	2010	2011
				(Billions of euros)					
Current account	20.9	60.8	10.9	-12.7	7.3	-143.4	-22.0	-6.9	-3.2
Goods	98.7	94.1	42.2	8.1	42.3	-21.8	31.2	15.0	4.9
Services	22.5	32.9	39.6	42.5	47.9	42.0	36.5	49.6	61.0
Income	-44.8	-6.8	2.4	16.6	5.3	-66.8	3.4	31.7	31.8
Current transfers	-56.1	-59.5	-73.4	-79.6	-87.9	-97.1	-93.1	-103.3	-100.6
Capital account	12.2	16.6	12.0	9.6	4.8	10.0	6.5	6.4	10.8
Financial account	-14.0	-78.6	-35.2	-6.2	3.1	121.3	9.4	-2.7	-24.6
Direct investment	-9.7	-79.4	-203.9	-159.6	-90.4	-231.2	-105.1	-113.8	-151.0
Portfolio investment	54.4	44.1	106.4	186.0	126.8	261.4	265.8	165.1	308.1
Equity	32.8	-2.3	103.7	89.2	102.0	-14.7	71.8	67.4	189.5
Debt instruments	21.3	46.7	2.4	96.5	24.9	276.3	193.9	97.8	118.9
Financial derivatives	-13.7	-8.3	-17.3	-0.7	-67.0	-84.6	19.9	18.4	-20.8
Other investment	-72.8	-47.9	62.1	-30.9	38.7	178.8	-175.7	-61.7	-150.8
Reserve assets	28.0	12.6	18.2	-1.1	-4.9	-3.4	4.6	-10.5	-10.1
Errors and omissions	-19.1	1.1	12.4	9.4	-15.1	12.2	5.7	2.9	17.0
				(Percent of GDP)					
Current account	0.3	0.8	0.1	-0.1	0.1	-1.6	-0.2	-0.1	0.0
Goods	1.3	1.2	0.5	0.1	0.5	-0.2	0.3	0.2	0.1
Services	0.3	0.4	0.5	0.5	0.5	0.5	0.4	0.5	0.6
Income	-0.6	-0.1	0.0	0.2	0.1	-0.7	0.0	0.3	0.3
Current transfers	-0.7	-0.8	-0.9	-0.9	-1.0	-1.1	-1.0	-1.1	-1.1
Capital account	0.2	0.2	0.1	0.1	0.1	0.1	0.1	0.1	0.1
Financial account	-0.2	-1.0	-0.4	-0.1	0.0	1.3	0.1	0.0	-0.3
Direct investment	-0.1	-1.0	-2.5	-1.9	-1.0	-2.5	-1.2	-1.2	-1.6
Portfolio investment	0.7	0.6	1.3	2.2	1.4	2.8	3.0	1.8	3.3
Equity	0.4	0.0	1.3	1.0	1.1	-0.2	0.8	0.7	2.0
Debt instruments	0.3	0.6	0.0	1.1	0.3	3.0	2.2	1.1	1.3
Financial derivatives	-0.2	-0.1	-0.2	0.0	-0.7	-0.9	0.2	0.2	-0.2
Other investment	-1.0	-0.6	0.8	-0.4	0.4	1.9	-2.0	-0.7	-1.6
Reserve assets	0.4	0.2	0.2	0.0	-0.1	0.0	0.1	-0.1	-0.1
Errors and omissions	-0.3	0.0	0.2	0.1	-0.2	0.1	0.1	0.0	0.2
Memorandum items:									
GDP (billions of euros)	7,546.9	7,860.4	8,145.4	8,564.9	9,030.2	9,244.3	8,930.1	9,160.9	9,425.8
Reserves of the eurosystem 1/ (billions of euros)	306.7	281	320.1	325.8	347.2	374.2	462.4	591.2	667.1

Source: ECB.

1/ End of period stocks.

APPENDIX

Table-4.A-3:Euro Area:Main Economic Indicators(% change)

	2007	2008	2009	2010	2011	2012	2013
						staff projection	
Demand and Supply							
Real GDP	3.0	0.4	-4.3	1.9	1.5	-0.3	0.7
Private consumption	1.7	0.4	-1.2	0.9	0.2	-0.5	0.5
Public consumption	2.2	2.3	2.5	0.5	0.0	-0.7	-0.4
Gross fixed investment	4.7	-1.1	-12.1	-0.5	1.3	-2.4	1.1
Final domestic demand	2.4	0.5	-2.8	0.5	0.4	-0.9	0.4
Stockbuilding 1/	0.4	-0.1	-1.0	0.7	0.1	-0.5	-0.1
Domestic Demand	2.8	0.3	-3.7	1.2	0.4	-1.3	0.4
Foreign balance 1/	0.2	0.1	-0.6	0.7	1.1	1.0	0.3
Exports 2/	6.6	1.0	-12.7	11.2	6.2	2.1	3.1
Imports 2/	6.2	0.9	-11.7	9.6	3.8	-0.2	2.7
Resource Utilization							
Potential GDP	1.7	1.4	0.8	0.7	0.6	0.5	0.7
Output gap	2.7	1.6	-3.6	-2.4	-1.5	-2.3	-2.3
Employment	1.8	0.7	-1.8	-0.5	0.1	-0.7	0.1
Unemployment rate 3/	7.6	7.7	9.6	10.1	10.2	11.1	11.3
Prices							
GDP deflator	2.4	2.0	0.9	0.7	1.3	1.9	1.4
Consumer prices	2.1	3.3	0.3	1.6	2.7	2.2	1.6
Public Finance 4/							
General government balance	-0.7	-2.1	-6.4	-6.2	-4.1	-3.2	-2.5
General government structural balance	-2.3	-2.9	-4.4	-4.2	-3.1	-1.7	-1.1
General government gross debt	66.4	70.2	80.0	85.8	88.1	91.4	92.4
Interest Rates 3/ 5/							
EURIBOR 3-month offered rate	4.3	4.6	1.2	0.8	1.4	0.7	...
10-year government benchmark bond yield	4.3	4.4	4.0	3.8	4.3	3.5	...
Exchange Rates 5/							
U.S. dollar per euro	1.37	1.47	1.39	1.33	1.39	1.28	...
Nominal effective rate (2000=100)	103.7	108.7	110.9	103.2	104.2	99.3	...
Real effective rate (2000=100) 6/	100.9	103.4	104.0	95.3	95.0	89.8	...
External Sector 4/ 7/							
Current account balance	0.1	-1.6	-0.2	-0.1	0.0	0.9	1.0

Sources: IMF, World Economic Outlook; Global Data Source; DataStream; and Eurostat.

CHAPTER 5

EURO CRISIS : AN EFFECT ON THE DEVELOPING COUNTRIES

Introduction

The Euro's global share in International currency reserves according to Recent COFER data from the IMF suggests that 25% of global reserves are denominated in Euros, 19% of global central bank deposits are Euro-denominated, according to the BIS. The BIS also reports that 34% of all cross-border bank loans are denominated in Euros, although this figure includes intra-Eurozone cross border activity and 39% of forex market turnover involves the Euro, according to the BIS's tri-annual survey. It is observed that 7% of sovereign bonds issued in the Eurozone are issued under foreign law, a more substantial 30% of non-sovereign bonds are issued under foreign law, and the foreign law share of Euro denominated derivatives amounts to around 95%.

Moreover, more than one third international trade is dominated by the EU.Therefore,the spill over effects of euro shortage must be huge and economic impact is costly.We cannot deny that Euro crisis has huge spillover effects on both developed and developing countries through trade , capital flows, finance , exchange rate adjustment and employment opportunities and these phenomenon would be studied in this chapter.

Spillover effects on the developing countries

As the global economy is rebounding from the crisis, there is widespread belief that the worst of the global crisis is over as output and trade are back to pre-crisis levels in 2010 in most of the emerging and developing world. However, the OECD countries still suffer from low growth and high fiscal deficits. The key issues that the world faces today are unsustainable fiscal expansion, inflationary pressure in some countries, deciding on the appropriate time to exit the extraordinary levels of public intervention in the immediate aftermath of the crisis, global co-operation to check macroeconomic imbalances and the quest for a new global economic regime.

Against this backdrop, ICRIER and Inwent jointly organised a two-day conference on "Policies for Growth and Financial Stability: Beyond the Crisis - The Scope for Global Co-operation", which brought together distinguished policy makers, regulators, practitioners and academicians for a dialogue on these issues. The conference focused on two specific issues. First, it took stock of major reports on the reform of the global financial system and the implementation of their recommendations through the G20 process. The second was an assessment of major fiscal, monetary and regulatory initiatives undertaken around the world after the crisis. The consensus was that the G20 had been quite successful in limiting the damage caused when the crisis initially broke out as well as in ironing out medium term issues like IMF and FSB reform.

A lecture on "Dealing with the Global Financial Crisis in Developing East and Southeast Asia" was delivered by Mr. C. Lawrence Greenwood at ICRIER on November 4, 2010. According to Mr. Greenwood, of the countries in the developing East and Southeast Asia, the two countries that escaped relatively unscathed from the crisis were India and Vietnam.

Mr. Greenwood pointed out that one of the continuing after effects of the global crisis has been a sharp rise in inflation rates in countries like China, India and Vietnam. This had prompted the adoption of tight money policies, flexible exchange rate management and fiscal measures to ward off a possible falling off in demand. He also pointed out that in countries like China, where the savings level is considered excessive, measures to transfer money to households have been introduced through increased expenditure on health, education and social safety nets. While structural reforms would take time to bear fruit, Mr. Greenwood said these, along with measures to promote regional co-ordination and the opening of intra-regional trade to reduce dependence on western economies, need to be pushed through to ensure sustained recovery.

In Fig-5.1, it was shown that on the inception of Euro crisis, the exports in intra-EU trade, extra-EU trade, and with USA, Asia and OPEC have tremendously fallen and started to increase since first quarter of 2010. In some trading partners , the index rose above the baseline 2008.It was happened due to depreciation of Euro in nominal terms. The most affected destination is USA and Japan but less affected area is in Asia.

Fig-5.1: Euro Area export;2008=100

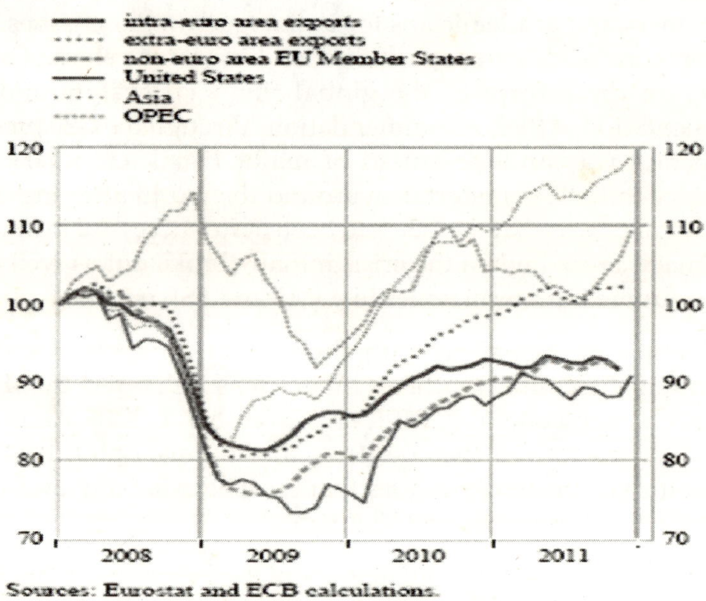

In recent years the geographical composition of euro area trade has undergone significant change, which is also reflected in the trade weights of the effective exchange rates (EERs) of the euro calculated by the ECB. In particular, the growing importance of emerging economies and the steadily intensifying integration of economies in Europe are increasingly shaping the trade linkages of the euro area.The Table -5.1,presents the trade weights over all available periods for each of the countries included in the broad EER-40 (listed in the order of their average trade weight over all periods). Advanced economies continue to account for a sizeable share of euro area trade, although the weight of the largest advanced economies in the EER-40 of the euro has been declining over time. Between 1995 and 2009 the two individual countries with the largest weights were, on average, the United States and the United Kingdom, which together accounted for almost a third of the EER-40. These countries, together with Japan, were also the three largest individual trading partners of the euro area in the period 1995-2000, with a combined weight of, on average, around 45% of the EER-40 basket. However, for the period 2007-09 their combined share in the basket of the EER-40 declined to around 30%.

The combined weight of trading partners from emerging Asia in the EER-40 rose from below 19% in the period 1995-97 to above 27% in the period 2007-09. This rise resulted mainly from a substantial increase in the weight of China, which became the euro area's largest individual trading partner in the period 2007-09. The share of other emerging Asian economies has remained broadly unchanged over time, as can be seen in Table-5.1,which presents developments in the trade weights of major regions of the world economy, as well as of some of the euro area's largest individual trading partners.

The opposite holds true for economies in emerging Asia with which the euro area has an aggregate bilateral trade deficit, as a reflection of the strong export orientation of these economies. At the same time, accounting for third-market effects lead to some adjustment in the overall trade weights through the double export weights. In particular, in the case of China, as well as Japan and other Asian economies, competition between euro area and Asian exporters in third countries results in a significant increase in the overall trade weight beyond the levels implied by direct export linkages. Based on the previous weighting scheme, the index would have reached a value of 96.9 and would thus have been 5.6% lower than in January 2007. The update of the trade weights therefore reveals that the increase in competitiveness of the euro area owing to the real depreciation of the single currency since 2007 was slightly more pronounced if changes in the geographical composition of euro area trade are taken into account.

Fig-5.2: Real Exchange rate,CPI deflated, Q1,1999=100

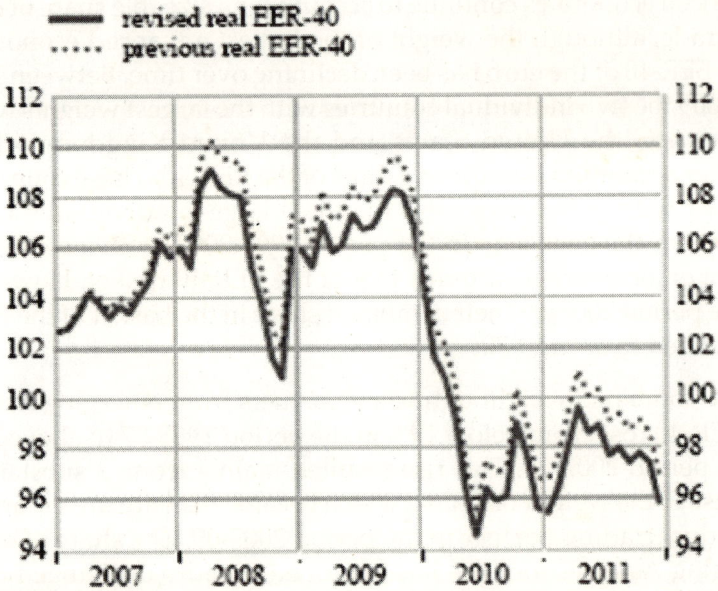

Source: ECB.

This potential for major spillovers can be seen in market reaction to developments in the EA over the past year (Fig-5.3). CDS spreads and bond yields for the EA program countries have risen to historically high levels, and their correlation with financial market spreads for other EA economies remains very high. In the run up to the approval of the Greece program, correlations of EA program country CDS spreads and bond yields with global asset prices rose sharply, highlighting the contagion potential. Marked pickups in correlations were also evident around the time the Ireland and Portugal programs were being finalized. While the increased correlations between EA and non-EA asset prices could partly reflect reactions to common risk factors they underscore the risk that an intensification of stress in the EA could have sizable effects on global markets.

Table-5.1:Trade weights for the EER-40

(percentages)

Country	Period					
	1995-1997	1998-2000	2001-2003	2004-2006	2007-2009	Average
United States	16.9	19.4	18.6	15.5	13.5	16.8
United Kingdom	18.3	17.7	16.7	14.2	11.9	15.8
China	4.4	5.3	7.6	11.4	15.0	8.7
Japan	9.7	8.8	7.6	6.7	5.8	7.7
Switzerland	6.6	5.9	5.7	5.2	5.2	5.7
Sweden	4.7	4.3	3.8	4.0	3.7	4.1
Poland	2.4	2.8	3.3	3.9	4.9	3.4
Czech Republic	2.2	2.4	3.0	3.4	4.0	3.0
Korea	2.9	2.7	2.8	3.2	3.1	2.9
Turkey	2.1	2.2	2.3	3.0	3.1	2.6
Russia	2.4	1.8	2.2	2.9	3.4	2.6
Denmark	2.6	2.3	2.3	2.2	2.1	2.3
Hungary	1.5	2.2	2.5	2.6	2.6	2.3
Taiwan	2.3	2.4	2.1	1.8	1.4	2.0
India	1.5	1.3	1.5	1.8	2.1	1.6
Hong Kong	2.0	1.7	1.5	1.5	1.3	1.6
Canada	1.5	1.6	1.6	1.4	1.3	1.5
Singapore	1.8	1.6	1.4	1.4	1.2	1.5
Brazil	1.5	1.4	1.2	1.2	1.4	1.3
Mexico	0.9	1.2	1.3	1.2	1.2	1.2
Malaysia	1.2	1.1	1.2	1.1	1.0	1.1
Norway	1.3	1.2	1.0	1.1	1.1	1.1
Romania	0.7	0.8	1.1	1.4	1.6	1.1
Thailand	1.2	1.0	1.0	1.0	1.1	1.1
South Africa	0.9	0.9	0.9	1.0	1.0	0.9
Israel	1.0	1.0	0.9	0.7	0.7	0.9
Australia	0.8	0.8	0.8	0.8	0.8	0.8
Indonesia	1.0	0.8	0.7	0.6	0.6	0.7
Morocco	0.6	0.6	0.6	0.6	0.6	0.6
Croatia	0.5	0.4	0.5	0.5	0.5	0.5
Philippines	0.4	0.5	0.5	0.4	0.3	0.4
Bulgaria	0.3	0.3	0.4	0.4	0.5	0.4
Argentina	0.6	0.5	0.3	0.3	0.3	0.4
Chile	0.3	0.3	0.3	0.4	0.4	0.4
Algeria	0.3	0.3	0.3	0.3	0.4	0.3
Lithuania	0.2	0.2	0.2	0.3	0.3	0.2
Venezuela	0.2	0.2	0.2	0.2	0.2	0.2
Latvia	0.1	0.1	0.1	0.2	0.2	0.1
New Zealand	0.1	0.1	0.1	0.1	0.1	0.1
Iceland	0.0	0.1	0.1	0.1	0.1	0.1
Total	100.0	100.0	100.0	100.0	100.0	100.0

Source: ECB.

Fig-5.3: Sovereign CDS spreads

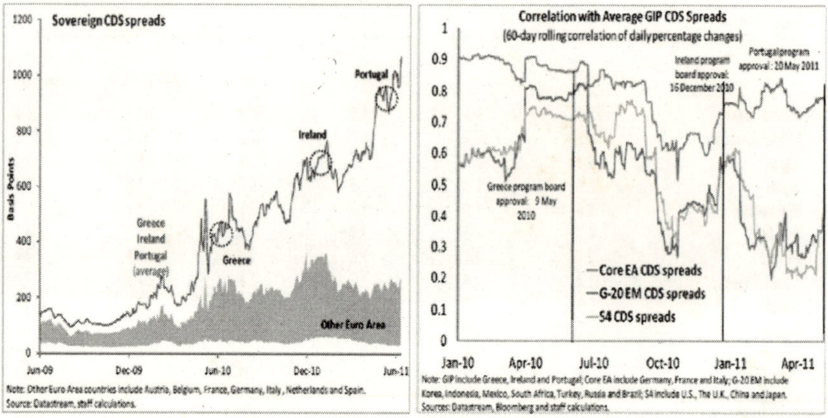

[i] Most partner authorities focused on financial spillovers from the EA, with spillovers seen as escalating sharply if the sovereign debt difficulties in the EA were to intensify.

[ii] Other spillovers discussed included the impact of EA macroeconomic policies, trade and FDI links, and regulatory changes on partner countries.

[iii] Economic growth in the S-5 has, apart from China, been highly correlated Growth in the U.S., U.K., and EA economies was particularly highly synchronized over the past decade. The financial crisis subjected the S-5 countries to a synchronous, sharp contraction in 2008, and all have since embarked on the recovery process. The co-movement of growth in China with the EA and the rest of the S-5 has been weaker as China's economic performance outpaced that of the rest of the S-5 countries, including during the recent crisis.(Fig-5.4)

[iv] A closer look at these growth links suggests that Euro Area output shocks have had generally moderate spillovers.

[v] Moving beyond the S-5, countries geographically closer to the EA—generally those with stronger trade links—are affected more by the area's economic fluctuations

Fig-5.4: Growth rate of S-5

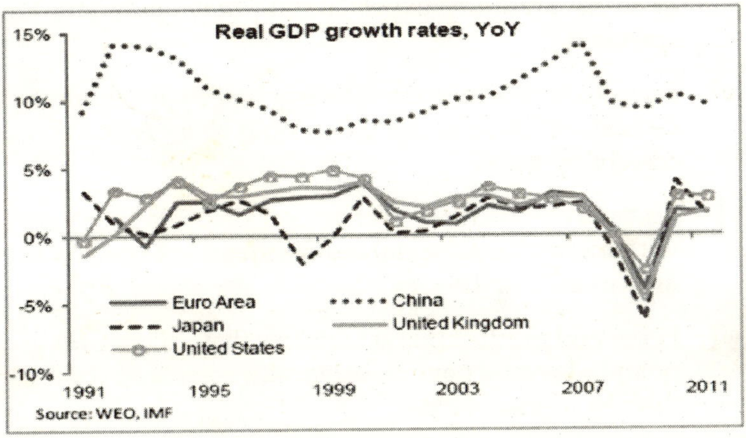

[vi] A implication of this analysis is that EA growth shocks are likely to have the largest spillover effects on non-EA European and North African economies.

[vii] Analysis of global risk factor movements across different asset classes suggests strong spillovers from the EA.

[viii] Direct spillovers from further stress in the EA program countries would likely remain manageable, but the potential to affect the rest of the world is much larger if stress spreads to the core EA.

[ix] Financial markets signal that spillovers of further stress in the EA would be large if the core is affected.

[x] Analysis of global bank interconnectedness also suggests that further EA stress would have negative spillovers that are sharply exacerbated if core Europe is affected.

[xi] The importance of spillovers from shocks to the core EA are further underscored by results from a broader macroeconomic modeling approach.

[xii] ECB exceptional liquidity provision has helped contain deleveraging by EA banks and corresponding spillover effects.

[xiii] A slightly faster pace of monetary tightening in the EA than markets presently expect would have generally limited spillovers.

[xiv] Projected EA fiscal consolidation should have modest global demand spillovers, and these could be more than offset by credibility gains.

[xv] Turning to structural reforms, any deleveraging associated with higher bank capital requirements is expected to have only modest spillovers.

[xvi] Labor and product market reforms that enhance EA growth potential would have positive, albeit modest, spillovers to the rest of the world.

[xvii] Further trade liberalization would also have positive spillovers.

[xviii] The prospect of large spillovers—particularly if recent stress in EA program countries were to spread to the core—underscores the urgent need for actions to contain, and eventually overcome, the ongoing crisis.

Now, if we analyse , the spillover effect of trade, we would find the loss of EU zone volume of trade. In analyzing data of EU, we can say that both export shares of EU and Euro zone started to decline from 2005 which were 33.93% and 26.39% of the world respectively in 2010.Besides the import shares of EU and Euro zone reached the peak level in 2007 and then declined to 34.21% and 25.72% in 2010 respectively.(Table-5.2).

Table-5.2: Export and import of EU and Euro zone (value in million US$)

	1990	*2000*	*2005*	*2007*	*2009*	*2010*
Export/EU	1549094	2447635	4064021	5339902	4576065	5149361
% share	44.52	37.96	38.72	38.15	36.58	33.93
Euro area	1223684	1915380	3176885	4187862	3588796	4004355
% share	35.16	29.71	30.27	29.92	28.68	26.39
Import/EU	1606837	2508665	4131559	5515271	4632700	5253044
% share	44.78	37.65	38.25	38.70	36.56	34.21
Euro area	1250184	1900613	3103428	4123476	3513394	3949383
% share	34.84	28.53	28.74	28.93	27.73	25.72

Source: UNCTAD-2011

Moreover, it is clear that the intra-trade of EU and Euro area had been fallen marginally with respect to 2000 but slightly improved in 2010 compared with 2009 when crisis began .(Table-5.3)

Table-5.3: Intra trade of EU(% of regional total)

	1980	*1995*	*2000*	*2005*	*2009*	*2010*
EU	62.2	67.2	67.7	67.4	66.5	67.2
Euro area	51.9	54.2	51.8	51.5	50.2	50.4

Source: UNCTAD-2011

The crisis has an impact on developing countries too in terms of trade shares. The exports and imports from the developing economies to EU sharply fell to 16.2% and 14.7% respectively in 2010 in comparison to 18.2% and 16.5% respectively in 2005. Therefore, huge loss in trade incurred with Euro crisis to the developing countries. The most affected developing region is Asia whose exports to EU declined to 15.1% in 2010 compared to 17.0% in 2005 and Asia's imports to EU fell to 12.9% in 2010 with respect to 14.8% in 2005.But,only 1% fell of both export and import shares from Eastern, Southern and Southeast Asian nations were observed. But, Western Asia lost too much as a result of Euro crisis. Because the export share from the region to EU declined to 13.5% in 2010 from 19.6% in 2005 and import shares fell to 27.9% in 2010 from 34.6% in 2005 respectively.

The export share from African developing countries to EU dropped sharply to 34.3% in 2010 from 39.9% in 2005 .On the other hand, the import share from African developing countries to EU fell down to 33.7% in 2010 with respect to 36.6% in 2005 respectively. On the contrary, the American developing countries lost only 1% trade share both in export and import shares in 2010 compared with 2005. India, too, confronted with severe effects of Euro crisis. Its export and import shares have drastically fell down to 18.4% and 12.0% respectively in 2010 compared with 22.4% and 17.4% respectively in 2005.(Table-5.4).

Table-5.4: EU Trade with developing countries (% of total regional shares)

	Export/ Import shares	*1995*	*2005*	*2010*
Developing countries to EU	Export/	18.7	18.2	16.2
	Import	20.0	16.5	14.7
African developing countries to EU	Export/	43.9	39.9	34.3
	Import	43.5	36.6	33.7
American developing countries to EU	Export/	16.9	12.7	12.6
	Import	18.6	14.4	13.5
Asia's developing countries to EU	Export/	16.4	17.0	15.1
	Import	17.7	14.8	12.9
Eastern, Southern, South Eastern developing countries to EU	Export/	15.8	16.4	15.4
	Import	15.2	11.6	10.4
Developing countries of Oceania to EU	Export/	18.3	19.2	15.8
	Import	19.9	20.3	16.4
Developing countries of Western Asia to EU	Export/	21.0	19.6	13.5
	Import	37.9	34.6	27.9
India to EU	Export	27.6	22.4	18.4
	Import	26.9	17.4	12.0

Source: UNCTAD-2011

Low-income countries (LICs) are affected by developments in the Euro Area (EA) through several channels. Direct channels include trade, remittances, FDI and aid flows. At the same time, the EA also has indirect spillover effects on LICs, especially through global commodity prices.

- **The EA receives about 20 percent of LIC exports.** About 30 percent of exports from LICs in Sub-Saharan Africa and 20 percent of exports from Asia and CIS countries go to the EA.

Commodity exports, in particular, play an important role in LIC bilateral trade links with Europe where fuel and crude material make up roughly 60 percent of LIC exports to Europe in 2008.

Remittances and FDI from the EA are particularly important for LICs in Sub-Sahara Africa. Over 30 percent of SSA's remittance inflows originate from EA. In other regions, the U.S.'s remittance role is generally larger. In addition, EA FDI dominates flows to CIS and SSA countries.

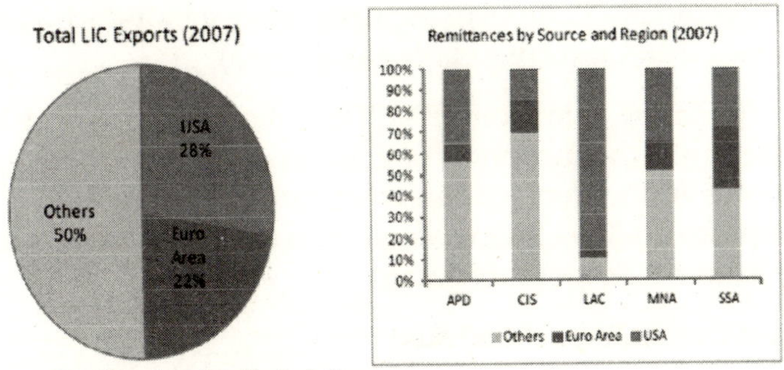

Sources: DOTS, World Bank and staff calculations

Fig-5.5: Total LIC export

- **The EA is the largest donor across LICs, particularly for LAC and SSA** where EA aid makes up more than 40 percent of total aid to these regions.

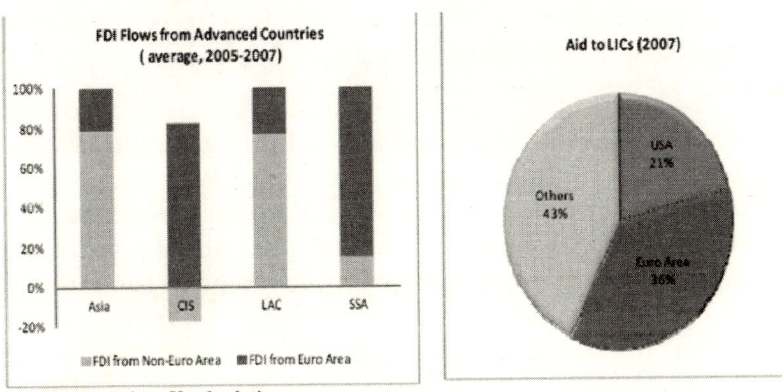

Sources: OECD and staff calculations

Fig-5.6: FDI flows from advanced countries

Empirical evidence suggest that developments in EA could have significant spillovers on LICs. Estimates from growth regressions suggest that trading partner growth has a significant impact on LIC growth. An empirical study using bilateral FDI data between EA and LICs suggests that EA growth is one driver of FDI flows to LICs, although the effect is much weaker than the size of the recipient economy. In addition, there is evidence that aid flows are pro-cyclical with respect to the donors' business cycle and could be influenced by donors' fiscal situation, particularly when donors face a large negative shock.(IMF Country Report No. 11/185)

The latest data from UNCTAD World Investment Report-2012 stated that the inception of Euro crisis had a severe crisis in FDI inflows in the debt ridden countries of EU zone ,the developing countries and also in India and even the FDI outflows had an equal effect like inflows.(Table-5.5)

Euro Crisis: Impact on India

It is evident that the crisis in the Euro zone has already impacted emerging markets in general and India in particular. As global investors seek safe havens, liquidity has been removed from emerging markets. Many emerging markets, and especially India are dependent on this liquidity to finance the current account deficit and provide capital for investment. India is particularly vernarable due to its large current account deficit which is financed to large degree by shorter term portfolio flows. As these have dried up the equity market have struggled and rupee has depreciated sharply.

"The Indian Government has introduced focused market schemes to diversify exports. So, the crisis in Europe should be seen as an opportunities for India to break into the market where they export", says Rammu Deora, chairman, All India Shippers council. If the Euro zone crisis is not averted, India which has about a sixth of its total exports to the EU, will face unemployment in the lower income category, such as textiles, one of the biggest employers in textiles, including readymade garments, accounts for about a fifth of the total exports to Europe. The Euro zone crisis has eliminated the benefits of a weak rupee, which is down 20% in a year, to Indian exporters as the spend-thrift consumers in the continent do something they are not used to three decades-save.

Companies that enjoyed cheap money from European Banks, such as Deutsche Bank and BNP Paribus, for expansion and acquisitions are beginning to feel the pinch as battered lenders in the continent slam the doors on Indian firms.

If the Euro zone collapsed the impact on Indian growth will be severe, said Enrico Atanasio, Fiat India Automobile Ltd.

Table- 5.5: FDI flows of Euro Area

	FDI inflows %						*FDI outflows %*					
	2006	2007	2008	2009	2010	2011	2006	2007	2008	2009	2010	2011
Eurozone% world	39.97	43.22	30.28	29.77	24.31	27.59	48.88	54.81	48.63	33.49	33.27	33.15
Greece %EUzone	0.91	0.24	0.82	0.68	0.11	0.43	0.58	0.43	0.25	0.52	0.20	0.31
Italy%EUzone	7.27	5.13	-1.99	5.62	2.88	69.07	6.33	7.98	6.99	5.4	6.76	8.4
Portugal%EUzone	1.86	0.35	0.86	0.75	0.83	2.45	1.03	0.45	0.28	0.20	-1.55	2.24
Spain%Eurozone	5.26	7.52	14.19	2.918	12.8	7.0	15.06	11.37	7.8	3.32	7.93	6.63
Developing nations%world	29.19	29.07	36.29	43.34	47.10	44.89	16.91	14.41	16.66	22.84	27.57	22.64
India % world	1.38	1.29	2.42	2.97	1.84	2.06	1.0	0.89	0.977	1.35	0.906	0.87

Source: UNCTAD-WIR-2012

Table-5.6: Indo-EU Trade

	Exports ($million)	*Growth rate*	*Imports ($million)*	*Growth rate*
2006-07	26831	15.51	29856	14.84
2007-08	34535	28.71	38450	28.78
2008-09	39351	13.95	42733	11.14
2009-10	36028	-8.45	38433	-10.06
2010-11	46819	29.95	44540	15.89
2011-12	26421		24473	

Source: ET-15/6/2012

Moreover, Indian exports fell 4.2% to $25.7 billion in May from a year ago, pilling on more bad news for the economy struggling with the nine year low growth and facing rating downward to junk status. The outlook for exports for the coming months is uncertain as the Euro zone teeters on the brink of serious crisis, prompting the government to announce sops last week to push up exports. Imports also dropped 7.4% in May from a year ago to $41.9 billion leaving a trade deficit of $16.3 billion , a higher than the $13.9 billion in April but less than $18.5 billion in May last year. To note that 51% fall in Gold and Silver imports in May because of price rise.

The data suggest that sharp rupee depreciation has not helped exports as it has coincided with decelerated in global growth, particularly Europe. All the key exports sectors like engineering goods(-15.67%),petroleum products(-26.07%),gems and jewellery (-9%) and readymade garments(-15.82%) reported negative growth.(ET-15/6/2012).The top three exports to the EU are Mineral fuels and products, electrical machinery and parts and apparel & clothing accessories amounting to 8646.81 million dollar,3770.30 million dollars and 3147.17 million dollars respectively in 2010-11.On the other hand ,the top three imports from EU are pearls & semi precious stones, nuclear reactors, boilers etc and electrical machinery & equipments amounting to 9417.56 million dollar,8844.84 million dollar, and 5252.34 million dollar respectively in 2010-11.

On the liquidity issue, India's external debt denominated in Euros was found as 3.8% and FDI from EU is 3.0 billion Euro in 2010.Moreover, about 26% of India's reserves are held in Euro. So,

India would face massive inverse effects due to break down of Euro in the offing.(ET-18/6/12)

Last but not the least, the EU debt crisis was originated from the global financial which had an international impact too which quickened the spillover effect to the rest of the world.

Between the record high posted in July 2008 and May 2009, the value of world trade diminished by 37%, of which 16% was accounted for by the drop in prices. Exports have fallen in every region of the world. Between November 2008 and March 2009, for example, over 90% of OECD countries experienced monthly decreases of over 10% in their imports and exports in comparison with the same period the previous year. As a group, the emerging economies have witnessed the sharpest decline in export prices (21%) and a slightly smaller dip in export volumes (18%). **Exports plummeted in nearly every country around the globe**. The worst hit were those that exported manufactures to the United States or the European Union, or to both markets, such as Hong Kong Special Administrative Region of China, Japan, Taiwan Province of China, the Republic of Korea and Singapore in Asia, and Belgium, Finland, Germany, Hungary and the Netherlands in Europe. World trade in manufactures dumped and industrial output with it. Part of the plunge was associated with a contraction of consumer spending as expectations worsened suddenly among households and businesses around the globe and unemployment rose. Thanks to the buoyancy of the Chinese economy, international demand for mining and energy commodities remained high in the first half of 2009. The novel aspect of this crisis for South America, which specializes in exporting commodities, is that it is hastening the shift from reliance on the business cycle of the United States towards reliance on that of China and Asia as a whole.

The drop in world trade in goods has been steeper and has occurred faster than in previous crises, even than in the Great Depression of the 1930s (Fig-5.7). During the Asian crisis, the decline in world trade was no more than 6% after 10 months. During the United States recession of 2001, it shrank 12% in 11 months. In the first nine months of this crisis, world trade plummeted 37%. A similar downturn was recorded during the Great Depression, but only 20 months into the crisis.

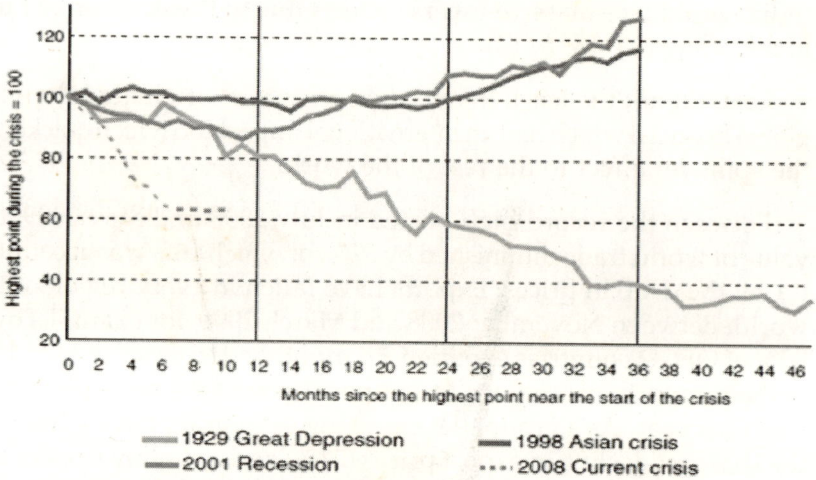

Source: CBP Netherlands Bureau of Economic Policy Analysis, "World-trade monitor", 2009; League of Nations 1934 *Monthly Bulletin of Statistics.*

Note: Does not include services. Constant dollars. The starting point is the month at which trade peaked before the crisis.

Fig-5.7: World Trade in Major Global crises (Pre crisis level=100)

In Fig-5.8, the loss of world GDP due to financial crisis since World War-I up till recent crisis are clearly signifies our conclusion about the gravity of the crises and their effects where we found that the current financial crisis affected largest loss of world GDP after the World War-II.

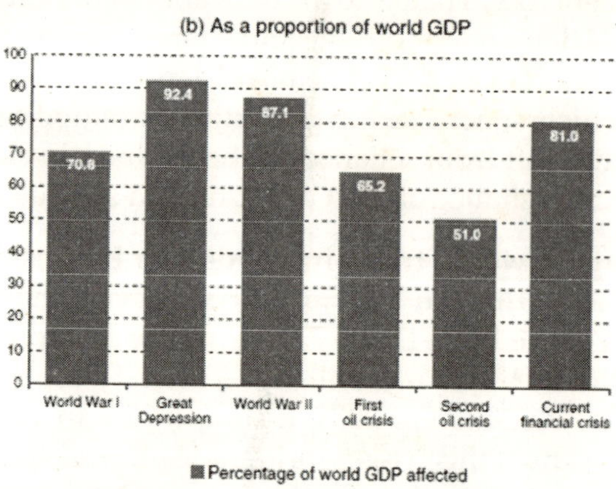

Fig-5.8: Proportion of the world economy in recession,1901-2008(in %)

Source: IMF and Maddison,2011

Conclusion

Euro debt crisis turned into financial crisis in EU which spill over into the international economies in which the developing countries had been suffering too much through imbalance in BOPs between EU and developing countries including in employment opportunities and exchange rate market which fell short of international liquidity in terms of Euro. ECB-IMFs bail out package, Draghi's bond buying plan, banking union, restructuring convergence criteria might be likely to control debt crisis and fiscal deficit which must have impact on debt financing in developing countries too.

References

Economic Times- 18/6/2012 , 15/6/2012.

ECB, 2011, *Eurostat.*

IMF, 2011, *WEO-2011.*

IMF, 2011,*IMF country report 185/2011.*

Maddison, Angus., 2011, *The World Economy*, Academic Foundation.

Nordvig, Jens., and Nick Firoozye., 2012, Rethinking the European Monetary Union,Wolfson Economics Prize,2012. 5-6-2012.

UNCTAD, 2011, *UNCTAD Report-2011.*

CHAPTER 6

EURO CRISIS : IMPACT ON MONEY MARKET

Introduction

During 2011, and increasingly in the second part of the year, the euro area financial system was strongly affected by the intensification of the sovereign bond market crisis. Cross-border yield spreads increased sharply in a number of countries, while access to primary markets by the more distressed sovereigns became increasingly difficult. Investors' portfolio choices and capital flows were dominated by risk aversion, as well as a search for quality and liquidity, especially during the periods of most acute market tension. Overall, the integration of the euro area financial system deteriorated further, especially in the money and bond market segments. A part of the euro area banking system was virtually cut off from market-based funding sources, but continued to be refinanced through Euro system operations.

Some critical findings:

Volatility in Euro short-term interest rates, as measured by the implied volatility derived from options on 3-month EURIBOR future contracts rose sharply in October 2008 (Fig-6.1) after the collapse of Lehman Brothers. This indicator of volatility, however, only actually peaked in May 2010 when concerns about sovereign debt in the Euro area were also at their most serious. The 3-month EURIBOR rate fell from 2.89% at the end of 2008 to 0.70% at the end of 2009 and then fell further to as low as 0.63% at the end of March 2010 (Fig-6.1). Since then EURIBOR rates have followed a rising trend as the surplus liquidity environment in the interbank market has declined in line with less recourse by banks to Euro system liquidity-providing operations. The 3-month EURIBOR rate reached the 1% level again in October 2010.

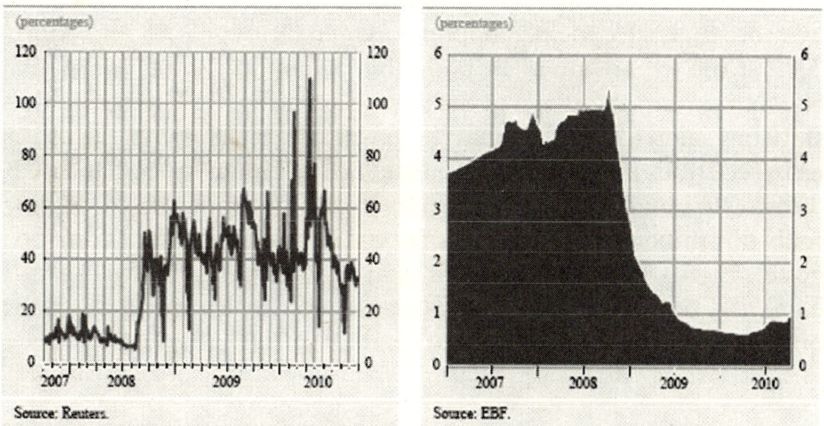

Fig-6.1: Implied volatility on 3-month EURIBOR rate and Evolution of 3 month EURIBOR rate

As regards the perception of liquidity conditions in the options market, the share of those who reported that liquidity had worsened continued to decrease from the 2008 peak (27%), to 16% in 2010 (Fig-6.2)

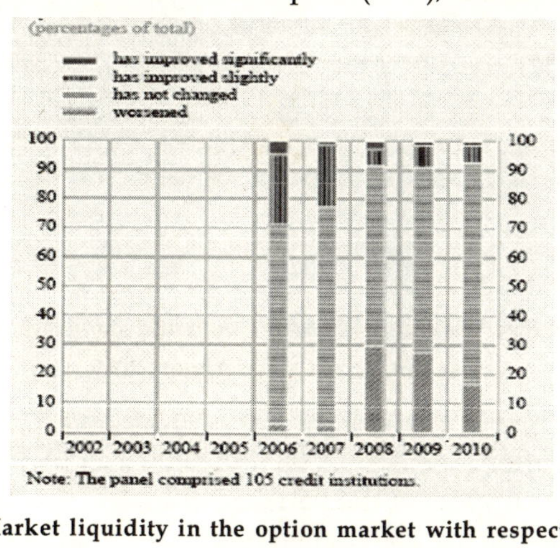

Fig-6.2: Market liquidity in the option market with respect to last year.

Source: ECB

According to ECB monthly statistical data on securities issuance, the outstanding nominal amounts of Euro-denominated short-term securities issued by Euro-area residents decreased slightly from €1,525 billion in May 2009 to €1,435 billion in August 2010. According to ECB statistics, developments in the gross issuance volumes of short-term securities exhibited some volatility. Issuance volumes decreased by more than 45% to €678 billion between October 2008 and August 2010. If the expansion of ECB-eligible collateral gave an immediate boost to certain segments of the market (e.g. the STEP market), these statistics seem to indicate that the positive impact on the euro short-term securities market as a whole did not last long. Indeed, the ECB's decision to broaden the list of eligible collateral temporarily, combined with a number of other supportive measures taken by European governments in favour of their domestic banking sector, seem to have had the most impact on issuance volumes around the fourth quarter of market 2008 and first quarter of 2009. (Fig-6.3)

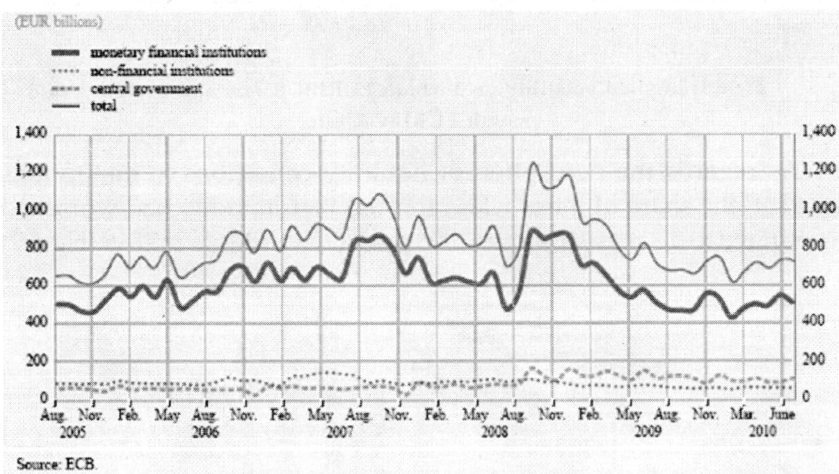

Fig-6.3: Gross issuance of Euro-denominated short term securities by issuing sector since August-2005

A slow decline in the issuance of central government securities was observed after a peak in 2008 and 2009 as a result of European rescue plans in support of the banking industry. The boosting effect was observable during 2009 when issuance remained at high levels of up to €160 billion. Since the beginning of 2010 issuance volumes have declined even if they remain higher than before the crisis. Since early 2010 monthly issuance volumes have been in the range of €100 billion to €125 billion. The declining trend in government issuances can be linked to the more restrictive budget policies in Europe and the shift to longer-maturity issuances by governments. MFI total Issuance by non-financial corporations declined. Levels of issuance were around €50 billion in 2010, whereas they had been above €100 billion in 2008.

The STEP initiative was designed and implemented to unite market standards and practices in the short-term commercial paper market. It supports financial integration, standardisation and a broadening of the investor base. The STEP initiative has indeed been successful in fostering the integration of the short-term paper market in Europe. The current outstanding amount of STEP labeled programmes of around €405 billion also points to increased liquidity. It is being used by both financial and non-financial corporations and the issuers comprise both large and complex banking groups and smaller entities across the EU. All these developments reflect the fundamental role STEP short-term paper plays as a funding and investment tool at the short end of the yield curve. (Fig-6.4)

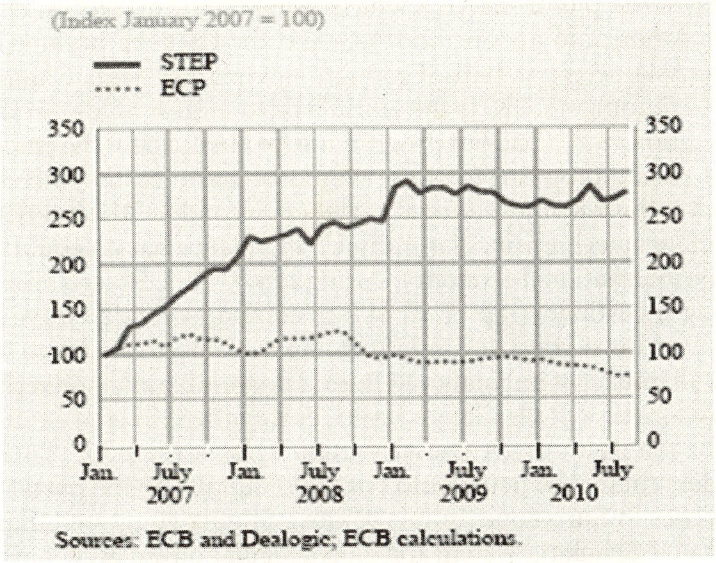

Fig-6.4: Growth in STEP and ECP outstanding amount

In 2010 turnover concentration among market participants increased in several market segments. This may reflect the important re-structuring that has taken place in the European banking industry as a result of the crisis and the significant reduction in the balance sheets and market-making activity of many banking institutions. The market share of the top 20 credit institutions increased in the unsecured market, in some of the OTC derivatives segments (OIS and other IRS) and in the short-term securities segment .Conversely, the remaining OTC derivatives showed a slight decrease in concentration, which may signal that a few more players were attracted to these segments due to the better conditions in these instruments for currencies other than the Euro. The proportion of business carried out with counterparties from the same country decreased in the unsecured market and in the Foreign exchange swaps and short-term securities segments, the latter changing most significantly in terms of geographical structure (down from 46% to 25%, in favour of the increase in trade with Euro-area counterparties). In most of the OTC derivatives segments the share of trading with "national" counterparties increased. In the unsecured and secured markets this share remains comparatively high (32% and 35% respectively).

Now, of late, the Standard and Poor's downgraded the US credit rating to AA-plus from AAA which created share market index falling from America to Europe and Asia and the US debt became dearer since Asia accounts half of foreign –owned US debt(China holds $1.16 trillion),and UK is the world's third largest holder of US debt . Therefore,ECB 's bail out programme for Greece debt,the emergency fund rescue program for Italy would be more costly since the US dollar is the key international currency to conduct the international paymants mechanism. Naturally,US imbalance has an equal impact on the international economy.During 1989-2012,US faced an average saving investment gap of - 3.34% in comparison to positive gap of 0.33% of Euro zone and 2.74% in Japan respectively.So to say,the over all impact of imbalance in Euro is favourable as against USA but unfavourable to Itally,Greece,Spain , Portugal and Ireland etc. It affects on inequality through re-distribution against the poor. Thus why, the debt finance policy would not affect equally on the participating countries in Euro zone. In this context, Stiglitz suggested that more centralized banking system and global regulation are urgent including new capital account management. Since rising debt and deficit also come from the financial crisis itself, so debt financing management along with reserve management are to be crucially handled with care so that cross border transactions may not be de-stabilizing. Also, he suggested to replace present international monetary system which is dollar based international payment system. So ECB should re-think about the essence and solution of the international liquidity problem in which euro debt problem lies.

In managing the above problems, we have seen that during the world financial crisis, Euro crisis also emerged and ECB found that during 2008-2010,the sovereign credit swap spread of Ireland , Greece and Portugal which are mostly indebted countries, damaged heavily and the five year tenor could not able to reach 400 basis points. In other words, these reached up to 1500pts after 2010 when EC emphasized to swap. This was seen in Fig-6.5

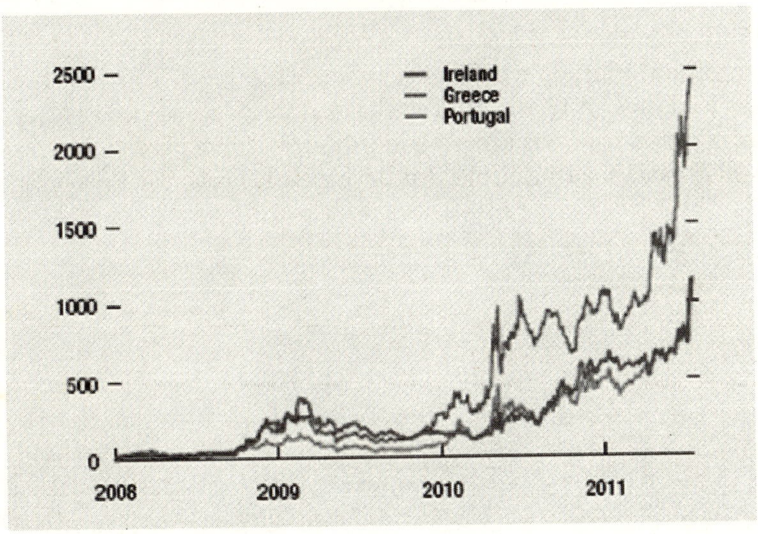

Fig-6.5: Sovereign Credit Default Swap Spreads (five year tenor, in basis points)
Source: Global Financial Stability Report-2011

Consequently, the monetary policy of ECB to counteract Euro crisis was very encouraging, in the sense that it started to swapping in the international financial market and EU revived more speedily than the USA and Japan since 2008 which were observed in the Fig-6.6.

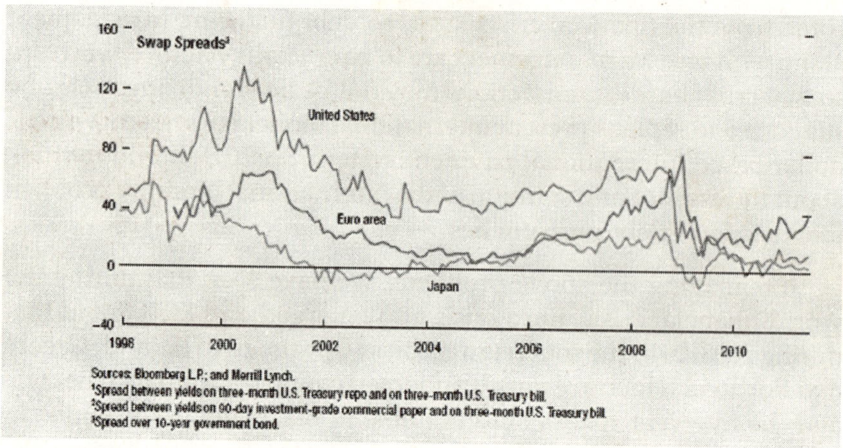

Fig-6.6: Swap spreads of EU

Moreover, the ECB also started to buy and sell Euro bonds in the international market which was seen in the Fig-6.7 in which Euro bonds issuance in terms of US billion dollars were rising after the financial crisis vis-à-vis Euro crisis although it sharply fell down since mid 2009 because of double dip depression arose for Euro crisis in EU.

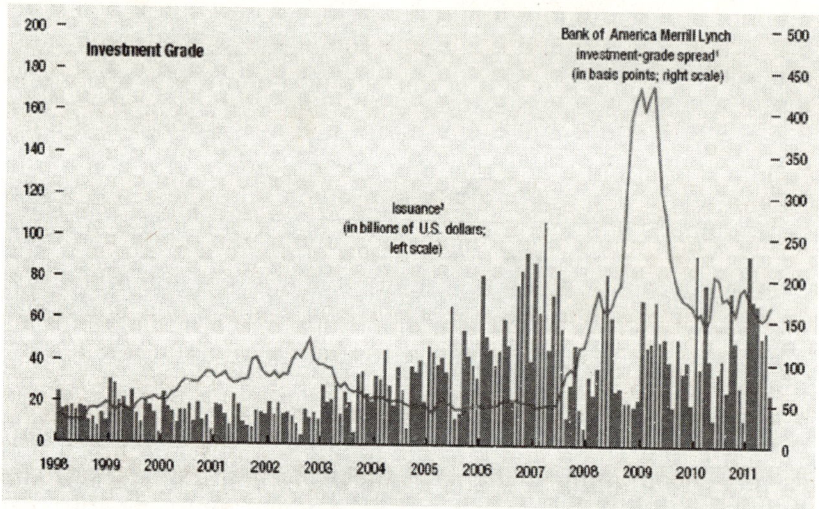

Fig-6.7: Euro Area: Corporate Bond Market.

Source: Global Financial Stability Report-2011

In particular, the Greek crisis and the hesitant political response from the other European countries raised concerns over the debt situation and the structural and competitiveness problems of the economically weaker periphery member countries of the euro area, which—in a slightly derogatory fashion—have been named PIIGS (Portugal, Ireland, Italy, Greece, and Spain). As a consequence, the borrowing costs for the PIIGS increased significantly and the cost of insuring sovereign debt against default soared (Fig-6.8) as trust in their ability to repay vanished. The crisis also raised awareness of the existing imbalances within the Euro area, which constitute a serious problem.

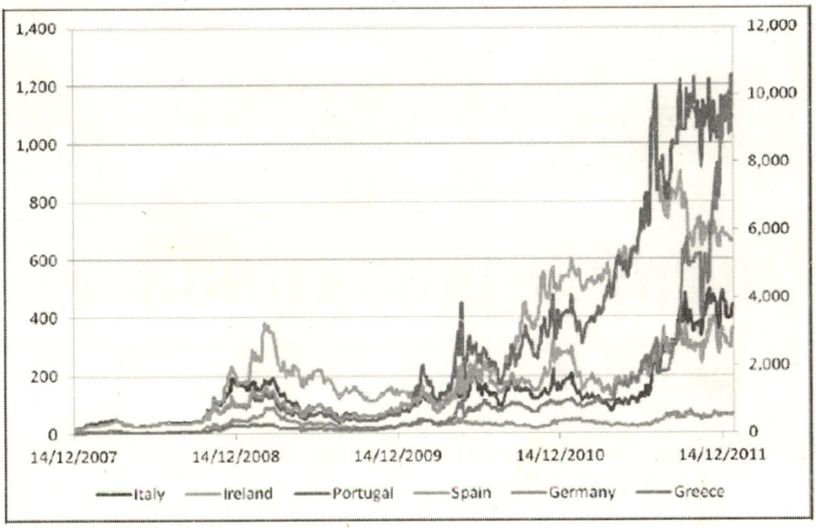

Source: Datastream.

Fig-6.8: Sovereign Credit Default Swaps, 2007 Dec-2012 Jan.

An important element that contributed to the crisis was a mispricing of risk by capital markets and an ensuing misallocation of capital in the decade before the outbreak of the crisis. European monetary unification brought about a convergence of interest rates among Euro area members. Spreads of sovereign bonds of the PIIGS over Germany narrowed rapidly in the run-up to EMU membership and almost disappeared once they had become members of the Euro area (Fig-6.9). By January 2001, the time of Greece's entry into the Euro area, the yields on 10-year Greek bonds had fallen to 5%—

from 25% in 1992. Sovereign risk of virtually all Euro area countries, including the PIIGS, was priced more or less the same as German sovereign debt. This was not least because the risk of Euro area central government bonds was weighted at zero in regulatory capital calculations and because the Euro system (the ECB and the national central banks of the Euro area) treated such debt with no haircut—basically as risk-free collateral—when these were offered as collateral for repos and other collateral financing trades.

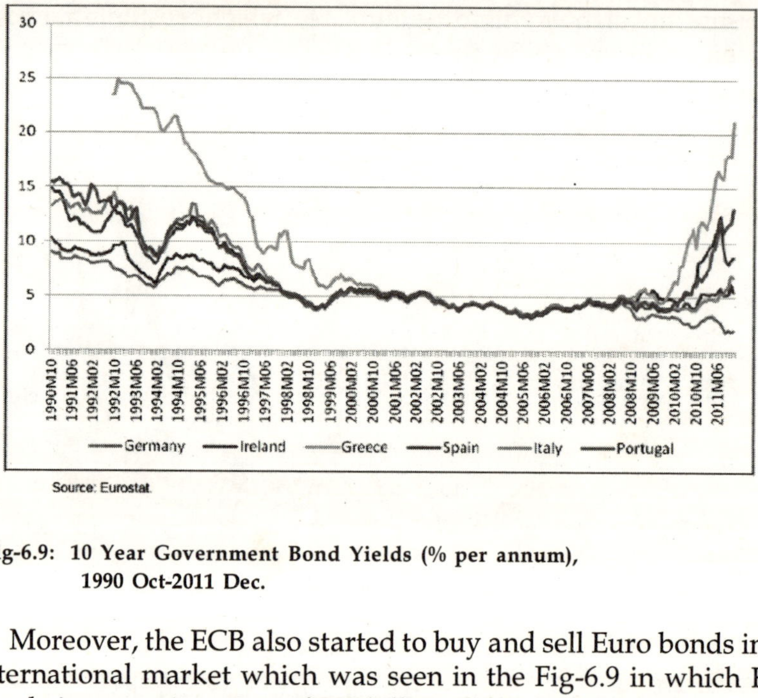

Fig-6.9: 10 Year Government Bond Yields (% per annum), 1990 Oct-2011 Dec.

Moreover, the ECB also started to buy and sell Euro bonds in the international market which was seen in the Fig-6.9 in which Euro bonds issuance in terms of US billion dollars were rising after the financial crisis vis-à-vis Euro crisis although it sharply fell down since mid 2009 because of double dip depression arose for Euro crisis in EU.

As the recent financial crisis highlighted, liquidity risk is of key importance to the functioning of money markets and the stability of the banking sector. Proposals on international liquidity regulation were put forward by the Basel Committee on Banking Supervision (BCBS), which are by far the most important initiative in this area to have emerged from the experience of the crisis.

The proposals include a minimum liquidity standard for internationally active banks based on two key regulatory ratios: the liquidity coverage ratio (LCR) and the net stable-funding ratio (NSFR). They also outline a set of four liquidity risk monitoring tools involving contractual maturity mismatch, funding concentration (with regard to counterparties, instruments and currencies), availability of unencumbered assets, and market-related monitoring tools. The LCR identifies the minimum amount, to be specified by the supervisors, of unencumbered, high-quality liquid assets to be held by a bank for use in offsetting the net cash outflows that the bank might encounter under an acute stress scenario lasting 30 days. The new proposed standard would require that the value of the ratio be no lower than 100% (i.e. the stock of liquid assets should at least equal the estimated net cash outflows).

The definition of "liquid assets" encompasses cash, central bank reserves, marketable securities issued or guaranteed by international bodies 3 and government or central bank debt issued in domestic currencies. Moreover, it was agreed by the GHOS to split such assets into so-called level 1 and level 2 categories. Level 1 liquid assets are defined as: 1) government and public sector entity assets qualifying for the 0% risk weight under Basel II and 2) sovereign debt that does not have a 0% risk weight, issued in foreign currency, provided that the currency matches the currency needs of the bank's operations in that jurisdiction. Level 2 liquid assets may only account for a maximum share of 40% of the total stock of liquid assets and consist of:

1) government and public sector entity assets qualifying for the 20% risk weight under Basel II and 2) corporate and covered bonds (not self-issued) rated at least AA-. A 15% haircut will apply on the level 2 liquid assets.

The euro area crisis has reached a new, critical level

1. **Market tensions have increased further.** Still-pressing banking problems and continuing sovereign funding concerns in some euro area countries have raised doubts about the viability of the monetary union itself. This has driven sovereign borrowing costs and risk premiums to very high levels in several countries, adding to the already-severe pressures on many bank and sovereign balance sheets in an environment of very low confidence and growth.

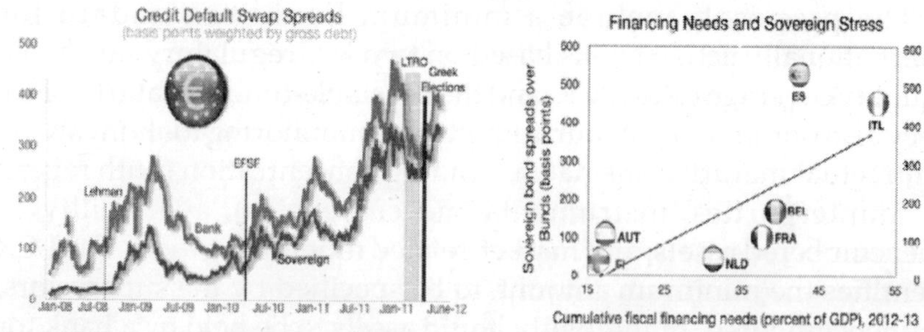

Sources: Bloomberg L.P.; IMF, World Economic outlook database; and IMF staff calculations

Sources: Bloomberg L.P.; and IMF staff calculations

Fig-6.10: Credit default

2. The adverse bank-sovereign feedback loops at the heart of the crisis have intensified.

Concerns about banks' solvency have increased because of large sovereign exposures, particularly in periphery countries. Some sovereigns, in turn, are struggling to backstop weak banks on their own. Depositor confidence is increasingly fragile. As investors have moved capital "north" and abroad to perceived safer assets, official financing—including in the form of programs and ECB liquidity support—has become more important. This is largely mirrored in widening Target 2 balances between euro area national central banks.

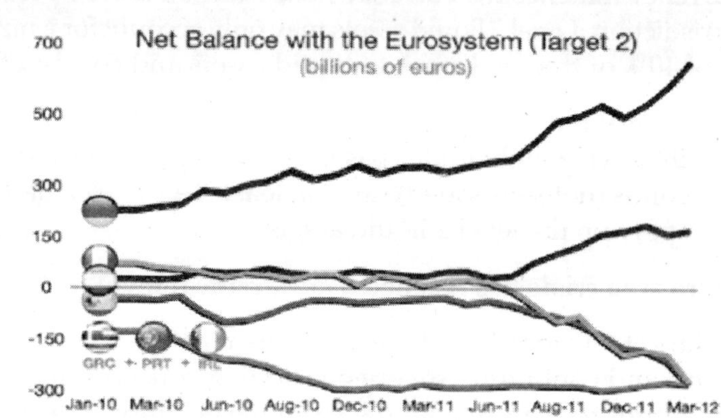

Source: National Central Banks

Fig-6.11: Net Balance with Euro system

3. **And the single financial market has become increasingly fragmented.** Despite low policy rates, credit conditions vary widely among euro area countries. This is mainly due to starkly diverging perceptions of sovereign and banking risks, as well as a drastic decline in interbank activity (as banks reduce cross-border funding, shore up capital and liquidity buffers in their home jurisdiction, and accumulate overnight deposits at the ECB). As a consequence, financing conditions are now the least supportive in countries where the crisis is the most acute.

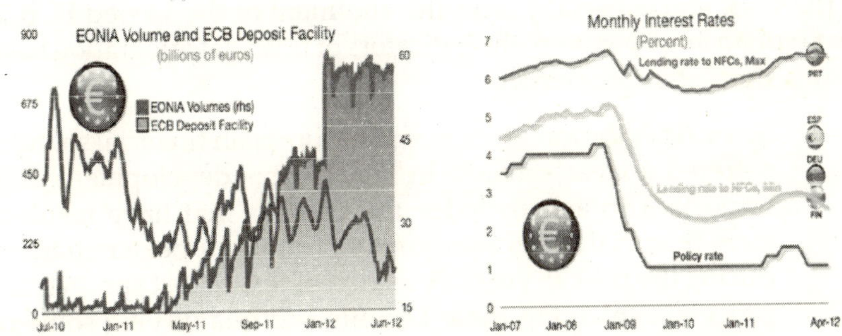

Source: European Central Bank

Sources: Haver Analytics; and European Central Bank

Fig-6.12: Eonia Volume and ECB Deposit Facility and Interest Rate

4. **Against this backdrop, the real economy has been weak, reinforcing adverse bank sovereign feedback loops**. GDP was flat in the first quarter of 2012, after contracting at an annualized rate of almost 1 percent in the last quarter of 2011. Demand was depressed, particularly in the periphery countries (Fig-6.12). Tightening financing conditions and weak confidence held back private investment and consumption, and fiscal consolidation dampened demand further. Consequently, the euro area unemployment rate increased further, to over 11 percent in May, its highest level since the start of EMU. In turn, the weakness in real activity has added to budgetary pressures and the deterioration in banks' loan portfolios.

Concluding Remarks

European debt crisis had a quick spill over on the bond, equity and capital market both at home and in abroad and in some countries credit rating fell sharply along with banking crisis. There is every possibility of financial contagion if proper corrective measures in time were not taken and implemented. Up till now, the initiatives of Markel and Sarkozy, on behalf of ECB and EC, are at all not promising for revival of Euro.

In short, we can say that , in the recent years, the financial crisis has led to a marked deterioration in European financial integration. Specifically, during 2011 the intensification of the European sovereign bond market crisis strongly affected the euro area financial system, whose degree of integration has deteriorated further. After the turn of the year, and especially after the allotment of the second ECB 3-year refinancing operation, the indicators of financial integration have shown signs of improvement.

- Since 2007, the integration of pan-European financial services suffered a clear setback. In light of this development, it is important to acknowledge the benefits that have resulted from financial integration coming from European initiatives during the past 25 years. A section of this report surveys this process, explaining these benefits and quantifying some of them.

- The enhancements of the Single Market Programme, the strengthening of the euro area policy frameworks regarding prudential supervision as well as macroeconomic and fiscal policies accompanied by policy actions at national level, need to be brought forward. The completion of the current institutional reforms, constituting a first step towards a fiscal union as well as an even more European set-up of supervision, is desirable as it should contribute to a better environment that can surpass the crisis.

- In money market ,due to the intensification of the sovereign euro area bond market crisis, secured and unsecured money markets have become increasingly impaired, especially across borders. The pricing of risk in the repo market has become more dependent on the geographic origin of both the counterparty and the collateral, in particular when these were from the same country, which contributed to additional money market segmentation and fuelled country and financial risks. With the aim of preserving the integrity of the monetary policy transmission process, the ECB provided intense liquidity and credit support to financial institutions and undertook a number of monetary policy measures to alleviate funding tensions and market uncertainty.

- In bond market ,euro area sovereign bond markets experienced severe tensions, giving rise to concerns of systemic nature. Wealth holders are now acutely aware of sovereign credit risks and price them accordingly. Euro area sovereign yields have diverged further, overall, in 2011. In the most intense phases of the sovereign debt crisis, there may have been an overestimation of risk regarding some euro area sovereigns, leading to an overshooting of the respective yields.
- Corporate bond markets have also experienced significant tensions, in both the financial and non-financial sector. Indicators suggest that country-level effects have become more important in driving yield developments, reflecting the differences in the fiscal situation and economic outlook of euro area sovereigns.
- In equity market too, the impact of the sovereign crisis on cross-border integration seems to have been limited in equity markets, relative to bond markets. Cross-border holdings are not displaying significant discrimination with regard to the country of origin. Also national stock price indices seem to be reacting without an overwhelming country-specific influence.
- Moreover, the indicators of the euro area banking market integration generally signalled a lower pace of deterioration during the financial crisis, relative to other markets. However, more recently in both the retail and wholesale euro area banking markets there is evidence suggesting a slow erosion of the earlier - equally slow - progress towards financial integration.

At last,we should mention that the financial crisis has given rise to significant challenges to the Euro system operational framework. The impairment of financial integration has adversely affected the functioning of money markets, a key part of the transmission mechanism of monetary policy. To mitigate this adverse impact, the Euro system has intervened in market segments that are outside its usual area of operation (specifically, the sovereign debt and covered bond markets).

While the operational framework has performed well, exhibiting both robustness and flexibility, important challenges remain that may require further adaptation. Four areas have been mentioned in which further reflection will be required in the near future.

The first area concerns the implications of the sizeable shift in money market transactions from the unsecured to the secured segments. This phenomenon suggests that increasing emphasis should be placed on repo markets in the conduct of monetary policy operations, though the full implications of this transition need to be explored further. The second concerns the breadth and scope of the operational framework. During the crisis, the Eurosystem expanded the scope of its operations, performing to some extent an intermediary to capture the most relevant types of bank loans in each individual jurisdiction. Due to the fact that knowledge of the domestic economy and of the national legal framework is essential, the responsibility to assess the eligibility of the bank loans and specifically their creditworthiness lies with the relevant NCB, also in order to ensure a swift and efficient implementation of the measure.

The third concerns the issue of the appropriate size of the liquidity deficit of the banking system with the central bank in future. During the crisis, certain Euro system instruments resulted in a reduction in the liquidity deficit. If the deficit remains permanently lower, or even turns into an occasional surplus, the nature of the monetary policy instruments may have to change.

The fourth concerns the new regulation of bank liquidity risk contained in Basel III and how it should interact with the Euro system collateral framework. Both liquidity regulation and the collateral framework are important elements of the financial architecture, capable of affecting market practices. Hence the importance of ensuring their mutual consistency and synergy over time in the interest of preserving bank liquidity and guaranteeing effective monetary policy implementation.

References

Bhowmik, Debesh., 1997, Problems and prospects of Maastricht Treaty: Its impact on Indian and LIEs Raj Kumar Sen, Kartik c.Roy and Clement A.Tisdell (Ed) *World Trade and Development* (Atlantic Publishers & Distributors, Delhi,1997, 114- 128

................., 2003, *Essays on International Money*. (Deep and Deep, NewDelhi)

................, 2003, International Financial Institutions, European Central Bank and International Monetary System.86th IEA Conference Volume,Kolhapur, 2003, 997-1006.

.................., 2003, The convergence criteria towards the Euro:An analysis. *Vision*-Vol-XXII, No-3-4 Jan-June, 36-54

.............., 2006, New Horizon in International Financial Institutions and Stability in The international Monetary System (2006)-*Political Economy Journal Of India* Vol-15,Issues 3, 4 , July-December 2006, 18-27.

..................,2011, International Financial Institution, European Central Bank and the International Monetary System (2011)-this paper was published in V.Shanmugasundaram edt *"The New Institutional Economics"*.Deep and Deep,NewDelhi,288-301

..............,2011, US Financial crisis , Recovery packages and dollar Hegemony-Paper published in *Modern Indian Economy –Essays in honour of Prof. Alak Ghosh* –Ed by Raj Kumar Sen (Deep and Deep, New Delhi, 2010), 126-137

.................., 2012, Reform of International Monetary System-Paper will be published in edt volume in honour of Amalesh Banerjee, to be published by BEA.

..................., 2012, Analytical Framework of Euro Crisis, *International Journal of Business, Management and Social Sciences,*Vol-1, Issue 7(III), March, 111-116.

Celani, Claudio., 2012,The EU Fiscal Pact: Euro Crisis Continues As Nations Crumble, *EIR*, April 6,10-13

Eichengreen, Barry., 2011, The Euro's Never-Ending Crisis, *Current History* , March, 91-96

ECB, 2011, *Annual Report-2011*

.............:, *EuroStat-2011*

..........., 2011, *Euro Money Market Survey-2010*

..........., 2012, *Financial Integration in Europe,*April,Germany

IMF, 2009, *IFS-2007and 2011*

.........., 2012, *Global Financial Stability Report-2011*

Salai-i-Martin,X.,1986,Regional Cohesion: Evidence and Theories of Regional Growth and Convergence, *European Economic Review*,Vol-40, 1325-52

Torres,F.,Amy Verdun.,Hubert Zimmermann.,2006,EMU Rules: The Political and Economic Consequences of European Monetary System. (Suippet view)

Volz, Ulrich., 2012, Lessons of the European Crisis for Regional Monetary and Financial Integration in East Asia,*ADBIWP-347*, February.

www.debeshbhowmik.weebly.com

www.dbhowmik.blog.com

www.economist.com

www.econ.berkley.edu/Eichengreen

www.ecb.int

www.imsreform.org

APPENDIX

Fig-6A.1: Bank lending to corporations and private households for selected countries in the Euro area

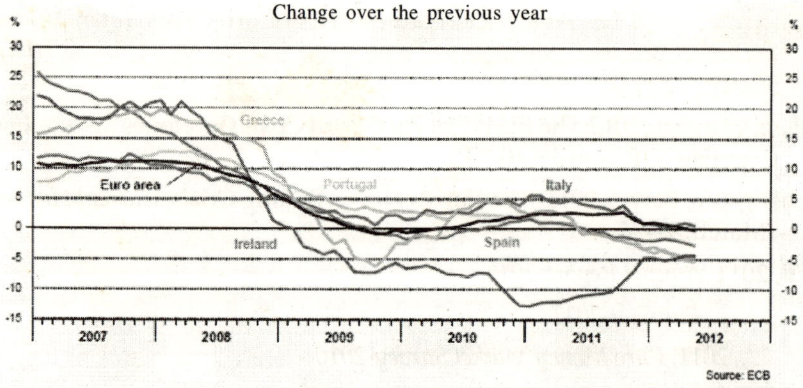

CHAPTER 7

DIAGNOSTIC TEST THROUGH ECONOMETRIC MODELS

[A] A SHORT NOTE ON THE BEHAVIOUR OF US$/EURO EXCHANGE RATE DURING 1999-2012

Introduction

Recent Euro Crisis is clouded over the universe and has diverged the convergence criterion of EU and made unstable the international monetary and financial situation for which the exchange rate US$/Euro is quite responsible to some extent. Therefore, I endeavour to study the exchange rate of US$/Euro behavior in the time series analysis from 1999 to 2012.

The Methodology

Semilog linear model is used for calculating trend line. To check the stationarity, Box-Jenkins (1976) estimation of time series model is taken for showing ARIMA(1,1,1) , AR(1),AR(2), ACF,PACF. Bollerslev (1986) was used for calculating ARCH and GARCH models. The methodology of Dickey and Fuller (1979, 1981) was used for testing unit root. The data were collected from European Central Bank. The EViews 3.0 software is used for computation.

The Findings of the time series analysis

On the inception of the single currency Euro since 1999, the Euro has gone a clear set back in international market because US Dollar has gained 3.33% per year against the Euro according to the semilog linear model which showed below:

$$\text{Log}(X) = -0.069120 + 0.033306\, t + U_i$$
$$(-1.319) \qquad (5.412)^*$$

R^2= 0.7093 , DW = 0.8616 , F= 29.291 (Significant) , X= US$/Euro

This growth rate of US$/Euro rate is seen in the Fig-7.A.1 in linear form as well as in the actual data.

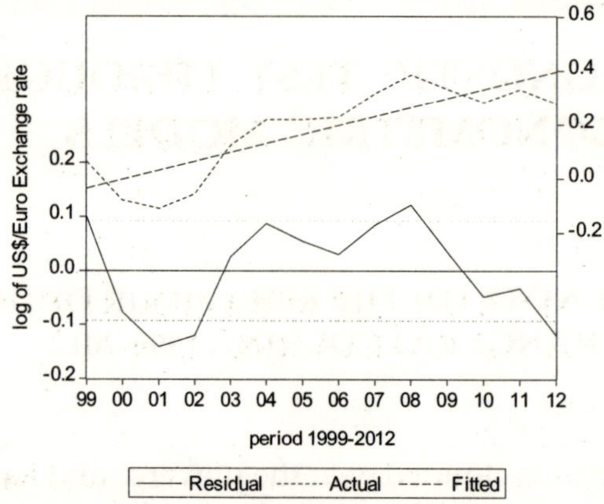

Fig- 7.A.1: Linear trend line of US$/Euro

The US$/Euro rate from 1999 to 2011 is plotted below where the rate is upward since prior to 2002. So, loosing Euro is clear in Fig-7.A.2.

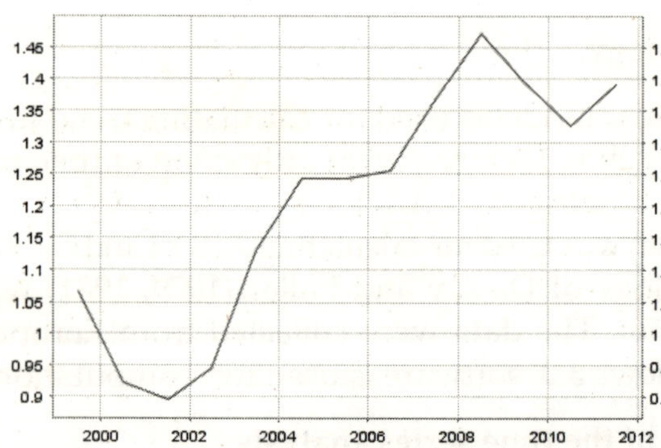

Fig-7: A.2 : US$/Euro exchange rate .

The quarterly data is also seen in the Fig-7.A.3 so nicely that the path the exchange rate is cleary explainable.

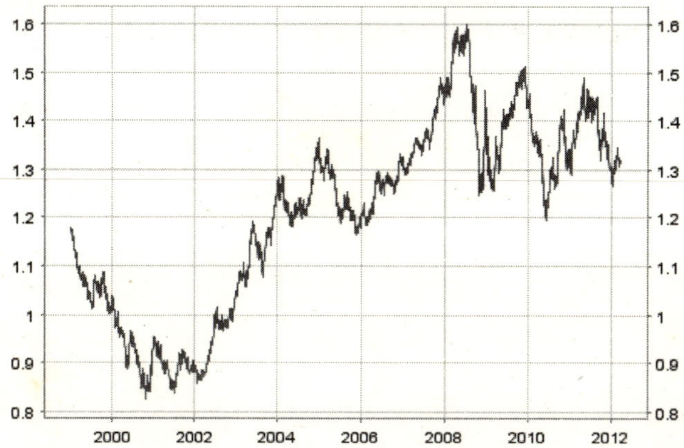

Fig-7.A.3: US$/Euro exchange rate on quarterly data

European Central Bank (ECB) has calculated the Nominal effective exchange rate, Euro area-17 countries vis-a-vis the EER-12 group of trading partners (AU, CA, DK, HK, JP, NO, SG, KR, SE, CH, GB and US) against US dollar which showed downward but proves the volatility of the ERM in the field of international trade. It is seen in the Fig-7.A.4.

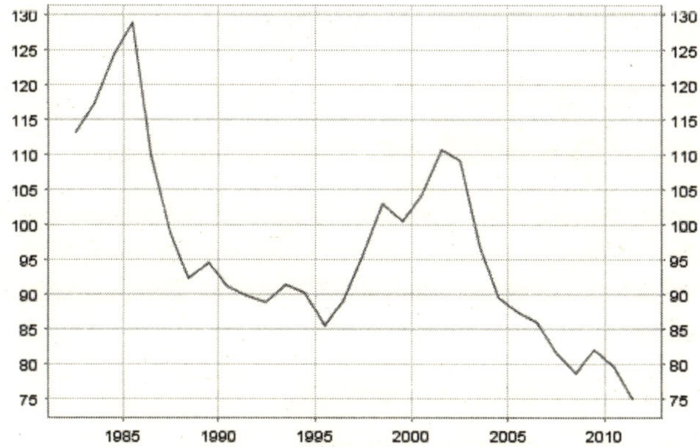

Fig-7.A.4. Nominal Effective Exchange Rate of Euro

Even , the Real Effective Exchange Rate of Euro is found more volatile than the NEER. This proves that EU in competing international trade and payment mechanism, lags behind the US, and other developed countries. In Fig-7.A.5, it is shown clearly.

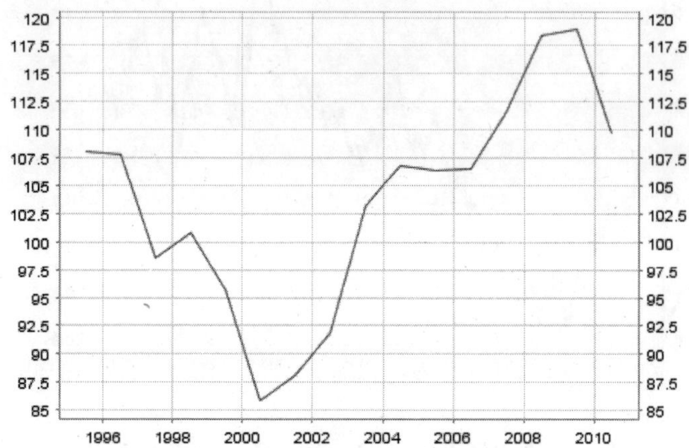

Fig-7.A.5: REER of Euro

The exchange rate US$/Euro is negatively skewed and its coefficient of variation was found to be 15.65% during 1999-2012 in which the exchange rate has unit root in the level series because the ADF statistic showed insignificant and equals -1.529583 which is less than tabulated value. The estimated value of the Unit Root Test is given below.

$$\Delta X_t = 0.499028 - 0.476287\, X_{t-1} + 0.467821 \Delta X_{t-1}$$

(1.8743)* (-1.529) (1.674)

R^2=0.4102 , DW= 1.8719 , F=1.85489 (insignificant)

The Augmented Dicky Fuller Unit Root Test of the first difference series of the exchange rate found no sign of unit root.ADF statistic = -3.507215 which is significant at least 10% level. The estimated equation is given below,

$$\Delta X_t = 0.1526 - 1.1736 \Delta X_{t-1} + 0.3380 \Delta X_{t-2}$$

(2.214)* (-3.507)* (1.299)

R^2=0.6654 , F= 4.64 (significant) , DW = 2.165

The level series of the exchange rate was found Autocorrelation and Partial Auto Correlation Problems since Q statistics which followed χ^2 distribution were significant whose values are seen in the Table-7.A.1 and ACF and PACF of the level series are shown in the Fig-7.A.6.

Table-7A.1: AC, PAC and Q Stat

AC	*PAC*	*Q-Stat*	*Prob*	
1	0.843	0.843	12.241	0.000
2	0.552	-0.546	17.934	0.000
3	0.310	0.251	19.896	0.000
4	0.092	-0.443	20.086	0.000
5	-0.121	0.062	20.450	0.001
6	-0.293	-0.231	22.847	0.001
7	-0.390	0.091	27.709	0.000
8	-0.420	-0.175	34.308	0.000
9	-0.391	0.169	41.141	0.000
10	-0.309	-0.164	46.492	0.000
11	-0.218	0.021	50.056	0.000
12	-0.122	0.033	51.730	0.000

Source: Author's calculation

ACF: US$/EURO exchange rate, 1999-2012

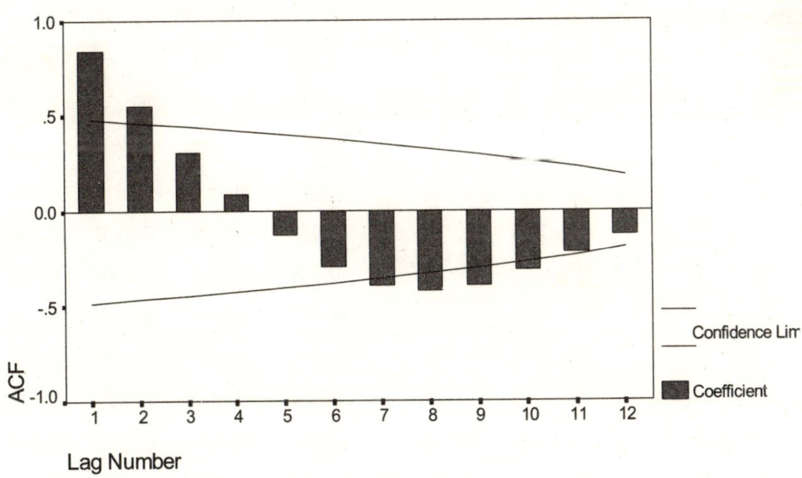

Source: Author's calculation

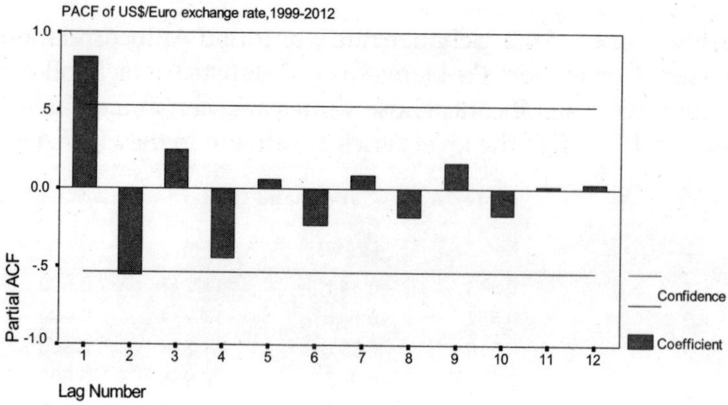

Source: Author's calculation

Fig-7.A.6: ACF and PACF of US$/Euro

Also the first difference series of the exchange rate of US$/Euro found Auto Correlation and Partial Auto Correlation Problems whose values including Q statistics are shown in Table-7.A.2 and plotted in Fig-7.A.7

Table 7.A.2:ACF and PACF of ΔUS$/Euro

Autocorrelation	*Partial Correlation*		*AC*	*PAC*	*Q-Stat*	*Prob*
. |** . |	. |** . |	1	0.223	0.223	0.8091	0.368
. **| . |	.***| . |	2	-0.266	-0.332	2.0619	0.357
. **| . |	. | . |	3	-0.193	-0.047	2.7847	0.426
. |* . |	. |* . |	4	0.079	0.069	2.9183	0.572
. | . |	. *| . |	5	0.032	-0.096	2.9435	0.709
. **| . |	. **| . |	6	-0.229	-0.224	4.4098	0.621
. **| . |	. **| . |	7	-0.282	-0.195	6.9868	0.430
. *| . |	. *| . |	8	-0.110	-0.167	7.4575	0.488
. | . |	. *| . |	9	0.054	-0.110	7.5976	0.575
. |* . |	. | . |	10	0.085	-0.045	8.0706	0.622
. | . |	. *| . |	11	-0.029	-0.133	8.1543	0.699

Source: Author's calculation

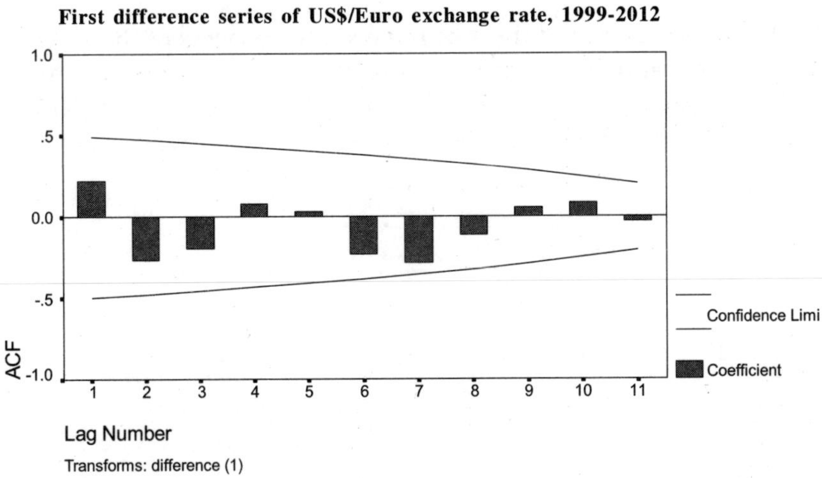

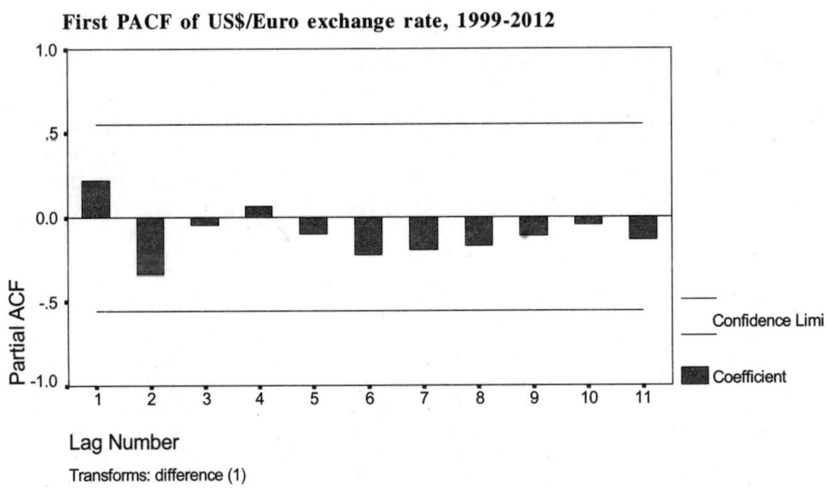

Fig-7.A.7: ACF and PACF of first difference series of US$/Euro

Source: Author's calculation

We have calculated the Auto Regressive process of the exchange rate in lag 1 and lag 2 which showed that it is non-stationary where AR(1) is significant but AR(2) is not in the least square method. In Table-7.A.3,it is shown in detail. There is a serial correlation problem.

Table-7.A.3: AR(1) and AR(2)

Variable	*Coefficient*	*Std. Error*	*t-Statistic*	*Prob.*
AR(1)	1.261194	0.278911	4.521851	0.0011
AR(2)	-0.245485	0.285271	-0.860531	0.4097
R-squared	0.771439	Mean dependent var	1.249133	
Adjusted R-squared	0.748583	S.D. dependent var	0.177731	
S.E. of regression	0.089117	Akaike info criterion	-1.846718	
Sum squared resid	0.079419	Schwarz criterion	-1.765900	
Log likelihood	13.08031	F-statistic	33.75205	
Durbin-Watson stat	1.655775	Prob (F-statistic)	0.000171	
Inverted AR Roots	1.02	.24		

Source: Calculated by author

Estimated AR process is nonstationary

On the contrary, the AR (1) and AR(2) process of the log of the exchange rate series are significant and stationary having inverted AR roots and the F statistic is significant in the least square method. It is shown in Table-7.A.4.No serial correlation problem was found.

Table 7.A.4:AR(1) and AR(2) in log

Variable	*Coefficient*	*Std. Error*	*t-Statistic*	*Prob.*
C	0.262363	0.081026	3.238020	0.0102
AR(1)	1.175445	0.215367	5.457879	0.0004
AR(2)	-0.428169	0.220007	-1.946163	0.0835
R-squared	0.878082	Mean dependent var	0.212105	
Adjusted R-squared	0.850989	S.D. dependent var	0.154494	
S.E. of regression	0.059638	Akaike info criterion	-2.588743	
Sum squared resid	0.032010	Schwarz criterion	-2.467517	
Log likelihood	18.53246	F-statistic	32.40992	
Durbin-Watson stat	2.079602	Prob(F-statistic)	0.000077	
Inverted AR Roots	.59 -.29i	.59+.29i		

Source: Calculated by author

In the ARMA process, the AR(1) and MA(1) are both significant and stationary showing significant F statistic in the log exchange rate series of US$/Euro and both have inverted roots of 0.72 for AR and -0.92 for MA. F statistics = 46.487 is significant too.

The estimated equation is given below;

$$Y_t = 1.293492 + 0.7193Y_{t-1} + \varepsilon_t + 0.9241\,\varepsilon_{t-1}$$

(9.587)* (4.171)* (28.913)* , * = significant at 10% level

R^2= 0.902 , DW=1.788 , F= 46.487 (sig) The ARCH-LM test is given by the values as follows: F=0.964 (insignificant) , TR^2= 1.0556 (insignificant)The serial correlation test assures that F = 3.167 (significant), $TR^2 = nR^2$=5.7442 (significant)

Thus, the AR is convergent, exponential and decaying. And there is serial correlation in the AR process.

In the next step, we have found the estimated equation of conditional variance which is given below.

$$\varepsilon_t^2 = 1.27062 + 1.6952\,\varepsilon^2_{t-1} + 0.81466\,\varepsilon^2_{t-2} + v_t$$

(50.307)* (9.596)* (4.599)* , * = significant at 10% level

R^2 = 0.825 ,F=26.01(significant), DW=1.401

Therefore, the ARCH-LM test confirms that the convergence is insignificant in the ARCH process because TR^2= 0.0702(insig) , F= 0.059(insig.) and DW = 2.12.

Conclusion

Euro crisis had made the exchange rate more volatile than before in both nominal and real terms. The Euro dollar rate went in favour of dollar, so that Euro Area had suffered in international payments in all cases.

APPENDIX

Fig-7AA.1: CYCLES OF DOLLAR-EURO AND DOLLAR-YEN

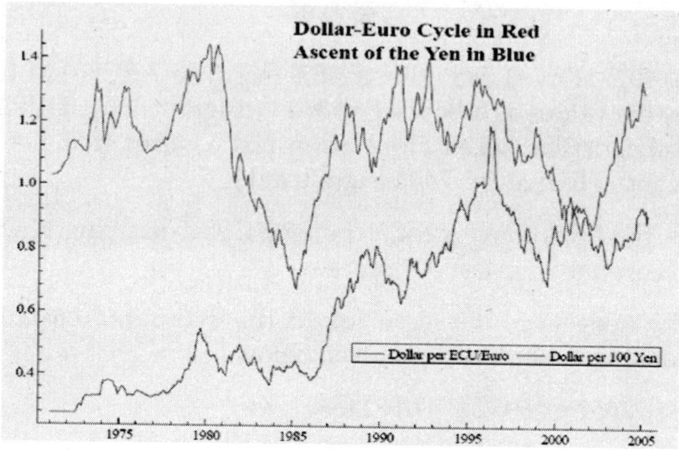

References

Anderson,T.W., 1971,*The Statistical Analysis of Time Series*,Wiley, NewYork.

Bhowmik,D., 2003, *Essays on International Money*, Deep and Deep, NewDelhi

............., 1989, Exchange Rate Behaviour in India during 1968-1997- 82nd Conference Volume of IEA,Amritsar,pp. 352- 362. Also in Alak Ghosh and Rakesh Mohan (Ed) *Exchange Rate Behaviour in Developing Countries.*(2000)(Deep and Deep , NewDelhi), pp. 87-104.

..............., 2001, Exchange Rate Policy ,IMF and the Developing Countries- 84th Conference Volume of IEA, Vellore, pp. 404-418.

Bollerslev,T.,1986, Generalised Autoregressive Conditional Heteroscedasticity, *Journal of Econometrics*, Vol-31, pp. 307-27.

Box, G.E.P. and G.M.Jenkins., 1976,*Time Series Analysis*, Forecasting and Control, Holden-Day, San Francisco.

Dickey. D.A. and W.A.Fuller., 1979, Distribution of the estimators for Autoregressive Time Series with a unit root, *Journal of the American Statistical Association*, Vol-74, p 427-31

...............,1981, Likelihood ratio statistics for autoregressive time series with a unit root,*Econometrica*, Vol. 49, pp. 1057-72.

Enders,W.,1995,*Applied Econometric Time Series*, John Wiley &Sons, NewYork.

[B] EURO CRISIS : CO-INTEGRATION OF FISCAL DEFICIT OF EURO AREA

Introduction

One of the root causes of the Euro crisis is the disruption of fiscal convergence of Euro area since a few years. This chapter will endeavour to show the econometric relationship between fiscal deficit of Euro area and the co-integrating variables of the fiscal deficit during 1999-2011.

Methodology

Basically, we tried to follow Engle and Granger (1987) technique of co-integration test for fiscal deficit of Euro area.

Structure of Fiscal deficit of Euro Area

The fiscal convergence of Euro Area broke down after 2007 although it was volatile since the inception of Euro. The nature of fiscal deficit as percent of GDP of Euro Area is plotted in Fig-7.B.1 where the path is not seen declining.

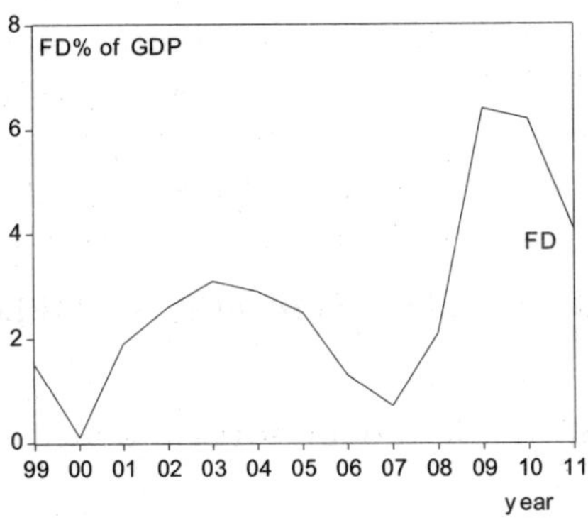

Fig-7.B.1: The path of fiscal deficit of Euro area

Taking the semi-linear model Log(y) = $a+bt+u_i$ to show the growth rate of fiscal deficit and the trend line of fiscal deficit of Euro area , we found that the fiscal deficit as percent of GDP has been stepping up at the rate of 14.85% per year from 1999 to 2011.The estimated equation is statistically significant as shown below.

$$Log(y) = -0.3847 + 0.1489\ t + Ui$$
$$(-0.689) \quad (2.1187)^*$$

DW=1.976 R^2=0.2898 F=4.489* where y= fiscal deficit % of GDP *=significant

In Fig-7.B.2, the trend line is plotted and is shown upward rising.

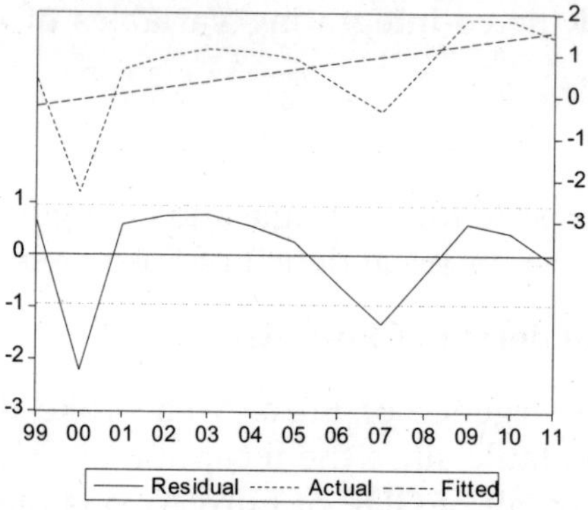

Fig-7.B.2: Trend line of Fiscal deficit of Euro area.

The fiscal deficit series of Euro area consists of no unit root since the value of ADF = -3.48473 but it has auto-correlation and partial auto-correlation problem too. Again, the level series of the fiscal deficit suffers from auto regressive conditional homoscedasticity and generalised auto regressive conditional homoscedasticity problem .

CO-INTEGRATION TEST FOR FISCAL DEFICIT IN EURO AREA

Let us assume a simple model of fiscal deficit in the following manner,

$$Y=\beta_0+\beta_1X_1+\beta_2X_2+\beta_3X_3+\beta_4X_4+\beta_5X_5+\beta_6X_6+\beta_7X_7+\beta_8X_8+e_t$$

Where Y= fiscal deficit % of GDP , X_1= GDP growth % per year,X_2=debt GDP ratio per year,X_3= inflation rate,X_4=money supply % of GDP,X_5=current account deficit % of GDP,X_6=net FDI outflow % of GDP,X_7=revenue deficit % of GDP,X_8= tax revenue % GDP and e_t=random variable

Let us assume, β_0=constant,β_1=coefficient of X_1which is<0,β_2=coefficient of X_2which is >0,β_3 is the coefficient of X_3 which is >0,β_4 =coefficient of X_4 which is >0,β_5= coefficient of X_5which is >0,β_6=coefficient of X_6 which is <0,β_7= coefficient of X_7 which is <0,and β_8>0 respectively

Solving for error term as,

$$e_t=Y-(\beta_0+\beta_1X_1+\beta_2X_2+\beta_3X_3+\beta_4X_4+\beta_5X_5+\beta_6X_6+\beta_7X_7+\beta_8X_8)$$

Since e_t must be stationary, it follows that the linear combination of integrated variables (x_1............X_8) must also be stationary. According to Engle and Granger (1987), the co-integration considers the set of variables in the long run equilibrium when,

$$\beta_1X_1+\beta_2X_2+\beta_3X_3+\beta_4X_4+\beta_5X_5+\beta_6X_6+\beta_7X_{7+}+\beta_8X_8=0$$

If we denote β and X_t the vectors ($\beta_1,\beta_2,\beta_3,\beta_4,\beta_5,\beta_6,\beta_7,\beta_8$) and ($x_{1t},X_{2t},X_{3t},X_{4t},X_{5t},X_{6t},X_{7t},X_{8t}$),then equilibrium error is $e_t=\beta X_t$.. Now, following Engle and Granger(1987) test for co-integration ,let us have OLS regression of the parameters. If the long run equilibrium is stationary then it is co-integrated in the order of (1,1).

$$\underset{(-0.965)}{Y=-21.1498} - \underset{(-2.656)^*}{0.5521X_1} + \underset{(1.856)}{0.2659X_2} + \underset{(0.279)}{0.1297X_3} + \underset{(1.0343)}{0.02779X_4}$$

$$+ \underset{(2.349)^*}{1.3455X_5} - \underset{(-0.2008)}{0.04502X_6} - \underset{(-0.7014)}{0.6482X_7} + \underset{(0.9403)}{1.3415X_8}+Ui$$

R^2=0.975 DW=2.0918 F=20.3316* *=significant

This OLS is statistically significant and GDP growth rate and fiscal deficit inverse relation and current account deficit and fiscal deficit positive correlation have been found to be statistically significant.

Now the Unit Root Test of the level series of residual showed the following results;

$$\Delta e_t= 0.20738 - 1.819e_{t-1}+0.54047\ \Delta e_{t-1}+ \varepsilon_t$$

(1.0801) (-3.6768)* (1.6102)

R^2=0.693 DW=2.455 F=5.286* ADF = -3.676* *=significant

Again, the Unit Root Test of the first difference series of the residual became,

$$\Delta e_{t-1} = -0.2966 - 2.245e_{t-2} + 0.2258'' e_{t-2} + \varepsilon_t$$

(-0.664) (-3.527)* (0.491) and R^2=0.708 DW=2.36 F=4.864* ADF=-3.5277* *=significant

In both level series and first difference series, ADF became significant ,so that co-integration test is found significant. In the level series,-2<-1.819<0 is proved ,so that the series is stationary and the variables assumed in the model are co-integrated in the order of (1,1).On the other hand, in the first difference series, -2>-2.245<0 is proved , therefore, the series is non-stationary and the variables are not co-integrated in the order of (1,1).

Hence, the equilibrium error of the level series of the co-integrated model is shown in the Fig-7.B.3,where we found the fitted line and the actual line crossed more than once, so the model is stable.

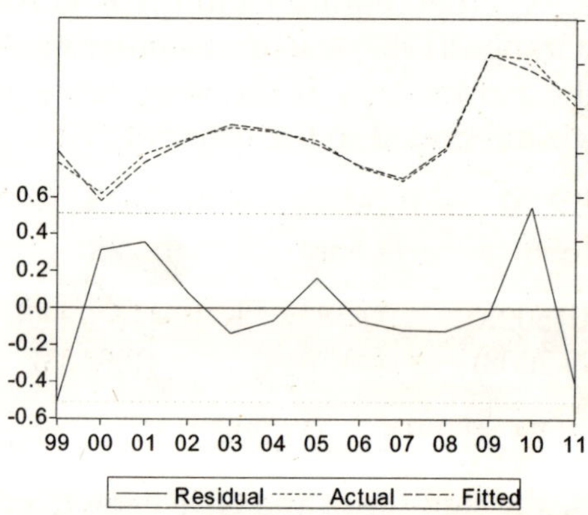

Fig-7.B.3: The equilibrium error of co-integration

Equilibrium In terms of log

The co-integration model can be found out in terms of logarithm which is given below,

$$Log(Y) = -85.13471 + 0.18271\log(X_1) - 2.357\log(X_2) -$$

(-0.864) (0.645) (-0.1907)

$$0.3599\log(X_3) + 11.5209\log(X_4) + 0.2436\log(X_5)$$

(-0.395) (2.0518)* (2.0995)*

$$-2.2088\log(X_6) + 8.343\log(X_7) + 4.8733\log(X_8) + \varepsilon_t$$

$$(-1.7165) \qquad (0.1837) \qquad (0.147)$$

$R^2=0.864$ DW=2.288 F=3.191

The Unit Root Test of the residual level series showed that

$$\Delta e_t = 0.1336 - 1.89079e_{t-1} + 0.68937\,\Delta e_{t-1} + \varepsilon$$

$$(0.6217) \qquad (-5.7023)^* \qquad (3.1656)^*$$

and $R^2= 0.843$ DW=2.343 F=12.58* ADF=-5.702313* *=significant

The logarithmic co-integration model is significant because ADF became significant .Note that the association between current account deficit and fiscal deficit and association between money supply and fiscal deficit were found significant. From the unit root test we have $-2<-1.89079<0$, so that the series becomes stationary and the variables assumed are co-integrated in the order of (1,1). Hence, the equilibrium error was stable which is shown in the Fig-7.B.4.

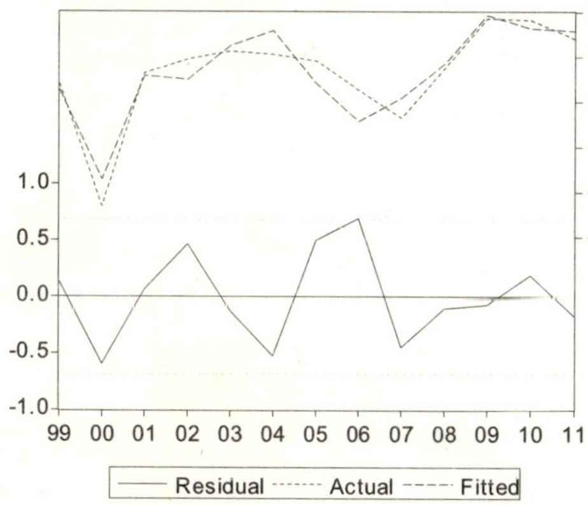

Fig-7.B.4: Equilibrium error of logarithmic model

Finally, the Error Correction Model was also found statistically significant but the association between change in inflation rate , change in GDP growth rate and the change in fiscal deficit became significant.

$$\Delta Y = 0.0446 - 0.5539\Delta X_1 + 0.0553\Delta X_2 - 0.9452\Delta X_3 + 0.000655\Delta X_4 - 0.0875\Delta X_5$$

$$(0.058) \qquad (-2.263)^* \qquad (0.715) \qquad (-2.8347)^* \qquad (0.0048) \qquad (-0.1126)$$

$$0.24841\Delta X_6 + 0.2651\Delta X_7 - 0.3557\Delta X_8 + \varepsilon_t$$

$$(-1.579) \quad (0.2198) \quad (-0.2485)$$

R^2=0.9472 DW=1.844, F=8.971* *=significant

Unit Root Test of the residual is as follows,

$$\Delta\varepsilon_t = 0.4387 - 1.70219\varepsilon_{tt-1} + 0.4015\,\Delta\varepsilon_{t-1} + \varepsilon_t$$

$$(1.13) \quad (-2.867)^* \quad (0.9314)$$

and R^2= 0.658, DW=2.25 , F=4.493* and ADF=-2.8673

Since ADF became insignificant , therefore ECM model has unit root but -2<-1.70219<0 proved that the series is stationary and variables are co-integrated in the order of (1,1).But, the ECM model suggests that the relation between change in growth and change in fiscal deficit and change in inflation and change in fiscal deficit are inversely related and showed significant. In Fig-7.B.5, the equilibrium error of ECM is seen stable.

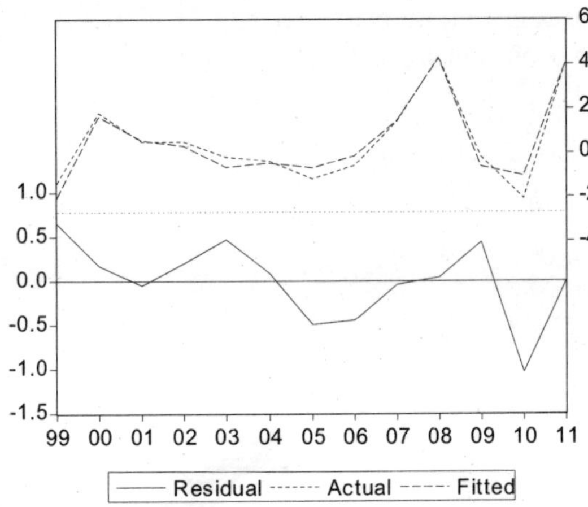

Fig-7.B.5, Equilibrium of ECM model.

Conclusion

We know that Euro crisis began with the break down of convergence criteria of fiscal deficit and debt/GDP ratio where we were able to find through co-integration test that GDP growth, inflation rate, current account deficit and money supply are the significant co-integrating variables and even other variables are co-integrated with fiscal deficit in the Euro Area from 1999 to 2011.

References

Bhowmik, Debesh,& S.Pramanik.,2002, Fiscal Policy Reform Towards the Behaviour of Fiscal Deficit of the States in India,.85th Conference Volume of IEA, Trivandrum, 649-664., Also published in D.K.Srivastava & M.Narasimhulu (edt)(2006)-*State Level Fiscal Reforms in the Indian Economy,* (Deep and Deep,New Delhi.), 373-392.

Bhowmik, Debesh., 2003, The convergence criteria towards the Euro: An Analysis, *Vision,* Vol-XXII, No-2-4, 36-54.

Bhowmik,Debesh.,2004,Behaviour of Fiscal Deficit and the Reform Policy in India, published in S.Murty (edt) *Fiscal and Monetary State in India: Some Aspect.*(RBSA Publishers, Jaipur), 59-94.

Bhowmik, Debesh., 2012, Analytical Framework of Euro Crisis-2012-*International Journal of Business, Management and Social Sciences,* Vol-1,Issue 7(III), March, pp111-116.

Bhowmik, Debesh., 2012, A short note on the behavior of US$/Euro exchange rate during 1999-2012 – *International Journal Of Business, Management and Social Sciences,* Vol-I, Issue 8(II), April 2012, 15-21.

Enders, Walter., 1990, *Applied Econometric Time Series* (John Wiley and Sons, NY)

Engle, R.F. and C.W.J.Granger., 1987, Co-integration and Error correction: Representation, estimation and testing ,*Econometrica,* Vol.55 , 251-76.

Sala-i-Martin, X.,1996, Regional cohesion :Evidence and Theories of regional growth and convergence, *European Economic Review,* Vol-40, 1325-1352

[C] EURO CRISIS : THE NEXUS BETWEEN GROWTH AND EMPLOYMENT IN EU

Introduction

The debt crisis in the Euro Area remains the biggest threat to the world economy leading to fall of growth of output and employment.Employment to population ratios remain below 2007 level except in Brazil,China and Germany.Unemployment rate in most of the countries in Europe,USA,Asia and Latin America remain high above the pre-crisis level.At the same time ,the Eurozone has continued to slide more deeply into recession.A mild recession in the Eurozone would have benign supply effects on the US,but a breack up of the Eurozone or a European depression would transmit negative supply effects including collapsing banking sectors.Spreading lower employment and growth injected into structural tragilities which matter for sovereign risk and changed each country's economic fundamentals.

So to say, the Euro crisis has distorted the general economic relationships in most of the macro variables in Euro Area. The employment and growth nexus was positive before the beginning of the Euro crisis and international financial crisis. But, the relationship turned into negative during 1999-2012 in the Euro Area because of the impact of Euro crisis. Although,there are so many factors like wage rate, trade unionism,order of vacancies,inflation structure of the economy that determined the employment ,yet modern approaches tried to show the nexus between the employment and growth rates. In this chapter, we will endeavour to explain the relationship through the econometric model using co-integration test and VAR model.

The methodology

We have used the Engle-Granger Methodology of Co-Integration test(1987) and also applied the Johansen M.L.Method of cointegration(1996) including the Error Correction Model for significance of the relationship between employment and growth in Euro zone during 1999-2012.Applying the VAR model , we have justified the relationship more appropriately.The data of growth rate of unemployment and growth rate of GDP of Euro Area from 1999 to 2012 were collected from Euro Stat.

The Literature reviewed

According to Walterskirchen (1999) there was a very close relationship between GDP growth and employment in EU, in the 1988-1998 period, under the conditions in which employment elasticity, compared to GDP growth, was of 0.8. The analysis of the relationship between economic growth and employment, in order to catch the effect of growth on employment at the level of the entire European Union, in the 2000-2010 period, highlights a positive elasticity (+0.37), under the conditions of an annual average growth in GDP of 1.5% and in employment of 0.6%. The low value of the employment elasticity coefficient of +0.37 reflects the fact that for an average GDP growth of 1 percentage point (p.p.) there was an average employment growth of 0.37 p.p. The European Union is characterized by an economic growth, accompanied by a less proportional increase in jobs, but also by a labour productivity growth (de +0.9%), fact which creates the conditions of an intensive - extensive growth.

Walterskirchen(1999) showed that there is a very close relationship between GDP growth and employment in time-series as well as in cross-county analyses. The coefficients are highly significant. In cross-country analysis (1988-1998), the employment elasticity vis-à-vis GDP-growth is 0.65 (Table -7.C.1). In time-series analysis the employment elasticity in the EU is 0.8 for the period 1988-1998 and it is highly significant (Table-7.C. 2).

Table-7.C.1: Cross Country Analysis of all EU countries (1988-1998)

$$E = -1.03 + \underset{(6.3)}{0.65g}$$

R^2=0.75 , DW = 2.04

$$U = 0.51 \underset{(-3.5)}{-0.17g}$$

R^2=0.49 , DW =1.81

Where E= relative change in employment per year, g= GDP growth rate per year , U= change in the unemployment rate per year.

Source: Walterskirchen, 1999

Table-7.C.2:Time series analysis-growth, employment , unemployment rate in EU

Employment Elasticity with respect to GDP			
1968-1978	0.20	t=2.8	R^2=0.5
1978-1988	0.63	t=5.3	R^2=0.8
1988-1998	0.84	t=4.3	R^2=0.7
Unemployment rate with respect to GDP			
1968-1978	-0.17	t=-3.8	R^2=0.6
1978-1988	-0.59	t=-5.9	R^2=0.8
1988-1998	-0.52	t=-4.8	R^2=0.7

Source: Walterskirchen,1999

There can be no negative relation between economic growth and unemployment, because GDP and unemployment are both rising in the long run. It is evident that employment will only increase if GDP is rising faster than productivity. In the EU, during the nineties a GDP-growth rate of 1.8 percent was necessary to keep employment constant and, as labour supply increased, a rate of 2.3 percent was necessary to keep unemployment constant at existing labour market regimes.There is obviously a strong negative linear correlation between real output growth and the change in the unemployment rates.There is still a strong and positive relation between GDP-growth and employment. But employment, of course, will rise only if economic growth rates are out stripping productivity gains (tautology).

Perugini(2005) observed that for the period 1995-2003, the national differences in GDP growth rates, annual changes in hours worked and annual changes in GDP per hour worked, distinguishing the EU-15 countries and maintaining the comparison with US. Five European countries (Ireland, Luxembourg, Greece, Finland and Spain) had an annual GDP growth rate higher than US,the annual changes in total hours worked were higher in six EU countries (Luxembourg, Ireland, Spain, Netherlands, Finland and Italy) compared to US. Finally, only four EU countries (Ireland, Greece, Sweden and Finland) had an annual change in GDP per hour worked higher than in US. The changes in total employment rates between 1997 and 2003 are all positive for the "old" EU-15 members (especially Spain, Ireland, The Netherlands, Italy and Finland), whereas five "new" EU members (Poland, the Slovak Republic, the Czech Republic, Estonia and Lithuania) plus Romania show a negative variation. In Table-7.C.3, it is clear that the correlation coefficient between GDP and employment in Euro area was estimated as 0.88 compared to USA as 0.76 during 1995-2003.

Table-7.C.3:GDP and Employment annual change in EU-15 and US(1995-2003)

Table 3 – GDP and Employment annual changes in EU-15 and US (1995-2003)

		1995	1996	1997	1998	1999	2000	2001	2002	2003	correlation coefficient
EU-15	GDP	2.4	1.6	2.5	2.9	2.9	3.5	1.6	1.0	0.7	0.88
	Employment	0.8	0.6	0.9	1.8	1.7	2.0	1.2	0.5	0.3	
US	GDP	2.5	3.7	4.5	4.2	4.5	3.7	0.5	2.2	3.1	0.76
	Employment	2.1	1.7	2.1	2.2	2.0	2.0	-0.2	-0.9	0.9	

Source: elaboration on Annual Macroeconomic Database (AMECO) based on ESA 95 national accounts; Employment Outlook, OECD.

The positive association between GDP and employment changes in Euro zone during 1995-2003 was recorded in the fitted equation in the form of Y=0.5747X-0.1307 and R^2= 0.7751 where Y= employment changes and X= GDP growth rate. This fitted equation is shown in Fig-7.C.1below.

Fig-7.C.1 :The correlation between GDP growth and employment change:EU-15

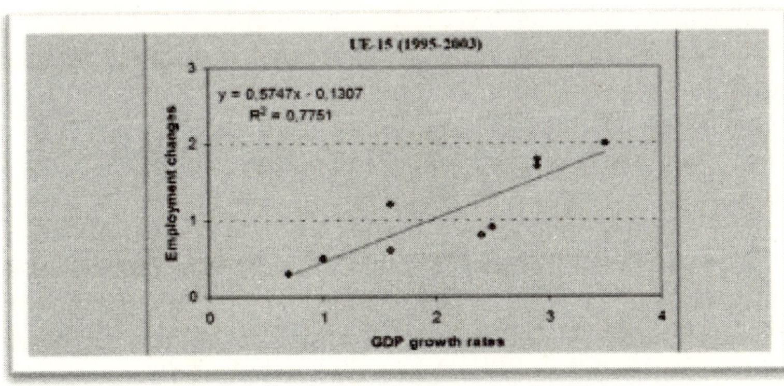

Source: As Fig-7.C.2

Similarly, the regression equation was estimated between GDP growth rate and employment changes in USA during 1995-2003 , which was found as Y=0.6678X – 0.8221 and R^2=0.58 where Y=employment changes and X= GDP growth rate of USA. The positive association was significantly observed, but the impact is higher than Euro Area in the specified period. The association is shown in the Fig-7.C.2.below.

Fig-7.C.2:The correlation between GDP growth and employment change: USA

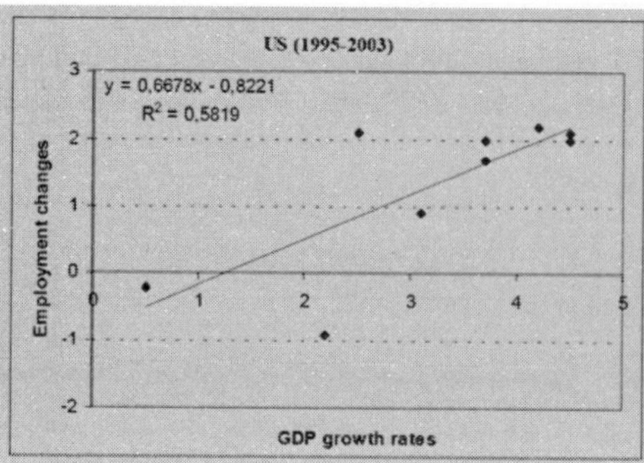

Source: elaboration on Annual Macroeconomic Database (AMECO) based on ESA 95 national accounts.

Signorelli(2005) clarified that during the period 1995-2003, EU-15 countries have been characterised by lower GDP growth rates compared to US, with a worsening in the second half of the period, accompanied by a remarkable and generalised net job creations (*rich-job low-growth*) and reductions in unemployment rates. It should be noted that in the previous 25 years the European countries experimented a worsening of employment performance (increase and persistence of unemployment), also during the more favourable economic cycles (*job-less growth*).The changes in total employment rates between 1997 and 2003 are all positive for the "old" EU-15 members (especially Spain, Ireland, The Netherlands, Italy and Finland), whereas five "new" EU members (Poland, the Slovak Republic, the Czech Republic, Estonia and Lithuania) plus Romania show a negative variation.As already highlighted, since the "EU White Paper on competitiveness, growth and employment" (1993) the target of increasing the employment intensity of growth has been clearly posed. In this EU document has been also stated that a GDP growth rate of about 2% would be just enough to keep employment constant. If one takes this statement (GDP growth threshold) as given, the employment increase in EU-15, during the period 1995-2003, must be taken as a surprise. In fact an annual employment growth average of about 1.1% (about 14.7 million new jobs, with an increase in total employment rate from 60.1 in 1995 to 64.3 in 2003) has been obtained with an average annual GDP growth rate of just 2.2%.In contrasting the world scenario of unemployment in USA,Japan and EU during 2000-2012,we should have a quick look at the Fig.-7.C.3, for considering cyclical nature and high rates since the inception of financial crisis.

Herman (2011) proved that during the period of 2000-2010, in five countries (Estonia, Latvia, Lithuania, Hungary, Romania), economic growth was obtained only due to the increase in productivity, because employment fell. In 11 countries, the increase in employment as well as the one in productivity contributed to economic growth. Italy is an exception, because in this country, in the period of 2000-2010, an average economic growth of +0.6% was recorded, under the conditions of an increase in employment (of +0.8)and a fall in labour productivity of 0.3%. In the five European countries like Malta, Luxembourg, Cyprus, Spain employment growth was superior to the labour productivity growth, and economic growth was much more labour-intensive, with employment growth contributing by 75% to the output growth. Unlike these countries, in other ones (Slovakia, Slovenia, Czech R., Poland, Bulgaria, Austria and Denmark) productivity growth was the one that contributed by over 75% to economic growth. Overall, at the EU-27 level, in the period of 2000-2010 , output growth was generated with a low employment intensity. This means that annual average economic growth of 1.5% was generated by an annual average productivity growth of 0.9% and by an average employment growth of 0.6%.After using the correlation analysis on data regarding the employment growth and labour productivity growth (Fig-7.C.3) for EU-27 countries, 2000-2010, we have found a negative significant relationship between productivity and employment growth (Spearman correlation= -0.599), which confirms the existence of trade-off between employment and productivity.

Fig-7.C. 3: Trend of unemployment of EU

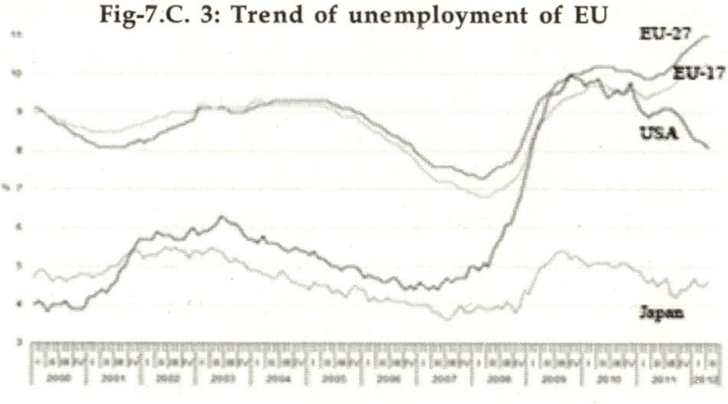

Source: Eurostat

Stehrer and Ward(2012) explained sectoral employment and income growth in EU in comparison to US and Japan as a result of crisis.According to them, the financial crisis that started off in 2008 has had a severe and sustained impact on the economic situation around the world and particularly in the more developed countries such as the US and Europe. As has become evident recently, though there have been signs of recovery in 2009 or 2010, growth prospects with respect to GDP have again deteriorated due to increasing economic and financial uncertainty in particular countries. Prospects for employment recovery in general are therefore again less favourable, implying that one expects sustained high unemployment rates and little or no recovery in terms of employment levels. Additionally, the impact of the crisis itself and the period after the crisis with a tendency towards recovery both in terms of GDP growth and employment was quite heterogeneous across the EU Member States. This heterogeneity of economic developments and prospects is still in place if not increasing further. Similarly, economic sectors suffered differently - both in terms of output and employment - from the crisis and recovered unevenly if at all. The again unfavourable outlook for the next year and maybe the years to come will also show in a differentiated impact on activity and employment across sectors and countries.

In brief, there is little sign of the crisis which first beset the EU economies in 2008 coming to an end and growth is forecast to be sluggish across the EU over the next two years. In this context, the rate of net job creation is likely to remain low and unemployment to remain high in most parts of the EU at least in the short-to-medium-term, particularly in the construction industry and manufacturing sectors most affected by the recession. Even in the longer-term, the prospects for any significant increase in employment in the manufacturing sectors are limited by the 'overhang' of productivity built up over the crisis as well as by apparent overcapacity in some industries (motor vehicles in particular) which was evident even before the crisis hit. While growth of employment is likely in services in both the short and longer-term, it is likely to be lower than before the crisis unless there is a significant pick-up of growth in manufacturing to generate the increase in income required to support the creation of jobs elsewhere in the economy. While there might be a short-term trade-off between productivity and employment, in the longer-term, employment growth depends on growth of productivity, though specifically in manufacturing sectors in order to maintain their global competitiveness so that they can generate the growth in income on which employment growth depends. On the evidence of the years preceding the onset of the recession and of what has happened since, Italy and Spain are likely to experience slower growth of manufacturing in the future, together with France. This has implications for the balanced growth of the EU economy. Young people have been hit particularly hard by the crisis and the lack of job creation which has accompanied it and employment rates of those aged 15-24 have fallen in all EU countries, in many considerably. This could have damaging long-term consequences for both the young people concerned and the economy. There is likely to be a continuing shift of manufacturing from the EU15 to the EU12, especially of engineering industries, though there are signs of production beginning to shift out of the EU12 to lower wage economies.

Mckinsey Global Institute(2010) made three clusters based on geography and took into account common patterns in terms of both productivity and labour market institutions.In cluster-1,it took Denmark,Finland,Ireland ,Sweden and UK which have higher labour utilization rates than EU average and almost on a par with US.Each economy has experienced strong increases in labour utilization since mid 1990s and productivity is in line with EU-15 average.Finland and UK have caught up with that average over the past 10 years and Irelands' productivity has had a significant boost from productive FDI.Denmark is the outlier in this point,its productivity has seen a large drop in recent years.Ireland also stands out for the fact that unemployment has risen particularly sharply in response to the severe hit the economy experienced during the global economic crisis.

In cluster-2, it took Austria,Belgium,France,Germany,Luxembourg and the Netherland which have above average productivity. Netherlands,Belgium and Luxembourg had higher productivity than in US in the run-up to the financial crisis.Productivity in France and Germany slightly exceeds US levels in the past but has recently fallen below US levels again. Incontrast, labour utilization is generally substantially below the EU-15 average due to low annual hours worked per employee and a mixed picture on employment. Austria is a modest exception,with labour utilization almost matching rates in Nordic countries and productivity on a par with the EU-15 average. The Netherlands, too, stands out positively in terms of employment rates and Germany in terms of Senior participation.

Cluster-3 consists of Greece, Italy, Portuguese and Spain and is the least homogeneous group of countries. Portugal and Greece have very high labour utilization rates driven by extraordinary high working hours.In Greece,employment remain low,driven by low female and senior participation .Spain had a very significant increase in labour utilization until crisis,when rising unemployment caused the rate of utilization to drop back again.Italy continues to most below average labour utilization as relatively long annual hours per employee fails to compensate for the lowest employment rate in the EU-15.On productivity,this group of countries still severely lags behind EU-15 levels.While Greece and Portugal have made up considerable ground from very low starting levels but have fallen behind.All countries in this cluster lag behind other groupings on innovation-related indicators as well as those related to the development of service sectors.

Observations from the Econometric models

The Nexus-The Euro crisis is although financial ,yet it is partially related with unemployment rate because it has an equal effect on low realized output growth with lower demand generated by them.However,the unemployment rate varies from one EU nation to other.

Euro zone unemployment rate showed negative association with the growth rate of GDP as a whole during 1999-2012 which was found statistically insignificant with very low R^2 and F statistic.The estimated regression is given below,

$$U = 8.9634 - 0.09736\, G + U_i$$

$$(30.1513)^{*} \quad (-0.83666)$$

$$R^2 = 0.0598, \; DW = 0.742086, \; F = 0.70$$

Fig-7.C.4:Scatter Diagram of U and G

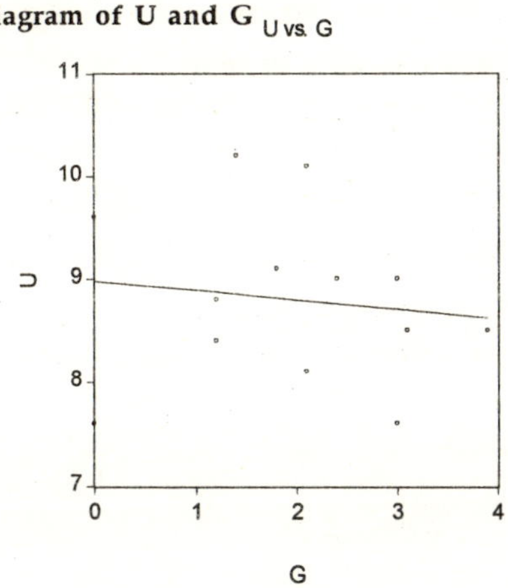

Source: Author

The scatter points have been fitted through Loess fit with degree one and 0.3000 span and is shown below where it is seen clearly insignificant with no linear association. (Fig-7.C.5)

Fig-7.C.5:Losess Fit

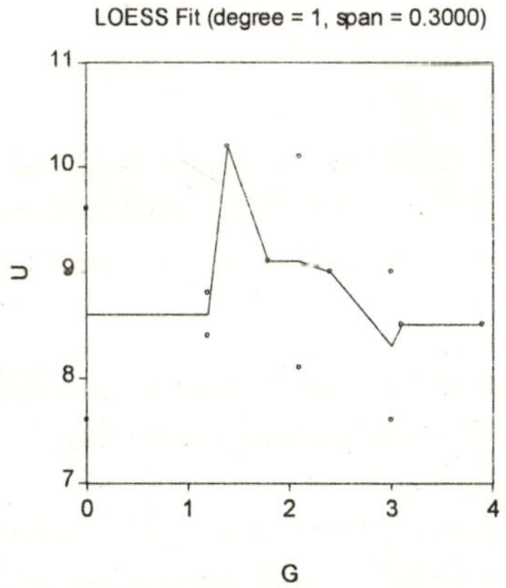

Source: Author

Fig-7.C.6: Kernel Fit

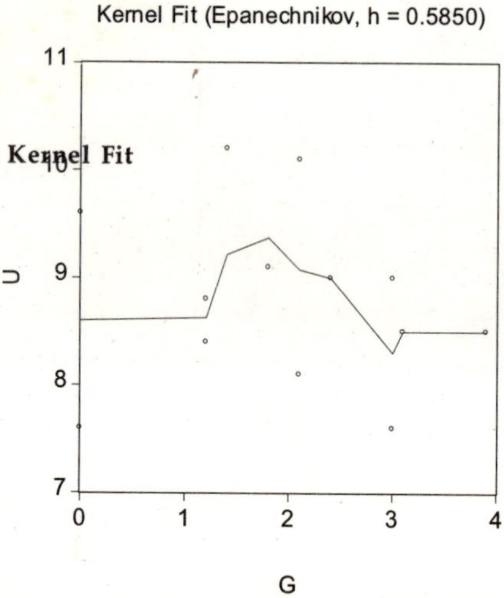

Source: Author

Similarly,the scatter points have been fitted through Kernel Methodology assuming Epanechikov ,h=0.5850 and is shown above which do not prove any positive or negative linear association.(Fig-7.C.6)

If we estimate Euro zone unemployment rate with GDP growth rate through double logarithm model which specified that 1% increase in GDP per year induced unemployment rate to grow a marginal increase of 0.002447% per year during 1999-2011 although it is found statistically insignificant with low R^2,DW and F.The estimated equation is given below,

$$\text{Log}(U) = 2.1734 + 0.002447 \log(G) + U_i$$

(78.89)* (0.3283)

$R^2 = 0.0097$, DW = 0.800 , F= 0.1077 *=significant

In Fig-7.C.7 , the fitted line showed that it is negligibly increased over time with respect to growth which means increase in GDP in EU is less sig rate in the inception of Euro crisi

Fig-7.C.7: Fitte

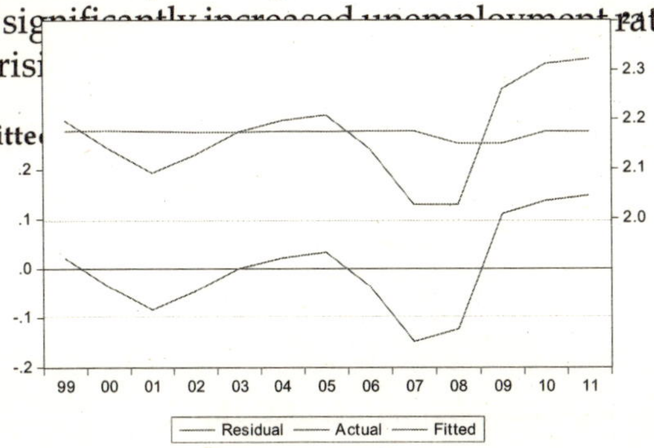

Source: Author

We can estimate nonlinear regression models with autoregressive error terms which showed the following result in case unemployment and GDP growth rate nexus of Euro zone from 1999 to 2011.

The estimated equations were found significant having high R^2 ,F and DW.

$$U_t = 7.655 + G_t^{-0.04149} + u_t$$

(41.709)* (-1.280)

$$u_t = 0.9494u_{t-1} - 0.9932u_{t-2} + \varepsilon_t$$

(3.9421)* (-3.2956)*

R^2=0.7173 , DW= 2.7709 , , F= 5.920* ,AIC= 1.987 , SC = 2.135

The model suggests that as the growth rate GDP of Euro zone increases the rate of unemployment diminishes which showed significant after 11 iterations with AR errors (which was shown by the second equation whose t statistics of the coefficients are significant)and the equilibrium errors converges in the long run which is clearly shown in the Fig-7.C.8 below.

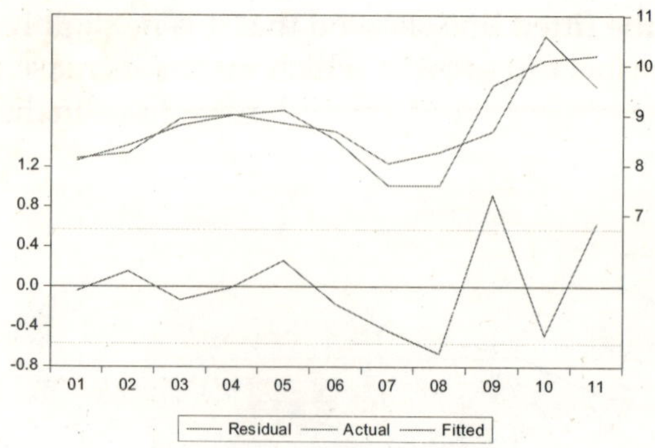

Fig-7.C.8: Equilibrium of U and G

Source: Author.

Co-integration Test

We have applied the Engle-Granger Methodology of Co-Integration test of the simple linear model in which we have the following estimated equation by OLS method;

$$Ut = 8.9634 - 0.09736\,G_t + U_i$$

(30.1513)* (-0.83666)

R^2=0.0598 ,DW=0.742086 ,F=0.70

So, we can infer that the relationship is very weak since R^2 is very low and F is insignificant. The value DW confirmed that it has serial correlation and t statistic of the coefficient is insignificant.

Now, the Augmented Dickey Fuller Test for co-integration suggests the following results.

$$\Delta e_t = \beta_0 + \beta_1 e_{t-1} + \beta_2 \Delta e_{t-1} + \beta_3 \Delta e_{t-2} + \varepsilon_t$$

$$= -0.402808 - 2.8359e_{t-1} + 1.76507\Delta e_{t-1} + 1.4937\Delta e_{t-2} + \varepsilon_t$$

(-0.951) (-3.6138)* (3.906)* (2.4763)*

R^2 = 0.821 , DW= 2.467 , F = 5.735

We have to reject the null hypothesis of a unit root since the value of β_1 is less than zero but less than -2.0 and β_2 is also greater than one. The residual long run series is not stationary ,so that the series U_t

and G_t are not co-integrated of order (1,1). Moreover, the value of ADF= -3.61388 which is less than the tabulated value of -3.46079 (10% critical value). So ADF is not significant and it has unit root.

Johansen test for co-integration

When we used the Johansen M.L.Method of cointegration,we found that the cointegrating relationship between Ut and Gt was significant at the 5% level. When Null hypothesis H0 of r=0 is tested against r=1 ,the trace test statistic turns out to be 22.2833 which is less than the critical value of 25.8721 at 5% level and it is true when $r\leq1$.So,the null hypothesis of at most 0 cointegrating vectors is accepted ie, there is no co-integration. (Table-7.C.4).On the other hand,when null hypothesis of r=0 is tested against r=1,the maximum Eigenvalue statistic turns out to be 14.48463 which is smaller than the critical value of 19.38704 of 5% level.When $r\leq1$,the same results hold good. The acceptance of null hypothesis can be stated that the ,Ut and Gt are not cointegrated in the order of I(1,1). In the Table-7.C.5,the test statistic of Max-Eigen values are given below.

Table-7.C.4 : Trace Statistic

Unrestricted Cointegration Rank Test (Trace)

Hypothesized No. of CE(s)	Eigenvalue	Trace Statistic	0.05 Critical Value	Prob.**
None *	0.732004	22.2833	25.87211	0.1312
At most 1 *	0.507849	7.798665	12.51798	0.2686

Trace test indicates nocointegrationat the 0.05 level
 * denotes rejection of the hypothesis at the 0.05 level
 **MacKinnon-Haug-Michelis (1999) p-values
Source: Estimated by Author.

Table-7.C.5: Max-Eigen Statistic

Unrestricted Cointegration Rank Test (Maximum Eigenvalue)

Hypothesized No. of CE(s)	Eigenvalue	Max-Eigen Statistic	0.05 Critical Value	Prob.**
None *	0.732004	14.48463	19.38704	0.2232
At most 1 *	0.507849	7.798665	12.51798	0.2686

Max-Eigenvalue test indicates no co -integration at the 0.05 level
 * denotes rejection of the hypothesis at the 0.05 level**MacKinnon-Haug-Michelis (1999) p-values
Source: Estimated by Author.

Thus, prior to the inception of Euro, the positive correlation between GDP growth and employment growth in EU-15 was observed until the financial crisis began, so the co-integration between the two in the order of CI(1,1) was the genuine possibility by which macro fundamentals for convergence were realized. But, the Euro exchange in Euro zone have been facing strong convergence problems with low macro fundamentals and imbalance along with the financial and debt crisis for which co-integration between employment growth and GDP growth in the order of CI(1,1) was not fulfilled.

We have also conducted the **Error Correction Model** for the above result of co-integration test for further clarification of integration between the variables. The ECM is given below.

$$\Delta U_t = -0.2251 - 1.7756\Delta e_{t-1} + 0.18177\Delta G_{t-1} - 0.33237\Delta U_{t-1} + \varepsilon_t$$

(-1.140) (-3.007)* (1.603) (-1.199)*

$R^2=0.6624$,DW=2.53 ,F=4.58* , AIC=1.808 , SC=1.953

ADF=-3.201 (not significant at 10% level),so it has unit root

$$\Delta G_t = 0.3029 + 4.106\Delta e_{t-1} - 0.7226\Delta G_{t-1} + 0.1872\Delta U_{t-1} + \varepsilon_t$$

(0.558) (2.529)* (-2.318)* (5.25)*

$R^2=0.816$, DW=2.426 , F=10.354* , *=significant

AIC=3.831 and SC=3.976

ADF=-3.936 (not significant at 10% level. The residual test did not find unit root).

Therefore, ΔG_t and ΔU_t were found to be I(0) and the residuals are not stationary ,we can conclude that the series are not cointegrated of order (1,1).

Since ECM model is near VAR model,so we can apply VAR methodology to test co-integration of order (1,1).

$$\Delta U_t = 0.235142 + 0.161099\Delta U_{t-1} - 0.1156084\Delta G_{t-1} + e_{1t}$$

(1.00041) (0.47165) (-1.22801)

$R^2=0.6349$, AIC=-21.831 , SC= -12.094 , loglikelihood=-12.715

ΔG_t=-0.624166+2.844719ΔU_{t-1} -0.047704ΔG_{t-1}+ε_{2t}

(-1.19156) (3.737)* (-0.22737)

R^2=0.6349 , AIC=-21.831 , SC=-21.71 , loglikelihood= -22.33

Using lag operator, we find,

ΔU_t=0.268690/(1-0.113395L+0.32118L^2)

$L_{1,2}$=0.176520±1.75565 √(-i)

So,ρ=1.76534 and θ=$\tan^{-1}$ 9.9458 = 84.258,therefore , $L_1=\rho e^{i\theta}$ and $L_2=\rho e^{-i\theta}$

Now, ΔU_t=0.268690/$\rho^{t\cos(84.258t-\varepsilon)}$

As t→α, So, $\rho^{t\cos(84.258t-\varepsilon)}$ →α, and ΔU_t→0 , similarly , ΔG_t→0 ,Therefore,the sequences ΔU_t and ΔG_t both converge each other.

The stability condition of the Impulse Response Function is

$$X_i = \mu + \sum_0^{\alpha} A^i \varepsilon_{i-1}$$

for all values of i=0 to α and $A^i=\begin{pmatrix} 0.161099 & -0.115608 \\ 2.844719 & -0.047704 \end{pmatrix}$ and $\mu=\begin{vmatrix} \overline{G} \\ \overline{U} \end{vmatrix}$

As i→α, $\Sigma A^i \to 0$ because $a_{ij}^m \to 0$ as m→α

Therefore , the convergence condition is assured for ΔG_t and ΔU_t sequences , that is impulse response function converges to zero.

The correlation and covariance matrices were found as

	ΔG	ΔU
ΔG	1	-0.9258
ΔU	-0.9258	1

	ΔG	ΔU
ΔG	0.487408	-1.0057
ΔU	-1.0057	2.4208

The Cholesky decomposition constrain is such that ε_{gt} shock has no direct effect on ΔU_t ,there is an indirect effect in the lagged value of ΔG_t affect the contemporaneous values of ΔG_t.The decomposition forces potentially important asymmetry on the system since an ε_{ut} shock has contemporaneous effect on both ΔG_t and ΔU_t. Since correlation coefficient =0.9258,hence decomposed error can be written as $e_{1t}=\varepsilon_{ut}+0.9258\varepsilon_{gt}$ and $e_{2t}=\varepsilon_{gt}$.In panel (a), a one unit shock in ε_{ut} causes ΔU_t to jump by one unit and ΔGt to jump by 0.96348. The values of the characteristic roots prove that ΔG_t and ΔU_tconverge in the long run. The impulse response of an ε_{gt} would be similar to those in panel (b).

So,after the error correction in VAR model ,the first difference series of growth and unemployment in EU-15 during 1999-2011 tended to each other.(Fig-7.C.9)and (Fig-7.C.10).

Fig-7.C.9: Impulse response function of ΔG and ΔU

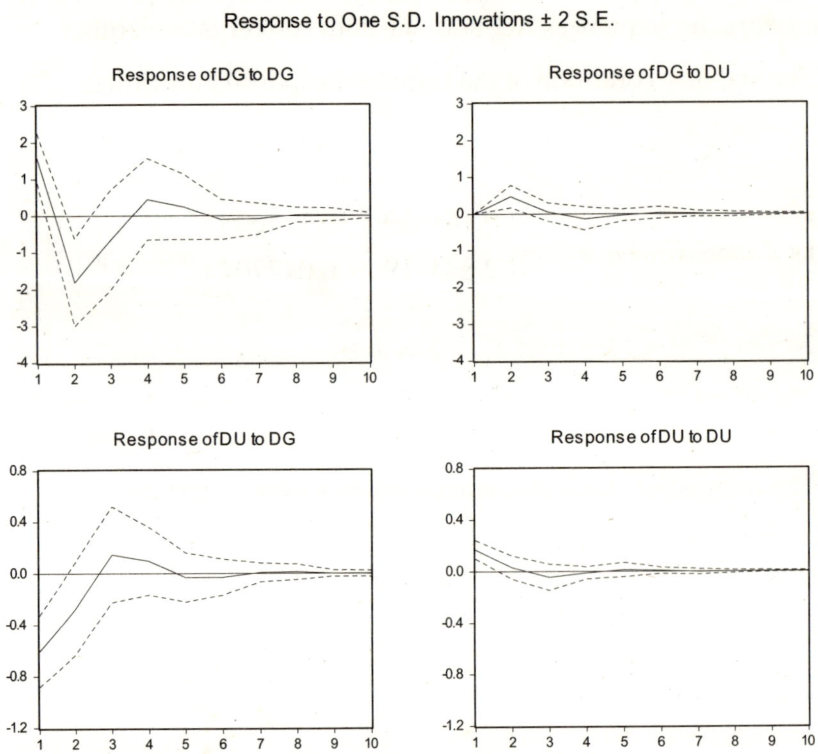

Fig-7.C.10:Impulse response function in two graphs and variance decomposition

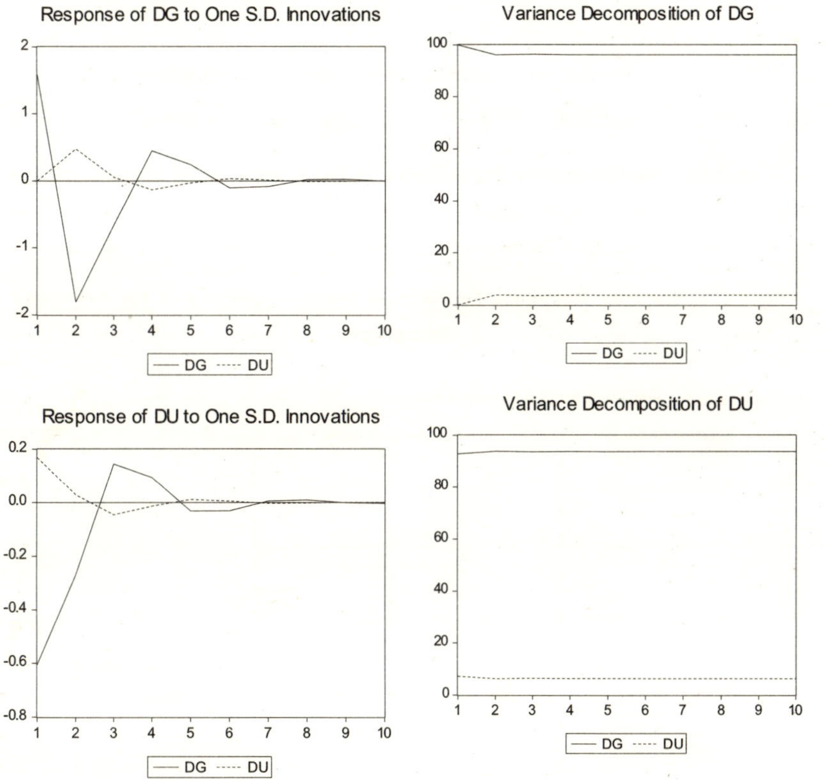

Source: Computed by author

The VAR Model

The first order estimated VAR model of unemployment and growth of Euro Area during 1999-2012 is given below;

$U_t = 1.625087 + 0.874932U_{t-1} - 0.197398G_{t-1} + e_{1t}$

(0.640) (3.146)* (-1.7832)

$R^2=0.6272$, AIC=-12.89 , SC= -12.76 , loglikelihood= -13.35

$G_t = -9.2683 + 1.147245U_{t-1} + 0.328339G_{t-1} + e_{2t}$

(-1.438) (1.6054) (1.1543)

$R^2=0.242$, AIC=-25.169 , SC=-25.032 , loglikelihood= -25.62

The residual correlation matrix and co-variance matrix are given below

	U	G	U	G
U	1	-0.9247	0.4569	-1.08578
G	-0.9247	1	-1.08578	3.01708

The Impulse Response Function to Cholesky one SD innovation±SE under multiple graphs and two graphs (RHS) were shown below which clearly signify no sign of convergence towards long run level.

Fig-7.C.11:Impulse Response Function in multiple graph and Fig-7.C.12:IRF in two graph

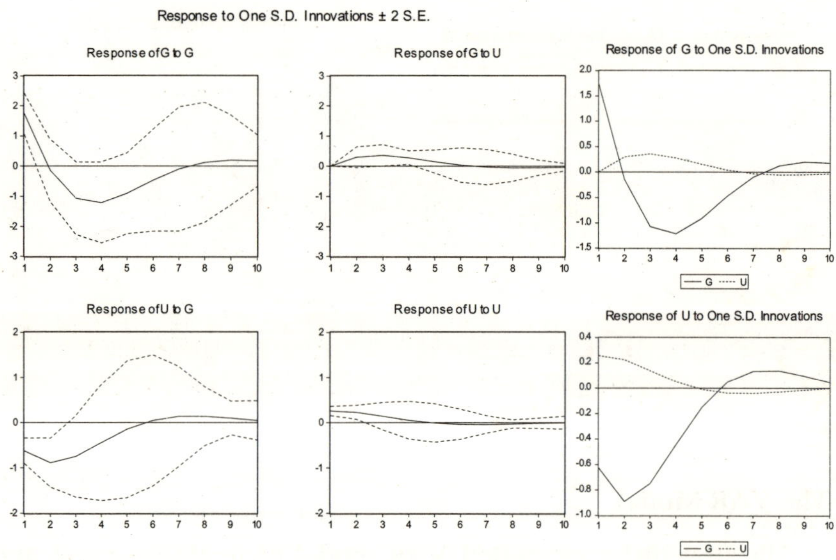

Source: Author

Using lag operator, we found that the characteristic roots are imaginary and complex,so the sequences Ut and Gt are converging which were shown in above and below in impulse response functions figures.

Using lag operator, we found that the values of G_t and U_t are such that

$U_t = -1.62/(1-1.20337L+0.513738L^2)$

Therefore, the characteristics roots are are complex and imaginary, $L_{1,2} = 1.17114 \pm 0.7791\sqrt{(-i)}$

Hence, $\rho = \sqrt{1.1714^2 + 0.7791^2} = 1.40682$ and $\theta = 33.63$

So, $U_t = -1.62631/\rho^{t\cos(t\grave{e}-\varepsilon)}$ As $t \to \alpha$, $\rho^t \to \alpha$, because $L_1 = \rho e^i\theta$ and $L_2 = \rho e^{-i}\theta$

$U_t \to 0$, Similarly, $G_t \to 0$, Therefore, the sequences U_t and G_t are converging each other.

The stability condition of Impulse response function is

$X_i = \upsilon + \sum_0^\alpha A^i \varepsilon_{i-1}$

for all values of i=0 to α and $A^i = \begin{pmatrix} 0.0874932 - & 0.197398 \\ 1.147245 & 0.328339 \end{pmatrix}$ and $\upsilon = \begin{vmatrix} \overline{G} \\ U \end{vmatrix}$

As $i \to \infty$, $\Sigma A^i \to 0$ because $a_{ij}^m \to 0$ as $m \to \infty$

Therefore , the convergence condition is assured for G_t and U_t sequences , that is impulse response function converges to zero.(Fig- 7.C.11 and Fig- 7.C.12)

Consideration of Policies.

The European Parliament has taken the resolution in favour of rising employment and has viewed that in most European economies, the share of wages in national income has fallen dramatically in the last 30 years, widening economic equalities, leading to over reliance on credit to sustain demand, and laying the ground for the financial meltdown of 2008. Moreover, the weakening of collective bargaining will intensify downward pressure on wages, therefore delaying recovery further. Reversal of this imbalance should be an explicit target of European economic governance. Especially during this crisis time, maintaining or raising the purchasing power of wage earners and especially low wage earners should be seen as a factor for social cohesion and the maintenance of internal demand, notably in countries experiencing trade surpluses. In the longer term, evolution of aggregate wages should be in line with productivity growth.

The Synthesis report has opined that Post-crisis Europe can revitalize its economy by tackling the climate challenge. Raising the European climate target from 20% to 30% emissions reductions can open the way towards higher growth and increased employment. The financial crisis has reduced European GDP by several percentage points; if business as usual prevails, the EU growth path will proceed at a lower level than before the crisis. What is more, under business as usual it will be hard to even maintain the growth rate of the pre-crisis times. As a result, unemployment across Europe is likely to stay high, with major disparities between different regions. Sticking to the 20% target in a situation where this target has become too weak to mobilize innovations and to stabilize political will is the equivalent of digging deeper while being stuck in a hole.

It is to be noted that "Europe 2020 strategy" needs "An Agenda for new skill and jobs" that can be work through [i] National Reform Programme describing national employment policy,[ii] Joint Employment Report containing Annual Growth Survey guided by Employment Committee,[iii] country specific recommendation by EU commission,[iv] Employment and Social Developments in Europe examining Joint Employment Report,[v] institutions like[a] European Employment Observatory Network and [b] Mutual Learning Programme,[vi] EU commission should lauch "New Momemtum for flexibility" developing "Quality of work", exploring impact of employment policies, namely wages, taxation,and make work play, supporting job creation, exploring the impact of climate change on labour market and strengthening youth and self employment.

Netherland Government suggests that social welfare systems redesigned to be more job friendly; and training provided to increase labour market skills. These investments are also key to mirror competiveness concerns. The more important is that European economies should focus even more on education, qualification and skills as a top political priority. The second challenge is bringing government finances back on track. The euro area public debt-to-GDP ratio is around 95%, close to the OECD average, and rising. This is almost 25 percentage points above the pre-crisis level. Deep and prolonged fiscal consolidation process will be needed in most countries in the coming years to stabilise and then to reduce debt levels to the pre-crisis level. The third challenge is to recover the potential output lost due to the crisis and to return to sustainable improvements in living standards. OECD projections suggest that, if nothing is done, the pace of growth in the euro area over the next fifteen years will be around half what it has been since 1995. Clearly it is a bad scenario. The EU 2020 agenda, the Euro Plus Pact and strict monitoring at the EU level will help to bring these above goals.

The European Council has agreed on the key elements of the new strategy for jobs and growth, the EU 2020 strategy. The strategy sets out to boost competitiveness and productivity without hampering social cohesion. To reach this objective, five headline targets have been established:

- reduction of poverty;
- an employment rate of 75 % of the working age population;
- meeting the EU's climate and energy targets: reduction of green house gas emissions, increased share of renewables in energy consumption and improved energy efficiency;
- reduction of school drop-out rates and more students in higher education; and
- 3% of the EU's GDP should be invested in research and innovation.

These headline targets will be converted into national goals to be set by member states.

Welfens,andAddision (2009) stated that during 1996-2001,Eurozone achieved around 2% growth rate a high employment greater than EU-27 some of which achieved full employment at turn of the century -has gradually came down after 2001,where cyclical or structural influence have been decisive.Enlargement of Euro Area had affected too.Pension reform,social security reform are equally urgent where innovative policy is a key challenge along with energy security policy.Some economists cast some doubts on explanations of employment gap which stress the lack of wage flexibility on the labour market.He also favours the ongoing trends in skill -biased technical progress and globalization and wage differentiation at the low end of the wage distribution.

Europe's growth (smart, sustainable and inclusive) strategy would be achieved by:

- improving skills levels and (life-long) education
- boosting research and innovation
- more use of smart networks and the digital economy
- modernising industry
- greater energy and resource efficiency.

Where EU target for inclusive growth include:

- 75% employment rate for women and men aged 20-64 by 2020–achieved by getting more people into work, especially women, the young, older and low-skilled people and legal migrants
- better educational attainment - in particular:
- reducing school drop-out rates below 10%
- at least 40% of 30-34–year-olds completing third level education (or equivalent)
- at least 20 million fewer people in or at risk of poverty and social exclusion

The **initiatives** of inclusive growth are

1. Agenda for new skills and jobs

- for individuals - helping people acquire **new skills,** adapt to a changing labour market and make successful career shifts
- collectively - modernising **labour markets** to raise employment levels, reduce unemployment, raise labour productivity and ensuring the sustainability of our social models

2. European platform against poverty

- ensuring **economic, social and territorial cohesion**
- guaranteeing respect for the fundamental rights of people experiencing poverty and social exclusion, and enabling them to live in dignity and take an active part in society

- mobilising support to help people integrate in the communities where they live, get training and help to find a job and have access to social benefits
- The EU mustincrease its overall employment rate: The employment rate is particularly low for women (63% against 76% for men aged 20-64) and older workers, aged 55-64 (46% against 62% in the US and Japan).
- Europeans work short hours - 10% less than their US or Japanese counterparts.
- The economic crisis has brought high youth unemployment - over 21% - and made it harder for out-of-work people to find jobs.
- The EU has around 80 million people with low or basic skills - benefiting less from lifelong learning than more educated people.
- By 2020, 16m more jobs will require high qualifications, with 12m fewer jobs requiring low skill-levels.
- Acquiring and building on new skills is ever more important.
- Europe needs strong economic growth and high levels of employment to sustain its levels of social protection, especially with its ageing population.
- This means giving people the skills to succeed in new economic circumstances, hence the reform proposals for education and training in the strategy is urgent.

As the recession bites, the European Commission and national governments have begun to reflect on replacing the EU's overarching strategy for growth and jobs, known as the Lisbon Strategy. 'Green growth', innovation and education are likely to feature highly among the strategy's new priorities. Under Lisbon strategy, EU countries have agreed on a number of precise targets and indicators for their joint efforts to create more jobs and growth. The main ones are that by 2010 the employment rate should have increased to 70 % and investment in research should have risen to 3 % of GDP (gross domestic product).

Recently,the Commission felt to reform the employment policy in the following manner;

1. A pan-European emergency programme to combat youth unemployment A European emergency programme to combat youth unemployment can be financed at short notice by utilizing unallocated resources, especially from the European Social Fund (ESF). First and foremost, political priority must be agreed upon and applied to the following:

- facilitation of mobility within Europe, especially for young people seeking employment, among other things by improving recognition of qualifications and establishing a mobility fund which might offer language courses, for example;
- a "youth guarantee", which ensures the right to obtain training or further training within four months of obtaining a school-leaving certificate, with the aim of providing vocational or company-oriented training leading to a qualification; incentives for companies to train young people or give them jobs, among other things by offering short-term subsidies from the ESF;
- a European "Alliance for training and jobs" geared specially towards young job seekers and in which the EU Commission gets trade unions and European companies together at round-table negotiations with the aim of finding jobs for young people through cross-border training and employment programmes;
- supporting young people to set up their own business;
- a quality charter for work placements and internships and
- expansion of the European voluntary service and the ERASMUS and LEONARDO programmes.

2. Effective measures to combat the financial market and banking crisis:

3. Swift implementation of a European growth and employment programme. The following core areas are central to this demand:

- Growth and employment by promoting technical innovation and higher public and private investment in the fields of education, research and development.
- Growth and employment by ecological industrial policies which promote the development of renewable energies, create modern energy networks, increase energy efficiency and support more local generation of energy, such as solar energy in southern Europe.
- Growth and employment by expanding modern trans-european infrastructure networks, especially in the fields of energy, transport and information technology. Some specific examples here are the development of renewable energy sources in southern Europe, including the DC lines required to transport electricity to central and northern Europe; the creation of a "North Sea grid", i.e. central connections between the wind farms; modernisation of port systems of numerous European maritime traffic interfaces; introduction and expansion of programmes for energy-efficient building renovation

4.Creating a European investment and reconstruction fund:

[i] More effective use of the EU structural funds:

[ii] Strengthening the European Investment Bank (EIB):

[iii] Insisting on taxation of the financial markets

[iv] Introduction of European project bonds:

5. Supporting public administration:

6. Creation of a European social union

7. A social stability pact for Europe:

8. Industrial renewal – a strong common industrial policy

Conclusion

The chapter concludes that due to Euro crisis the nexus between employment and GDP growth rates in Euro Area turned negative instead of positive where as from 1995 to 2003 , or 1988-1998 ,the relation was positive in Euro Area as well as in many EU member countries. Moreover, the co-integration between employment and GDP growth rate in the order of CI(1,1) had failed during 1999-2012.VAR model confirmed that the Impulse Response Functions of the first difference series and the level series of growth and unemployment have been found convergent. High growth (emphasizing inclusive growth) with low unemployment target through the "Europe 2020 strategy" might be partial solution , but the remodeling of convergence criteria including banking union might be the solution of Euro stability/ revival that could have equal impact on the co-integration between employment and GDP growth rate in Euro Area.Yet,the commission prescribed the series of reform policies to combat high unemployment rate.

References

Bhowmik, Debesh.,2012,The nexus between the employment and GDP growth rate.Paper presented in IEA conference at Vishakhapattanam on27-29 Dec.2012 and published in Indian Economic Journal, Dec 2012, 23-35.

.............., 2012, Analytical Framework of Euro Crisis,*International Journal of Business, Management and Social Sciences*,Vol-1,Issue 7(III),March, pp111-116.

............, 2012, A short note on the behavior of US$/Euro exchange rate during 1999-2012 – *International Journal Of Business, Management and Social Sciences*,Vol-I,Issue 8(II), April, 15-21.

Enders, W.,2004, *Applied Econometric Time Series*. Wiley India.New Delhi.

Engle, R.F. and C.W.J. Granger, 1987, Cointegration and error correction: Representation, estimation, and testing. Econometrica 55(2), 251-276.

European Commission,2008, *Jobs and Growth in the EU:A roadmap to a sustainable tomorrow*. (European Commission, Brussels).

Herman,Emilia.,2011,The Impact of Economic Growth Process on Employment in EU countries.*The Romanian Economic Journal*,Year-xiv,No-42,Dec,47-67.

Johonsen, S., 1996, Likelihood Based Inference in Cointegrated Vector Autoregressive Models, OUP, Oxford.

Mckinsey Global Institute.,2010,Beyond austerity:A path to economic growth and renewal in Europe., October.

Nachane,Dilip.M.,2006, *Econometrics:Theoretical Foundations and Empirical Perspectives*.Oxford.

Perugini,Cristiano.and Marcello Singnorelli.,2005,Growth and Employment in EU countries and Rregions.XX "ConvegnoNazionaledegli Economist del Lavoro"Rome,Sep 22-23.

Signorelli,Marcello., 2005, Growth and Employment: Comparative Performance, convergence and Co-movements.Conference"Europe Day 2005".University of Perugie 4-5-05.

Stehrer,Robert and Terry Ward.et al.,2012,Sectoral employment Effects of Economic Downturns.,Vienna *Institute for International Economic Studies Research Reports*, 379, August.

Walterskirchen,Ewald.,1999,The relationship between growth ,employment and unemployment in the EU.Workshop in Bercelona,16-18 September, 1999.

Welfens,Paul J.J. and Addition,John.T.(ed), 2009, *Innovation,Employment and Growth Policy Issues in the EU and the USA*.Springer Book.

APPENDIX

Table-7CA.1: Growth Rates of Euro Area

	Average 1993–2002	2003	2004	2006	2006	2007	2008	2009	2010	Projections 2011	2012	2016
Real GDP												
Advanced Economies	**2.8**	**1.9**	**3.1**	**2.7**	**3.0**	**2.7**	**0.2**	**–3.4**	**3.0**	**2.4**	**2.6**	**2.4**
United States	3.4	2.5	3.6	3.1	2.7	1.9	0.0	–2.6	2.8	2.8	2.9	2.7
Euro Area[3]	2.1	0.8	2.2	1.7	3.1	2.9	0.4	–4.1	1.7	1.6	1.8	1.7
Germany	1.5	–0.2	0.7	0.9	3.6	2.8	0.7	–4.7	3.5	2.5	2.1	1.3
France	2.0	1.1	2.3	2.0	2.4	2.3	0.1	–2.5	1.5	1.6	1.8	2.1
Italy	1.6	0.0	1.5	0.7	2.0	1.5	–1.3	–5.2	1.3	1.1	1.3	1.4
Spain	3.2	3.1	3.3	3.6	4.0	3.6	0.9	–3.7	–0.1	0.8	1.6	1.7
Netherlands	2.9	0.3	2.2	2.0	3.4	3.9	1.9	–3.9	1.7	1.5	1.5	1.8
Belgium	2.3	0.8	3.1	2.0	2.7	2.8	0.8	–2.7	2.0	1.7	1.9	1.9
Austria	2.2	0.8	2.5	2.5	3.6	3.7	2.2	–3.9	2.0	2.4	2.3	1.8
Greece	2.7	5.9	4.4	2.3	5.2	4.3	1.0	–2.0	–4.5	–3.0	1.1	2.9
Portugal	2.7	–0.9	1.6	0.8	1.4	2.4	0.0	–2.5	1.4	–1.5	–0.5	1.2
Finland	3.5	2.0	4.1	2.9	4.4	5.3	0.9	–8.2	3.1	3.1	2.5	2.0
Ireland	7.7	4.4	4.6	6.0	5.3	5.6	–3.5	–7.6	–1.0	0.5	1.9	3.4

Source: IMF World Economic Outlook, April 2011.

Table-7CA.2: Unemployment Rate of EU-16 During 2001-2010

Unemployment rate, annual average (%)										
Euro area 16	8.1	8.5	8.9	9.0	9.2	8.5	7.6	7.6	9.6	10.1
Germany	7.6	8.4	9.3	9.8	11.2	10.3	8.7	7.5	7.8	7.1
Ireland	3.9	4.5	4.6	4.5	4.4	4.5	4.6	6.3	11.9	13.7
Greece	10.7	10.3	9.7	10.5	9.9	8.9	8.3	7.7	9.5	12.6
Spain	10.3	11.1	11.1	10.6	9.2	8.5	8.3	11.3	18.0	20.1
Italy	9.1	8.6	8.4	8.0	7.7	6.8	6.1	6.7	7.8	8.4
Portugal	4.6	5.7	7.1	7.5	8.6	8.6	8.9	8.5	10.6	12.0
Source: Eurostat										

CHAPTER 8

POLICIES RELATING TO EURO CRISIS

Introduction

Every crisis should have policies to way out from that situation. There are series of policies either from public or private or from institutions who were constantly trying to find out possible solutions of the euro crisis. We saw innumerable controversies from those solutions. In this chapter, we would discuss about the policy issues relating to Euro crisis as well as we would place some critical debates, analysis, comments, recommendations on such policy issues.

The Policy Issues

Stiglitz (2012) remarked the following in context of policy framework of Euro crisis,viz,

[i] European Commission emphasised the recapitalization of the European Investment Bank, part of the growth package of some &150 billion .But, it is too little and too late. The markets are more pragmatic:as austerity weakens economic growth, and undermines the capacity to service debt, interest rates will not fall.In fact ,investment will decline-a vicious downward spiral on which Greece and Spain have already embarked.

[ii] Euro bonds and a solidarity fund could promote growth and stabilize the interest rate faced by governments in crisis.

Lower interest rate, for example, would free up money so that even countries with tight budget constraints could spend more on growth, enhancing investment.

[iii] Matters are worse in banking since each country's banking system is backed by its own government.

[iv] Europe leaders did not recognize this rising danger of money flee the weaker countries going to financial institution in the stronger countries, it could be easily averted by a common guarantee which would simultaneously correct the market distortions arising from the differential implicit subsidy.

[v] Politically and economically, the Euro came with the best intentions but was flawed. The flaws, it was clear, would become apparent only in a crisis. The single market principle was supposed to promote the efficient allocation of capital and labour.

[vi] Germany's cost will be high if either the Euro or the economies on the periphery collapse.

[vii] Europe's weaknesses today reflect flawed policies and institutional arrangements, which can be changed , only if their fundamental weaknesses are recognized. While structural problems have hurt particular countries, they did not bring about the crisis, and addressing them will not resolve it. It is not just confidence in Europe's periphery that is wanting.The survival of the Euro itself is being put in doubt.

Marc Jones(2012) also remarked that [i] The ECB also faces a conflict of interest minefield with the new role, where policy makers' knowledge about a bank or group of banks could influence their monetary policy decisions." Any new task in the supervisory area should be rigorously separate from monetary policy task", said Draghi.[ii] The local specialists would do much of the day to day monitoring of banks' health and also remain in charge of less sensitive decisions such as a bank opening a new branch .It is a 'hub and spoke' model that is already being used in the US where the Federal Reserve oversees heavy weights like JP Morgan,Citi and Wells Fargo with regional regulators covering the rest.[iii] Another crucial detail still to be decided is who will pay to rescue a bank that fails under the new set up.[iv] The ECB's preference is to have a central Eurozone deposit guarantee fund - paid for with proceeds from a bank tax and public money. But again, there is much work to be done.

Henning and Kessler(2012) clarified that European debates over reform of the fiscal governance of the euro area frequently reference fiscal federalism in the United States. The "fiscal compact" agreed by the European Council during 2011 provided for the introduction of, among other things, constitutional rules or framework laws known as " debt brakes" in the member states of the euro area. Therefore, the euro area should unify bank regulation and create a common fiscal pool for restructuring the banking system.

Ansgar Belke (2012) opined that the mutualisation of the euro zone's debt to bring about the convergence of interest rates will not, in the long run, tackle the roots of the problem. Instead it will sow the seeds of an even larger crisis in the future.

We have seen what happened in the early years of the euro, when interest rates largely converged. Paradoxically, perhaps, this paved the way for a greater divergence of national fiscal policies. A reckless lack of discipline in countries such as Greece and Portugal—be they more (Greece) or less (Portugal) insolvent—was matched by the build-up of asset bubbles in other member countries, such Spain and Ireland, deemed merely illiquid. Structural reforms were delayed, while wages outstripped productivity growth. The consequence was a huge loss of competitiveness in the periphery, which will not be resolved by the mutualisation of debt.

Debt mutualisation can take different forms. One is to mutualise new sovereign debt through Eurobonds. Another is to merge part of the old debt, as advocated by the German Council of Economic Experts with its proposal for a European Redemption Fund. A third is to activate the euro zone's "firewall" by using the rescue funds—either the temporary European Financial Stability Facility (EFSF) or the soon-to-be permanent European Stability Mechanism (ESM)—to buy bonds on the secondary market, or to inject capital directly into distressed banks. Indeed, the ECB is already engaged in a hidden form of mutualisation—of risk if not (yet) of actual debt—through its programme of bond purchases and its long-term refinancing operations for banks.

Almost all these are bound to fail for economic or political reasons, or both. The governments of even financially strong countries cannot agree to open-ended commitments that could endanger their own financial stability or, given that they are the main guarantors, that of the bail-out funds. And the danger of moral hazard is ever-present.

Any form of mutualisation involves an element of subsidy, which severely weakens fiscal discipline: the interest-rate premium on bonds of fiscally weaker countries declines and the premium for stronger countries increases. Fiscally solid countries are punished and less solid ones, in turn, are rewarded for their lack of fiscal discipline and excess private and public consumption.

If yields are too low, there is no incentive for private investors to buy sovereign bonds. The countries become decoupled from the capital markets permanently and the debt problems become increasingly structural.

This is true of the ECB's bond-buying. The credit risk is thus just rolled over from the bonds of the weaker countries to those of the stronger ones, and the ECB is made responsible for its liability. Over time, the ECB's measures might be inflationary. Allowing the rescue funds to buy bonds is little different, except that they lack the lending capacity to be credible. If they are given a banking licence, as some argue, it would be no different from the ECB buying bonds directly.

What of the European Redemption Fund (ERF)? This could be of particular help to Italy, which could unload half of its debt. But its partners could not force it to tax its citizens to ensure it pays back the dormant debt. And with the assumption of debt, Germany's credit rating might drop, due to the increase in the German interest burden. The pressure on Italy and Spain to consolidate their budgets sustainably would be reduced. The problems of Greece, Ireland and Portugal would not be resolved, since these countries are unlikely to qualify for the ERP.

On top of moral hazard, there are the political obstacles, which would be most acute in the case of Eurobonds. Germany demands political union before Eurobonds can be considered. But this is to put the cart before the horse: a political union would be created simply to justify Eurobonds. Advocates say treaty changes and high-level political agreements would be sufficient to make sure that euro-zone member countries comply with all decisions taken at the euro-zone level. But the experience of Greece's adjustment casts severe doubt on such optimism.

A quick glance at the World Bank's databank of "governance indicators" shows that differences between euro-zone members, on everything from respect for the rule of law to administrative capacity, are so great that political union is unlikely to work, at least in the next couple of years. It follows that the basis for Eurobonds is extremely thin.

The introduction of Eurobonds would have to be backed by tight oversight of national fiscal and economic policies. But there is no true enforcement as long as the euro-zone members remain sovereign. Intervening directly in the fiscal sovereignty of member states would require a functioning pan-European democratic legitimacy, but we are far away from that. Voters in southern countries can at any time reject the strong conditionality demanded by Brussels, while those of northern countries can refuse to keep paying for the south. And either can choose to exit the euro zone.

The emphasis on debt mutualisation means the debate, at least in Germany, has become a question of "all or nothing": either deeper political union or deep chaos. But there is an alternative to the notion of co-operative fiscal federalism involving bail-outs and debt mutualisation: competition-based fiscal federalism, of the sort successfully operating in America, Canada and Switzerland, among others. These countries have largely avoided serious and sustained public debt in their component states. The sub-federal entities, faced with insolvency, have a great incentive to take early corrective action—without having to be forced into a corset of centralised fiscal policy co-ordination.

To achieve this sort of federalism, it is necessary to separate the fate of the banks from that of the sovereigns. What is needed is not a fiscal union, but a banking union. It should be based on four elements: reformed banking regulation with significantly higher equity capital standards; European banking oversight with far-reaching powers to intervene; a banking resolution fund; and a European deposit insurance scheme.

Banking union – a less comprehensive, more clearly delineated and rather technical task – should be much more acceptable than the Europeanisation of fiscal policy as a whole. Only a small fraction of fiscal policy areas would have to be subordinated to central control in a fiscal union.

Obviously, a central resolution authority has to be given the resources to wind up large cross-border banks. Where does the money for this come from? In the long run, a resolution authority would exist alongside a deposit insurance scheme for cross-border banks. This should be funded partly by the banking industry. But there should also be a backstop provided by the euro-zone governments through the EFSF or ESM to cope with systemic bank failure.

As a temporary transition measure, limited debt mutualisation may be necessary – but only to recapitalise banks that cannot be sustained by their sovereigns. However, the amounts required are much smaller than for, say, Eurobonds.

With the banking system and the debt crisis thus disentangled, banking-sector losses will no longer threaten to destroy the solvency of solid sovereigns such as Ireland and Spain. Eurobonds will not be needed, and neither will the bail-out of sovereigns. The debt of over-indebted states could be restructured, which means that the capital market could exert stronger discipline on borrowers.

Drafted with three others – José Manuel Barroso, president of the European Commission, Mario Draghi, president of the European Central Bank, and Jean-Claude Juncker, president of the Euro group (made up of finance ministers of the euro zone) – the report is thus a delicate piece of diplomacy at a time of sharp differences between Germany and France; indeed between Germany and many of the euro zone's biggest countries.

It sets out four "building blocks" for deeper euro-zone integration: a European system to guarantee bank deposits and manage troubled banks; fiscal integration to exert greater control on national budgets and steps towards issuing joint debt; more integration in economic policy-making to boost competitiveness; and more democratic accountability in European-level decisions. Precisely what these building blocks consist of, how the steps should be sequenced and how much can be done within existing treaties is all left a bit vague. The paper is peppered with words like "appropriate" and "commensurate" without attempting to define them.

On what many in Brussels call "banking union", it proposes creating a fund, "primarily funded" through contributions from banks, to help guarantee deposits and wind up failed banks. To be credible the fund should be backstopped by the euro zone's permanent rescue fund, the European Stability Mechanism (ESM), expected to be activated in the coming weeks.

Even further in the future, the euro zone could create a common treasury with some kind of central budget.

The report has been toned down in drafting, and some contentious ideas have been dropped. Gone is the call, made in an earlier version, for an "immediate and permanent" mutualisation of risk to backstop the banking sector. Ditto for the idea that the ESM could recapitalise banks directly (so relieving some troubled sovereigns like Spain from having to take on a big additional debt burden). The report is also silent on the question of a financial-transactions tax, no doubt to avoid upsetting a British government that is wary of stronger European bank supervision.

It is worth comparing the wooliness of Mr Van Rompuy's paper with the detail of the more convincingly worked-out proposal issued on the same day by a group of prominent economists under the aegis of Jacques Delors, the former commission president, and Helmut Schmidt, the former German chancellor. It calls, for instance, for the creation of a special fund to help countries weather cyclical downturns. It also proposes a European debt agency to oversee the issuance of limited amounts of joint Eurobonds (typically up to 10% of GDP, with more possible if a country is willing to cede ever more budgetary decision-making powers).

Mr Van Rompuy's report does not pretend to be a "roadmap" to greater fiscal federalism. It is, instead, a proposal to talk about one. European officials argue that just getting Mrs Merkel to agree in principle to discuss things like the mutualisation of debt would be a big achievement, as would getting the French to talk about surrendering the powers of the Fifth Republic. Yet talking is one thing, agreeing quite another—and there is still no sign of accord among leaders.

Mr Van Rompuy says a detailed plan for integration could be presented in December, with perhaps an interim version issued in October. But will the markets be ready to wait that long? After all, this is the week that Cyprus asked for a bail-out, and Spain confirmed it would seek up to €100 billion to recapitalise its banks.

The likelihood is that this week's European summit will disappoint, and that could set off another round of panic in the markets. If the euro is to survive, Mr Van Rompuy may have to draft his roadmap rather sooner than he expects.(Economist.com,26/6/2012)

The euro-zone chiefs were far from agreeing on anything like a banking union—but let that pass. The 172 academics are indignant and warn of dire consequences for German citizens when they end up guaranteeing balance-sheets three times the size of all euro-zone public debt.

A banking union means assuming "collective liability for the debts of the banks in the euro-system" thunder the professors. "Dear fellow citizens, please relay these concerns to your constituent MPs; our elected representatives must be alerted to the dangers that are threatening our economy," they say.

Europe's leaders actually agreed on two things: to work towards joint bank supervision by the European Central Bank, and that euro-zone banks may be recapitalised directly by the European Financial Stability Facility and its future replacement, the European Stability Mechanism.

The most a banking union, if it indeed comes, is likely to guarantee is the deposits of private savers up to €100,000—no more than each EU member state already guarantees at a national level. True, even that would be a lot of cash if there were a systemic bank run, but avoiding one is precisely the goal of joint supervision.

Predictably, the government has come out fighting. Angela Merkel, the chancellor, urged people to study the actual decisions taken in Brussels. Wolfgang Schäuble, the finance minister, spluttered: "I find it outrageous. Economists should be more responsible in the way they handle the concept of bank debt."

Only a handful of the signatories are much known outside their faculties, including Hans-Werner Sinn, head of the Institute for Economic Research in Munich, and Klaus Zimmermann, former head of the German Institute for Economic Research in Berlin.

A riposte from seven economic heavy weights (including Peter Bofinger and Bert Rürup, member and former member respectively of the Council of Economic Experts, which advises the government) has been posted on the website of the *Handelsblatt*, a business daily, under the headline "No bogeymen!" In these uncertain times, they write, "it cannot be the job of economists to unsettle the public even more with cliché-ridden assertions and questionable arguments."

The 172 professors have certainly broken new ground. The most remarkable thing, says one *FAZ* reader, is that "so many economists could agree on a single text - incredible." (Economist.com-6/7/2012)

Critical Policy Issues and debates of Euro crisis-

Mr. Cameron vetoed the so-called "fiscal compact" to toughen budget rules, may have been a foretaste of rows to come. Events may redefine Britain's relations with the rest of Europe rather sooner. A summit in June decided, with Mr. Cameron's assent, to create a single bank supervisor for the euro area, based on the European Central Bank (ECB), by the end of the year. Rescue funds could then be used directly to recapitalise ailing banks. This could be an important move towards greater risk-sharing. Britain wants the ECB to take the supervisory role to ensure its remit extends only to the euro zone. Moreover, the legal instrument needed to create it gives Britain a veto.

Even if banking union can be enacted with existing powers, other forms of integration would require changes to the EU's treaties. This includes "economic union" (to enforce common economic policies), "fiscal union" (with a path to joint Eurobonds) and "political union" (including boosting the European Parliament).

How to resolve the euro's woes? Angela Merkel says Germany will not agree to pool sovereign debt or share banking liabilities with other countries until there is greater political union. It sets out four "building blocks" for deeper euro-zone integration: a European system to guarantee bank deposits and manage troubled banks; fiscal integration to exert greater control on national budgets and steps towards issuing joint debt; more integration in economic policy-making to boost competitiveness; and more democratic accountability in European-level decisions. On what many in Brussels call "banking union", it proposes creating a fund, "primarily funded" through contributions from banks, to help guarantee deposits and wind up failed banks. To be credible the fund should be backstopped by the euro zone's permanent rescue fund, the European Stability Mechanism (ESM), expected to be activated in the coming weeks.

On fiscal union, the report goes beyond the current system of euro-zone controls on national budget. It suggests jointly setting the ceiling for each country's debt and deficit. Governments would have to seek permission to break these limits, and Brussels could demand changes. Greater budget controls could, later on, lead to some form of Eurobonds (or "Eurobills" for short-dated debt). This is how the report puts the delicate issue.

In a medium term perspective, the issuance of common debt could be explored as an element of such a fiscal union and subject to progress on fiscal integration. Steps towards the introduction of joint and several sovereign liabilities could be considered as long as a robust framework for budgetary discipline and competitiveness is in place to avoid moral hazard and foster responsibility and compliance.. Several options for partial common debt issuance have been proposed, such as the pooling of some short-term funding instruments on a limited and conditional basis, or the gradual roll-over into a redemption fund. Different forms of fiscal solidarity could also be envisaged.

Jacques Delors, the former commission president, and Helmut Schmidt, the former German chancellor calls, for instance, the creation of a special fund to help countries weather cyclical downturns. It also proposes a European debt agency to oversee the issuance of limited amounts of joint Eurobonds (typically up to 10% of GDP, with more possible if a country is willing to cede ever more budgetary decision-making powers).

One plan to resolve the euro zone debt crisis is for the common issue of euro bonds - each country's debt would be guaranteed by all the others. The rationale is that the overall level of European debt is not that high, when compared with the US; it is just distributed in an awkward way.

David Owen of Jefferies has come up with a ready reckoner, by assuming that euro zone debt would trade at the weighted average (based on issuance) of current yields (excluding Greece). Thus the cost of annual issuance for Germany would rise from the current 1.4% to 3.7%, while yields in Italy, Spain etc would fall. The result would be an annual cost for Germany of €49 billion, or around 1.9% of GDP. France would pay an extra €16 billion, or 0.8% of GDP. the Netherlands, Austria and Finland would all face costs of around 1% of GDP. That may not seem too bad a deal, given the predictions of the pain caused by a Greek exit, although it is worth pointing out it is an annual cost, not a one-off.

The biggest savings would accrue to Portugal and Cyprus, which would save 8.7% and 8.1% of GDP respectively. Ireland's borrowing costs would fall by 3.6% of GDP. Italy would save €37 billion, or 2.4% of GDP and Spain €18 billion, or 1.7%. Such a deal would knock a significant lump off their annual budget deficits.

An alternative scheme would involve the joint underwriting of that debt which is more than 60% of GDP. Because of the mix (less German debt, more Italian), the weighted interest rate would be higher, at 4.2%. The costs and benefits of such a scheme would be much lower. Germany would lose 0.6% of GDP, France 0.4%. Portugal would gain 3.6% and Ireland 1.4%.

Can Greece leave the euro quietly? Its size would suggest so: the Greek economy is just 2% of the euro area's GDP. But so far the Greek crisis has had plenty of noisy knock-on effects. A few years later Barry Eichengreen and Andrew Rose of the University of California, Berkeley, and Charles Wyplosz of the Geneva Graduate Institute looked at 20 currency crises in industrial economies between 1959 and 1993. They found that a crisis in one country increased the probability of crises in others.

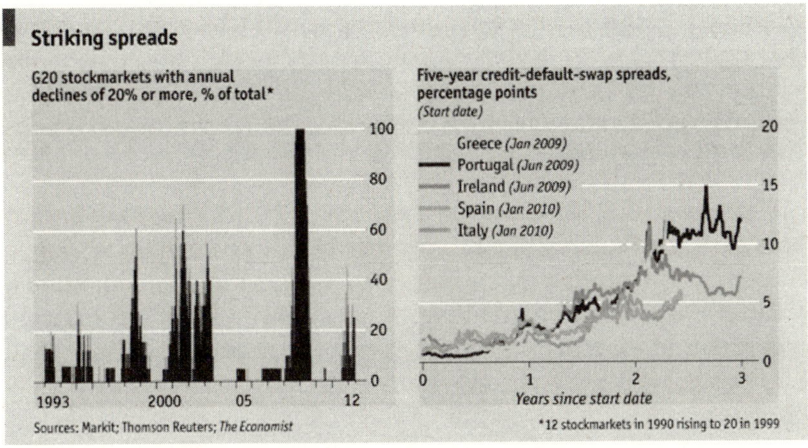

Fig-8.1: Stock market and swap spread

Crises in much smaller countries began infecting the global economy (see left-hand Fig.). A 1994 crash in Mexico led to unexpectedly large stock market slumps across Latin America. Then, in June 1997, Thai markets dropped suddenly, dragging down Indonesia, Hong Kong and even seemingly unrelated economies such as Canada's. This created a contagion puzzle: how do shocks in small countries spread so far?

Vítor Constâncio, a vice-president at the European Central Bank (ECB), examines what investors have to pay to insure themselves against the risk that a euro-area country will default on its debts (credit-default swap spreads, or CDSs). The cost of this insurance has been rising for many euro countries since 2009, with Greece leading the way (see right-hand Fig.). Mr. Constâncio crunched CDS data to estimate market perceptions of the probability of another country defaulting if Greece defaults. Markets now put a much higher probability – sometimes up to 45 percentage points more – on Ireland and Portugal also defaulting if Greece fails. The CDS spreads thus not only document contagion across Europe, but show that the risk of further contagion has grown.

Some contagion may be caused by markets waking up to the possibility that the euro zone could indeed fall apart. But contagion doesn't spread evenly: risks are high for Ireland, Spain and Portugal, but much lower for France. Country-specific factors, as well as euro-wide concerns, seem to play a role. Worryingly, Italy, which some believe will be next in line for a bail-out, could go either way. Pessimists argue that it is more vulnerable than its trade and financial links with Greece suggest.

There is a final lesson: expect the unexpected. The path for pure contagion is devilishly hard to predict. In 2004 Stefan Straetmans of Maastricht University, in co-operation with Philipp Hartmann of the ECB and Casper de Vries of Erasmus University Rotterdam, examined weekly slumps of at least 20% in different financial markets to measure links between these markets, both within a country and between countries.

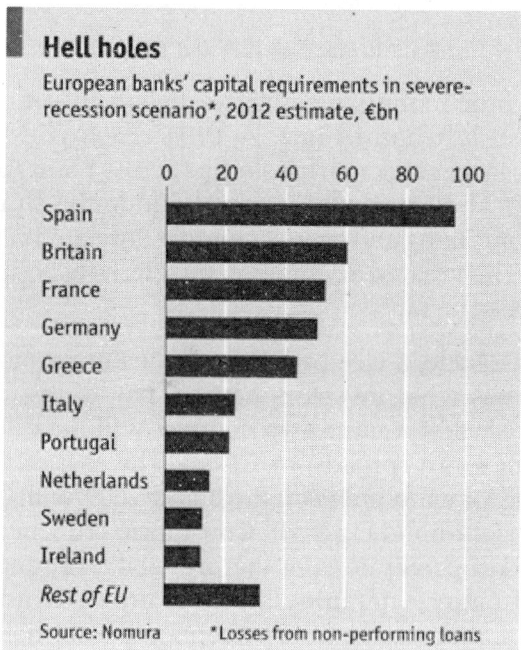

Fig-8.2:Hell holes

The euro zone bound diverse economies in a single exchange rate and a single interest rate. Plainly, it is far from being an optimal currency area. That said, most currency unions are not optimal. The difference between the euro and other currency areas is that it lacks the flexibility to make it work (labour mobility in Europe is lower than in the US or Canada) as well as the tools to absorb asymmetric shocks. It took a British prime minister, David Cameron, a self-declared Eurosceptic, to sum up the problem. Successful currency unions, he said, had some vital features in common: a lender of last resort for the state, economic integration and flexibility to deal with shocks, fiscal transfers and collective debt. "Currently it's not that the euro zone doesn't have all of these; it's that it doesn't have any of these," Cameron said. The most passionate Euro idealist could not have put it better.

The result has been perverse. If the European Union and its single market were once a great 'convergence machine' for the economies of its members, as a recent World Bank report put it, the single currency has become an infernal engine pulling them apart. Spain and Greece are suffering from mass unemployment, yet joblessness in Germany is at a record low. The bond yields of peripheral European states may have blown out; but Germany enjoys remarkably low borrowing costs.

Southern Europe, in particular, has suffered a triple blow: the Mediterranean countries were hit hard by globalisation and the loss of low-tech industries such as textiles; they faced competition from cheaper labour in ex-communist member states when the EU was enlarged eastward; and the adoption of the euro made it hard for southern countries with a tradition of high inflation to adjust through the time-tested method of devaluation.

The euro zone's response to the crisis so far has been slow, hesitating and erratic. That said, countries in danger of collapse have been rescued with hundreds of billions' worth of loans. Greek debt has been belatedly restructured. Financial firewalls have been built and expanded. Brussels has been given greater powers to monitor national economies, and demand changes of policy backed with the threat of 'semi-automatic' sanctions. A fiscal compact, enshrining balanced-budget rules, has been negotiated and signed. The European Central Bank has intervened sporadically and controversially, buying up government bonds in secondary markets and spraying banks with €1 trillion worth of cheap three-year liquidity.

It is possible that, had all this been done sooner and more decisively, the euro crisis might have been arrested. If Greece's debt had been recognised immediately as unsustainable and restructured rapidly, if its first loans had been granted on concessionary rather than punitive terms, if it had been told to concentrate on structural reforms rather than drastic budget-cutting, if the ECB had been willing to wield the big bazooka more convincingly, if...if...then perhaps financial contagion might not have spread so far.

As matters stand, the crisis goes on. Indeed, in some ways it is getting worse. Spain is a far larger problem than Greece, Ireland or Portugal, and it could drag down Italy and perhaps even France. The firewalls, though enhanced, are inadequate to deal with this scale of problem. The relief from the central bank's liquidity was short-lived, and loaded banks with even more dodgy sovereign bonds. Above all, the patient has not responded to the austerity medicine.

Some of this therapy is needed. But the problem is more complex. The euro zone is afflicted by three interconnected ills: a sovereign-debt crisis, a banking crisis and a growth crisis. Dealing with one often makes the others worse. Weak banks weaken sovereigns that are called upon to bail them out; weak sovereigns impair banks that hold their bonds. Poor growth enfeebles both the sovereigns and the banks. In turn, cutting deficits reduces growth, as does reduced lending by banks trying to restore their balance-sheets.

Structural reforms are vital to boosting growth, but these are unlikely to produce big results in the short term.

Deficit countries could cut payroll taxes to reduce labour costs and raise VAT to discourage imports; the effect would be magnified if surplus states did the opposite.

A 'banking union', with a European system to wind down or recapitalise troubled banks and a Europe-wide bank-deposit insurance scheme, would help break the feedback loop between weak banks and weak sovereigns. A 'fiscal union' in which all or part of the national debts are mutualised as joint Eurobonds would stop markets pushing sovereigns into insolvency, and would create a European asset that banks could hold.

A euro area banking union could combine three main elements:

- *A pan-European deposit guarantee scheme.* A deposit guarantee scheme can increase depositor confidence by reducing the dependence of banks on their sovereigns and thereby also reduce the risk of sudden deposit movements across the currency area. Eventually, such a scheme could (and should) be funded by a levy on the industry but, to be effective, it would need ready recourse to additional funding in times of stress, from a common pool of government-provided resources or—for the euro area— an ECB credit line.
- *A pan-European bank resolution mechanism.* A bank resolution authority, established with powers to bail in private creditors and support directly the resolution of banks, would facilitate an orderly wind-down of failing institutions and smooth the deleveraging process across the region. As with the deposit scheme, resolution could be backed by a common fund financed by an industry levy with recourse to government-provided resources or the ECB.
- *Common supervision.* In addition to deposit guarantee and bank resolution schemes, an effective banking union will need the support of a common supervisory framework to foster stability and deter fragmentation. The framework would be most effective if it encompassed the entire banking system but could at first focus on cross-border banks and large systemically-important financial institutions in the euro area. To this end, the June 28-29 summit plan to establish a single supervisory mechanism for euro area banks—to be considered by the Council by end-2012—is an important first step toward a banking union.

But it will be important that the necessary decisions be taken and implemented quickly.(IMF country report-12/181 ,2012). The big test will come if France is deemed to be missing its target to bring the deficit below 3% of GDP next year.

The European Commission must be a mere arbiter between members, messy as this may be. But if the EU, or maybe just the euro zone, is a proto-federation, then the problems are more easily resolved. More fiscal federalism will stabilise the euro, and more political federalism will grant a greater democratic mandate to European institutions.

The crisis has confirmed countries in their prejudices. Germans see Greeks as indolent and corrupt; do they really want to commit the German cheque book to Greece fully and indefinitely? And having portrayed Angela Merkel and Wolfgang Schauble as the embodiment of the old Nazi invader, are Greeks ready to be forever bound to German strictures?

If the euro zone cannot, or will not commit to deeper integration, then it would be wise to consider how disintegration might take place, and how best to manage it. Would it be better for strong states like Germany to leave? Or would it be best to cut off the weakest members? This is an uncomfortable discussion. Merely being heard to talk about such things may exacerbate the crisis.

The most hopeful scenario for the euro zone is that it faces a long and unnecessarily painful road to recovery, with the adjustment placed almost entirely on deficit countries. But the euro could just as well face a long and painful death.

Cline (2012) examined by his model and concluded that the policy context for his study is the centrality of debt sustainability in both Italy and Spain in determining whether the euro area can resolve its debt problem without far more severe economic disruption than has already taken place in the region. If either or especially both countries were forced into some form of sovereign default and/or exit from the euro, the likely damage to the euro area economy and the world economy would be large. Earlier he argued that Spain's initially low ratio of debt to GDP gave it considerable room for maneuver. Even, he conducted selected simulations of the EDSM to examine Italy's debt, and concluded that because of a relatively favorable maturity structure of medium-term debt Italy could sustain even relatively high interest rates (over 7 percent) for a number of years so long as it met its primary surplus targets, but that some form of firewall would be highly desirable to ensure that the interest rates did not surge far higher and impose a self-fulfilling prophecy of insolvency.

Bergsten & Kirkegaard(2012) explained that the European Commission proposals for so-called project bonds, the Europe 2020 Project Bond Initiative, has already been accepted by the EU Council and EU Parliament and will in all probability begin to be implemented by the European Investment Bank (EIB) later in 2012. These project bonds, which will be backed by the entire EU-27 (i.e., not just the euro area), are intended to "fund pre-identified transport, energy and ICT priority infrastructures of EU interest, and both physical and information technology infrastructures, consistent with sustainable development criteria" but are in the pilot phase not presently intended to exceed more than €400 million to €500 million. Viewed in the context of the euro area's much broader financial problems, these bonds are inconsequential. However, when seen as a step toward more joint liability debt issuance in the euro area, its precedent setting effect should not be underestimated. Other potential gradualist proposals include eurobills (i.e., the issuance of joint liability debt in the euro area for only the short end of the yield curve); the European Debt Redemption Fund (i.e., pooling all national sovereign debt above 60 percent of GDP into joint liability euro bonds); the Red Bond/Blue Bond proposal (i.e., only the first 60 percent of national debt to GDP would be euro bonds); the European Commission's Stability Bond proposals; and William Cline's recent proposal to rely on euro area bond insurance. The common denominator in all these proposals is that they entail a partial mutualization of euro area sovereign debt, which would require transfer of only parts of member states' remaining national sovereignty over fiscal policies to the euro area. Looking at the long history of European integration, it would be a mistake to underestimate the ability of European policymakers to engineer such partial but ongoing transfers of fiscal sovereignty.

As euro area banking sector integration also needs the same proportional transfer of national sovereignty and joint euro area underwriting of contingent liabilities. Here the shift toward a single euro area deposit insurance scheme and resolution fund (e.g., joint euro area contingent liabilities) will take place only with the simultaneous shift toward a common euro area resolution authority, a single euro area banking supervisor with ultimate decision making powers, and a uniform single rulebook for prudential banking supervision (preferably for the entire European Union). Again, it is a mistake to underestimate the ability of euro area policymakers to engineer such a gradual process, even if starting with consolidating the framework for only the largest (cross-border) euro area banks. The euro area crisis, as we have established, is a political crisis. In broad political terms, euro area member states need to hand over more of their national sovereignty to new euro area institutions to begin the process of completing the economic and monetary union. This handover, as laid out earlier, must be accompanied by a synchronized and proportional mutualization of euro area government debt liabilities and contingent liabilities. This political-financial quid pro quo will dictate the progress expected at the June EU Summit on the two key areas for further deepening of euro area integration: banking union and fiscal union.

On the break down of EMU, Aslund (2012) stated that The Economic and Monetary Union must be maintained at almost any cost. All the economic problems in the current crisis can be resolved within the EMU. A devaluation may be only a palliative or a postponement of resolution of the real problem, as has so often been the case, while the costs of the dissolution of the euro area could be truly monumental. The exit of any single country from the EMU, at the present time when large imbalances have been accumulated, would likely lead to a bank run, which would cause the EMU payments system to break down and with it the EMU itself. In order to maintain the euro area, EMU-wide clearing must be maintained in full. The exponential rise in the accumulated Target2 ("Target2 is the grid through which the liquidity in the euro area circulates. With this payments system cross-border central bank money is transferred between the national central banks within the currency union. This liquidity arises in the individual countries predominantly through the national central banks' refinancing operations with commercial banks.") balances is a major concern because the resulting strains within the EMU may lead to its breakup. The Target2 balances should be resolved by reforms such as a banking union, fiscal adjustments, and guarantees so that the EMU will be maintained. The natural way of resolving the Target2 issue would probably be to truly consolidate the balance sheets of the European System of Central Banks, akin to the US system. Any attempt to cap national clearing balances would lead to differing values of a euro in various countries, which would be a dangerous step toward the breakup of the euro area. Finally, the reasons that would prompt the euro area to break up would be

Table8.1: IMF policy recommendation

	Fiscal Policies and Reforms	Financial Sector Reforms	Structural Reforms
Greece	• Specify and legislate remaining revenue and expenditure measures necessary to achieve the medium-term fiscal target • Undertake fiscal institutional reforms to improve revenue collection and prevent expenditure arrears	• Finalize recapitalization strategy for viable banks and establish timeframe for capital raising • Finalize plans to address state-owned banks in a least cost manner (while protecting depositors)	• Improve competitiveness through labor market reforms, product and service market liberalization, and business environment reforms
Ireland	• Accommodate a revenue shortfall if growth weakens notably in 2012 to help protect the fragile recovery • Specify the measures to underpin the 2013-15 fiscal consolidation by Budget 2013, including targeting of social welfare • Implement fiscal institutional reforms through the Fiscal Responsibility Bill and give a statutory basis to the medium-term expenditure ceilings	• Implement PTSB restructuring carefully to put it on a sound footing, including through timely separation of certain legacy assets • Strengthen banks' capacity to manage distressed loans to help restore their viability and restart lending • Prepare the new personal insolvency framework to address household debt distress while protecting debt service discipline	• Fully implement Pathways to Work strategy, and increase resources for engaging with jobseekers, possibly through private employment services • Implement asset sales in 201 and reinvest a portion of proceeds, but strengthen competition enforcement to harness the full growth benefit • Review the structure of social payments to avoid unemployment traps, especiall for the long-term unemployed
Portugal	• Adhere to programmed fiscal targets, but avoid excessive structural adjustment in case of weaker growth and employment • Ensure timely implementation of PFM reform agenda • Reduce contingent liabilities through timely, planned SOE restructuring	• Avert a credit crunch by ensuring alignment of bank deleveraging plans with available credit supply • Strengthen the capital buffers of the largest banks in line with program targets • Strengthen the supervision and resolution framework	• Ensure competitiveness gains through accelerated supply sid reforms, notably the labor cod and product market reforms • Address structural weaknesse in wage setting mechanisms and the judicial system
Italy	• Lower taxes supported by expenditure cuts to better distribute the burden of adjustment and help growth • To build buffers, target an overall structural surplus of 1 percent of GDP as the anchor for the new fiscal rule; legislate medium-term	• Strengthen capital and liquidity buffers by raising equity and/or disposing of noncore assets • Conduct and publish stress tests on banks not covered by the EBA • Encourage banks to devise	• Raise productivity in services by accelerating reforms in the energy, local public, and professional services sectors t reduce the cost of doing business and increase competition • Curb state involvement in th

	expenditure cuts in next year's budget to lock in gains • Strengthen fiscal institutions by ensuring independence of fiscal council, adopting multi-year expenditure frameworks, and merging the various spending reviews into a central role in the budget process	strategies for selling, restructuring or writing down impaired loans • Strengthen the crisis management framework in line with the forthcoming EU Directive	economy • Implement labor market reform to reduce duality, increase participation, and decentralize wage setting • Promote SME growth by improving access to financing and reducing start-up costs and regulatory hurdles
Spain	• Make the fiscal adjustment less front loaded and embed in a more prudent macro framework • Increase role of revenue measures, especially indirect taxes • Apply sanctions on regional government finances and improve their transparency	• Communicate comprehensive strategy, including triaging banks according to the independent valuations, and managing legacy assets • Enhance crisis management and resolution framework	• Implement approved labor market reforms • Implement other planned structural reforms

Source: IMF

that EMU governance has failed completely, that one nation decided to leave, or that speculative forces broke it before policymakers could act. The exit EMU of any country is not likely to be isolated. Therefore, if the breakup starts, it would be better to agree on a complete and speedy dissolution into the old national currencies, because a stub euro is not likely to gain credibility fast enough. Either none or all leave the EMU.

Veron (2012) argued that the euro area has many problems. Based on the lessons from the past five years, he argued that the core of the current crisis, what makes it unique, is Europe's insufficient ability to make authoritative policy and political decisions for the region as a whole. To correct this weakness, Europe must build a fourfold union that would allow such executive decisions to be made. The four components are: (1) a banking union, (2) a fiscal union, (3) a competitiveness union, and (4) a political union, i.e. institutional reform to embed democratic accountability more solidly in decision making.

Johnson(2012) firmly prescribed that Five measures are needed to enable the euro area to survive: (1) an immediate program to deal with excessive sovereign debt, (2) far more aggressive plans to reduce budget deficits and make peripheral nations "hypercompetitive" in the near future, (3) supportive monetary policy from the ECB, (4) the introduction of mechanisms that credibly achieve medium-term fiscal sustainability, and (5) institutional change that reduces the scope for excessive leverage and consequent instability in the financial sector.

Conclusion

The ECB shows its muscle and decides to intervene directly in the market to solve the short term liquidity needs with a medium-term QE programme. The intervention also succeeds in designing an appropriate burden-sharing among NCBs through greater contribution to capital and reserves, and it also stimulates member states to find greater coordination of fiscal policies. In effect, in parallel to the ECB intervention, Euro zone member states - feeling they are losing direct control on burden sharing mechanisms in the European Monetary Union - and the European Commission decide to seek political agreement on a process of greater economic integration via a Euro zone federal budget (supported by Eurobond issuances). In the meantime, the Commission will inject new resources for long-term investments (to support austerity measures) and - jointly with the ECB – will supervise the implementation of austerity measures and predispose an official exit procedure from the Euro zone, threatening to use the procedure and stop the QE and other liquidity support for countries that do not comply. Additionally, member states will be forced to find a broad and stable political agreement by the indirect burden-sharing imposed by the independent ECB intervention. Once a more federal budget is agreed, the Commission (with the support of national governments) will elaborate a long-term strategy to boost competitiveness in troubled countries and to implement even more structural reforms and investments in innovation. Essential to this broader action is the definition of an effective mechanism of sanctioning/ rewarding for 'net receiver' countries, as well as an exit procedure from the Euro zone if sanctions are not enough.

The Euro zone is at a turning point. We can either sink in the mire of our debt and go back to weak national policies that will destroy the euro area, or decide to build a more integrated European economy by strengthening efforts towards more coordinated fiscal policies. In effect, monetary union has been a great tool with which to increase financial integration in the euro area, but it has not seriously addressed issues of economic integration and competitiveness. Despite high level commitments, the original sin of the crisis lay in the decision to harmonise monetary policies without harmonising or strengthening Euro zone fiscal policies. The way forward must be designed around three actions: redefining institutional competences among international organisations; strengthening ECB policy as 'lender of last resort' for its members; and increasing coordination among euro area members around fiscal policies. The whole Euro zone has been built on the implicit guarantees of stronger countries. If markets feel at any stage that these guarantees may no longer be there, because certain countries are not using all possible means to avoid a default, they withdraw capital and investments in weaker countries in favour of the stronger ones or other regional areas of the global economy.

Alternatives to the two-tier long-term exit strategy (quantitative easing and a more federal budget) described above seem so far unable to tackle the financial instability and structural regional imbalances that lie behind the inception of the monetary union. The role of European monetary fund and the IMF cannot be elevated to a panacea for this crisis, as they are tools to help countries in very specific and limited circumstances. The time for endless political compromises is up. Now is the time to push our leaders to take their responsibilities by embracing a new age for the euro area that could avert an unsettling and rather painful decline (Valiante,2011).

Last but not the least, the foreign ministers of EU-11 prepared a Final Report of the Future of Europe Group reaching a decisive juncture is as follows;[1] strengthening the economic and monetary union has absolute priority,[2] To improve the overall functioning of the EU by enhancing the coherence and political clout, improving policies with institutional reform which necessitates,[i] an integrated budgetary framework,[ii] an integrated economic policy framework,[iii] an integrated financial framework,[iv] strengthening democratic legitimacy and accountability,[3] facilitating further integration steps and the long-term governance structure of the EU considering [i] Europe as a global player,[ii] strengthening the EU's effectiveness and democratic legitimacy,[iii] strengthening the EU as a community of values,[iv] improving the long term overall function of the EU.

Above all, the policies to resolve or revive the Euro crisis is an never -ending process since the sources of the crisis could not be eliminated with in a very short time because those are structural, political and also policy failures and some of are exogeneous. Therefore, success and failures depends on mainly political integration and co-ordinations among the economic and political institutions.

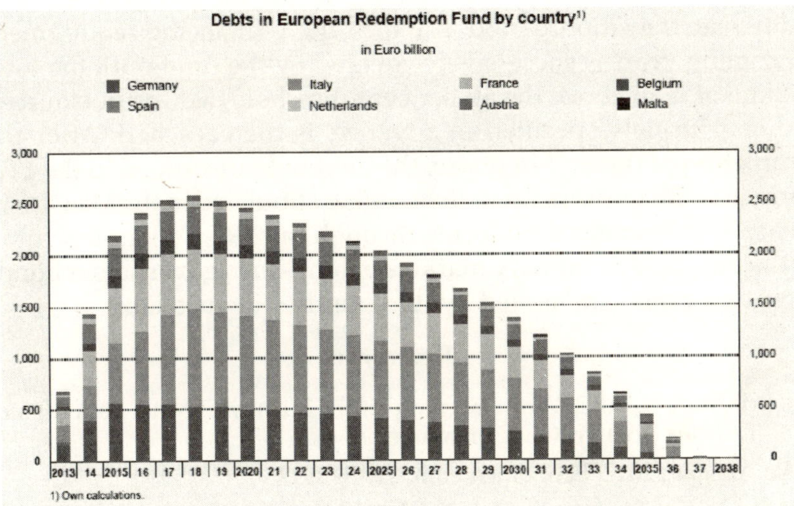

Fig-8.3: Debts in European Redemption Fund

European Redemption Fund - European Redemption Pact (ERP) is based on three pillars: a European Redemption Fund (ERF) that envisages temporary and limited joint and several liability for debt in Europe; the Fiscal Pact, which is meant to give national fiscal policy enduring soundness by imposing suitable restrictions; and an insolvency regime for states to come into force after the reduction of debt in the ERF. The objective behind the proposal is to restore national responsibility in fiscal policy in line with the bail-out clause in the Treaty of Lisbon. Access to the ERF is contingent on translation of the Fiscal Pact into national (constitutional) law, in particular the introduction of debt brakes. Joint and several liability for part of the debt will be temporal and of limited scale. The ERP features a series of safety barriers and sanctioning mechanisms to ensure a successful transition to sound public finances.

The proposal for the ERP hinges on the Euro area member states, which are not already on an adjustment programme, to outsource their debt which exceeds the Maastricht Treaty limit of 60 per cent of GDP at a specific date to a European Redemption Fund (ERF) for which there is joint and several liability. In return, the member states taking part assume payment obligations to the ERF that depend on the scale of debt outsourced and shall be set such that the debt can be completely repaid in about 25 years. In this way, each country itself fully repays the debt it outsources and remains liable for the debt it has entrusted to the ERF. Outsourcing debt to the ERF occurs over a multi-year transition period in which the refinancing requirement for coming years is successively covered by the fund until the total volume of debt above the 60 per cent threshold, as was outsourced and conclusively specified in advance, is then reached. After the completion of this roll-in phase, the debt not outsourced to the ERF complies with the 60 per cent debt ceiling stipulated in the Maastricht Treaty. Government refinancing through the ERF is then structured by the purchase in primary markets of long-term government bonds (over two years) and issued by the countries in question.

References

Åslund, Anders., 2012, Why a Breakup of the Euro Area Must Be Avoided: Lessons from Previous Breakups.

Belke,Ansgar., 2012, Economist.com, 11/7/2012

Bergsten, C . Fred and Jacob Funk Kirkegaard., (2012): The Coming Resolution of the European Crisis: An Update.*PB12-18*,June,PIIE.

Cline, William R., 2012, Sovereign debt sustainability in Italy and Spain:A probabilistic approach .*WP-12-12*,August, PIIE.

Economist.com., 2012, "The Future of Eurozone: outlook and lessons." August 1, 2012.

Eurozone: Outlook and Lessons" on August 1, 2012

German Council of Economic Experts,2012,After the Euro Area Summit :Time to implement Longterm Solutions-Special Report, 30July, 2012, Germany

Henning, C.Randall & Martin Kessler ., (2012): Fiscal Federalism: US History of Architects of Europe's Fiscal Union.*WP-12-1*,Jan,PIIE

Johnson, Simon., 2012., The Future of the Euro Area, The statement presented before the US Senate Committee on Foreign Relations Subcommittee on European Affairs hearing on "The Future of the Eurozone: Outlook and Lessons", August 1, 2012.

Mark, Jones., 2012, Economic Times, 8/7/2012, Also see article of Mark, Jones., PB-12-20, August, PIIE.

Stiglitz, J.E., 2012, EconomicTimes, 8/7/2012

Valiante, Diego., 2011, The Euro Debt Crisis:From its Origins to a way forward.*CEPS Policy Brief No-251*,August, Brussels.

Veron, Nicolus., 2012, Challenges of Europe's Fourfold Union. Statement presented before the US Senate Committee on Foreign Relations Subcommittee on European Affairs hearing on "The Future of the Eurozone: outlook and lessons."

Appendix

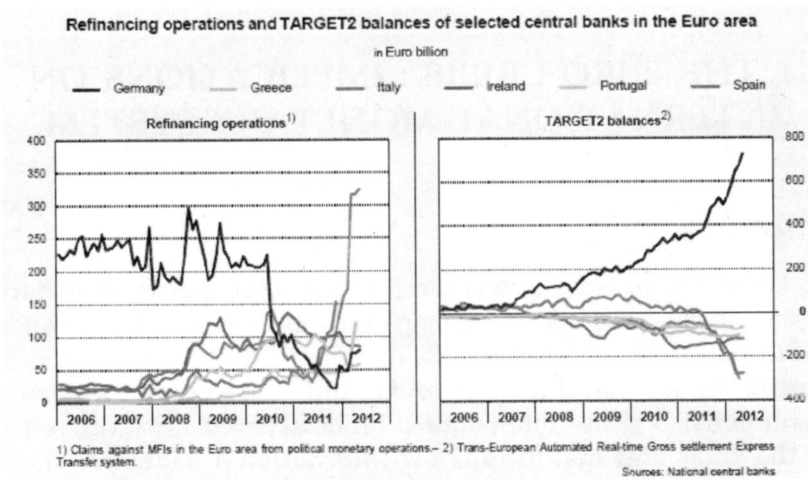

Fig. 8.A.1: Target 2

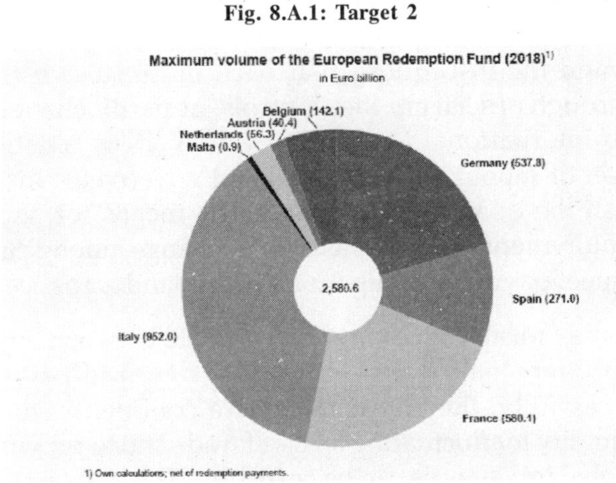

Fig. 8.A.2: European Redemption Fund

CHAPTER 9

THE EURO CRISIS : IMPLICATIONS ON INTERNATIONAL MONETARY SYSTEM

Introduction

According to Gold (1981) the international (global) monetary system manages the rules governing the relations of countries through their balance of payments and the monetary authorities (treasuries, central banks, stabilization funds, and other country-specific institutions). or, The "International Monetary System" (IMS) refers to the rules and institutions for international payments. Less abstractly, it refers to the currency/monetary regimes of countries, the rules for intervention if an exchange rate is fixed or managed in some way, and the institutions that back those rules if there is a problem (through official credits, controls, or parity changes).More simply, The International Monetary System (IMS) constitutes an integrated set of money flows and related governance institutions that establish the quantities of money, the means for supporting currency requirements and the basis for exchange among currencies in order to meet payments obligations within and across countries.

They provide means of payment acceptable between buyers and sellers of different nationality, including deferred payment. To operate successfully, they need to inspire confidence, to provide sufficient liquidity for fluctuating levels of trade and to provide means by which global imbalances can be corrected. The systems can grow organically as the collective result of numerous individual agreements between international economic actors spread over several decades. Alternatively, they can arise from a single architectural vision as happened at Bretton Woods in 1944.

The inception of Euro

The introduction of the euro will represent the most dramatic change in the international monetary system since President Nixon took the dollar off gold in 1971 [and when] the era of flexible exchange rates began...the euro is likely to challenge the position of the dollar [and hence] this may be the most important event in the history of the international monetary system since the dollar took over from the pound the role of dominant currency in World War I (Mundell ,1998).

The creation of the euro will be the most important development in the evolution of the international monetary system since the widespread adoption of flexible exchange rates in the early 1970s. It will almost certainly be the most important development for the monetary (as opposed to adjustment) dimension of the system since the dollar succeeded sterling as the world's top currency during the interwar period. (Bergsten ,1997a).

The advent of a new global currency based on a European economy as large as that of the United States clearly indicates that the international monetary system will look very different in the 21st century than it did in the dollar dominated world of the 20th century or the sterling-dominated world of the 19th century.

The present Euro land is 20-30 percent smaller than the United States in terms of total output and about 25 percent higher in its share of world trade. For all practical purposes, the two currency areas are close enough to be regarded as rough equivalents.

Expansion of the euro to include all fifteen members of the current European Union would take the numbers modestly (10-20 percent) above the United States in output terms. Inclusion of the ten new EU members would add at least another 10 percent or so to Euro land's output superiority (as well as bringing its population to about two-thirds greater than that of the United States).In short, it is clear that the euro provides the first real competition for the dollar since the latter's ascent to global currency dominance.

Given sufficient time, the creation of a euro area whose share of world trade is larger than that of the United States will make the euro more attractive as a vehicle and invoicing currency. But the attractions of shifting to the euro are a function of how many other market participants also shift.

There is little incentive to be first, lending the international role of currencies a strong element of inertia. This is the implication of both economic theory and historical evidence (Eichengreen ,1998).

Euro As International Money

As Peter Kenen (1995) has argued, the ''introduction of the ECU [euro] may reduce the demand for the ECU [euro] as money. By helping to unify capital markets within the EC, however, EMU may produce a long-lasting increase in the demand for ECU-denominated claims. That is why the ECU [euro] is likely to appreciate after Stage Three begins...The ECB can readily offset a once-and-for-all reduction in the demand for ECU [euro] balances by reducing the supply. It will be harder to offset the exchange-rate effects of an ongoing capital flow.''

Bergsten (1997) suggested that the euro would quickly be pushed up by 35 to 70 per cent against the dollar by the portfolio shift of central banks, governments, and market participants into the new European currency. The euro, in other words, would quickly come to rival the dollar in the international domain, in ways that had profound implications for equilibrium exchange rates. This has not happened. In the long run, there remains every prospect of the euro becoming an increasingly important reserve, vehicle and invoicing currency.

The same conclusion applies to the invoicing and vehicle-currency roles of the euro. Given sufficient time, the creation of a euro area whose share of world trade is larger than that of the United States will make the euro more attractive as a vehicle and invoicing currency. But the attractions of shifting to the euro are a function of how many other market participants also shift. There is little incentive to be first, lending the international role of currencies a strong element of inertia. This is the implication of both economic theory and historical evidence (Eichengreen ,1998).

As of 2009, the euro accounted for 27 percent of stock of global reserves and 20 percent of stock of cross-border loans, served as the currency anchor for 12 countries, and more than 31 percent of international debt was denominated in the euro. In 2010,the world export share of USA , EU and Euro Area were 8.419%, 33.93%, and 26.39% and world imports shares were 12.82%,34.21% and 25.72% respectively. Moreover, the world GDP shares of them were 23.08%, 24.09% and 19.3% respectively in 2010 (UNCTAD, 2012). The EuroArea produces about a fifth of global output, second only to the US. With its exports and imports together adding to almost 30 percent of GDP, the area accounts for a larger share of world trade than any other economy. Its financial sector is also one of the world's largest, with banking exposures to other countries exceeding those of all other economies, although its debt and equity markets—as measured by turnover—are dwarfed by those in the US. The dollar is currently used in 83% of two-way transactions in foreign exchange markets, while the DM is used in only 37%; other EMS currencies are used in 21% of transactions, and sterling in 10%; the yen is used in 24% of transactions (BIS ,1996).The following two pie charts clarified that the US share in trade and GDP are higher than EU in 2009 and 2010 respectively although EU had improved gradually since 1999.Again,if we look at Fig-9.1, we could think that the world share of GDP of India and China are rising upward, on the other hand, Euro Area, UK, USA and Japan have been falling steadily up to 2050.In 2010,the share of export of EU in world trade was 33.93% and the world share of import of EU was 34.21% which fell marginally since 2007.But,the share of EU in world GDP :US share of world GDP was 32:25.In case of stock market capitalization, the shares of USA,EU and Euro area were 31.36%,19.39% and 11.31% respectively in 2010 and in the world share of bond, equity and bank asset , they had 441.6%,551.4% and 484.2% of GDP respectively in 2010 .

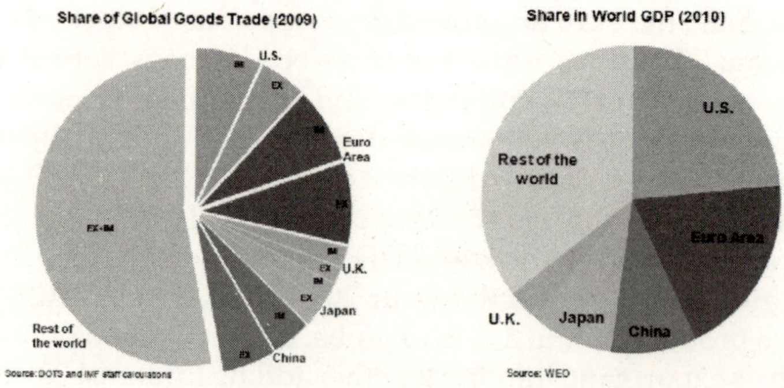

Fig-9.1: Share of trade and GDP

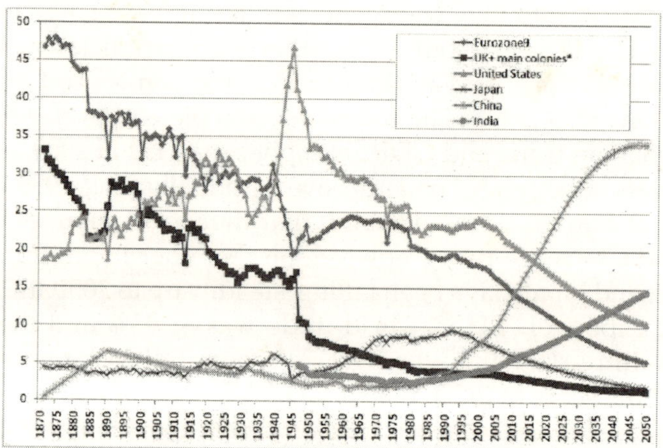

Sources: Angus Maddison's historical statistics and CEPII projections.

* Australia (up to 1900), New Zealand (up to 1939), India (up to 1946). Canada is not included as it was already granted significant autonomy in 1867.

Fig-9.2: Percentage share of selected countries and areas in world GDP,1870-2050(at 2005PPP exchange rate)

This is despite the fact that the EU accounts for a higher proportion of world trade than the US (even netting our intra-EU trade): in 1992, the EU accounted for 17% of the world exports, the US 12%, and Japan 9%. But the dollar intermediates in the financing of trade between the EU and third countries, as well as trade of third countries among themselves, partly because of lower transaction costs in the inter-bank market. The lower transaction costs in all markets involving the euro will make some substitution likely (Kenen ,1996). Hartmann (1996a) estimates that the initial post-EMU position would see 59% of world trade denominated in dollars and, on his 'euro optimistic' scenario, 28% in Euros. The euro replaces the dollar as the main international currency for financial asset transactions, but the transactions between the dollar bloc and the Asian bloc are still dominated by the dollar. The euro has taken the role of vehicle currency on the foreign exchange markets. In the Fig-9.3, the share of US Dollar in world foreign exchange reserves is greater than the Euro although the share is falling down marginally.

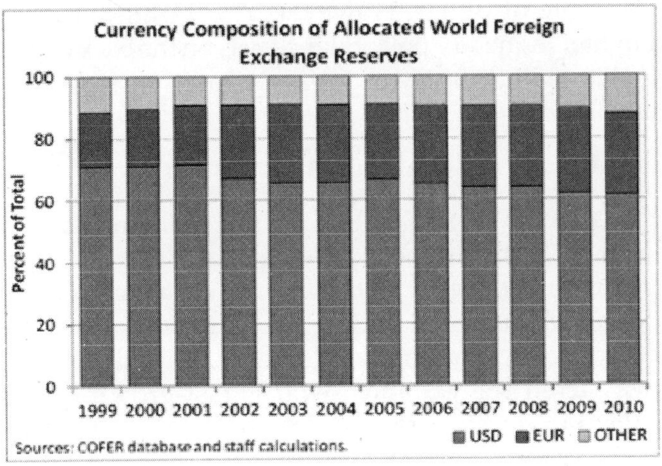

Fig-9.3: Currency composition and foreign claims

The euro could serve as a more credible anchor currency and store of value ,as the resulting seignirorage gains could be used to solve the current EU debt crisis. Reducing the intra-EMU asset and liability position would allow for a reconstitution of the stability oriented ECB monetary policy framework.A stronger focus on the second pillar of the ECB monetary policy strategy would allow putting a larger weight on the impact of money growth on financial market volatility and exerberance.

In this environment of enhanced competition for the previleges of an international currency Euro Area could assume the role of a mediator.A stronger diversification of East Asian foreign reserve holdings and exchange rate stabilization based on dollar and euro based currency baskets with changing weights could create a discilplinary mechanism concerning undue monetary expansion in the US or the euro area. By stabilizing the internal and external value of the currency , more seigniorage gains could be attracted.This system of monetary checks and balances could path the way towards credible monetary reform to create more global financial, economic and political stability.

An incentive towards a move of the US towards monetary policy reform could be created by a stability oriented monetary policy stance in EU.A tight monetary policy by the ECB would enhance the international role of euro as a store value thereby challenging the international role of dollar. However, also in Europe, the move towards a tighter monetary policy stance was on the back of a decisive monetary policy within the EMU. These are based on intra-EU current account imbalance.

Implications in International Monetary System

Since the end of World War II, the world economy has relied on the US dollar to lubricate the flow of global trade and finance. It accounts for the majority of global foreign exchange reserves and worldwide foreign currency trading and is the dominant currency for invoicing international trade. However, the shift in economic weight away from the US and towards fast-growing emerging markets calls into question the world's reliance on the US dollar. Many experts foresee a movement towards a multi polar currency system in which both the euro and the Yuan play a bigger role. Since its introduction in 2001, the euro has grown to 27% of global reserves and accounts for some 12% of global trade settlements. In early 2009, the Chinese authorities started to promote the international use of the Yuan in trade settlements with key trading partners and the development of offshore markets in Hong Kong. Developments over recent years have challenged this multi polar view. The European debt crisis threatened to evolve into a source of severe instability for the world economy; a growing need for structural adjustments in the Chinese economy and possible contagion from Europe raised new questions about the path and pace of Yuan internationalization; and despite persistent fiscal challenges, the dollar continued to play the role of a safe haven currency for global investors. The Euro zone, the

United States and China all face policy choices while adjusting to internal and external imbalances, affecting the stability of the international monetary system. How these choices play out and are influenced by developments at the global level will determine whether the individual currencies will be able to function as anchors for global economic stability. While the individual challenges for each currency area are widely acknowledged, there is a high level of uncertainty about how policy-makers will respond to their being interlinked in a complex two-level game between domestic priorities and international impacts (see deep dive on the dynamics of imbalances). In the past, policy choices within the Euro zone, China and the United States have all contributed to the build-up of substantial macroeconomic imbalances at the regional and global levels (Deep Dive I and II), both contributing to and highlighting the vulnerabilities of the current international monetary system through adjustments and interactions in the future by,

Deep Dive I: The current dynamics of US-China imbalances
Deep Dive II: The current dynamics of Eurozone imbalances

The way policy-makers deal with these internal adjustment challenges will significantly influence the context for the future of the international monetary system. The dominant narrative of how these adjustments will play out is that the continued growth of imbalances will progressively undermine international faith in the US dollar, leading to a gradual rebalancing towards the euro and eventually the Yuan. The result will be a multipolar "tripod" of reserve currencies, which under cooperative management, creates a self-supporting system that is more resilient to the build-up of imbalances than a system characterized by a single reserve currency. The international monetary system has fragmented into various regional systems and there is little coordination of policy beyond the regional level. Barriers to trade have significantly increased and there is limited capital mobility between regions. The International Monetary Fund has been rendered largely obsolete, while various regional initiatives have flourished, such as the Chiang Mai Initiative in Asia. Growth has stagnated and there are rising fears that economic conditions will deteriorate further. The importance of an international currency and the need for global macroeconomic coordination has been decreased by this ongoing reversion to regionalism. With sustained challenges and a gradual disintegration of the Euro zone, Europe is no longer a meaningful player on the international stage from both an economic and political perspective. The US dollar remains the dominant invoicing currency for oil and other commodities, but the RMB is the currency of choice in inter-Asian trade and, to a lesser degree, trade between Asia and other emerging economies. Unprecedented levels of global consumption make natural resource scarcity an increasingly serious global problem.

While observers had long called the RMB a possible regional currency for Asia, it has now become the de facto BRICS currency. Within emerging economies, Bretton Woods institutions have been largely bypassed by the China-led BRICS Development Bank and Monetary Fund, which is aggressively expanding RMB-denominated trade financing. Even though the euro has successfully overcome its internal governance challenges and emerged as a true fiscal union, the expansion of its international use has been limited. Policy discussions are dominated by the question of how to reconcile this two-speed world.

As Europe's leaders struggled to preserve the Euro zone in the early 2010 decade, they converged around the idea that only a fundamental redesign of the monetary union could ultimately bring stability. Arduous negotiations led to a multilateral accord establishing a European Finance Ministry with sweeping competences for fiscal and economic policies. The effort of establishing these new institutions while managing the subsequent political fallout that emerged in several key member states made European policy-makers largely disconnected from developments in the rest of the world. Many observers perceive a multi polar currency system as a better guarantor for global stability in an increasingly multi polar world economy than the current Dollar-based system. But the pathway towards such a multi polar system will necessarily be slow and fraught with political challenges. It presupposes significant structural adjustments in the main currency areas, the Euro, Dollar and Yuan, so that they can individually become anchors of global stability. (World economic forum,2012). The European Union and the United States both have major interests in constructing and implementing a "finance G-2." A "*finance G-2*" (whether or not part of a broader G-2) would constantly remind the United States that unilateralism is not an option for it in the economic domain, even in the financial component thereof where dollar supremacy has prevailed for so long. It would constantly remind Europe that its external affairs had to be managed carefully and constantly. It will inevitably become a necessary feature of the international monetary policy of both and thus a central element of the global monetary system of the 21st Century.(Bergsten,2004).In the Table-9.1,it is vividly clear that the US share in world foreign exchange reserves was decreasing since 2000 although it is too higher than the Euro whose share was only 25% as against 63% of US Dollar.

Table-9.1:Currency shares of foreign exchange reserves holding, by %,1923-2010

	1923	1965	1995	2000	2005	2010
			All countries			
U.S. dollar	33.0	56.1	59.0	71.1	66.9	63.0
Euro[a]	-	-	18.5	18.3	24.1	25.0
U.K. pound	66.0	20.0	2.1	2.8	3.6	4.0
Japanese yen	-	-	6.8	6.1	3.6	4.0
Other (including Swiss franc)	-	-	13.7	1.8	1.9	4.0
			Advanced Countries			
U.S. dollar	-	-	53.9	69.8	69.3	66.0
Euro[a]	-	-	19.5	18.4	21.2	23.0
U.K. pound	-	-	2.1	2.8	2.7	3.0
Japanese yen	-	-	7.1	7.3	4.7	4.0
Other (including Swiss franc)	-	-	17.5	1.8	2.1	4.0
			Emerging and developing countries			
U.S. dollar	-	-	73.7	74.8	62.7	57.5
Euro[a]	-	-	17.4	18.1	29.2	27.5
U.K. pound	-	-	2.2	2.6	5.1	5.0
Japanese yen	-	-	6.0	2.8	1.5	3.0
Other (including Swiss franc)	-	-	2.8	1.7	1.5	7.0

Source: Global Development Horizon. 2011. World Bank. IMF. "Currency Composition of Official Foreign

In Fig-9.4, the trend lines of the exchange rate of US dollar with respect to Yen, Euro,Swiss Franc, Pound Sterling, and Renminbi were shown where it is clear that US dollar is loosing against Yen but it is gaining against all other currencies showing in the figure which means exchange rate went in favour of USA.

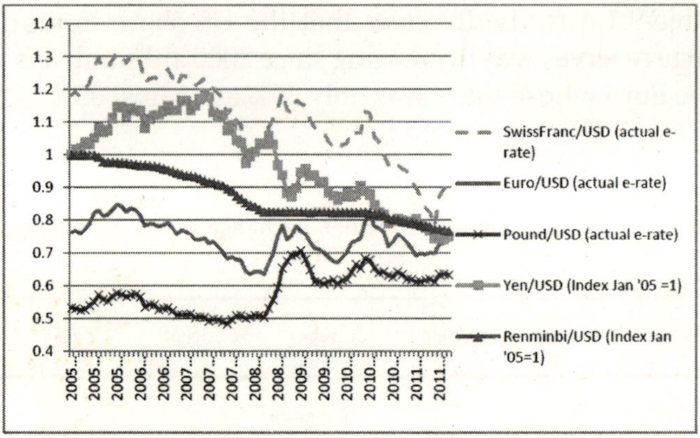

Source: Data from World Bank Global Economic Monitor database.

Fig-9.4: Nominal exchange rate of currencies against dollar,*2005-2011*

In the Table-9.2,it is shown that US dollar is holding 60.2% of world foreign exchange reserves as against 28.4% of Euro as of March,2010.So,thus,the supremacy of US Dollar is proved.

Again, in Table-9.3,it is clear that the Dollar is holding highest forex market turnover, outstanding international debt securities and outstanding international bank loans as against Euro, Yen and other currencies in 2009,so that dollar hegemony in international liquidity against Euro is still unchallenged.

Table-9.2: Currency composition of world foreign exchange reserves(%)

	2002	*2003*	*2004*	*2005*	*2006*	*2007*	*2008*	*2009*	*2010*
US$	60.8	63.4	65.1	63.6	63.9	64.7	63.3	62.2	60.2
Euro	29.6	27.6	25.9	27.7	26.8	25.9	27.0	27.3	28.4
Yen	5.1	4.4	4.2	4.3	3.9	3.6	3.0	3.0	3.1
Pound Sterling	2.6	2.4	2.8	3.2	3.5	3.8	.4	4.3	4.6
Other	1.9	2.2	2.0	1.8	1.9	2.0	2.3	3.2	3.7

Source: IMF & ECB

Table-9.3: Selected Indicators of the international use of key currencies in respect of world totals

	Dollar	Euro	Yen	Other
Forex market turnover, April 2010 (/200%)	84.9	39.1	19.0	57.0
Outstanding international debt securities, end 2009 (excluding domestic issues)	45.8	21.4	5.8	17.0
Outstanding international bank loans, end 2009 (excluding trans-European loans)	53.8	15.7	3.6	26.9
Allocated foreign exchange reserves, end 2009	62.2	27.3	3.0	7.5

Sources: ECB (2010), BIS (2010).

Jeffrey Frankel (1995), now on the Council of the Economic Advisers, argued recently that "there is little likelihood that some other currency will supplant the dollar as the world's premier reserve currency by 2020. One national currency or another must occupy the number-one position, and there is simply no plausible alternative". Similarly, Deputy Treasury Secretary Lawrence Summers said, "The dollar will remain the primary reserve currency for the foreseeable future .... We expect the impact of the euro on the monetary system to be quite limited initially and to occur only gradually ... (speech to Euromoney Conference, New York, 30 April 1997.)".

Even if the Euro does achieve the status of an international currency rivalling the dollar, does it matter? International currency hegemony has long been regarded as bringing political and economic benefits to the hegemon. We do not analyse or measure most of them here, but we do assess the likelihood of alternative scenarios in which hegemony shifts partly to the euro zone. Policy-makers may care more about the international status of their currency and its determinants than our quantitative estimates of some of the consequences. We have something to say about both, and it is important to understand why they care. Kunz (1995), writing in *Foreign Affairs*, "Geopolitical power depends on financial power, each of which supports the other. To ignore the real benefits of controlling the international currency system is [unfortunate]...The death of the dollar order will drastically increase the price of the American dream while simultaneously shattering American global influence."

The progress towards the organization of an International Monetary System functional to a stable and expansionary global economy will require the creation of large monetary areas with convertible currencies and Central Banks that will be able to target inflation in the respective areas. At the sametime, the system would contribute through monetary policy coordination to preserve price, monetary and financial stability in the global economy. The immediate consequence of the crisis in the Euro zone is to delay this process of global monetary coordination; but once the Euro zone shows that the Euro survives the current crisis and the European nations find a way to improve their monetary and fiscal institutions as to reduce the risk of future crises, the experience accumulated by the Euro zone Nations will help to guide the process of monetary integration for the Global Economy on sounder grounds. Hopefully, the current crises, which originated not only in excessive leverage of government, banks, firms and household in several countries of the Eurozone, but also in excessive leverage in the UK and the US, will help to find better monetary and financial regimes for the global economy. These regimes will for sure incorporate greater efforts of monetary and fiscal policy coordination and a more integrated financial regulatory framework.

Concluding remarks

The global financial crisis is the first major challenge for the euro as a multinational currency. Many wonder whether it will also be the last. Although early indications suggest that the euro zone countries are weathering the storm, this has not stopped prominent economists such as Martin Feldstein from cautioning that 'the current financial crisis may provide a severe test of the euro's ability to survive'.The euro as a multinational currency is not as vulnerable as it may first appear. Indeed, it provides a bulwark against the forces currently wreaking havoc in the global economy. The simple conclusion is that Europe's economic and monetary union is not only much stronger than many fear, it is also much better than the system of fixed but adjustable exchange rates that it replaced. Far from engendering conflicts, the single currency has diffused them. Along the way, it has also insulated politicians from being forced to make inevitably unpopular and difficult choices. Thus, the euro zone is more likely to get larger than it is to get smaller.

References

Bergsten, C. Fred., 1997a., The Impact of the Euro on Exchange Rates and International Policy Coordination. In Paul R. Masson, Thomas H. Krueger and Bart G. Turtelboom, *EMU and the International Monetary System*. Washington: International Monetary Fund: 17-48.

Bergsten, C.Fred., 2004, The Euro and the Dollar: Toward a "Finance G-2"?Prepared for The Euro at Five: Ready for a Global Role? February 26, 2004.

Bergsten, C. Fred., 1997b., The Dollar and the Euro. *Foreign Affairs* Volume 76, Number 4(July/August): 83-95

Bergsten, C.Fred., 2002, The Euro Versus the Dollar: Will There be a Struggle for Dominance? Director, Institute for International Economics, Presented to a Roundtable at the Annual Meeting of the American Economic Association, Atlanta, January 4, 2002

Bhowmik, Debesh., 2003, *Essays on International Money*, Deep and Deep, New Delhi.

Bhowmik, Debesh., 2011,International Financial Institution, European Central Bank and the International Monetary System (2011), V. Shanmugasundaram edt "*The New Institutional Economics*". Deep and Deep,NewDelhi, pp. 288-301

Bhowmik, Debesh., 2012, Reform of International Monetary System-Paper sent to edt volume in honour of Amalesh Banerjee. Ed.by Prof. Dhirendra Nath Konar, (Deep and Deep, New Delhi.)

BIS (1996): Changing financial system in small open economies.*Policy Papers.*

Eichengreen, Barry and Jeffrey Frankel., 1996, The SDR, Reserve Currencies and the Future of the International Monetary System. In Michael Mussa, James D. Boughton and Peter Isard, *The Future of the SDR in Light of Changes in the International Financial System*. Washington: International Monetary Fund: 337-78.

Eichengreen, Barry., 2012, "Implications of the Euro Crisis for the International Monetary System," Paper to be presented at the Allied Social Science Associated Meetings and forthcoming in the *Journal of Policy Modeling*.

Eichengreen, Barry., 1997, Comments on Bergsten. In Masson, Krueger, and Turtelboom, *EMU and the International Monetary System*: 49-57.

Eichengreen, Barry., 1998, Transatlantic Economic Relations in the Post Cold War Era. A council on Foreign Relation Book.

Eichengreen, Barry., 2000, T*he Euro One Year On1,University of California*, Berkeley

Gold, Joseph., 1981, The multilateral system of payments.*OP-6*,IMF.

Hartmann, P., 1996a, *The future of the Euro as an International Currency*. Mimeo. Institute for International Economics, Washington D.C.

IMF, 2011, Euro Area Policies: Spillover Report for the 2011 Article IV Consultation and Selected Issues , *IMF Country Report No. 11/185*, July 2011.

IMF, 2011, How should the crisis affect our views of the international monetary system? Background Note for Session VI – Monetary Policy, Conference on ¯Macro and Growth Policies in the Wake of the Crisis, March 7-8, 2011 – Washington, DC

Kenen, P.B., 1995, Capital Controls,the EMS and EMU.*The Economic Journal* 105, January, 181-192

Kunz,Diane B., 1995, The fall of the dollar order: The world of the United States is loosing.July/ August, *Foreign Affairs*.

Lago, Isabelle Mateos Y., 2010, The Debate on the International Monetary System.KDI/IMF Conference on Reconstructing the world economy.25/ 2/2010,Korea.

Lin,Justin.,Shahrokh Fardoust and David Rosenbhatt., 2012: Reform of the International Monetary System:A Jagged History and uncertain prospects. *Policy Research Working Paper 6070*.May,World Bank.

Maddison, Angus., 2003, The World Economy: Historical Statistics, OECD, Paris.

Mundell, Robert., 1998., The Case for the Euro – I and II. *Wall Street Journal*, March 24 and 25.Portes,

Richard and Helene Rey., 1997, The Emergence of the Euro as an International Currency. *CEPR* Workshop,4-5April.

Schinasi, GarryJ. and Edwin M. Truman., 2010, Reform of the Global Financial Architecture, WP 10-14 September, 2010.

UNCTAD, 2012, UNCTAD Trade & Development Report, 2012.

World Economic Forum, 2012, Global Competitiveness Report, 2012-2013.

CHAPTER 10

EURO CRISIS: THE CONCEPT OF POLITICAL ECONOMY

Introduction

Political institutions, social and geopolitical hegemony sometimes determined the economic limitations and conflicts of political super structure which lies behind the economic crises.EU suffers from social, economic and historical conflicts among the sovereignty of nations. Hegemonic war is the history of EU. So, economic issues had no concrete solutions without political solutions. Economic integration becomes incomplete without political integration. Therefore, common currency in Euro area had been confronting with asymmetric shocks in fulfilling criteria of optimum currency area as well as monetary integration where political policy decisions in the hands of the individual government under the currency areas are crucial for stability and success of the common currency.

Concept of political economy

Casimir Dadak (2011) claims that the Numerous economists, claim that the European monetary union is rather a political than an economic endeavor. This conclusion originates in the fact that the countries admitted to the union do not meet the criteria of Optimum Currency Area (OCA) theory as spelled out in Robert A. Mundell (1961), Ronald I. McKinnon (1963), and Peter B. Kenen (1969). If nations that form a monetary union do not form an OCA, then the costs related to the loss of control over monetary policy and exchange rates may outweigh the benefits resulting from the elimination of foreign exchange risk (greater volume of trade and closer economic integration). Many economists claim that the monetary union in Europe is a political rather than an economic enterprise, because the region does not meet OCA requirements, has low labor mobility and lacks a central fiscal authority. For these reasons, the euro area is prone to asymmetric demand-side shocks and lacks effective defenses against such adverse developments, except for deflation. The current crisis in several member- states, especially in Greece, Ireland, and Portugal supports these views and casts a shadow over the future of the euro.

The steps that the leaders of the euro area undertook to address the present crisis show that the region lacks political unity. The proposed ESM is designed to be an emergency facility; its funds will be disbursed only under very strict conditions and exclusively to members of the euro area. Consequently, in breach of European solidarity, the European Union is divided into two economic tiers, the euro area and the rest. The governance of ESM is based solely on economic power of a member-state. The position of the European Commission and, especially, of the European Parliament is weakened; it is the individual state that wields power. Moreover, the mechanism cannot be used to turn the region into a transfer union and, thus, make it more cohesive and competitive.

Johanna Croon and Miguel Poiares Maduro (2012) described that at the GGP High-Level Policy Seminar, policy recommendations to strengthen democratic participation and legitimacy in the European Union in the context of the current crisis were debated., Amongst the participants, there was general consensus that more and deeper integration is needed to respond to the challenges posed by the Euro crisis. Building on this commonly shared view, the seminar debate turned on ways and models to reach such higher level of integration in a democratically legitimate manner. This seminar highlights the following five of the discussed options - non-exclusionary and interrelated in nature - to enhance democratic governance of the Euro:

(1) Politicizing the EU by politicizing the European Commission through the transformation of the next election to the European

Parliament into an electoral competition on the presidency of the European Commission;

(2) Introducing a tax at the European level to equip the European Union with resources independent from Member States and to make citizens aware of the existing benefits of integration;

(3) Adding an institutional reform component to European policies, so that grant of European funds becomes conditional on targeted institutional reforms;

(4) Strengthening the relation between the European Union and national parliaments by furthering exchange and making European institutions more accountable towards national constituents;

(5) Increasing transparency and accountability of the European Stability Mechanism (ESM).

The fiscal crisis has exposed the most important element of the European Union's democratic deficit: the scope and level of politics has not followed the scope and level of political problems in Europe. Throughout the last decades, the European integration project has generated a deep interdependence between national policies.

Many citizens do not see European institutions as reacting soundly to the crisis. Instead, they blame primarily the European Union for the current problems, although it has played an only minor role in their creation. Treaty on European Union (TEU) still entrusts the choice of President of the Commission to the Heads of government of the Member States, the proposal proponents argue that the political dynamic and legitimacy generated by such electoral process, together with the fact that the President of the Commission needs to be approved by Parliament, would give national governments no choice but to appoint the candidate having "won" the elections. In addition, they argued that this proposal will preserve some hybrid character of the Commission: a pluralist composition of the Commission and influence by Member States will be insured by the fact that Member States continue to put forward candidates for the College of Commissioners. This should not be seen as a problem but as part of the gradual evolution of the EU political system.

The fourth option discussed to increase democratic governance within Europe was to establish a relation of stronger cooperation between European institutions, such as Commission and Parliament, and national parliaments. Given that the Commission has now the power to control national budgets, therefore a fundamental part of the work of national parliaments, it is important to strengthen the direct dialogue amongst those actors. Fora of debate could be established to increase the sense of ownership by national parliaments as well as a sense of accountability by the Commission. For example, one could initiate debates within national parliaments under the label of 'the state of the States in the Union'. In these debates, the President of the Commission or a European Commissioner would be required to present a summary of the reports, recommendations and assessments that the Union will produce for each State.

Furthermore, several participants stressed how important it would be for national politicians to change their conduct of externalizing political costs to the EU and internalizing the accomplishments and successes of integration to their own advantage. It was thought that political debates, at national level, involving both EU and national political actors may help remedying this situation.

According to Maria Damanaki (2011), as opposed to the markets, which can react in no time, the policy makers are by definition much slower. Political power needs democratic legitimacy, something that the financial markets can forego. The democratic process means that we should enable an open debate, aimed to reach a synthesis of different opinions and a socially acceptable outcome. It is a gradual process. But that is the way our democratic system works. I absolutely insist on this point: we need this system. We have, of course, to work on how to simplify and improve it. But, sacrificing our democratic values, not only for ideological, but even for social and economic reasons, is totally out of question.

We live in a globalised world. The current international context is complicated. The national economies across the world are interconnected. Still, they operate in very different ways. The principles applied are not the same everywhere. The risk of contagion remains too high. Throughout the world, regulatory approaches are different. The supervision of the international financial markets is fragmented. The lack of solid governance structures at global level is all too evident. There is also a competitiveness issue. There is a growing gap among nations. There are countries which have sustained high rates of growth. And there are others whose economies are trapped in a stagnation and recession spiral. The economy needs both the markets and the politicians to operate in what I would call an equilibrium. The political power should supervise the markets appropriately. The markets should benefit from the merits of forward-looking regulatory oversight. The political power should try to reconcile the needs of the markets with the needs of the majority of the citizens and the needs of the real economy. We have to heal our wounds and we need simplicity, efficiency, credibility and accountability.

However, this was not the case. The political reaction, during this crisis management period, was not up to the challenge. It was inadequate and it suffered from short-termism. It was a relief. But it was definitely not the solution. Europe has already taken a lot of major steps towards integration. The European currency has been the fundamental one - but not the only one. Despite the problems, the process of political coordination is already in motion.

But now we are very reluctant to go the extra mile. Why? Let us face the truth here. Under today's system, further integration steps will be very difficult. We are approaching fast those policy areas which touch upon the core of national sovereignty. This will require a major rethink of our political and institutional set-up. Above all, it is a question of leadership. Europe's political class needs to make brave decisions. This will mean that the politicians will need to avoid responding only to national short-term interests.

I have been in politics for almost all my adult life. I am fully aware of the difficulties and the constraints involved. But crisis time is leadership time. It is time for Europe's leaders to leave the sidelines. I am convinced that "more Europe" is the way to go.

The EU can tackle the Euro area debt crisis and the other challenges ahead only if it moves in the direction of more integration. This means that this is the moment for a political and fiscal union. This is not about idealistic federalism. It is about offering the right and most powerful solution to a persisting systemic crisis. This means that we have to accept transfers of national sovereignty. There will be resistance. But I hope that the political class in Europe will find the strength and courage to move forward.

Svetlozar A. Andreev(2007) showed that it can be demonstrated however that the EU does not suffer from a 'democracy deficit' as some have assumed simply by juxtaposing the democratic political experience at the national level with that at the supranational one. However as a consequence of both endogenous and exogenous developments, it is the case that the EU finds it increasingly difficult to build support on the basis of three forms of legitimacy:

- Traditional liberal democratic institutions and values, usually associated with the functioning of the state and sub-state political entities, as well as transnational society (i.e. a European demos) - '*borrowed*' legitimacy;
- Results, i.e. by acting as a 'benevolent bureaucracy', which is efficient and produces solely 'goods' - and almost never 'bads' - for the wider European public - *output* legitimacy;
- The 'rule of law', i.e. by relying on the power of the existing European and international laws - *constitutional* legitimacy.

The need for greater input legitimacy ('government by the people') - relating to increased citizen participation and better representation, as well as improved accountability on the part of the rulers and EU elites - has been *Political Perspectives.* Thus it has been pointed out that in order to alleviate the alleged 'democratic deficit,' as well as to address many of the legitimacy problems in the EU, one of the key principles of national democracy, 'inclusiveness of citizenship', has to be fulfilled at the supranational level.

Sara Hagemann (2012) opined that the political and economic crisis in Europe has meant a step back for the EU's major institutions. Solutions in 2012 must not come at the expense of democracy.His analysis consists of [i] Trapped in compromises ,[ii] Guarantees for democracy .

[i] Trapped in compromises

Since its very beginning the EU has been a compromise between, on the one hand, a vision of a supranational collaboration with independent institutions acting on a mandate to promote and develop Europe's common interests, and, on the other hand, the idea of an intergovernmental organization controlled and steered by its participating governments.

The compromise between supranational and intergovernmental preferences is apparent in all sections of the EU's structures. Its supranational institutions - the European Parliament, European Commission and the European Court of Justice - are responses to a need for delegating a number of core tasks to independent institutions that can promote and protect the collective interests of the member states. They are to ensure that the political and legal agenda is handled efficiently and to avoid a (complete) dominance by the largest and richer countries. As a counter balance to this delegation, the governments have made sure to keep control over the overall political direction by establishing the European Council, as well as over policy-making through the Council of the European Union ('Council of Ministers').

The result is an impressive, but highly complicated, set-up, which has proved advantageous for smaller and poorer member states. But there is a muddled picture when it comes to power and responsibilities at a time of crisis, with an unfortunate reliance on personalities. When the EU institutions - and in particular the Commission - are headed by strong leaders, Europe's common interests are well looked after. When the Commission is weak, it is not necessarily a shared European 'good' that drives decisions, and political actions may be dictated by government representatives' shorter political time horizons and party political convictions.

[ii] Guarantees for democracy

The euro crisis and the political crisis of the EU have meant a step backwards for both the European Commission and the European Parliament. Both institutions have failed to influence decisions about everything from bail-outs to general financial and economic structures and regulation. Furthermore, a new round of treaty changes and the suggested creation of separate governance structures for the Euro zone are likely to result in a further decline in their role and influence in the future.

These developments are highly problematic. While the Commission and Parliament each have their respective problems to address, they are the only guarantees against the domination of the interests of large (and rich) member countries. The past months' intense negotiations have led to a predominantly German-conservative conclusion for the further management of the Euro zone, without consideration of potential alternatives. Of course the situation during the past months has necessitated 'quick and convincing' political announcements (although the political leaders did drag their feet for quite a while), but the Commission, European Parliament and national parliaments should be included to a much greater extent. Much of the mess Europe finds itself in has to do with the lack of transparency in different actors' decisions and behaviour, both in the financial markets and with respect to the economic and financial politics of the respective governments. Hence, it is very important that the Euro zone, as well as the whole of the EU, ensures that it continues to keep a watchful eye over governments' decisions in the coming months' negotiations over a blueprint for the Euro zone.

But a more convincing signal of a new, strong and democratic economic 'regime' in Europe would be a detailed - and binding - agreement on the involvement of the European Commission in the governance of the Euro zone, as well as greater parliamentary participation in debates over Europe's economic future.

According to Kirsty Hughes(2011), political leadership and democratic aspects of the crisis are closely interlinked. But while some of the failures identified below suggest weaknesses in, or even contempt for, the role of democracy, others are failures of leadership and strategy not of democracy per se. He had given 10 failures of EU,namely,

Failure No. 1: Lack of European political vision and strategy

Failure No. 2: Mishandling political relations between member states - directoire of two, inner core of 17, or EU of 27?

Failure No. 3: Geopolitical failure - neglecting the EU's role in its region and globally

Failure No. 4: National and EU failures - lack of policy choices and debate

Failure No. 5: Failure to prioritise people and societies over markets - hopelessness and democracy are not good bedfellows

Failure No. 6: Emergence of technocratic Governments

Failure No. 7: The EU's democratic deficits

Failure No. 8: Macro-economic failures - neo-liberalism still dominates

Failure No. 9: Failure to confront financial Markets

Failure No. 10: Micro-economic failures - misunderstanding competitiveness, inadequate industrial policies

Addressing these ten failures would open up a route to a more strategic approach to the crisis and one that promotes and defends the EU as a whole and not only the euro. There is a pressing need for a genuine overarching political strategy that emphasises democracy, political vision, and social inclusiveness and that recognises that economies, societies and political processes are all intertwined instead of presuming democracy and social cohesion can take endless battering while economic policies are designed to appease financial markets. The EU's leaders and politicians - not just those in the euro zone - need to face up to the depth of this crisis and especially to recognise it as a political and democratic not just an economic crisis. They need to show that they have a clear and positive political strategy and vision for the EU, that the EU is more than just a single currency, that it has a current and future political and social as well as economic purpose and dynamic. Such a strategic approach would both help in tackling the euro crisis itself and in limiting the wider damage to the EU.

The EU's leaders need to take a hard look at the damage much of the current handling of the crisis is doing to democratic processes across the EU - and start to respect again member state and EU fundamental democratic norms, processes and values. Political parties across the EU need to challenge themselves as to whether they are rising to the challenge of the crisis - and to the end of the neoliberal decades - and whether they are producing vibrant and viable policy alternatives to debate with the public. They need to ask whether and how they can find policies that will build cohesive, dynamic societies that sustain democratic and political as well as economic life rather than undermine it. For now, the euro zone is heading in the wrong direction as the euro crisis deepens daily. It is an economic crisis that has become a political crisis, and the EU will come through the crisis successfully only if it finds new political vision, courage and imagination that today is sorely lacking.

Thanos Dokos (2012) argued that Greece's (and Europe's) crisis is mainly -but not exclusively- economic in nature, but the geopolitical dimensions should not be underestimated. If Greece fails to recover, it may well be forced to leave the Euro zone and, according to most experts, there will be a huge economic and political impact for the Euro and the EU. In addition, there will be severe repercussions for regional stability in Southeastern Europe and the Eastern Mediterranean, as well as the EU's and NATO's ability to play a substantial role in those regions.

Allowing Greece to become a weak or even a semi-failed state will have an impact well beyond its immediate borders. Greece is – or has the potential to become once more- a quite useful player in a number of foreign and security policy areas, including EU relations with Turkey, the Cyprus problem, EU enlargement in the Western Balkans, EU and NATO policies in the Eastern Mediterranean, energy security, and migration management. On all of those issues, the ability of Greece to make a positive contribution should no longer be taken for granted. If one agrees that geo-economics are increasingly important but nevertheless geopolitics still matter, then one cannot afford anymore to manage the Greek crisis without due consideration of its geopolitical consequences. No one is seriously arguing for giving Greece another free lunch (and obviously no one would be willing to). Instead, the EU should be looking for a highly pragmatic policy which would be reasonably effective in achieving Europe's geopolitical and geo-economic objectives and promoting its interests. A policy seeking to support and engage a country in deep trouble is much more likely to succeed than policies intended to punish such a country, as students of German history may remember from the periods after the two World Wars. What is needed is a policy that goes beyond bean-counting and tackles the Greek problem in the context of the EU's regional and global role, not merely its economic policies.

Admittedly, the stormy scenario outlined in the chapter is the least probable among the three presented (although several of its predictions may materialize in one form or another). But considering the potential costs of Greece becoming a weak state in terms of foreign and domestic policy and being a consumer rather than a producer of security, is it a risk worth taking for the EU (and also the US)?

Razeen Sally(2012)explained that the rootstock of the euro zone crisis is a failed political project: the euro itself. It was pushed through for political reasons – to further 'ever closer integration'. But the euro zone was never an 'optimum currency area', given its diverse economies. Further, there was no structural adjustment in most of the EU; rather, governments flouted common fiscal rules and went on a borrowing spree at artificially low interest rates. The global financial crisis exposed these flaws. The result is a triple crisis – of sovereign debt, banks and the common currency.

Anders Aslund (2011)tried to show that the current European leaders have largely proven immune to these elementary observations. The euro crisis is an illustrative collection of mistakes of political economy. It even took the European leaders several months before they accepted professional advice from the IMF. Few rulers in the developing world are that daft. Several unsuccessful political leaders have fortunately departed, but the two key players, Sarkozy and Merkel, persist. Since they have assumed most power in the European Union during the crisis, the main responsibility for this astounding disaster falls on them. As Sachs has noted, "Europe hangs on the words of Chancellor Angela Merkel, which are sporadic and often doled out on the eve of euro zone summits." After almost two years of crisis, neither Greece nor Italy has any plausible anti-crisis programs. The latest Italian "austerity" budget without any cuts is nothing but a bad joke. And the European Union is about to run out of credible sources of financing after its many failed anti-crisis programs. This folly has apparently driven Europe into an unnecessary recession.

Given the miserable performance of the current set of political leaders, they have lost all credibility. There is little reason to believe that they will be able to resolve the crisis. This is not a moral or political statement, but an assessment based on rather elementary political economy. In the end, crisis resolution is a matter of restoring confidence in the state. For that task, Europe needs new leaders, who can handle a crisis in a relevant way. Until then, the euro crisis is likely to persist.

Alan Mayhew, Kai Oppermann, Dan Hough Sussex (2011) wrote that at a time when German leadership in the EU is arguably more in demand than ever, in particular in the current Euro crisis, the willingness and ability of German governments to provide such leadership can subsequently no longer be taken for granted. The first part of their paper begins by sketching out the major changes in German European policy, putting them into the broader context of whether German foreign policy in general has normalised. It then analyses the main drivers of these changes: first, a shift in the international and European-level opportunity structures of German policy towards European integration; and second, a tightening of the political constraints and a reappraisal of the standards of appropriateness in the making of German European policy at the domestic level. It then moves on to analysing Germany's recent behaviour in dealing with the Euro zone crisis before concluding with some speculations on the implications that all of the above have for Germany's European Policy in the future. The second part of the their paper investigates the economic background to German leadership of the EU. In particular, it argues that Germany's swift recovery from the global financial crisis has once more demonstrated that the country is the major economic power in Europe. Given its economic strength, leadership in rescuing the Euro zone has been forced upon a reluctant Germany.

The Europeans have not been averse to the prospect of Chinese money. Member states have been keen to tout statements of Chinese support—or even talks with China—as votes of confidence in their economies, with Greece, Portugal, Spain, Italy and Hungary among the most conspicuous examples. At the EU level, policymakers have been divided throughout the crisis about the involvement of outside funding, even from the IMF. But the need for a large war-chest to hold the markets at bay, together with the political and legal wrangling over various financing mechanims, ultimately shifted the stance of the euro-group, and the European Council meeting in October 2011 gave the green light for leveraging the European Financial Stability Facility (EFSF). China is the only country other than Japan whose forex holdings exceed those in the euro zone itself, and Beijing and Tokyo were natural first destinations for EFSF head Klaus Regling after the summit.

Estimates of Chinese holdings in EFSF bonds—where the data is somewhat more transparent—have varied between 10-20% (less, for instance, than Japan). Although there have been offers of greater support, Beijing has made clear that this would largely be channeled through the IMF. While the lack of clear statistical information necessitates a certain level of educated guesswork, the general picture is still clear: no grand deals have been struck and Chinese involvement has been that of a normal market actor rather than a savior for the euro-zone.

Allan Drazen (2011) analysed that contagion will be intrinsically political, for in the absence of the political objective, devaluation in one country would not affect speculative pressure on another country's currency.

First, what does one mean by "primarily political" objectives in economic policy? Economic decisions are often made on the basis of largely political goals. Income distribution programs are a good case in point: transfers are made with the aim of maximizing votes for the incumbent party. The objective of a decision is clearly primarily political when it supports a political objective that is in conflict with economic objectives.

Hence, holding the exchange rate fixed for the purpose of enhanced political integration at significant economic cost is a primarily political decision.

The concept of political contagion in speculative attacks follows as an implication of the desire for political integration where maintenance of a fixed exchange rate is a membership condition on each potential member of the integrated unit. One must make one further assumption, namely, that the value of membership in the arrangement depends positively on who else is or may be a member. Hence, if a country learns that other potential members of the arrangement place less weight on meeting the conditions required to join and, hence, are less likely to participate, it will find less advantage in joining as well. It will therefore assign a lower value to maintaining a fixed exchange rate, especially when doing so requires sacrificing domestic goals. To complete the argument, suppose that speculators are uncertain about a country's commitment to a fixed rate because they are uncertain of the weight the country's policymakers put on conflicting objectives.

Speculators know, however, that the desire for integration subject to the no- devaluation membership condition is an important objective. Rational behavior on their part will then imply that a successful attack on one currency (or perhaps even speculative pressure on the currency), revealing a weaker commitment than previously believed, creates an externality in the form of a lower commitment of all other potential members. These countries will therefore be more vulnerable to attack term this contagious effect *membership contagion.*

The European Union Committee (2012) summarises that the euro area crisis is a complex blend of financial, economic, political and institutional problems. Over the past year, developments in these interwoven elements have dominated the political and news agenda. National governments and EU institutions have struggled to keep up with the pace of events. The EU, and the euro area in particular, face massive challenges and there is a need for effective and proactive leadership both from the EU institutions and Member States, in the interests of the wider Union.

The proposed 'fiscal compact' and economic policy coordination measures for the euro area have been highly controversial. In December 2011 the United Kingdom indicated it would stand aside, and at the end of January 2012, the Czech Republic stated that it would not participate for the time being. Eight of the ten non-euro Member States are likely to join the 17 euro area states in signing the new treaty at the next European Council on 1–2 March 2012. The proposed treaty makes clear that the key provisions apply only to euro area states (unless a non-euro state indicates that it will choose to be bound by them).

The proposed treaty is outside the treaty architecture of the EU, though it cites within it several obligations arising under the EU treaties and legislation made under the treaties. Under the fiscal compact, each state will undertake that it will not have a structural deficit of more than 0.5 per cent of GDP (or 1 per cent if certain conditions are met); that it will put in place an automatic correction mechanism if it is not on course to meet that objective; and that within 20 years the ratio of general government debt to GDP should not exceed 60 per cent. The EU Court of Justice will be allowed to rule on whether states have met the requirement to put into national law the balanced budget rule and, if they fail to comply with a judgment that they have not, to levy a fine of up to 0.1 per cent of a country's GDP. There are also treaty provisions on economic policy co-ordination and governance, including for summit meetings of the euro area states and the President of the European Commission and President of the European Parliament to be held at least twice a year.

The proposed treaty raises a number of other questions, particularly concerning the relationship between it and the EU treaties and laws made under those treaties; and the proper role of EU institutions. The history of the institutional development of the European Union is characterised by pragmatic flexibility, suggesting that some of the rough legal edges of the proposed treaty will be softened over time. With the United Kingdom reducing its objection to the use of the EU institutions under the proposed treaty, it might be argued that this process is already underway. But even so, the lack of clarity about whether it is legitimate for the proposed treaty to confer new functions on institutions of the European Union, and the extensive overlap between the provisions of this treaty and functions which have already been imposed by EU legislation, is undesirable. The United Kingdom Government, together with the other Member States of the Union, and the EU institutions, must devise a means of securing the fiscal integration desired by some of the euro area Member States while at the same time protecting the integrity of the single market, including its provisions for financial regulation, as an engine of economic growth for all 27 Member States of the Union.

We agree with the assessment of the United Kingdom Government that the "optimum outcome" at the December European Council would have been an agreement at the level of all 27 EU Member States, with the interests of the United Kingdom protected. Shifting discussions outside the main EU channels to forums where the United Kingdom has no voice risks marginalising the UK over time.

For the longer term, we note that the proposed treaty states in Article 16 that it remains the intention for its provisions to be folded in to the main EU treaty framework. We can see no reason in principle why this should not in due course be achieved.

Article 16 of the proposed treaty also provides for an assessment of experience with implementation, well within five years. We hope that this assessment will encompass a reflection on what is, in the fiscal compact, a major development in the fiscal policy of the euro area states.

It is clear that improved budgetary discipline is necessary in order to make progress in resolving the euro area crisis, but ultimately the resumption of sustainable economic growth will hold the key: both in general terms across the EU, and in facilitating attempts to resolve the serious imbalances in competitiveness between different countries in the euro area. Therefore, while we acknowledge the great difficulty of devising measures to support economic growth in a period of austerity, we are concerned that the potential of the development of the single market to enhance growth has faded from view during the crisis. We are heartened by the emphasis on job creation and the single market at the EU summit on 30 January 2012, but the real challenge for policymakers will be the sustained implementation of measures which are both effective in developing the single market and thus supporting economic growth, and which do not threaten the drive to improve budgetary discipline.

In analyzing the policy issues, the concept of political economy is very much important.

Because, the 27 EU members together have a voting power in the Executive Board of the IMF of more than 32 %. In combination with the fact that the managing director of the IMF has always been a European, this explains why IMF involvement has been approved so quickly. Thus, EU-IMF cooperation was facilitated by the numerical dominance of EU countries in the Executive Board as well as the regional identity of the managing director.

After EU countries and institutions could not agree on own rescue packages (either via EU institutions or the ECB), the cooperation with the IMF was established. Together with the EFSF and EFSM this twin-track approach created parallel (shadow) budgets and further liquidity to finance country-specific public deficits and overturned the no-bail-out clause of the EU Treaty. In this respect, the involvement of the IMF seems to be an attempt to circumvent the prohibition of direct financing of national budget deficits via central banks.

This view was corroborated by the decision at the EU summit in December 2011 of providing additional resources to the IMF of up to € 200 billion via bilateral loans from EU and other central banks. All this has to be assessed against the earlier decision of the IMF to nearly triple its quotas to US-$ 934 billion and the Intention to further increase Special Drawing Rights (SDRs). Thus, the European sovereign debt crisis seems to be the push to allow the IMF to become the ultimate lender of last resort through the issuance of SDRs and granting of credit.

If the IMF more and more develops as a lender of last resort and for that purpose demands and gets more and more funds, one may ask whether the deposits at the IMF are still safe. And if the answer is no, it is questionable whether SDRs can still function as international reserves. As already mentioned the scale of commitments by the IMF during the EMU debt crisis until the end of 2011 has already been unprecedented.

In March 2010, as Greek's problems worsened dramatically and European attempts to solve the crisis solely did not work, the IMF announced to participate in the rescue actions. This decision by the IMF was voluntarily as it was in the clear interest of the IMF to do so.

Together with the EC and the IMF, which will be it formed the IMF/ECB/EC-Troika responsible for negotiating and monitoring the economic adjustment programs for Greece, Ireland and Portugal. The Troika can be seen as a new institutional body that was formed on an ad hoc basis as the EU was not able to manage its problems alone and as politicians of the donor countries (above all the German Chancellor Merkel) did not trust the European institutions and tried to reduce the moral hazard problem that was connected with the bail-outs.

The risks of an IMF involvement in the EMU debt crisis are straightforward, but there seems to be no workable and convincing alternative. The EU countries have resisted in accepting the German economic model and its "stability culture". The Stability and Growth Pact didn't work and even if the EU countries can ratify the planned fiscal pact it will take a long time to install it and to re-gain credibility on financial markets. Another often proposed solution to the sovereign debt crisis by guaranteeing unlimited ECB support is facing tough German opposition and could pave the way for an inflationary process in the EMU. Financial support and the enforcement of reform steps by the Troika to solve the structural, budgetary and international competitiveness problems of the program countries seem to be the only solution for the near future.

Conclusion

Federalism should no longer mean technocracy. On the contrary, the financial crisis has heralded the end of the approach to world problems simply through the prism of expertise. This does not mean it should be given up completely; it simply means removing the political dimension from problems for which the States and representative institutions must again take responsibility. Europe, like the rest of the world, fell into this trap and it now has to escape it. The European crisis has highlighted this. Building the institutions of European budgetary federalism, especially if it occurs in stages, calls for major political change. It would be clumsy to subordinate the settlement of the present crisis to political reforms that have to be undertaken long term. The debate over political change desired by 21st century Europe is not restricted to settling the crisis in its financial aspect - even though the urgency or necessity and the future implications of this might be highlighted. Europe has the means to deal with its immediate problems. Therefore we have to stop Europe sitting down to wait for Godot. Europeans have seen more clearly, whether this was in Ireland, Greece or elsewhere, the limits of narrow ideas of sovereignty, when States threaten to default and depend entirely on their partners for salvation. Even the most virtuous countries are now aware of the extremely negative repercussions that the default of some would have on them. In this crisis Europe has shown that far from being the destroyer of national sovereignty, it is rather the catalyst, the condition for its real rehabilitation.

Dr Economides will argue that the current Euro-crisis is not simply a financial crisis with economic implications for the whole of Europe and beyond; rather it is essentially a political crisis that cuts to the very heart of the European edifice. What we are witnessing among the EU member states is a dialogue and debate which, while focusing on the possible short and long-term fiscal remedies for the twin problem of ballooning debt and deficit, is fundamentally about their relationship at a political level. Many of these questions can only be answered based on the understanding of sovereignty and its relationship to the evolution of the European Union. Dr Economides's lecture will therefore challenge the primacy of taking a purely economic approach to the crisis and cast the troubles of the euro zone in terms of the role of political sovereignty and European integration.

Finally, it is both misleading and superficial to summarise the current economic turbulence - as is now routine in mainstream media and politics - under the heading of 'public debt crisis'. What is happening now is rooted - to be sure, in a variety of ways, depending on the country - in the destabilisation of national models of capitalism due to the predominance of neo-liberalism since the demise of the post-war 'golden age'. More precisely, the combination of 'financialisation' , EU internal market policy and European Monetary Union, on the one hand, and the weakening of regulatory and welfare institutions within most EU countries, on the other, have given rise to serious imbalances within the EU and contributed to imbalances in the world economy . It is nothing less than the very concept and architecture of the Euro zone that have been overwhelmed by a deep crisis. It is expected that the 'unfolding contradictions between different national capitalisms, characterised by [broadly] financialised or by neo-mercantilist regimes of accumulation': in other words, a monetary union between an export-focused and surplus-oriented core and a periphery that is dependent on imports and capital inflow has proven to be fatally flawed and unsustainable (Lehnderff,2012).

References

Alain Fabre, Alain., 2011, The Euro and the Debt Crisis: Towards greater political integration- *European issues ,no-215*,3rd October 2011, Foundation Robert Schuman-Policy paper.

Andreev, Svetlozar A., 2007, *The EU 'Crisis of Legitimacy' Revisited: Concepts, Causes, and Possible Consequences for the European Politics and Citizens Political Perspectives,* Epru, 2007 Issue 2 (7).

Aslund, Anders., 2011, The Failed Political Economy of the Euro Crisis, November 18, 2011.

Bohn, Frank., & Eelke de Jong., 2011, The 2010 euro crisis stand-off between France and Germany: leadership styles and political culture-*International Economic Policy (2011)* 8:7–14.

Croon, Johanna., and Miguel Poiares Maduro., 2012, The Euro Crisis and the Democratic.

Dadak, Casimir.,2011, Political Economy of the Euro Area Crisis, *Panoeconomius*, 2011, 5, Special Issue, pp. 593-604

Damanaki,Maria., 2011, *Financial Markets versus Political Power: the European Response*, New York, September 12th, 2011.

Dokos, Thanos., 2012, Who Lost Greece? The Geopolitical Consequences of the Greek Crisis

Drazen,Allan., 2012, Political Contagion in Currency Crises.

Economides, Spyros.,2011, *Greece and the Euro-crisis – the end of sovereignty?* London School of Economics.

Emmanouilidis, Janis A., Josef Janning with Rosa Balfour,Hans Martens,Yves Pascouau., 2012, *Governance of the Euro: Legal and Political Issues of a Fiscal Crisis*, Policy Brief, Issue 2012/3 – July 2012

Fabian Zuleeg.,2012, Stronger after the crisis Strategic choices for Europe's way ahead., *ELIAMEP* -PP No 18 Feb-2012

Hacker,Bjorn.,2011,Contours of a political union-Recalibrating European Economic and Monetary Union through more integration, *International Policy Analysis*,November 2011.

John Grahl ,John., 2012, Politics and The Euro Crisis, *Discussion Paper*.No 147, March., Middlesex University Business School

Kirsty Hughes, Kirsty.,2011,European Politics and the Euro Crisis: Ten Failures-*policy paper-Centre for International Studies*, University of Oxford, UK-November, 2011.

Lehnderff, Steffen.,2012,A Triumph of Failed ideas European models of capitalism in the crisis.European Trade Union Institute, Brussels.

Mayhew, Alan., Kai Oppermann, Dan Hough.,2011, German foreign policy and leadership of the EU, *Sussex European Institute, University of Sussex*-Working Paper No 119-May 2011.

Sally, Razeen., 2012, A brief political economy of the euro zone crisis,March 20th, *ECIPE*

Sara Hagemann,Sara.,2012,Jan 9 2012-http://blogs.lse.ac.uk/politics and policy/2012/01/09/eu-crisis-instit

Sklias, Pantelis., and George Galatsidas.,2010, The Political Economy of the Greek Crisis: Roots, Causes and Perspectives for Sustainable Development, Middle *Eastern Finance and Economics* .Issue 7 (2010),Strategy Paper on the 'State of the Union', June-2011,European policy centre.

The European Union Committee.,2012,*The Euro area crisis*.,25th Report of Session 2010-2012, published 14-2-2012

CHAPTER 11

IMPACT OF EURO CRISIS ON INDIAN ECONOMY

Introduction

Bilateral relations between the European Union (EU) and the Republic of India date back to the 1960s, when India was one of the first countries to establish relations with what is now the European Union. The two signed bilateral agreements in 1973, when the United Kingdom joined. The most recent cooperation agreement was signed in 1994 and an action plan was signed in 2005. As of April 2007 the Commission is pursuing a free trade agreement with India.

Under the joint action plan, EU and India would enhance consultation and dialogue on human rights within the UN framework, strengthen cooperation in world peacekeeping mission, fight against terror and non-proliferation of arms, promote cooperation and exchange in developing civil nuclear energy and strike a free trade deal as soon as possible. France who relies heavily on nuclear power and is a major exporter of nuclear technology, is expected to sign a deal that would allow it to provide nuclear fuel to India.

"The 12th EU-India summit will confirm that EU and India are strengthening and rebalancing their partnership in its political dimension, thus bringing our relationship to new heights. It will demonstrate that increased cooperation between India and the EU can make a difference for the security and the prosperity of our continents." The EU is India's largest trading partner, accounting for 20% of Indian trade. However India accounts for only 1.8% of the EU's trade and attracts only 0.3% of European Foreign Direct Investment, although still provides India's largest source for finance. The bilateral trade between India and Europe, which stood at $74.5 bn in 2010, is likely to touch USD 207.6 billion by 2015.

European debt crisis which emerged during mid 2009-10 popularly known as Euro crisis began as a result of highly debt ridden in the countries like, Greece, Portugal, Ireland ,Spain and Italy respectively .It was ultimately transformed into banking and financial crisis in the Euro zone which had a spillover effects on the whole world although Asian economies were induced less than other economies. Therefore, India is not an exception to this spillover effects.

Euro crisis in India

There are five channels namely[i] trade,[ii] currency,[iii] investment,[iv] banking ,[v] commodity price , through which the development in Europe can percolate to the Indian Economy. In the Table-11.1,the transmission of the crisis through the various channels are given.

Table-11.1: The transmission of European crisis to the Indian Economy

[i] Trade channels	Merchandise exports	IT/ITES exports
[ii] Currency channels	Export competitiveness	Profit margin
[iii] Investment channels	Capital inflow	M&A
[iv] Banking Channels	International exposure	Borrowing cost
[v] Commodity Price channels	Crude oil price	Metals and other raw materials

[i] Around one fifth of India's mercantile exports and 10% of India's commercial service export go to EU-27.However, the share of the countries' exports worst affected by the crisis. The EU share in readymade garments, machinery and chemicals are significant. Among the commercial services, around 25% export of IT/ITES services went to EU but the exposure to the worst affected countries is relatively less.

Let us have a detail look over the India's trade with EU.

Table-11.2: Indo-EU Trade

	Exports ($million)	*Growth rate*	*Imports $million)*	*Growth rate Growth rate*
2006-07	26831	15.51	29856	14.84
2007-08	34535	28.71	38450	28.78
2008-09	39351	13.95	42733	11.14
2009-10	36028	-8.45	38433	-10.06
2010-11	46819	29.95	44540	15.89
2011-12	26421		24473	

Source-ET-15/6/2012

In Table-11.2, it is clear that Indian exports and imports to EU have been fallen drastically after the Euro crisis. In Indo-EU trade, export accounts 20% and import 13% .In 2010-11,EU imported $46.8 billion worth of agricultural products, fuel, minning, machinery, transport equipments, chemicals, textile and clothing.EU exports $44.5 billion of machinery, chemical products, semi manufactured products(2.6% of EU export) etc. In the Table-11.3 below, Indo-EU exports to countries of EU during 2010 and 2011 is shown and observed that their exports to India have dwindled in 2011.

Table-11.3: India's exports to EU

	Exports in 2010, (20.0%)	*Exports in 2011, (18.6%)*
Netherland	3.58	3.09
Germany	3.03	2.69
Belgium	2.10	2.51
France	2.17	2.02
Italy	1.90	1.81
Spain	1.14	1.02
Austria	0.14	0.43
Portugal	0.21	0.21
Greece	0.25	0.11
Ireland	0.15	0.11
Finland	0.12	0.10

Source: UNCTAD

The European Union accounts for nearly 21 per cent of India's total export and Exports to Greece, Spain and Portugal, including Italy, is only 4%.Indian finance minister rightly said that is Indian export to PIIGS are marginally low and will not have any impact on it. India export mainly textiles, pharmacy products, Gems etc to European countries but these sectors were not effected much on crisis.

The current global economic slowdown has its epicentre in the Euro-region but the contagion is being witnessed in all major economies of the world. Several countries are seeing a slowdown in their economic activities and overall pace of investments.

Despite the strong growth delineated by the Indian exports sector in the last few years (CAGR 2005-11 of 20.2%), India continues to be a domestic economy with the share of exports to its GDP being around 11% on an average for the last 5 years.

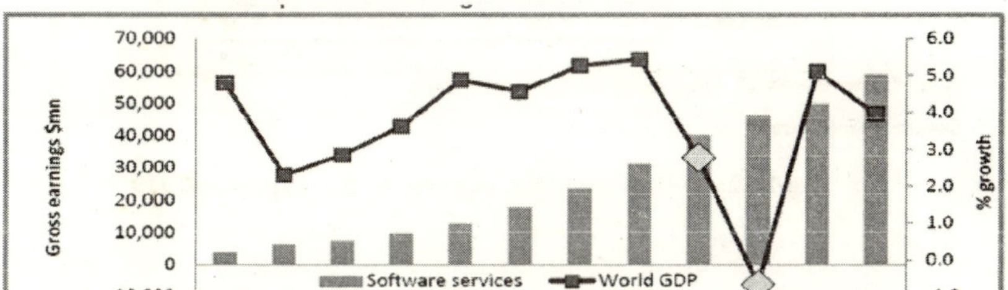

	FY00	FY01	FY02	FY03	FY04	FY05	FY06	FY07	FY08	FY09	FY10	FY11
Software services	4,016	6,341	7,556	9,600	12,800	17,700	23,600	31,300	40,300	46,300	49,705	59,001
World GDP	4.8	2.3	2.9	3.6	4.9	4.6	5.3	5.4	2.8	-0.7	5.1	4.0

Source: IMF, CMIE

Fig-11.1 India's earning from IT Sector

India's earning from the software sector have been increasing steadily over the years at a CAGR of 27.7%. In FY09, the world economic growth slowed to -0.7% but software services continued to increase, albeit at a slower rate. Net software earnings growth rate declined from 28.8% in 2007-08 to 14.9% in 2008-09 and further to 7.4% in 2009-10.

In the first eight months of 2011, the rupee had been stable in the range of Rs. 44-45 per dollar. A depreciating trend became stark since Aug 2011. The rupee has depreciated by 18% against the Dollar and by around 9% against the euro since Aug 2011. This trend is likely to improve the competitiveness of this sector. The negative impact, if any, will be marginal.

Although India's exports to US, Japan and EU started to decline since the beginning of the US financial crisis which shown in the Fig-11.2 and these were continued till date. India's trade openness thus declined since then and it is clearly shown in Fig-11.3.

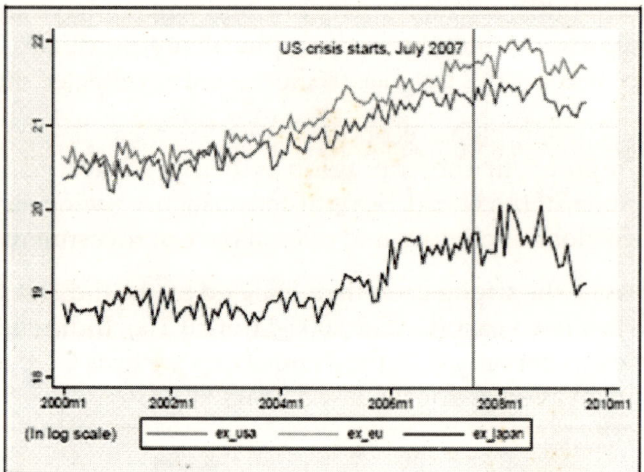

Note: EU represents 27 members of the European Union.

Source: IMF (2009a).

Fig-11.2: India's monthly exports to EU, Japan and US

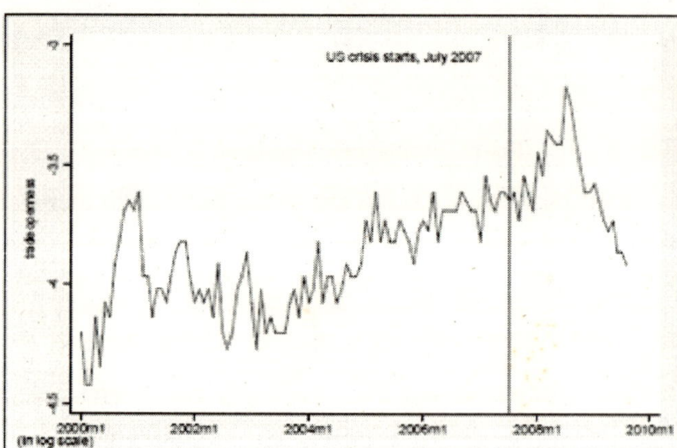

Note: *Trade as percentage of GDP.

Source: IMF (2009a).

Fig-11.3:India's monthly trade openness

[ii] Depreciation of Euro against Rupee, profit margin of Indian export would be negatively impacted but appreciation of Rupee could also undermine India's export competitiveness.

During 2010-11, the average monthly exchange rate of the rupee against the US dollar appreciated by 1.2 per cent from ` 45.50 per US dollar in March 2010 to ` 44.97 per US dollar in March 2011. Similarly, on point-to-point basis, the average exchange rate of the rupee [average of buying and selling rate of the Foreign Exchange Dealers Association of India (FEDAI)] appreciated by 1.1 per cent from ` 45.14 per US dollar on 31 March 2010 to ` 44.65 per US dollar on 31 March 2011. This was mainly on account of weakening of the US dollar in the international market in 2010-11. The monthly average exchange rate of the rupee vis-a-vis the pound sterling, euro, and Japanese yen, however, depreciated in 2010-11. The monthly average exchange rate of the rupee vis-a-vis the pound sterling was depreciated by 5.9 per cent from ` 68.44 per pound sterling in March 2010 to ` 72.71 in March 2011. Similarly, against the euro and Japanese yen, the monthly average exchange rate of the rupee depreciated by 1.9 per cent from ` 61.77 per euro in March 2010 to ` 62.97 per euro in March 2011 and by 8.7 per cent from ` 50.18 per 100 Japanese yen in March 2010 to ` 54.98 per 100 Japanese yen in March 2011. On an annual average basis, the rupee appreciated against major international currencies except the Japanese yen in fiscal 2010-11. The annual average exchange rate of the rupee was ` 47.44 per US dollar in 2009-10, appreciating by 4.1 per cent to ` 45.56 per US dollar in 2010-11.

Similarly, the annual average exchange rate of the rupee in 2009-10 was ` 75.76 per pound sterling and ` 67.03 per euro, which appreciated by 6.9 per cent and 11.3 per cent to ` 70.87 per pound sterling and ` 60.21 per euro respectively during 2010-11. The annual average exchange rate of the rupee per Japanese yen however was depreciated by 4.1 per cent from ` 51.11 per 100 Japanese yen in 2009-10 to ` 53.27 per 100 Japanese yen in 2010-11. In the current fiscal, there are two distinct phases in the exchange rate of the rupee. The rupee continued exhibiting a two-way movement with an appreciating trend till about July 2011, after which the trend reversed and it started declining sharply from September 2011 onwards, due to factors relating to the uncertain global economy. On month-to-month basis the rupee depreciated by 14.6 per cent from the level of ` 44.97 per US dollar in March 2011 to ` 52.68 per US dollar in December 2011. On point-to-point basis, it depreciated by 16.2 per cent from ` 44.65 per US dollar on 31 March 2011 to ` 53.26 per US dollar on 30 December 2011. The rupee reached a peak of ` 43.94 per US dollar on 27 July 2011, and a low of ` 54.23 per US dollar on 15 December 2011 indicating depreciation of 19.0 per cent. Similarly, the monthly average exchange rate of the rupee was depreciated by 11.5 per cent against the pound sterling, by 9.1 per cent against the euro, and by 18.7 per cent against the Japanese yen respectively during March 2011 and December 2011. As the rupee has been under pressure since July 2011, efforts have been made by the RBI to augment supply of foreign exchange and curb speculation in the foreign exchange market to stem rupee decline. (Table-11.4).As a result of these measures, and increase in capital inflows, the depreciating trend in rupee exchange rate reversed. The monthly average exchange rate of the rupee was appreciated by 2.6 per cent from ` 52.68 per US dollar in December 2011 to ` 51.34 per US dollar in January 2012. On point to-point basis, the average exchange rate of the rupee has appreciated by 9.2 per cent from its lowest value of ` 54.23 per US dollar on 15 December 2011 to ` 49.67 per US dollar on 31 January 2012.

Table-11.4: Exchange rate of Rupee per foreign currency and RBI's sale and purchase of US$ in the exchange market during 2010-11 and 2011-12

Month	Average exchange rates (₹ per foreign currency)*				RBI Net sale (-) / purchase (+) (US$ million)
	US dollar	Pound sterling	Euro	Japanese yen**	
1	2	3	4	5	6
2010-11 (annual average)	45.56	70.87	60.21	53.27	(+)1690
	(4.1)	(6.9)	(11.3)	(-4.1)	
March-2011	44.97	72.71	62.97	54.98	
	(1.0)	(0.8)	(-1.4)	(0.1)	
2011-12 (monthly average)					
April-2011	44.37	72.72	64.25	53.31	-
	(1.4)	(-0.02)	(-2.0)	(3.1)	
May-2011	44.90	73.41	64.48	55.32	-
	(-1.2)	(-0.9)	(-0.4)	(-3.6)	
June-2011	44.83	72.79	64.52	55.65	-
	(0.2)	(0.9)	(-0.1)	(-0.6)	
July-2011	44.42	71.65	63.46	55.91	-
	(0.9)	(1.6)	(1.7)	(-0.5)	
August-2011	45.25	74.11	64.94	58.68	-
	(-1.8)	(-3.3)	(-2.3)	(-4.7)	
September-2011	47.63	75.12	65.47	62.03	(-) 845.0
	(-5.0)	(-1.3)	(-0.8)	(-5.4)	
October-2011	49.26	77.49	67.45	64.11	(-) 943.0
	(-3.3)	(-3.1)	(-2.9)	(-3.2)	
November-2011	50.86	80.25	68.91	65.60	(-) 2,918.0
	(- 3.1)	(- 3.4)	(- 2.1)	(- 2.3)	
December-2011	52.68	82.13	69.29	67.63	(-)7809.0
	(- 3.5)	(- 2.3)	(- 0.6)	(- 3.0)	

Source : RBI.

Notes : * FEDAI indicative rate; ** Per 100 yen; Figures in parentheses indicate percentage appreciation (+) and depreciation (-) over the previous month / year. Some percentage figures may not tally due to rounding off.

The NEER and REER indices are used as indicators of external competitiveness of the country over a period of time. NEER is the weighted average of bilateral nominal exchange rates of the home currency in terms of foreign currencies, while REER is defined as a weighted average of nominal exchange rates, adjusted for home and foreign country relative price differentials. REER captures movements in cross-currency exchange rates as well as inflation differentials between India and its major trading partners. The RBI has been constructing six-currency (US dollar, euro for euro zone, pound sterling, Japanese yen, Chinese renminbi, and Hong Kong dollar) and 36-currency NEER and REER indices. The six-currency trade-based NEER (base: 2004-05=100) depreciated by 2.1 per cent between March 2010 and March 2011 and by 13.5 per cent between March 2011 and December 2011. As compared to this, the monthly average exchange rate of the rupee appreciated by 1.2 per cent between March 2010 and March 2011, while in the current fiscal it depreciated by 14.6 per cent against the US dollar from ` 44.97 per US dollar in March 2011 to ` 52.68 per US dollar in December 2011. The six-currency trade-based REER (base: 2004-5=100) of the rupee appreciated by 4.1 per cent between March 2010 and March 2011. During 2011- 12 (up to December 2011), the six-currency index showed depreciation of 10.8 per cent over March 2011 largely reflecting depreciation of the rupee in nominal terms, which mainly happened during the period August-December 2011.

[iii] The EU debt crisis could affect the EU investment in the Indian corporate sector's mergers and acquisitions activity. During last few years, EU companies have merged as significant partners for India's in bound and out bound M & A. With European companies for M&A in emerging markets including India is expected to decline. During the recent global crisis, it has been observed that the investment channels have assumed a more dominant role in transmitting the effects of global development in Indian economy during recent periods.

At end March 2011, India's external debt stock was US$ 306.4 billion (` 13,68,477 crore) recording an increase of US$ 45.4 billion (17.4 per cent) over the end March 2010 level of US$ 261.0 billion (` 11,78,994 crore). Component-wise, long-term debt increased by 15.7 per cent to US$ 241.4 billion at end March 2011 from US$ 208.7 billion at end March 2010 while short-term debt based on original maturity, showed an increase of 24.2 per cent to US$ 65.0 billion from US$ 52.3 billion at end March 2010.

India's external debt stock increased by US$ 20.2 billion (6.6 per cent) to US$ 326.6 billion at end September 2011 over end March 2011 estimates of US$ 306.4 billion. This increase was primarily on account of higher commercial borrowings and short term debt, which together contributed over 80 per cent of the total increase in external debt. The rise in short-term trade credits is in line with the increase in imports associated with reasonably strong domestic economic activity.

The maturity profile of India's external debt indicates the dominance of long-term borrowings.

Long-term external debt at US$ 255.1 billion on September 2011, accounted for 78.1 per cent of total external debt. Long-term debt on September 2011 increased by US$ 13.6 billion (5.6 per cent) over the end March 2011 level, while short-term debt (original maturity) registered an increase of US$ 6.5 billion (10.1 per cent) (Table -11.5).

Table-11.5: India's External debt stock

At end-March	In US$ million			In ₹ crore		
	Long-term	Short-term	Total	Long-term	Short-term	Total
1	2	3	4	5	6	7
2005	116279	17723	134002	508777	77528	586305
2006	119575	19539	139114	533367	87155	620522
2007	144230	28130	172360	628771	122631	751402
2008	178669	45738	224407	714409	182881	897290
2009	181185	43313	224498	921469	220656	1142125
2010	208685	52329	261014	942806	236188	1178994
2011PR	241448	64990	306438	1078330	290147	1368477
2011 (end-June) PR	249010	68474	317484	1116205	306248	1422453
2011 (end-Sept.) QE	255071	71530	326601	1247863	349889	1597752

Source : Ministry of Finance and RBI

Note : PR : Partially Revised QE : Quick Estimates.

Table-11.6: Composition of external debt(% of total external debt)

Sl. No.	Component	March 2010 PR	March 2011 PR	June 2011 PR	September 2011 QE
1	2	3	4	5	6
1	Multilateral	16.4	15.8	15.6	15.0
2	Bilateral	8.7	8.4	8.3	8.4
3	IMF	2.3	2.1	2.0	2.0
4	Export credit	6.5	6.1	5.9	6.0
5	Commercial borrowings	27.1	29.0	29.5	30.3
6	NRI deposits	18.3	16.9	16.6	16.0
7	Rupee debt	0.6	0.5	0.5	0.4
8	Long-term debt (1 to 7)	79.9	78.8	78.4	78.1
9	Short-term debt	20.1	21.2	21.6	21.9
10	Total external debt (8+9)	100.0	100.0	100.0	100.0

Source : Ministry of Finance and RBI. PR : Partially Revised. QE : Quick Estimates.

Since India's total external debt in terms of Euro is only 3.5% in September 2011 which dwindled from 3.7% in March 2011 as against 55.8% and 12.1% in terms of US$ and Yen which means that Euro crisis had less stress on India than previously faced from US financial crisis in 2008-09.It is shown in the Table -11.7,below.

Table-11.7: Currency composition of India's external debt and sovereign external debt

Sl. No.	Currency	Total external debt				Sovereign external debt			
		March 2010	March 2011PR	June 2011PR	Sept. 2011QE	March 2010	March 2011PR	June 2011PR	Sept. 2011QE
1	2	3	4	5	6	7	8	9	10
1	US dollar	53.2	53.6	54.3	55.8	26.5	26.8	26.7	26.5
2	SDR	10.7	9.7	9.5	9.1	41.7	38.1	38.2	37.3
3	Indian rupee	18.7	19.5	19.1	18.2	8.9	12.4	12.2	12.5
4	Japanese yen	11.5	11.4	11.1	12.1	18.6	18.8	18.9	19.9
5	Euro	3.6	3.7	3.7	3.5	4.3	3.9	3.9	3.8
6	Pound sterling	1.8	1.7	1.7	0.8	0.0	0.0	0.0	0.0
7	Others	0.5	0.5	0.6	0.5	0.0	0.0	0.0	0.0
	Total	100.0	100.0	100.0	100.0	100.0	100.0	100.0	100.0

Source : Ministry of Finance and RBI.

The share of ECBs in India's total external debt has increased substantially over the past few years. While between end March 2001 and end March 2006, the share of ECBs in total external debt declined from 24.1 per cent to 19.0 per cent, the compound annual growth in such borrowings was 1.7 per cent. However, between end March 2006 and end March 2011, ECBs have registered a compound annual growth rate of 27.4 per cent with the share in total external debt climbing up to 30.3 per cent at end September 2011. The increase in ECBs in the recent period caused some concern given the depreciation of the rupee as it would mean a higher debt service burden in rupee terms that could impact profitability and the balance sheets of corporate borrowers. The key external debt indicators are presented in Table-11.8. India's foreign exchange reserves provided a cover of 95.4 per cent to the total external debt stock at end September 2011 vis-à-vis 99.5 per cent at end March 2011. The ratio of short-term external debt to foreign exchange reserves was at 22.9 per cent at end September 2011 as compared to 21.3 per cent at end March 2011. The ratio of concessional debt to total external debt declined steadily and worked out to 14.7 per cent at end September 2011 as against 15.5 per cent at end March 2011.

India's external debt has remained within manageable limits as indicated by the external debt to GDP ratio of 17.8 per cent and debt service ratio of 4.2 per cent in 2010-11. This has been possible due to an external debt management policy of the government that emphasizes monitoring long and short-term debt, raising sovereign loans on concessional terms with long maturities, regulating ECBs through end-use and all-in-cost restrictions, and rationalizing interest rates on NRI deposits.(Table-11.8)

[iv] The Indian banking remain relatively well capitalized with greater exposure to domestic conventional assets. Even, with the over going European crisis, the direct effects on the Indian banking and financial system should remain negligible as the direct exposure of Indian banks to Europe. Although the Indian banking system would not come under the direct stress, the lending requirement of the Indian corporate sector might increase if alternative sources of funds such as external commercial borrowing become difficult in the offing. The international banks may once again get guarded on their

lending activity and companies may find it difficult to raise capital in the European financial market. Also, the increased risk averseness of the lenders would raise the base lending rate of LIBOR as well as premium lending to higher borrowing costs for the corporate sector. The lack of alternative resources for funding investment of the corporate sector may raise demand for and the price of bank credit in the domestic banking system.

Table-11.8: India's Key external debt Indicators(%)

Year	External Debt (US$ billion)	Total External Debt to GDP	Debt-Service Ratio	Foreign Exchange Reserves to Total External Debt	Concessional Debt to Total External Debt	Short-term External Debt* to Foreign Exchnage Reserves	Short-term External Debt* to Total Debt
1	2	3	4	5	6	7	8
1990-91	83.8	28.7	35.3	7.0	45.9	146.5	10.2
1995-96	93.7	26.9	26.2	23.1	44.7	23.2	5.4
2000-01	101.3	22.5	16.6	41.7	35.4	8.6	3.6
2005-06	139.1	16.8	10.1#	109.0	28.4	12.9	14.1
2006-07	172.4	17.5	4.7	115.6	23.0	14.1	16.4
2007-08	224.4	18.0	4.8	138.0	19.7	14.8	20.4
2008-09	224.5	20.3	4.4	112.1	18.7	17.2	19.2
2009-10	261.0	18.3	5.5	106.9	16.8	18.8	20.0
2010-11PR	306.4	17.8	4.2	99.5	15.5	21.3	21.2**
End-June 2011 PR	317.5	-	4.6	99.6	15.1	21.7	21.6
End-Sept. 2011 QE	326.6	-	-	95.4	14.7	22.9	21.9

Source : Ministry of Finance and RBI.

Notes: - Not worked out for the broken period. PR : Partially Revised QE-Quick Estimates.

*: Short-term debt is based on original maturity.

**: Based on residual maturity, the short-term debt (US$ 129.1 billion) accounted for 42.2 per cent of total external debt at end March 2011 (RBI Press Release, dated 30 June 2011). Short-term debt by residual maturity comprises all the components of short-term debt with original maturity of up to one year and amounts falling due under long-term debt including NRI deposits during the one-year reference period.

#: Works out to 6.3 per cent, with the exclusion of India millennium deposits (IMDs) repayments of US$ 7.1 billion and prepayment of US$ 23.5 million.Debt-service ratio is the proportion of gross debt service payments to external current receipts (net of official transfers).

European banks have higher exposure than banks in emerging markets, the US and Japan put together. If European banks collapse due to exposure to countries such as Greece, Ireland and Portugal, the supply of foreign credit to emerging markets will dry up. That will put pressure on investment spending in emerging markets — already struggling with high capital costs due to tight monetary policies — impacting investment, growth and employment. Early warning signs, such as low investor confidence and falling consumer demand across the board, signal a crisis at India's doorstep which it cannot completely avoid. So it is imperative that emerging markets, including India, look inward and boost domestic demand to compensate for the shrinking world market.

Europe is one of India's largest trading partners. Austerity measures in European countries and falling consumer expenditure may affect Indian exports, especially in services. Though China is India's largest trading partner, it mostly imports raw materials for manufactured goods produced for the rest of the world, now facing recession. So, the Euro zone crisis does not bode well for Indian exports. The Indian stock market has already fallen substantially, and if European banks become insolvent capital may return, leading to a sharp depreciation of the rupee, which is already in turmoil. Given increased intra-industry trade, and the import intensity of Indian exports, a rising rupee would hurt industries both within and outside the country.

Indian stock markets have corrected 10% from its recent peaks on the back of the jitters from the Greece-led European crisis. In fact, the concerns about the stability in the European region have once again resurfaced with the latest down grade of Spain by the Fitch. However, India has out-performed the global indices during this correction phase.

India has not corrected as much as have other global markets, during the phase of European debt crisis. The recent healthy correction in the stock markets is happening constantly trembling under the fear of worsening of the European crisis and a possibility of a double dip recession in the US.

Indian banking system has, however, not been impacted by current crisis as it does not have any significant presence in countries impacted by the current crisis nor Indian banks have any significant exposures to bonds issued by them. While there is no first order impact of the sovereign debt crisis, there could, however, be second-order impact through various channels including trade. There could be funding constraints for Indian bank branches operating overseas if European banks deleverage. The cost of borrowing for banks and corporates may, therefore, go up leading to concerns over refinancing foreign currency liabilities. Due to the slump in the overseas demand and the associated downturn in investment activity, there has already been some sluggishness in the credit as well as asset growth of Indian banking sector during 2011-12.

The crisis also had a measurable impact on the Indian financial markets, with equity prices witnessing sharp decline on account of large net sales by FIIs in the backdrop of worsening macroeconomic environment and bearish outlook on earning growth of Indian corporates. Further, moderation in capital flow coupled with widening trade deficit led to a sharp fall in the INR-USD exchange rate to touch an all time low of ` 54.30 on December 15, 2011.

Reserve Bank has taken a number of measures to contain the excessive volatility in the foreign exchange market. The prudential measures undertaken with a view to contain speculative activities included disallowing rebooking of cancelled forward transactions (involving the Rupee as one of the currencies which are booked to hedge current account transactions regardless of the tenor and capital account transactions falling due within one year), reduction in Net Overnight Open Position Limits of Authorised Dealer (AD) banks, curtailment in limit for cancellation of forward contracts booked on the basis of past performance route by the importers, prohibiting passing of exchange gains to the customers on cancellation of forward contracts booked under past performance route, disallowing FIIs to rebook cancelled forward contracts, stipulating all cash/tom/spot transactions to be delivery/ remittance based. With a view to encouraging inflows, measures such as raising the limits on FII investments in debt securities, further liberalisation of ECB policy, relaxation of interest rate ceilings on NRI and NRO deposits, have been taken.

[v] In the current episode, the troubles in Europe initially resulted in the drop in price of oil and going forward the oil price is not expected to rise sharply until the uncertainty about the European crisis persists which should result in savings for rising oil import bill.

Governance

India has emerged as the fourth largest economy globally with a high growth rate and has also improved its global ranking in terms of per capita income (as mentioned earlier). Yet the fact remains that its per capita income continues to be quite low (at current US $ 1527 in 2011). Nevertheless, India has a diverse set of factors, domestic as well as external, that could drive growth well into the future. Yet ,the euro crisis had a quick indirect impact toward adverse direction for which Planning commission had continually revised downward and now fixed to 6% only. In the Fig-11.4, how India and other countries reacted to GDP growth is given below. The Euro crisis has indirectly affected growth rate not only in Euro Area but also in other countries as well eg, India, China, Brazil, Japan, and USA where steady decline were observed since the beginning of the crisis although Russia and Japan revived the rate from the second quarter of 2011 and all other countries could not revive the rates which were initially targeted.

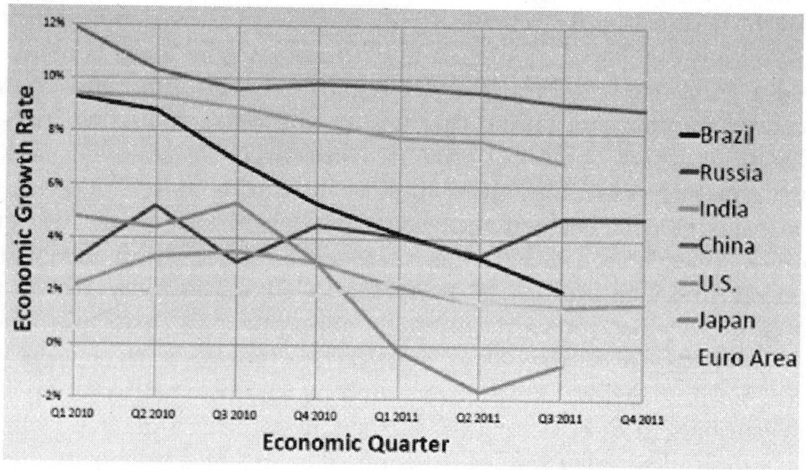

Fig-11.4: Impact on GDP growth during EU crisis
Source: IMF

It is observed that in majority cases there is a positive relation between the world economic growth and India's export growth. Any decrease (increase) in the world GDP has been reflected in India's trade with a fall (rise) in the exports. Two exceptions were 2006 and 2007 where the two variables were moving in opposite directions, albeit marginally. However, it comes to one's notice that the movement of India's export is directly correlated to the economic growth in the advanced economies and the euro region.

Despite the positive relation between India's exports and the world's economic activities, taking a look at the average elasticity between the two parameters shows a different picture. The average elasticity between India's exports and the word GDP is 0.29 which indicates positive low elasticity. Similarly, average elasticity between India's exports and the advanced nations or the euro region's GDP is 0.18.

Therefore it can be concluded that, with the advanced economies showing a slowdown on account of the US fiscal problem, Euro region debt crisis, Japanese unstable economy post the earth quake & tsunami and the rising inflation in the emerging economies, *India's exports are likely to be affected and the growth rate will slow down.*

After the financial crisis and even after the Euro crisis, Indian fiscal situation became more worse due to higher current account and capital account deficit.FDI inflows fell sharply, inflation up speedily and thus the fiscal deficit as percent of GDP grew uncontrolled and probably it will cross 10% in 2014-15.(Fig-11.5)

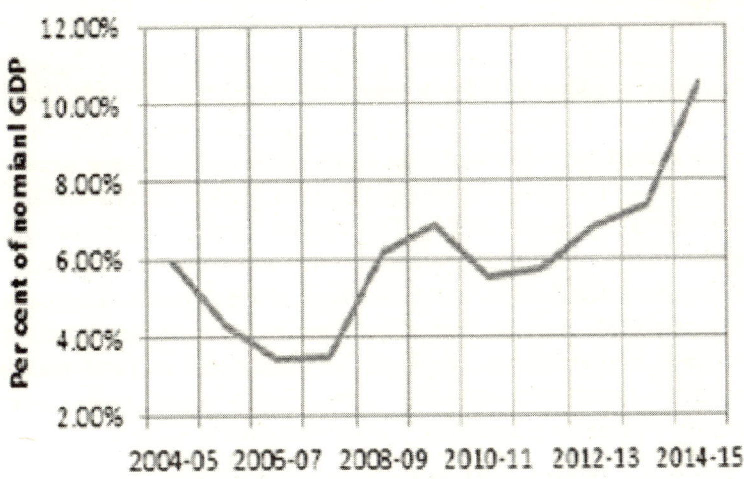

Fig-11.5: Indian Fiscal deficit % of GDP
Source: RBI Bulletin

To counter the international financial crisis which had immediately stepped up India's inflation and depreciation of rupee, RBI has increased repo rate and reverse repo rate and increasing bank rate but reduced CRR to protect financial scenario of India. These policies made Indian banking in a healthy situation (Table-11.9).

Table-11.9:Key rates/ratios

Rate	2009	2010	2011	2012
Repo	4.75	6.25	8.25	8.5
Reverse repo	3.25	5.25	7.25	7.5
Msf rate	9.25	9.25	9.25	9.5
Crr	6.00	6.00	6.00	5.5
Bank rate	6.00	6.00	6.00	9.50

Source: rbi bulletin

The impact of the current financial crisis on Indian banks may be limited as they do not have much exposure to vulnerable countries. However, with the worsening of the European crisis, the Indian banking industry may be impacted as trade with European markets slows down. As liquidity pressures rise, Indian banks and companies will face challenges in refinancing their foreign currency liabilities. The European banks which have been actively participating in funding Indian companies through external commercial borrowings (ECBs) and trade credit over the last two years have a significant exposure to India. As per the latest Financial Stability Report published by the Reserve Bank of India (RBI), European banks' claim on India constituted 8.6% of GDP. However, some analysts estimate that the figure may have reached 15% of GDP. As European banks de-leverage, Indian companies will be forced to borrow from Indian banks at a higher cost, and domestic liquidity would need to refinance the shrinking overseas debt of Indian firms. This will put pressure on to the already tightening liquidity scenario in India.

In the Table-11.10, we found that India's current account deficit had increased and FDI declined including portfolios, and even foreign exchange reserves dwindled to a large extent after the Euro crisis.

The foreign exchange reserves and capital flows have been given in details in Table-11.11.

Table-11.10: Balance of Payments summary (US million dollar)

Sl. No.	Item	2006-07	2007-08	2008-09	2009-10	2010-11 PR	2010-11 H1 (April-Sept. 2010) PR	2011-12 H1 (April-Sept. 2011) P
1	2	3	4	5	6	7	8	9
I	**Current Account**							
1	Exports	128888	166162	189001	182442	250468	107331	150909
2	Imports	190670	257629	308520	300644	381061	176213	236674
3	Trade balance	-61782	-91467	-119519	- 118203	-130593	-68883	-85765
4	Invisibles (net)	52217	75731	91604	80022	84647	39283	52923
	a Non-factor services	29469	38853	53916	36016	48816	21517	31060
	b Income	-7331	-5068	-7110	-8038	-17309	-8238	-9025
	c Transfers	30079	41945	44798	52045	53140	26004	30887
5	Goods & services balance	-32313	-52614	-65603	-82187	-81777	-47366	-54705
6	Current account balance	-9565	-15737	-27914	-38181	-45945	-29599	-32842
II	**Capital Account**							
1	Capital account balance	45203	106585	7395	51634	61989	38950	41061
	i External assistance (net)	1775	2114	2439	2890	4941	3036	705
	i External commercial borrowings (net)	16103	22609	7861	2000	12506	5674	10592
	iii Short-term debt	6612	15930	-1985	7558	10990	6937	5940
	iv Banking capital (net)	1913	11759	-3245	2083	4962	839	19344
	of which Non-resident deposits (net)	4321	179	4290	2922	3238	2163	3937
	v Foreign investment (net)	14753	43326	8342	50362	39652	30836	13657
	of which							
	a FDI (net)	7693	15893	22372	17966	9360	7040	12311
	b Portfolio (net)	7060	27433	-14030	32396	30293	23796	1346
	vi Rupee debt service	-162	-122	-100	-97	-68	-16	-32
	vii Other flows (net)	4209	10060	6916	-13162	-10994	-8356	-9145
III	**Errors and omissions**	968	1316	440	-12	-2993	-2320	-2500
IV	**Overall balance**	**36606**	**92164**	**-20080**	**13441**	**13050**	**7030**	**5719**
V	**Reserves [increase (-) / decrease (+)]**	(-) 36606	(-) 92164	20080	(-) 13441	(-)13050	(-)7030	(-)5719

Source : RBI. *Notes* : PR: Partially Revised. P: Preliminary.

FDI inflows in India during 2011-12 (Apr-Sept) increased by 74% to $19,136 million from $11,005 million for the same period last year. FDI inflows peaked to $5,656 million in Jun 2011 and declined thereafter. Mauritius has been the top investing country in India through FDI in equity, with a historical share of around 41%. Considering the share of euro zone in FDI equity inflows for cumulative period of Apr 2000 to Feb 2011 was 14.7% with share of Netherlands, Cyprus and Germany has been around 4.4% and 3.7% and 2.9% respectively. The share of the other euro zone countries has been marginal. Further, the share of the euro countries in distress namely, Italy (0.7%), Spain (0.6%) and Greece (0%) together contribute a marginal share of 1.3% to India's FDI flows. Hence, it can be drawn that euro zone slowdown would not have a significant impact on the

India economy. In analyzing the Table-11.12 where the FDI inflows and outflows from EU to India were shown, we can see that the world financial crisis and beginning of the Euro crisis, the capital flows from EU to India had tremendously fallen however small it was in comparison to the percent of the total flows.

Table-11.11: Foreign exchange Reserves on BOP(US$ billion)

Sl. No.	Items	2009-10	2010-11PR	April-September 2010-11PR	April-September 2011-12P
1	2	3	4	5	6
I	**Current account balance**	-38.2	- 45.9	-29.6	-32.8
II	**Capital account (net) (a to f)**	51.6	62.0	38.9	41.1
	a Foreign investment (i+ii)	50.4	39.7	30.8	13.6
	(i) FDI	18.0	9.4	7.0	12.3
	(ii) Portfolio investment	32.4	30.3	23.8	1.3
	of which:				
	FIIs	29.0	29.4	22.3	0.9
	ADRs/GDRs	3.3	2.0	1.6	0.5
	b ECBs	2.0	12.5	5.7	10.6
	c Banking capital	2.1	5.0	0.8	19.3
	of which: NRI deposits	2.9	3.2	2.2	3.9
	d Short-term trade credit	7.6	11.0	6.9	5.9
	e External assistance	2.9	4.9	3.0	0.7
	f Other items in capital account (includes Rupee Debt Service)	-13.3	- 11.1	-8.4	-9.2
III	**Errors and omissions**	-0.01	- 3.0	-2.3	-2.5
IV	**Overall balance (I+II+III)**	13.4	13.1	7.0	5.7
V	**Reserve change on BoP basis [increase (-) / decrease (+)]**	-13.4	- 13.1	-7.0	-5.7
VI	**Valuation change**	13.7	12.6	6.8	1.0
VII	**Total reserve change (V+VI)** (increase in reserves (+) / decrease in reserves (-)	27.1	25.7	13.8	6.7

Source : RBI. PR: Partially Revised. P: Preliminary.

India is a member of the Basel Committee on Banking Supervision (BCBS) and FSB and is actively participating in post crisis reforms of the international regulatory and supervisory framework. The Indian financial sector is well regulated and India remains committed to adopting international standards and best practices *calibrated to its conditions.* As such, banks in India are well capitalized and it is expected that the Basel III norms are unlikely to put undue pressure on the banking system on aggregate. India had even earlier implemented some countercyclical policies like provisioning norms and differential risk weights (for example for the real estate sector, capital markets, and personal loans) to control build-up of risks even before these were internationally proposed. Given its size and its profile in the global economy, India will inevitably need to play an active role at global level, not just in debates about how to resolve the continuing crisis and prevent the recurrence of similar crises in the future, but in influencing the rules for the global economy on overarching macroeconomic issues such as trade, capital flows, financial regulation, climate change, and governance of global financial institutions.

Table-11.12: EU FDI flows to India and China

	Outwards flows from the EU (billion €)				Inward flows into the EU (billion €)			
FDI partners	2007	2008	2009	2010*	2007	2008	2009	2010*
China	7.2	5.2	5.8	4.9	0.8	-0.2	0.3	0.9
Hong Kong	7.2	5.6	2.0	3.0	5.9	2.7	1.3	11.3
India	4.6	3.7	3.4	3.0	1.2	3.6	0.9	0.6
Total EU extra 27	550.7	387.3	280.6	106.7	423.8	170.7	215.7	54.2

*Preliminary data for 2010.
Source: Eurostat (June 2011).

Conclusion

In concluding remarks, we can add the summary of FICCI survey which stated the following;

[i] On the current economic crisis in Greece, Spain, Ireland, Portugal and now in Italy, there has been absolute unanimity in the surveyed companies that the ongoing crisis is the manifestation of larger issues and economic ills plaguing the European economies today.

[ii] 53% of the companies have said that the ongoing crisis has already resulted in their businesses prospects in the region adversely impacted.

[iii] The concern point is that over 75% of the surveyed companies have quoted a loss of 10- 15% in terms of business generation from the European region.

[iv] To keep their balance sheets stable, over 30% of the Indian companies surveyed have already begun to look beyond Europe. They have begun to gradually look for greener

pastures in African countries, Middle East, South Asia and even in North America.

[v] To further compound the situation, over 25% respondents have pointed out that during the current economic turmoil, rather than facilitating foreign investments and businesses, the respective European Governments have made its processes more stringent in obtaining and renewing long-term visas, work permits, family and dependent visas and overall ease of doing business in the region.

[vi] In the short to medium term, the European economic crisis is bound to impact the business prospects and the investment plans of Indian companies doing business in the region.

[vii] As the survey indicates, despite the number of policy and regulatory impediments, India's outbound investments in the EU may see smaller deals but the activity will continue. Number of Indian companies are viewing the current economic crisis as an opportunity to enhance their investments.

[viii] To maximize their benefits and to alleviate their business losses in terms of reduced demands in European markets, Indian manufacturers are aggressively pursuing new business plans. This includes increased imports of high-end machinery and technology from Europe due to highly competitive prices being offered by European exporters. This could have long-term spin-offs for Indian industry in terms of added capacities and reduced capital expenditures.

[ix] Indian companies will always be on the lookout for good buys with a strategic fit as the fundamental reasons to invest in the EU have not changed .

From the 9th GTA Report-2011,it was observed that India was given rank of 50 when imposing discriminatory measures but India ranked 369 of the tariff lines affected by discriminatory measures and India ranked 153 by the number of trading partners affected by discriminatory measures. So, Euro crisis did not harm too much to Indian economy after discriminatory measures than the other developed countries in the world .(Table-11.13).

Table-11.13: Which countries have imposed the most harm?

Rank	Ranked by number of (almost certainly) discriminatory measures imposed	Ranked by the number of tariff lines (product categories) affected by (almost certainly) discriminatory measures	Ranked by the number of sectors affected by (almost certainly) discriminatory measures	Ranked by the number of trading partners affected by(almost certainly) discriminatory measures
1	EU27 (227)	Vietnam (927)	Algeria (62)	EU27 (180)
2	Russian Federation (105)	Venezuela (785)	EU27 (58)	Argentina (175)
3	Argentina (88)	Kazakhstan (729)	Nigeria (45)	China (172)
4	UK (53)	Nigeria (599)	Kazakhstan (43)	Germany (161)
5	Germany (52)	EU27 (549)	Germany (42)	UK (154)
6	India (50)	Algeria (476)	USA (42)	Belgium (153)
7	Brazil (44)	Russian Federation (438)	China (41)	Finland (153)
8	France (44)	Argentina (413)	Indonesia (40)	India (153)
9	China (42)	Indonesia (387)	Russian Federation (39)	Indonesia (151)
10	Italy (42)	India (369)	Venezuela (38)	France (149)

Source: The 9th GTA Report, July 2011.

Lastly, with the euro area appearing to head for a recession and the global growth slowing again after a short recovery, growth in India too has moderated more than was expected earlier. Increase in global uncertainty, weak industrial growth, slow down in investment activity and deceleration in the resource flow to commercial sector led to dip in output growth. Inflation risks emanating from suppressed domestic energy prices, incomplete pass-through of rupee depreciation and slippage in fiscal deficit, further fuelled by food and commodity inflation have led to policy tightening. All these factors have resulted in the growth projection for India for 2011-12 being revised downwards from 7.6 per cent to 6.9 per cent.

References

CARE RATINGS,2011,Impact of Euro crisis and global slowdown on India, *Global Update*, 5th December.

Christensen,Tim.,2012,Global Effects of the European Sovereign Debt Crisis.University of Iowa,*Centre for International Finance and Development.*

Crisil Rating.,2010,European Sovereign debt crisis:What Does it mean for India? *Economy View,* July.

De, Prabir and Chiranjib Neogi., 2011,Global Financial Crisis:Implications for Trade and Industrial Rerstructuring in India.*ADBI Working Paper Series no-294*,ADB Institute.

ECB,2012,*The International role of the Euro*,July.

FICCI, 2011, Current Economic Scenario in Europe and its impact on Indian Industry.*A FICCI Survey*, August.

Ghorudi,Dr.K.N.,2012,Eurozone crisis:Causes and Impact on Indian Economy.*Global Economic Research*,Vol-1,Issue-III, April-September.

GOI, 2009, Global Economic Crisis and its impact on India.Rajya Sabha Secretariat.ND,June.

GOI., 2012,*Economic Survey, 2011-12.*

Kulkerni, Suresh., 2012,The Eurozone crisis and its impact on India. *Kaleidoscope*, Vol-32,No-2, July.

Kumar G S, Aneesh and GS Gireesh Kumar.,2012,Global Financial crisis and impact on Indian Economy.THAVAN *IJREB*,Vol-1, No-2,Jan-Mar.

Prasad, A. and C.Panduranga Reddy., 2009, Global financial crisis and its impact on India, *Journal of Social Science*, 21(1):1-5

Rangasamy, Elango., 2012,Sovereign debt crisis in the Euro zone and its impact on the BRIC,s stock index returns and volatility. *Economics and Finance Review*,Vol-2(2), 37-46, April

Ratho,Aditi., 2012, Plans for the BRICS Delhi Summit, March 29.*BRICS Research Group*

Sinha,Ananda., 2012,Changing Contours of Global crisis-Impact on Indian Economy.BIS Central Bankers' Speech, IIM Kashipur, February.

............., 2012, Changing Contours of Global crisis-Impact on Indian Economy.*RBI Monthly Bulletin*, April.

TRAIDCRAFT,2009,The wrong direction:Why the EU-India from Trade Agreement will not help India through the economic crisis. March

Vergeron, Karine Lisbonne-de., 2011, *Chinese and Indian views of Europe since crisis:New perspectives from the emerging Asian Giants.* Konrad Adenauer Stiftung and the Global Policy Institute, UK.

CHAPER 12

INTERNATIONAL ROLE OF EURO

Introduction

The Euro has been playing as international currency next to US dollar since long and also has a significant role in SDR. With out Euro,the international payments mechanism is to be considered incomplete.Yet, the international role of the euro was relatively resilient in 2011when compared with other major international currencies, despite the impact of the euro area sovereign debt crisis on some financial market segments and foreign investors' reduced appetite for the securities issued by a number of euro area Member States. The international role of the euro is primarily the outcome of market forces. The ECB will continue to monitor developments and disseminate information to the public on a regular basis.

MAIN FINDINGS

[a] Development in the International Role of the Euro in 2011

In 2011, particularly the second half of the year, the financial system of Euro zone was strongly affected by the intensification of the sovereign debt crisis. Risk premia for certain sovereigns and financial institutions increased, while the most distressed euro area issuers found it increasingly difficult to access primary markets. Money market conditions deteriorated significantly in the second half of 2011, after temporarily easing in the first half of the year .At the same time, euro area bond markets showed increasing signs of segmentation across euro area countries in the second half of 2011.In order to ensure that euro area banks had access to adequate funding liquidity, the Governing Council of the ECB decided to reintroduce 12-month refinancing operations and conduct two 36-month refinancing operations and significantly extended the collateral base. It also decided to continue using fixed rate tender procedures with full allotment in its main and special-term refinancing operations. In this challenging environment, the international role of the euro remained relatively resilient in relatively stable exchange rates against the other major reserve currencies until end-2011. In particular, the euro's share in global foreign exchange reserves remained around 25% at end-2011. The data of non-euro area central banks' reserves suggests that the euro area sovereign debt crisis had composition effects within the segment of euro-denominated reserves, as evident in the divergence of government bond yields across euro area countries. In international debt markets, foreign demand for euro-denominated debt securities remained stable in the first half of 2011 (Table-12.1), but declined moderately towards the end of 2011.The euro's share in the "narrow measure" of international debt securities, i.e. those issued by non-residents declined further in 2011 (Table-12.1).

The first main theme is the impact of the global financial crisis, which is considered from two different angles: [i] from the perspective of issuers of international currencies, analysing foreigners' demand for their securities during periods of financial turbulence; and [ii]from the perspective of emerging markets, where international currencies are widely used for domestic lending, looking at whether unofficial euroisation/dollarization exacerbated the crisis. The second main theme is the changing landscape of the international currencies, which could progressively see a shift towards a multipolar system in which emerging market currencies (particularly the Chinese renminbi) play a greater role. The impact is that the recent sovereign debt crisis has had on foreign investors' demand for euro area securities and potential differences compared with the period following Lehman Brothers' default. The analysis finds evidence of a sharp decline of foreign interest in government debt securities issued by particular

Table-12.1:Key data on the international role of the Euro

Indicator	Share of the euro (percentages, unless otherwise indicated)			Total outstanding amounts (USD billions, unless otherwise indicated)		
	Latest	Comparison period	Difference (percentage points)	Latest	Comparison period	Difference (percentages)
Stock of global foreign exchange reserves with known currency composition, at constant exchange rates	25.0 *(Q4 2011)*	25.4 *(Q4 2010)*	-0.4	5,646 *(Q4 2011)*	5,158 *(Q4 2010)*	9.5
International debt securities: global measure, i.e. including home currency issuance, at constant exchange rates	25.7 *(Q4 2011)*	25.7 *(Q4 2010)*	0.0	98,388 *(Q4 2011)*	95,196 *(Q4 2010)*	3.4
International debt securities: narrow measure, i.e. including home currency issuance, at constant exchange rates	25.5 *(Q4 2011)*	26.8 *(Q4 2010)*	-1.3	10,965 *(Q4 2011)*	10,576 *(Q4 2010)*	3.7
Daily foreign exchange trading (settled by CLS) at current exchange rates, volumes in EUR billions	20.7 *(2011)*	19.2 *(2010)*	1.5	3,784 *(2011)*	3,146 *(2010)*	20.3
Foreign currency-denominated loans in CESEE countries, in percent of total foreign currency loans at current exchange rates	81.2 *(2011)*	80.2 *(2010)*	1.0			
Foreign currency-denominated deposits in CESEE countries, in percent of total foreign currency deposits at current exchange rates	83.3 *(2011)*	84.9 *(2010)*	-1.6			
Invoicing of goods exported from the euro area to non-euro area countries, at current exchange rates	66.7 *(2011)*	63.5 *(2010)*	3.2	... ...	... ...	... ...
Invoicing of goods imported by the euro area from non-euro area countries, at current exchange rates	50.2 *(2011)*	49.6 *(2010)*	0.6	... ...	... ...	... ...
Foreign holdings of euro area debt denominated in euro (EUR billions and as a percentage of total euro-denominated debt)	17 *(H1 2011)*	18 *(H1 2010)*	-1.0	14,434 *(H1 2011)*	13,897 *(H1 2010)*	3.9
Cumulative net shipments of euro banknotes to destinations outside the euro area (EUR billions, not seasonally adjusted)	... ...	... ...	... ...	118 *(Dec. 2011)*	107 *(Dec. 2010)*	10.3

Sources: BIS, ECB and national sources.

euro area countries and a moderate reduction for the euro area as a whole during the intensification of the crisis in the second half of 2011, contrasting with the strong resilience of foreign demand for euro area government securities in 2008. The second special feature offers a new perspective on the current global currency order. One salient feature of the international monetary system is that it is centred around the US dollar as a global reference currency and the euro as a regional bloc currency. What role does the Chinese renminbi play in this system? This analysis draws on a recent empirical study that gauges whether the international monetary system is already tri-polar and centred around the US dollar, the euro and the Chinese renminbi. It focuses on the "Chinese dominance hypothesis" – i.e. whether the renminbi is already the dominant currency in Asia, exerting considerable influence on exchange rate and monetary policies in the region, over and beyond that of the US dollar.

This hypothesis lies in the fact of "German dominance hypothesis", which suggested that the Deutsche Mark played a dominant role in European countries' monetary and exchange rate policies in the 1980s and 1990s. Empirical evidences are indeed consistent with this hypothesis, suggesting that, to some extent, the international monetary system is already on the verge of becoming tri-polar when it comes to international currencies acting as exchange rate anchors at the regional level. Indeed, a typical feature of many emerging market economies is that a significant share of assets and liabilities are denominated in foreign currencies, such as the US dollar and the euro. This may, in turn, increase financial vulnerabilities and limit the scope for macroeconomic policies to act counter-cyclically. This empirical investigation shows that unofficial euroisation/dollarization contributed significantly to the severity of the global crisis in emerging economies. Its adverse impact was transmitted mainly through heightened currency mismatches, reduced monetary policy autonomy and a limited ability to act as a lender of last resort, which imposed greater constraints in the midst of the crisis. Overall, these findings confirm that the use of foreign currencies in emerging economies can contribute to the build-up of financial stability risks and should be monitored closely by the authorities.

According to IMF data, the shares of major reserve currencies remained relatively stable throughout 2011which cover 55% global foreign exchange reserves. The euro's share in global foreign exchange reserves decreased slightly to 25.0% at the end of 2011 when adjusted for exchange rate effects (down from 25.4% at end-2010, at constant end-2011 exchange rates). During the same period the share of US dollar-denominated assets in global foreign exchange reserves remained almost stable at 62.1%, down from 62.2% at end-2010 (at constant end-2011 exchange rates), while the share of the Japanese yen slightly decreased to 3.7% from 3.9%. At the same time, the share of "other currencies" (comprising all currencies other than the special drawing right (SDR) currencies and the Swiss franc in global foreign

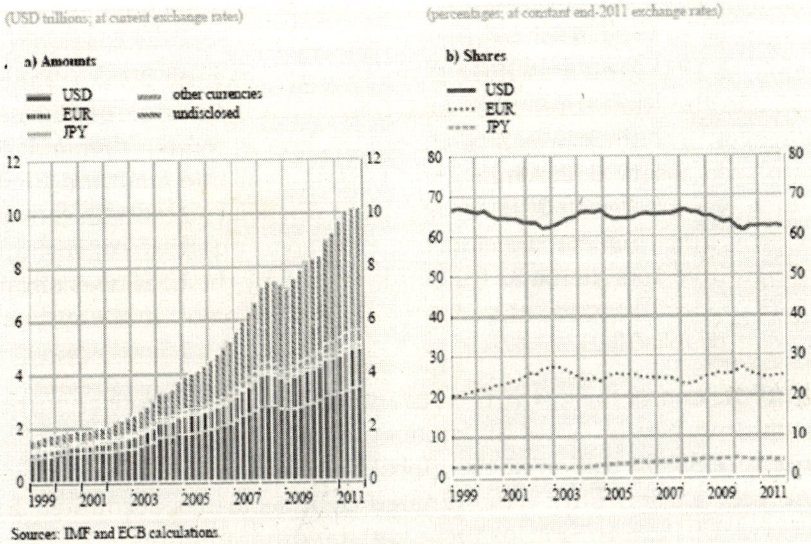

Fig-12.1: Currency composition of global foreign exchange reserves

exchange reserves rose by around half a percentage point (from 4.5% to 5.1% at end-2011) when adjusted for exchange rate effects. Among the non-euro area central banks which disclose the currency composition of their foreign exchange reserves (Table-12A.1 in Annexure), the euro's share remained relatively stable, with only a few exceptions. In accordance with this decision, Sveriges Riks bank increased the share of US government debt securities in its foreign exchange reserves, partly by selling euro-denominated assets. As a result, the euro's share declined to stand at 37% at end-2011 (down from 50% at end-2010). With the exception of the countries participating in ERM II, the decision to use the euro as an anchor currency is a unilateral one and does not involve any commitment on the part of the ECB. The US dollar, on the other hand, continues to be widely used as an exchange rate anchor both in Asia and in Central and South America.

[b] Foreign Demand for Euro Denominated Debt Securities

Foreign demand for euro-denominated debt securities remained unchanged in the first half of 2011, according data of ECB on a biannual basis. At end-June 2011 the share of euro-denominated debt securities in total debt securities held by non-euro area residents stood at 17% (down slightly from 18% at end-June 2010; (Table-12A.3 in the Annexure). Euro area financial account figures suggest, however, that there was a moderate decline in foreign demand for euro area assets at the end of 2011. Data available from the EFSF, which was created in 2010 to safeguard financial stability in Europe by providing financial assistance to euro area countries' suggest that foreign investors' demand for bonds issued by the EFSF was strong in 2011, accounting for more than half of all demand in the primary market (Table-12.2).

At the end of the Q4 2011 outstanding amounts of debt securities (including bonds, notes and money market instruments) reached around USD 98 trillion at the global level, up from USD 95 trillion one year earlier. Euro-denominated debt securities accounted for around USD 25 trillion of those outstanding amounts - 25.7% at current exchange rates (Table-12.3). When measured at constant exchange rates, this share shows remarkable stability over time, hovering between 25% and 26% over the past decade (Table-12A.2 in the Annexure). This figure, however, provides an estimate of the euro's "global" share in the debt market, including euro-denominated debt securities issued by euro-area residents and bought by euro area residents, which is a purely domestic transaction.

At the end of 2011, the total stock of debt securities stood, on the basis of this "narrow" measure, at around USD 11 trillion. Euro-denominated securities accounted for USD 2.8 trillion of that stock (- 25.5% of total outstanding amounts) (Table-12.3). At constant exchange rate, this was more than 1 percentage point lower than in the previous year, continuing a downward trend that began back in 2005 and was exacerbated by the global financial crisis (Fig. 12.2). By contrast, the US dollar's share in that narrow measure of international issuance rose further to stand at more than 50%.Moreover, it may be that the relatively large *domestic* sovereign euro area issuances since the beginning of the financial crisis, outstanding amounts of which increased from around USD 6 trillion at the end of 2008 to almost USD 8 trillion at end- 2011 (on the basis of BIS statistics) may have crowded out foreign borrowers, discouraging them from tapping the euro-denominated bond market.

Table-12.2: Primary market participation by foreign and official investors in EFSF bond issuance

Issue No	Issue date	Amount placed (EUR billions)	Maturity	Reoffer yield (percentages)	Programme country	Share of foreign investors (percentages)	Share of official investors (percentages)
1	25 Jan. 2011	5	18 July 2016	2.892	Ireland	54	44
2	15 June 2011	5	5 July 2021	3.493	Portugal	53	37
3	22 June 2011	3	5 Dec. 2016	2.825	Portugal	59	54
4	7 Nov. 2011	3	4 Feb. 2022	3.591	Ireland	45	32
5	5 Jan. 2012	3	4 Feb. 2015	1.77	Ireland (1.27); Portugal (1.73)	17	17
6	19 Mar. 2012	1.5	30 Mar. 2032	3.956	-	11	7
7	21 Mar. 2012	5	15 May 2017	2.061	-	39	11

Sources: EFSF and ECB calculations.

Table-12.3: Alternative measure of the supply of debt securities and the shares of major currencies

(fourth quarter of 2011; at current exchange rates)

	Amounts outstanding (USD billions)				Shares (percentages)		
	Total	Euro	US dollar	Japanese yen	Euro	US dollar	Japanese yen
"Narrow" measure	10,965	2,795	5,579	676	25.5	50.9	6.2
"Global" measure	98,388	25,259	37,950	15,731	25.7	38.6	16.0

Sources: BIS and ECB calculations.

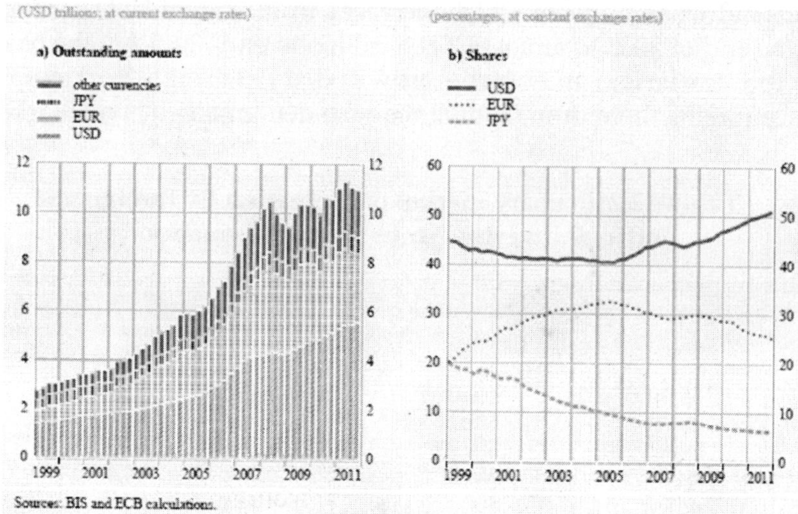

Fig.-12.2: Stock of international debt securities (narrow measure):outstanding amounts and currency shares

New forms of public debt were launched in 2011 in the euro area and EU. First, in order to fund loans to programme countries in the euro area, the European Financial Stability Facility (EFSF) issued debt with a total value of €18 billion in 2011, while the European Financial Stabilisation Mechanism (EFSM) issued debt with a total value of €28 billion. Second, in an effort to expand EU capital markets in order to finance large European infrastructure projects, a pilot phase was launched for the European Commission's Europe 2020 Project Bond Initiative. This aims to mobilise up to €4.6 billion in 2012 and 2013.

The EFSF and EFSM were both created in 2010 and are aimed at safeguarding financial stability in Europe by providing countries with financial assistance: euro area countries in the case of the EFSF; and all EU Member States in the case of the EFSM. While debt issued by the EFSF is backed by guarantees from euro area countries, debt issued by the EFSM is implicitly backed by the EU budget. The EFSM has a lending capacity of €60 billion, while the EFSF currently has a lending capacity of €440 billion. On the basis of the decisions taken at the euro area summit on 27 July 2011, the EFSF is authorised to provide financial assistance to euro area countries in financial difficulties - subject to the relevant requirements being met - by means of (i) loans; (ii) intervention in primary and secondary markets for sovereign debt; (iii) precautionary programmes; and (iv) the financing of recapitalisation for financial institutions (via loans to governments). The EFSF is currently involved in the financing of economic programmes for Ireland, Greece and Portugal.

The European Stability Mechanism (ESM) is scheduled to become operational in July 2012. The ESM will finance any new programmes for euro area countries. Although the EFSF could conceivably be involved in any new programmes beginning prior to mid-2013, it will - as a rule - only be involved in the financing of programmes beginning prior to July 2012. The maximum lending capacity of the ESM will be €500 billion, while the overall ceiling for lending by the EFSF and ESM will be €700 billion. The main difference between the EFSF and the ESM is that the ESM is established as a permanent mechanism and an intergovernmental organisation under public international law, in accordance with established IMF policies regarding private sector involvement. This implies that, in exceptional cases, an adequate and proportionate form of private sector involvement will be considered, where stability support is provided in tandem with relevant requirements in the form of a macroeconomic adjustment programme. The ESM will also have more efficient decision-making procedures, total subscribed capital of €700 billion and paid-in capital of €80 billion. This will be paid in five tranches, with paid-in capital totalling at least 15% of outstanding debt. As a result of the euro area summit decisions on 28 June 2012, it is intended that the ESM would also have the possibility to recapitalise banks directly by the end of 2012. As part of an effort to leverage the resources of the EFSF and the ESM, the European Sovereign Bond Protection Facility was approved on 17 February 2012, enabling the issuance of partial risk protection certificates in the form of insurance covering 20-30% of the principal of a sovereign bond issued by a Member State benefiting from EFSF financing. It is intended that such partial risk protection certificates will be used primarily in the context of precautionary EFSF programmes. Another leveraging option envisaged for the purchase of bonds in the primary and secondary markets is the establishment of co-investment funds under the European Sovereign Bond Investment Facility, with the EFSF/ ESM financing a first-loss tranche. This would allow a combination of private and public funding.

In foreign exchange markets, available data on average daily settlement values in CLS (Fig- 12.3) show that foreign exchange transactions, after a significant decline in 2008, began rising again in 2009 and finally surpassed their pre-crisis levels in July 2010. Since then, settlement values have kept rising, notwithstanding some interim volatility. The currency composition of trades settled in CLS remains stable: the US dollar was the counterpart in 90% of all currency exchanges, confirming its role as the main vehicle currency in foreign exchange markets, while the euro's share remains at 40%.

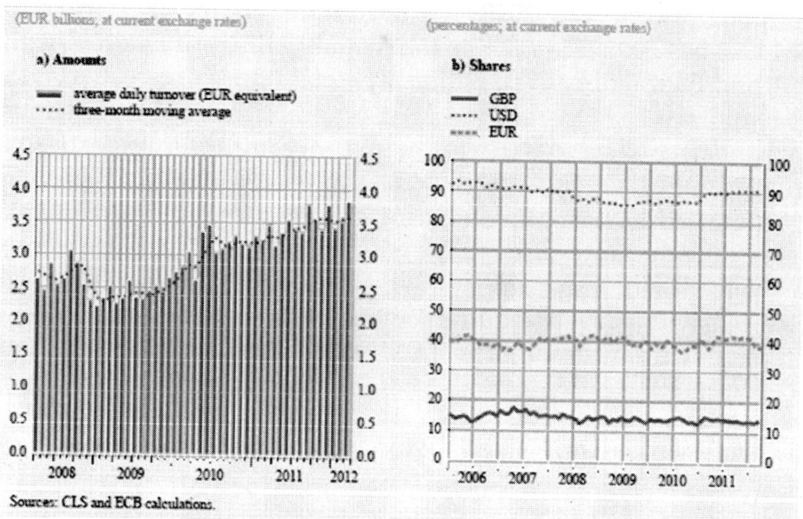

Fig-12.3: Settlement volumes and currency breakdown in the CLS system

The use of euro banknotes outside the euro area cannot be estimated with complete precision. One estimate of the amount of euro banknotes circulating abroad (published on a regular basis in this report) is based on the accumulation over time of net shipments of euro banknotes by euro area monetary financial institutions (MFIs) to destinations outside the euro area. On the basis of this method, some €117 billion worth of euro banknotes (after adjusting for seasonal effects) are estimated to have been in circulation outside the euro area at the end of December 2011 (Fig- 12.4). This was around 13% of the total euro currency in circulation in that month. This estimate is regarded as a clear lower bound, given that the banking channel is just one of a number of channels through which euro banknotes leave and re-enter the euro area.

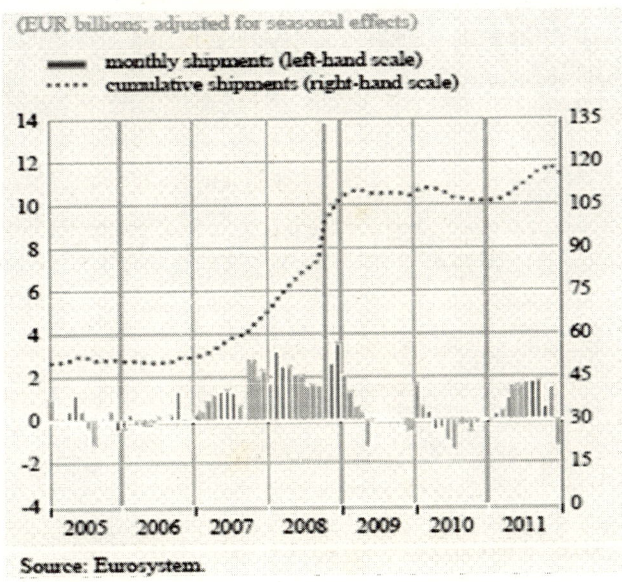

Fig-12.4: Net shipments of Euro banknotes to destinations outside the euro area.

Further evidence on the holdings of euro currency abroad can be derived from statistics provided by the monetary authorities of non-euro area countries. For example, the Central Bank of Russia publishes data on foreign currency brought into and taken out of the Russian Federation by authorised banks. These statistics show that net shipments of euro banknotes to Russia increased slightly in 2011 (Chart 12.5), following persistent net outflows during most of 2009 and 2010. However, the increase in euro banknotes held by Russian residents in 2011 remained below the average levels observed prior to Lehman Brothers' default. These data also reveal that the euro area sovereign debt crisis did not lead Russian residents to replace euro banknotes with US dollar banknotes in 2010.

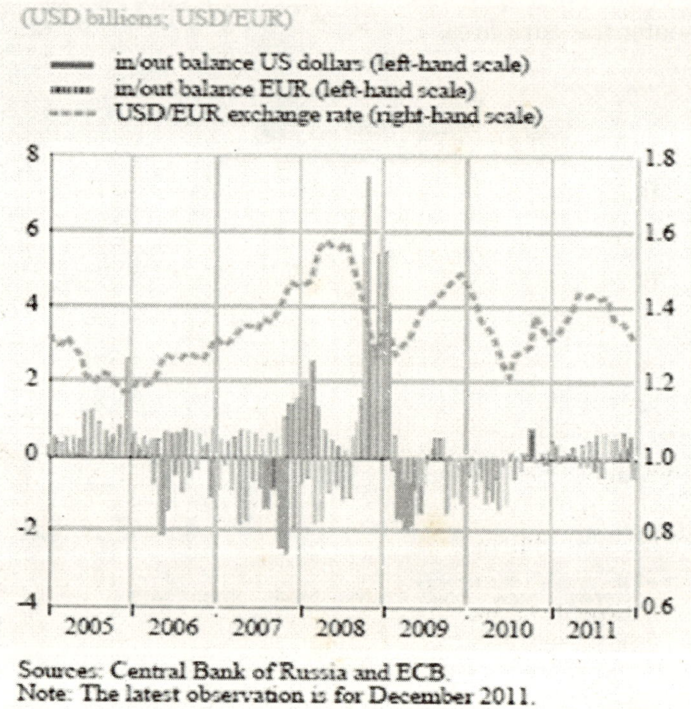

Fig-12.5: Foreign currency brought into and taken out of the Russian Federation by authorized banks.

The latest survey, which was conducted in autumn 2011, suggests that attitudes towards the euro on the part of households in central, eastern and south-east Europe may have been affected by the sovereign debt crisis. Among households participating in the survey, agreement with the statement "The euro will be a very stable and trustworthy currency over the next five years." declined in all countries relative to spring 2011 (Fig- 12.5).

[c] Foreigners' Appetite for Euro Area Securities During the Sovereign debt Crisis

The analysis finds evidence of a reallocation of foreign demand from euro area high-yield sovereign issuers towards euro area low-yield sovereign issuers, which was particularly pronounced during the euro area sovereign debt crisis in the second half of 2011 relative to the Lehman Brothers' default. For the euro area as a whole, foreign demand for euro area government debt securities was resilient in the face of the global shock in 2008, but declined in the last two quarters of 2011. Interestingly, the pattern of foreign demand for US and Japanese government debt securities is the mirror image of that for the euro area, declining in the aftermath of Lehman Brothers' default, but rising in 2011. This suggests that the response of foreign investors to the idiosyncratic shock to the euro area was indeed different from the previous global shock, lessening their appetite for euro area securities, in particular those of the high-yield sovereign issuers. Fig-12.6 shows total euro area liabilities for bonds, notes and equities over time. As noted, the flows from the balance of payments are scaled by the total stock of liabilities in each category, so that the shocks to the series in each period are comparable across different asset classes. Over the past decade, within portfolio inflows for the euro area, long-term debt securities have outpaced claims represented by equity securities. To provide some idea of the amounts involved, since 2001 the total stock of euro area portfolio liabilities has averaged €5.2 trillion (standing at €7.7 trillion at the end of 2011), of which equity liabilities have averaged €2.3 trillion (standing at €3.1 trillion at the end of 2011) and long-term debt securities have averaged €2.6 trillion (standing at €4.1 trillion at the end of 2011). Since 2001 quarterly equity flows have averaged around €33 billion, an average of 1.7% of the stock of equity liabilities, whereas quarterly flows for long-term debt securities have averaged €56 billion, an average of 2.6% of the stock of long-term debt securities.

In Fig-12.6, the two series are plotted against the VIX, a measure of the implied volatility of options on the Standard & Poor's 500 index and a good proxy for global risk and global risk aversion. This allows us to obtain a preliminary assessment of how foreigners' net demand for euro area securities behaved during these two periods of heightened financial market volatility.

In general, foreigners are net buyers of long term debt securities issued by euro area residents. However, foreigners retreated from the euro area bond market in the aftermath of Lehman Brothers' default, particularly in the fourth quarter of 2008, which corresponds to the largest negative spike in the series and an outflow of capital related to this asset category. In addition, since 2008, foreign purchases of euro area debt securities are generally below the average. Similarly, prior to mid-2007 foreigners were net buyers of equity securities issued by euro area residents. However, these equity flows then turn negative, suggesting capital outflows from the euro area at roughly the same time as the various crisis periods: the third quarter of 2007, when the liquidity crunch first became apparent; between the second quarter of 2008 and the first quarter of 2009, with a particularly protracted decline coinciding with the collapse of Lehman Brothers; and mid-2011, the second, sharper phase of the euro area sovereign debt crisis. It is therefore clear that foreigners display home bias during periods of financial turmoil.

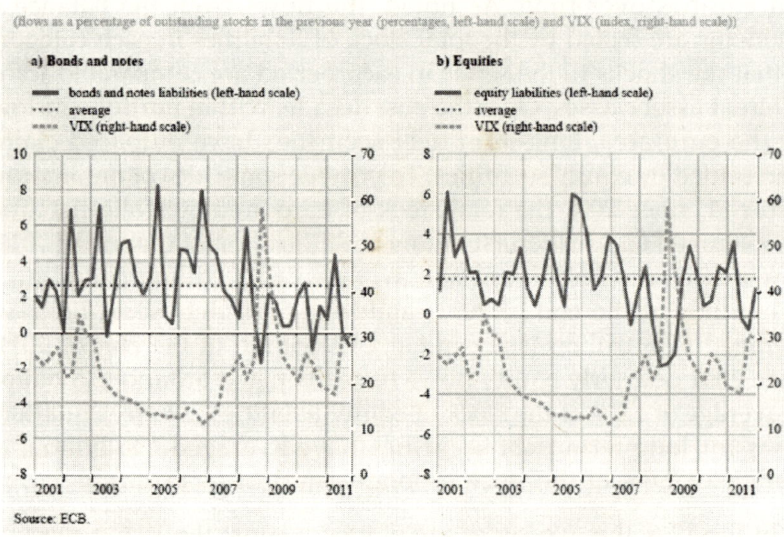

Fig–12.6: Euro Area Profile Liabilities(Q1-2001-Q42011)

Fig- 12.7 presents evidence on government liabilities held by non-residents, as recorded in the balance of payments, for the euro area as a whole (excluding intra-euro area flows), for high-yield and low-yield euro area sovereign issuers (aggregating national data, which include intra-euro area transactions), and for the United States and Japan (with data on Switzerland not available). Two stylised facts emerge from these data. First, euro area government securities continued to attract foreign interest during the Lehman Brothers' crisis, but there were large outflows from the government bonds of high-yield sovereign issuers of the euro area and an overall small outflow for the euro area as a whole during the recent euro area sovereign debt crisis. This confirms that the response of foreign investors to the idiosyncratic shock hitting the euro area was indeed different from the global shock in 2008. Second, the pattern of foreign demand for US and Japanese government debt securities is the mirror image of that for the euro area, declining in the aftermath of Lehman Brothers' default, but rising in 2011. The outflow of foreign investors from US government securities in the wake of Lehman Brothers' default is somewhat surprising, if compared to the euro area or Switzerland during the same episode. This suggests that the compression of government bond yields in the United States, which is often viewed as evidence of the safe-haven status of US Treasuries, may be the result of US residents displaying home bias, repatriating funds from abroad during such episodes, rather than a result of foreign investors buying US securities.

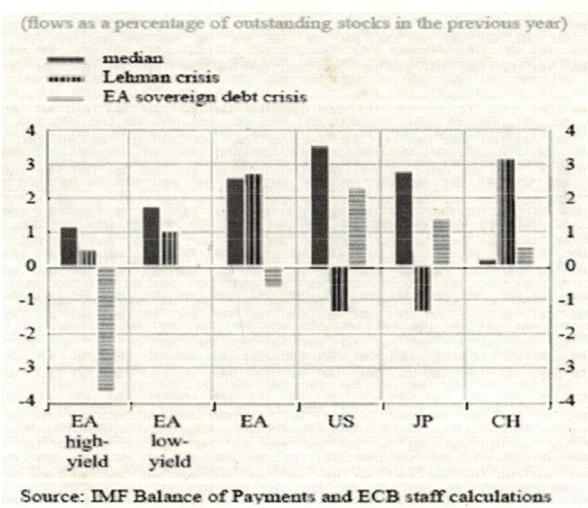

Fig-12.7 : External Liabilities: government bonds and notes(Q1 2001-Q4 2011 and crisis periods)

The patterns of flows are partly different when looking at total external holdings of bonds and notes, including private sector liabilities and equity liabilities. In the case of total long term debt securities (Fig- 12.8, Panel A), foreigners also withdrew from the euro area (particularly the high-yield countries) following Lehman Brothers' default. It is also interesting to note that, in all countries, net purchases of debt securities by foreigners, even where they remain positive, are always smaller than the median values for the sample as a whole, suggesting a declining appetite for foreign assets, irrespective of the country. This is further confirmation of the sharp increase in home bias described by Milesi- Ferretti and Tille (2011). In conclusion, these results confirm the special role of government debt securities during periods of rising global financial volatility, particularly for the euro area. Unsurprisingly, the same pattern of retrenchment of foreigners is magnified when looking at equity liabilities, a riskier asset class (Fig-12.8, Panel B). Foreigners appear to have shunned euro area and Japanese stock markets, particularly in the wake of Lehman Brothers' default, while remaining more neutral as regards

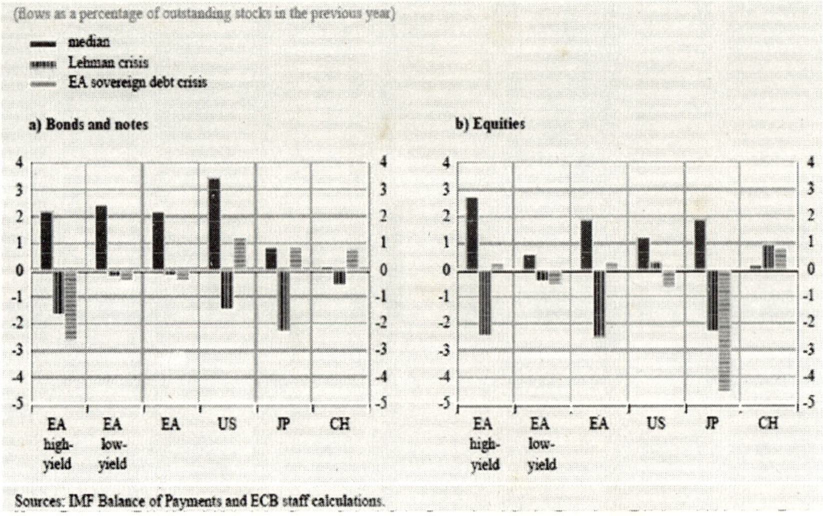

Fig-12.8 : External Portfolio Liabilities (Q1 2001-Q42011 and crisis period)

the United States. One interesting result is the increase, in times of considerable global financial market volatility, in foreigners' claims on Swiss equity. In the last two quarters of 2008 and 2011, foreigners' claims totalled around 1% of the outstanding amount of Swiss equity liabilities, a level higher than in normal periods . This atypical pattern, compared to other economies, is probably due to Switzerland's importance as a major international financial centre and, in particular, the weight of shares and units of investment funds and special-purpose entities based in Switzerland on the liability side of the financial account.

[d] The Chinese Dominance Hypothesis and the Potential Emergence of a Tripolar Global Currency System

A salient feature of the international monetary system is that it is centred around the US dollar as a global reference currency and the euro as a regional currency. At the Cannes summit of November 2011, G20 leaders made a commitment to work together to ensure that the international monetary system better reflects the increased weight of emerging market economies. This special feature draws on a recent empirical study that gauges whether the international monetary system is already tri-polar and centred around the US dollar, the euro and the Chinese renminbi. It focuses on the "Chinese dominance hypothesis" - i.e. the question of whether the renminbi is already the dominant currency in Asia, exerting considerable influence on exchange rate and monetary policies in the region. This hypothesis can, in turn, be traced back to the old "German dominance hypothesis", which ascribed to the Deutsche Mark a dominant role in Europe in the 1980s and 1990s. This special feature presents empirical findings which are consistent with this hypothesis, thus indicating that the international monetary system is already on the verge of becoming tri-polar when it comes to international currencies acting as exchange rate anchors at the regional level. This may not yet be the case when it comes to other aspects of international currency use - not least owing to the fact that China's capital account remains largely closed, which in turn limits the international use of the renminbi.

THE "NEW VIEW"

However, recent studies, referred to by Frankel (2011) as the "new view", have challenged this conventional account. Eichengreen and Flandreau (2009), relying on new data on the currency composition of global foreign exchange reserves, show that the US dollar overtook the pound sterling as the leading reserve currency as early as the mid-1920s - i.e. more than two decades earlier than was previously thought.

The "new view" also challenges the broader implications of the conventional narrative. First, it suggests that inertia and the advantages of incumbency are not as significant as they were previously thought to be. Moreover, it challenges the notion that there is room for only one international currency in the global system: on the contrary, the pound sterling and the US dollar accounted for roughly equal shares of global foreign exchange reserves throughout the 1920s. Finally, the "new view" challenges the assumption that, once lost, dominance is gone forever. Indeed, Eichengreen and Flandreau's data indicate that the pound sterling regained its dominant position for a brief period after 1931. This reinforces the point that the advantages of incumbency in the competition for reserve currency status may be less significant than is commonly thought. In a companion piece, Eichengreen and Flandreau (2010) show that what was true of reserve currencies was also true of the use of currencies for the financing of international trade. The US dollar overtook the pound sterling as the leading form of trade credit (as the currency of denomination for what were then known as "trade acceptances" or "bankers' acceptances") as early as the mid-1920s - not after the Second World War, as had been thought. The United States achieved this from a standing start - i.e. despite the fact that US dollar-denominated trade credits had been virtually unknown as recently as 1914.

Both market forces (i.e. the development of its financial markets) and policy support (with the Federal Reserve System acting as a market maker in the New York market for bankers' acceptances) were instrumental in helping the US dollar to overtake the pound sterling. Some critics have questioned the "new view". Ghosh, Ostry and Tsangarides (2011) suggest that the interwar gold standard was special in that gold – not foreign exchange – was the dominant reserve asset, accounting for some two-thirds of international reserves. The fact that gold played a significant monetary role at that time, but plays only a small one today, may limit the inferences regarding prospective changes in international currency status that can be drawn from this earlier episode. Forbes (2012) suggests that international financial transactions may now play a larger role in driving the decision as to which unit or units to use internationally, while goods transactions and the importance of a currency or market as a source of trade credit play a correspondingly smaller one. Thus, inferences regarding the future are also less convincing insofar as they are drawn from the past behaviour of trade credit, rather than the use of currencies in international financial transactions. Chiþu, Eichengreen and Mehl (2012) showed that, ignoring Commonwealth countries, the US dollar overtook the pound sterling as early as 1929 – at least 15 years earlier than the dates cited in previous accounts (Fig- 12.9, Panel A). Even including Commonwealth countries, which were wedded to the pound sterling for political and institutional reasons, the US dollar was already within hailing distance of sterling as a currency of denomination for international bonds by the late 1920s (Fig- 12.9, Panel B). Second, this new evidence also challenges the assumption that, once international monetary leadership is lost, it is gone forever. Indeed, although the pound sterling lost its leading position in the 1920s, it recovered after 1933 and was neck and neck with the US dollar at the end of that decade. And third, this new evidence challenges the assumption that there is room for only one dominant international currency owing to strong network externalities and economies of scope. In the 1920s and the 1930s international debt markets were characterised by a bipolar currency system, not a unipolar one. This is true even if account is taken of Commonwealth countries, which strongly favoured the pound sterling for institutional and political reasons.

As regards the determinants of these developments, the authors' empirical estimates point to the development of US financial markets as the main factor that helped the US dollar to overcome the pound sterling's incumbency advantage. According to their estimates, with the ratio of US banking assets to GDP rising from 70% to 100% of GDP between 1918 and 1932, the US dollar's share in global foreign public debt would have risen by almost 50 percentage points ceteris paribus (Fig- 12.10, Panel A). However, the impact of finance on international currency shares in global debt markets worked both ways during the interwar period. In particular, the authors find that the collapse of the US banking system and subsequent financial retrenchment was the most important factor contributing to the decline in the US dollar's share in global foreign public debt between 1932 and 1939. In the case of the United Kingdom, economic stagnation (i.e. declines in its relative economic size) was the most important factor accounting for the pound sterling's declining share over the period in question (Fig- 12.10, Panel B).

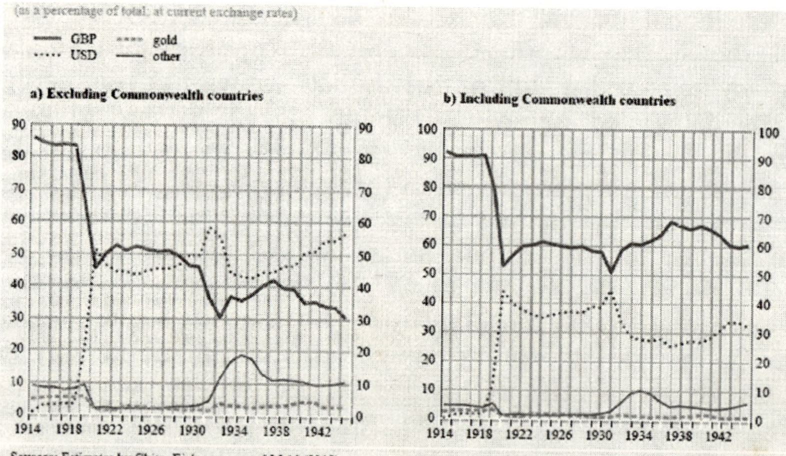

Sources: Estimates by Chițu, Eichengreen and Mehl (2012).
Note: This chart shows developments over time in the shares of the pound sterling, the US dollar, gold and other currencies in the global stock of foreign public debt between 1914 and 1946, based on a 28-country sample which excludes the Commonwealth countries India, Australia, Canada, New Zealand and South Africa.

Sources: Estimates by Chițu, Eichengreen and Mehl (2012).
Note: This chart shows developments over time in the shares of the pound sterling, the US dollar, gold and other currencies in the global stock of foreign public debt between 1914 and 1946, based on a 33-country sample.

Fig-12.9 : Global foreign public debt-selected currency shares

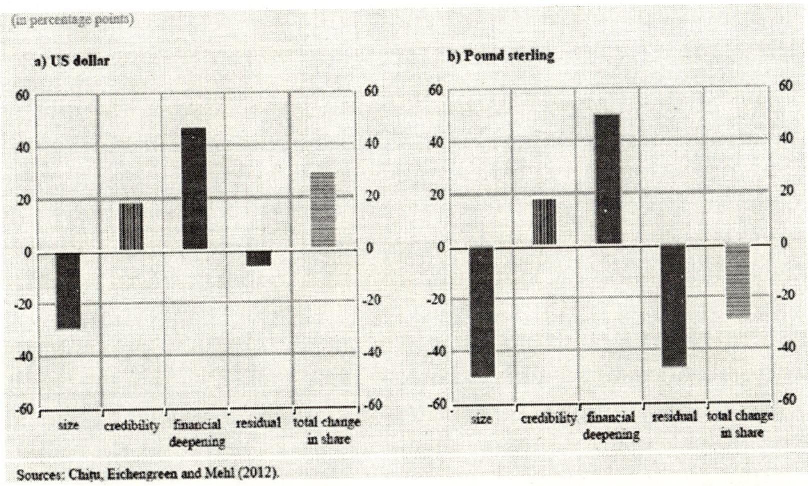

Fig-12.10 : Estimated contributions to changes in the shares of the US dollar and the pound sterling in global foreign public debt between 1918 and 1932.

[e] Was Unofficial Dollarisation/Euroisation an Amplifier of the Global Crisis of 2007-09 in Emerging Economies?

A typical feature of many emerging market economies is that a significant share of their assets and liabilities are denominated in foreign currencies, such as the US dollar and the euro, which is known as "unofficial dollarization/ euroisation". This may, in turn, increase financial vulnerabilities and limit the scope for macroeconomic policies to act counter cyclically. This special feature 30 draws on a recent empirical study which, building on a novel dataset, investigates whether - and if so, why - unofficially dollarised/euroised economies were harder hit by the recent global financial and economic crisis. It shows that conditional unofficial dollarisation/euroisation did indeed contribute to the severity of the global crisis in emerging economies. This adverse impact was transmitted mainly through heightened currency mismatches, reduced monetary policy autonomy and a limited ability to act as a lender of last resort, which became more binding constraints in the midst of the crisis. Unofficial dollarisation/

euroisation played a role in amplifying the severity of the Great Recession.

All of the major costs traditionally associated with unofficial dollarisation/euroisation became more apparent during the crisis. The key role found for currency mismatches as a transmission channel to the real economy of the adverse effects of loan dollarisation/euroisation gives support to the so-called "Fischer view", according to which a temporary tightening of monetary policy is not necessarily detrimental to growth in unofficially dollarised/euroised economies, as it can help to stabilise the exchange rate, thereby preventing the materialisation of adverse balance sheet effects. Overall, the findings presented here suggest that the use of foreign currencies in emerging economies can create financial stability risks and limit the scope for counter-cyclical policies.

Conclusion

In spite of resilient in international role of euro since the euro crisis, we cannot expect the collapse of euro zone and the abolition of the common currency euro if the deficiency of the convergence process is to be corrected gradually so far as statistical evidences of the euro area is concerned.

This view can be supported by Roth, Felix and others,(2012) who showed that the financial and sovereign debt crisis that started in Europe in 2008 has not affected popular support for the euro within the euro area. This finding is in contrast to the dramatic fall in public trust and support for European institutions, the European Union per se and in particular the ECB, the central bank issuing the euro. At the aggregate level, support for the euro can be explained adopting a popularity function approach, stressing the role of inflation and growth, when the economy runs smoothly as in normal times. During the recent crisis, only inflation still appears to drive the support for the euro. Furthermore, they find no evidence that omitted variables (exchange rates, budget deficits, trust in the EU and European institutions) change their estimates.

The crisis has not reduced the support for the euro within the euro area. However, outside the euro area, the public attitude towards the euro has become significantly more critical. Outside the euro area, the crisis is taken as proof that closer monetary integration is not the route to be taken. Inside the euro area, the opposite holds.

To conclude, the European single currency, the euro, has so far enjoyed an astonishing overall support throughout the crisis, in sharp contrast to the dramatic fall in public trust in the ECB and also to the negative response among EU countries outside the euro area. This pattern is consistent with the view that Europeans in the euro area want the euro to continue to be their currency while they are critical of the policies of the ECB during the crisis.

References

Beck, R. and Rahbari, E. , 2011, "Optimal reserve composition in the presence of sudden stops", *Journal of International Money and Finance*, 30, pp. 1107-1127.

Beck, R. and Weber, S., 2011, "Should larger reserve holdings be more diversifi ed?", *International Finance*, 14, pp. 415-444.

Chiþu, L., 2012, Was unofficial dollarisation/euroisation an amplifier of the global crisis of 2007/2009 in emerging economies?, mimeo.

Chiþu, L., Eichengreen, B. and Mehl, A., 2012, "When did the dollar overtake sterling as the leading international currency? Evidence from the bond markets", *Working Paper Series*, No 1433, ECB, May.

Eichengreen, B. , 2010, *Exorbitant Privilege – The Rise and Fall of the Dollar and the Future of the International Monetary System*, Oxford University Press, December.

Eichengreen, B. and Flandreau, M., 2010, "The Federal Reserve, the Bank of England and the rise of the dollar as an international currency, 1914-39", *BIS Working Paper Series*, No 328, BIS.

ECB, 2011, "What makes a currency a safe haven", *The international role of the euro*, Frankfurt am Main, July.

ECB, 2012, *Financial integration in Europe*, Frankfurt am Main, April.

European Commission., 2011, "Introduction of the euro in the new Member States - Analytical report", *Flash Eurobarometer Series*, No 329,August.

Forbes, K., 2012, *International monetary reform*, panel discussion at the AEA Annual Meetings, Chicago, 7 January.

Forbes, K.J. and Warnock, F.E., 2011, "Capital Flow Waves: Surges, Stops, Flight, and Retrenchment", *NBER Working Paper Series*, No 17351, August.

Frankel, J., 2011, *Historical precedents for the internationalization of the RMB*, paper written for a workshop organised by the Council of Foreign Relations and the China Development Research Foundation.

Fratzscher, M. and Mehl, A., 2011, "China's Dominance Hypothesis and the Emergence of a Tri-polar Global Currency System", *CEPR Discussion Paper Series*, No 8671, November 2011.

Ghosh, A., Ostry, J. and Tsangarides, C., 2011, "Exchange rate regimes and the stability of the international monetary system", IMF *Occasional Paper Series*, No 270, IMF.

Habib, M. and L. Stracca., 2012, "The geography of safe haven portfolio flows: The case of Lehman and the European debt crisis", mimeo, European Central Bank.

Kenen, P. , 2011, "Beyond the Dollar", paper presented at AEA Allied Social Science Association meetings, Denver, Colorado.

Milesi-Ferretti, G.M. and Tille, C., 2011, "The great retrenchment: international capital flows during the global financial crisis", *Economic Policy*, April, pp. 291-346.

Mondria, J., Wu, T. and Zhang, Y., 2010, "The determinants of international investment and attention allocation: Using internet search query data", *Journal of International Economics*, 82, pp. 85-95.

Roth,Felix.,Lars Jonung and Felicitas Nowak-Lehmann D., 2012, Public support for the Single European Currency ,the Euro,1990 to 2011.Does the Financial Crisis Matter?*Working Paper No-20*,Department of Economics, School of Economics and Management,Lund University, July.

Royal Bank of Scotland, 2012, *RBS Reserve Management Trends 2012*, Risks Books,London.

Sveriges Riksbank, 2011, *Annual Report 2011*.

Van Nieuwerburgh, S. and Veldkamp, L., 2010, "Information Acquisition and Under-Diversifi cation", *Review of Economics Studies*, 77, pp. 779-805.

ANNEXURE

Table-12A.1 : Currency composition of foreign exchange reserves for selected countries

(share of the euro in total foreign exchange reserve holdings; percentages, at current exchange rates)

	2007	2008	2009	2010	2011
Non-euro area EU Member States	68.6	61.3	63.7	61.6	60.9
of which					
Bulgaria	99.1	99.1	99.1	99.6	99.9
Czech Republic	54.0	62.6	61.3	57.4	60.1
Latvia	38.8	60.5	63.1	58.3	57.0
Lithuania	96.1	97.3	96.8	98.9	94.9
Poland	36.3	33.7	36.7	35.0	30.4
Romania	67.8	63.2	65.2	67.2	77.8
Sweden	46.9	48.5	48.1	50.0	37.0
United Kingdom	64.4	40.2	63.3	59.0	59.1
Acceding and candidate countries					
Croatia	84.1	76.6	71.7	73.7	75.9
Serbia	71.1	70.3	71.9		
Turkey	55.2	46	44.6	46.5	
Other industrial countries					
Canada	47.5	40.4	41.9	40.0	37.0
Norway	44.0	48.3	47.2	36.4	36.1
Russia	38.8	40.0	33.2		
Switzerland	40.2	47.9	55.6	54.9	57.0
United States	37.9	53.7	54.0	54.2	53.5
Latin American countries					
Chile	34.8	37.3	34.8	35.2	35.5
Peru	11.9	14.9	17.4	16.8	38.0
Uruguay	12.5	9.5	2.6		

Sources: National central banks and ECB calculations.

Table-12A.2 : Outstanding international debt securities by currency

		Global measure					Narrow measure				
		Total	EUR	USD	JPY	Other	Total	EUR	USD	JPY	Other
Outstanding amounts (in USD billions, at current exchange rates, end of period)											
2000		35,491	7,386	16,986	6,208	4,911	3,390	726	1,704	471	489
2001		37,120	7,644	18,450	5,936	5,091	3,567	822	1,802	426	516
2002		42,390	9,852	19,808	6,827	5,903	4,070	1,107	1,904	411	648
2003		50,145	13,162	21,416	8,321	7,247	4,963	1,560	2,136	439	828
2004		57,997	15,672	24,073	9,400	8,852	5,848	1,969	2,392	456	1,031
2005		59,481	14,879	26,110	8,851	9,641	6,166	1,924	2,712	401	1,128
2006		67,800	18,444	28,792	8,905	11,659	7,838	2,457	3,461	413	1,507
2007		78,301	22,779	31,768	9,464	14,290	9,660	3,111	4,186	510	1,853
2008		83,084	23,618	33,917	11,831	13,717	9,615	3,098	4,295	654	1,568
2009		90,965	26,402	35,354	12,232	16,978	10,341	3,249	4,737	600	1,756
2010	Q1	89,812	25,107	35,396	12,243	17,066	10,261	3,089	4,869	583	1,721
	Q2	88,632	22,918	35,639	13,172	16,904	9,937	2,777	4,883	604	1,672
	Q3	94,288	25,725	36,223	14,039	18,301	10,596	3,060	5,056	650	1,831
	Q4	95,196	25,205	36,675	14,516	18,799	10,576	2,907	5,146	666	1,857
2011	Q1	98,094	27,164	37,208	14,284	19,438	11,026	3,117	5,332	650	1,928
	Q2	100,216	27,863	37,424	14,942	19,987	11,294	3,161	5,450	665	2,017
	Q3	98,723	26,003	37,633	15,934	19,152	11,070	2,962	5,499	692	1,917
	Q4	98,388	25,259	37,950	15,731	19,448	10,965	2,795	5,579	676	1,916
Percentages of outstanding amounts (at constant exchange rates, end of period)											
2000		100.0	24.7	40.8	22.1	12.4	100.0	25.2	42.5	17.4	14.9
2001		100.0	24.9	40.9	22.2	12.0	100.0	27.6	41.3	16.5	14.6
2002		100.0	25.1	40.9	21.6	12.4	100.0	29.6	41.3	13.7	15.5
2003		100.0	25.2	40.0	21.5	13.4	100.0	30.9	41.3	11.7	16.2
2004		100.0	24.8	40.2	20.8	14.2	100.0	32.0	40.9	10.3	16.7
2005		100.0	24.9	39.9	20.6	14.7	100.0	32.0	41.1	9.3	17.6
2006		100.0	25.2	40.1	19.1	15.6	100.0	30.4	43.6	8.0	18.0
2007		100.0	25.3	40.1	17.3	17.3	100.0	29.2	44.7	7.9	18.3
2008		100.0	26.2	40.5	16.5	16.7	100.0	30.0	44.8	8.0	17.2
2009		100.0	26.2	39.0	16.1	18.6	100.0	28.8	46.8	7.1	17.4
2010	Q1	100.0	26.3	38.7	16.1	18.8	100.0	28.7	47.2	6.8	17.3
	Q2	100.0	26.3	38.7	16.4	18.6	100.0	28.6	47.6	6.7	17.1
	Q3	100.0	26.0	38.6	16.1	19.4	100.0	27.7	48.2	6.7	17.4
	Q4	100.0	25.7	38.6	16.0	19.8	100.0	26.8	48.9	6.7	17.6
2011	Q1	100.0	25.6	38.6	15.8	20.0	100.0	26.4	49.6	6.5	17.6
	Q2	100.0	25.5	38.3	15.9	20.2	100.0	25.9	49.9	6.3	17.8
	Q3	100.0	25.6	38.6	16.2	19.6	100.0	26.0	50.4	6.3	17.4
	Q4	100.0	25.7	38.6	16.0	19.8	100.0	25.5	50.9	6.2	17.5
Percentages of outstanding amounts (at current exchange rates, end of period)											
2000		100.0	20.8	47.9	17.5	13.8	100.0	21.4	50.2	13.9	14.4
2001		100.0	20.6	49.7	16.0	13.7	100.0	23.1	50.5	11.9	14.5
2002		100.0	23.2	46.7	16.1	13.9	100.0	27.2	46.8	10.1	15.9
2003		100.0	26.2	42.7	16.6	14.5	100.0	31.4	43.0	8.9	16.7
2004		100.0	27.0	41.5	16.2	15.3	100.0	33.7	40.9	7.8	17.6
2005		100.0	25.0	43.9	14.9	16.2	100.0	31.2	44.0	6.5	18.3
2006		100.0	27.2	42.5	13.1	17.2	100.0	31.3	44.2	5.3	19.2
2007		100.0	29.1	40.6	12.1	18.3	100.0	32.2	43.3	5.3	19.2
2008		100.0	28.4	40.8	14.2	16.5	100.0	32.2	44.7	6.8	16.3
2009		100.0	29.0	38.9	13.4	18.7	100.0	31.4	45.8	5.8	17.0
2010	Q1	100.0	28.0	39.4	13.6	19.0	100.0	30.1	47.4	5.7	16.8
	Q2	100.0	25.9	40.2	14.9	19.1	100.0	28.0	49.1	6.1	16.8
	Q3	100.0	27.3	38.4	14.9	19.4	100.0	28.9	47.7	6.1	17.3
	Q4	100.0	26.5	38.5	15.2	19.7	100.0	27.5	48.7	6.3	17.6
Percentages of outstanding amounts (at current exchange rates, end of period)											
2011	Q1	100.0	27.7	37.9	14.6	19.8	100.0	28.3	48.4	5.9	17.5
	Q2	100.0	27.8	37.3	14.9	19.9	100.0	28.0	48.3	5.9	17.9
	Q3	100.0	26.3	38.1	16.1	19.4	100.0	26.8	49.7	6.3	17.3
	Q4	100.0	25.7	38.6	16.0	19.8	100.0	25.5	50.9	6.2	17.5

Source: ECB

Table-12A.3:International dimensions of euro-denominated debt securities

(EUR billions; percentages)

	Held by residents	Held by non-residents	Total
a) As at end-June 2011			
Issued by residents	11,527 *69%*	2,906 *17%*	14,434 *87%*
Issued by non-residents	1,426 *9%*	760 *5%*	2,185 *13%*
Total	12,953 *78%*	3,666 *22%*	16,619 *100%*
b) As at end-June 2010			
Issued by residents	11,055 *68%*	2,843 *18%*	13,897 *86%*
Issued by nonresidents	1,476 *9%*	786 *5%*	2,262 *14%*
Total	12,530 *78%*	3,629 *22%*	16,159 *100%*

Source: ECB.

CHAPTER 13

THE EURO AS INTERNATIONAL MONEY

The central concept

Since 1971, when the Bretton Woods system of pegged exchange rates (centred on the dollar) broke down, the sustainability of the *de facto* dollar standard has been questioned at various times - in the 1980s when Japan was a rising star, in the late 1990s when the euro came into existence, and currently, in the aftermath of the global financial crisis of 2008-09. Each time, the dollar proved resilient as the global reserve currency for at least two reasons: its 'safe haven' status, and its role as the most preferred currency in international trade invoicing and cross-border financial/foreign exchange transactions. The choice of a reserve currency also tends to be highly influenced by the peg that a particular central bank chooses to maintain. Here too, the dollar remains hugely important as it still acts an exchange-rate anchor for more than 60 countries, accounting for nearly 14 per cent of the world economy.

On a structural basis, the dollar's share of global central banks' foreign exchange reserve holdings peaked at almost 85 per cent in the early 1970s shortly after it abandoned the convertibility of the dollar to gold. Since 1971, the dollar has remained the dominant reserve currency, although its share has been declining gradually, reaching 70 per cent of the global reserves of central banks by 2000, dropping further to 60 per cent by 2010 . Many observers contend that this declining share signals the beginning of the end of the dollar supremacy. The structural weakness of the US economy and the long-term decline of the dollar over the last decade have only fuelled the anxiety of central banks holding large dollar assets, particularly those of China and the rest of emerging Asia which constitute about three-fifths of the total foreign holdings of US Treasury securities (around US$ 2.5 trillion) . This has led to an intensified search for an alternative to the dollar.

Fig-13.1: Global Importance of the US Dollar (%)(as on November,2010)

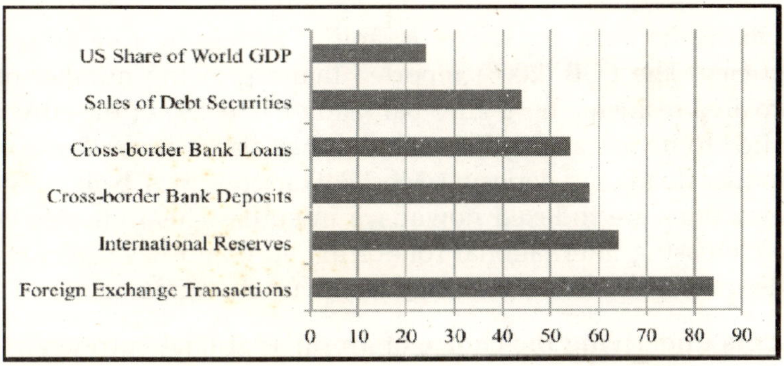

Source: Economist, November 2010, www. economist. com/mode/17414511

Most importantly, the euro has quickly established itself as a major international currency. This manifests itself in various forms.

First, many countries have decided to anchor their monetary policy vis-á-vis the single European currency . In addition many countries now peg their monies to basket of currencies where the euro has an important share (e.g. Russian Federation). While there is a strong regional pattern in the decisions of countries to anchor their monetary policies to the euro area, an increasing number of countries far away from Europe already do or may include the euro in basket-based peg systems.

Second, the share of the euro in international reserve holdings has substantially surpassed the sum of the legacy currencies and is slowly but steadily increasing.

Third, an increasing number of corporations and governments issue debt and equity in euros . Again, this pattern is not limited to countries geographically close to the euro area countries.

Fourth, while the dollar is still by far the dominant international currency, the euro is becoming increasingly important as an invoicing and quotation currency in international trade .

Fifth, the euro has spurred financial integration across Europe and has contributed to the development of pan-European liquid financial markets. Transaction costs in euro denominated securities are nowadays minimal, offering consumers a variety of financial instruments to smooth consumption and diversify risk.

Sixth, the euro is playing a rapidly increasing role as an asset currency. The ECB (2008) reported that a growing number of non euro area residents hold euro bank notes. The use of the euro is not limited to its use as parallel cash, but has also increased in banking activities (loans and deposits). Most Balkan countries' banking system transactions are indexed nowadays in euros. This indicates clearly the increasing international role of the euro and has direct welfare consequences as it implies larger gains from seigniorage.

Factors underlying the choice of an international currency

[i] First is economic strength and market size,[ii] Second, currency internationalization is positively associated with low inflation and exchange rate stability.,[iii] Third, broad, deep and efficient financial markets are also key determinants of currency international usage. The integration and development of euro-area financial markets since 1999 has been substantial.,[iv] Fourth, although hard to quantify, political power also contributes to currency internationalization.

The Political Determinants of International Currencies – The Economic literature agrees broadly on four main facilitating factors to achieve international currency status: (1) large economic size; (2) broad and deep financial markets; (3) confidence in the currency's value; and (4) network externalities . Taking an IPE approach that engages with this same framework, Helleiner (2010) reduces these economic factors to three: (1) confidence; (2) liquidity; and (3) transactional networks. Indirectly, politics can affect the main economic determinants through several channels. Confidence in a currency can be sustained by economic factors but also by 'the broader international security power of the issuing state' or by 'a consistent conservative monetary policy that is credibly embedded within domestic politics and institutions' .

Cohen's intense study of the euro's challenge to the dollar reaches two noteworthy conclusions. First, the euro is not yet a threat to the dollar. Secondly, the dollar is increasingly malfunctioning as the main anchor of the IMS. In other words, what Cohen says is that the euro might be catching up with the dollar, but that this is not so much a consequence of the euro's strengths, but that it has more to do with the dollar's weaknesses.

Cohen divides the euro's political shortcomings in three: (1) the fragmentation of the European financial markets; (2) the anti growth bias entrenched in the Maastricht Treaty; and (3) the governance difficulties associated with a decentralised monetary union.

The Euro's Geopolitical Limitations – Pointing to this leadership struggle and making a corollary between monetary power and consequent political and even military power, several authors in the wider field of International Relations (IR) saw in the creation of the euro the first step in the creation of a European superpower . Bellicose analogies to describe the birth of the euro were not lacking among these euro optimists in IR theory. Reid wrote that 'for the Europeans, the dreams of grandeur, the hope of creating "the weapon with which to fight back" against the might of the US dollar, are likely to come true'. In a similar vein, Haseler said that 'so integrated and centralised is the money of the EU that on monetary policy the Union speaks "with one voice", and with a vengeance!' for his part, said that the euro's 'success will push the EU towards rounding out its commercial and financial power with more effective and autonomous collective diplomatic and military power'. Finally, for Kupchan the creation of the euro is a stepping stone to establishing a European federal state more independent from the US economically and militarily, probably leading to friction between the two blocs in the future.

International Currencies as a Social Phenomenon-As we should be clear by now, to understand international currencies in their full complexity it is necessary to consider both economic variables and political factors. As Kirshner states, it would be a mistake to overlook the 'inescapable politics of money'. However, as Kirshner also hints, this is not comprehensive enough. There is more to money than just economics and politics. Money is socially constructed in everyday interactions. There is an inherent cultural symbolism in currencies that transcends narrow economic and political considerations. As Kindleberger once wrote, 'a country's exchange rate is more than a number. It is an emblem of its importance to the world, a sort of international status symbol'. In line with this, it is argued that money is not a culturally neutral or socially anonymous object, its value and reputation being profoundly shaped by cultural and social phenomena. Thus, for a full study of the euro challenge to the dollar it is necessary to explore this social context and attempt to grasp how this challenge is socially and culturally perceived worldwide.

The Euro's Socio Cultural Impact-It is generally accepted in the literature that the euro is the first real global competitor to the dollar since WWII. It poses a much greater challenge to the greenback than the Deutsche Mark and the Japanese Yen did in the 1970s and 1980s. This is acknowledged by respected economic historians who have studied the evolution of the IMS in depth, by financial elites, as will be shown below, and also in a wider social context, by the general public.

Euro Optimism seen from the Perspective of Key Financial Actors-This wider global social context, which impacts on the 'social mood' of market investors, as the socionomics literature has investigated, is mirrored in the narratives and behaviour of key private and public financial market actors and institutions, for whom the euro is also increasingly playing a bigger international role despite not being a challenge to the dollar. Goldman Sachs, for example, one of the most influential financial institutions of the world, considers EMU 'as a remarkable success so far, weathering widespread original scepticism, as well as a series of shocks –including 9/11 and the present market dislocations– while contributing to good and relatively stable growth throughout the Euro zone' over the past decade .

They calculate a further increase of the international role for the euro to between 30%-40% of the global share in the medium to long term. The view at Deutsche is that 'a bipolar system is not per se unstable... competition between the dollar and the euro regarding the international role is basically a good thing. Such a permanent beauty parade is expected to provide a big incentive for policymakers on both sides of the Atlantic to pursue sound economic and fiscal policies' (Deutsche Bank, 2008).

Some observations

Note that the investors outside the euro area hold 60% more euro equities compared to other (non-EMU) economies. Secondly, when both countries participate in the euro-zone, cross-border equity holdings increase by around 45%.

ECB figures released in 2008 by the European Commission (2008) show that only 5.3% of EZ trade with Asian countries such as Indonesia, Japan and South Korea is invoiced in euros, versus 80.1% in dollars. Nevertheless, it is important to highlight that these figures are mostly estimates. As recognised by the ECB in its 2009 report on the international role of the euro:

The ECB provides only 39.2% of currency denomination trade data for EZ countries (having only estimates for France and no export data for Germany, the two biggest economies of the EZ). Furthermore, for non EZ countries the share falls to 32.6% and for other regions of the world it drops to 5.4% (even though these account for 60% of global trade). This caveat is not acknowledged by many authors who rely on the same data to assess the performance of the euro, nor is it highlighted by De la Dehesa.

COFER ,IMF data, as of September 2010, show that the euro has steadily increased its share from 18% to 26.9% of total known reserves since 1999, versus a steady decline in dollar reserves from 71% to 61.3% in the same period. This indicates almost a 10% swing but, as mentioned, these numbers should be interpreted with caution because they miss around 40% of the total stock.

These estimates indicate that as of the end of 2009 the euro represented over 60% of UK, more than 40% of Canadian and close to 50% of US reserves. The ECB also gives 2008 figures for Russia, showing that the euro share was very close to 50%. This is in line with the 2009 report of the Russian Central Bank (RCB) which showed that the euro had surpassed the dollar as the main Russian reserve currency. The European currency now accounts for 47.5% of the share of total reserves, while the greenback accounts for 41.5% .

Fig.13.2:Global distribution of foreign exchange reserves

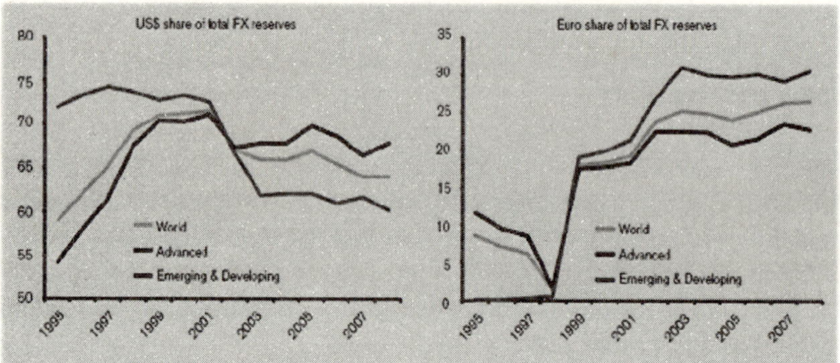

Source: IMF, COFER (reproduced in Benigno, 2010).

The latest Triennial BIS Survey on foreign exchange turnover released in December 2010 shows how in 2001 the shares were 89.9% for the dollar and 37.9% for the euro, while now they are 84.9% and 39.1% out of 200%, respectively .

Table 13.1: Currency distribution of global foreign exchange market turnover (%)

Currency	1998	2001	2004	2007	2010
US dollar	86.8	89.9	88.0	85.6	84.9
Euro	...	37.9	37.4	37.0	39.1
Japanese yen	21.7	23.5	20.8	17.2	19.0
Pound sterling	11.0	13.0	16.5	14.9	12.9
Australian dollar	3.0	4.3	6.0	6.6	7.6
Swiss franc	7.1	6.0	6.0	6.8	6.4
Canadian dollar	3.5	4.5	4.2	4.3	5.3
Hong Kong dollar	1.0	2.2	1.8	2.7	2.4
Swedish krona	0.3	2.5	2.2	2.7	2.2
New Zealand dollar	0.2	0.6	1.1	1.9	1.6
Korean won	0.2	0.8	1.1	1.2	1.5
Singapore dollar	1.1	1.1	0.9	1.2	1.4
Norwegian krone	0.2	1.5	1.4	2.1	1.3
Mexican peso	0.5	0.8	1.1	1.3	1.3
Indian rupee	0.1	0.2	0.3	0.7	0.9
Russian rouble	0.3	0.3	0.6	0.7	0.9
Chinese renminbi	0.0	0.0	0.1	0.5	0.9

Source: BIS (2010).

With about a quarter of allocated central bank reserves parked in euros, it seemed a logical competitor to the dollar up until a year ago, when the complex sovereign debt crisis that has engulfed the region raised concerns about the viability of the Euro zone. The threat of the 'disintegration' of the euro currency bloc – exaggerated or not – has brought the Euro zone to a crisis of confidence.

The crisis notwithstanding, observers also note that the euro has seen a dramatic expansion only in debt issuance, while the dollar dominates in cross-border foreign exchange or banking transactions. The internationalisation of the euro has also been concentrated within the Euro zone region, which reflects the limited and regional nature of its influence. Even though Europe's financial markets may have the required depth and liquidity, a number of 'structural' factors have held back the rise of the euro as a dominant reserve currency.

For instance, even prior to the Euro zone crisis, the euro's attractiveness was limited by the comparatively higher transaction costs, which stem primarily from the inability of the European Monetary Union (EMU) to supply an instrument on par with the US Treasury bill that ensures both liquidity and convenience. Second, the euro has functioned as a 'currency without a state', founded as a result of an inter-state treaty. The uncertainty associated with this governance arrangement has handicapped the euro, and thrown the Euro zone into a debate on the weak governance framework. Thus, absent significant structural and institutional changes within the Euro zone, it is rather unlikely that the euro will be a credible competitor

Table 13.2:Share of SDR:1981-2015

	Jan 1981 - Dec 1985	Jan 1986 - Dec 1990	Jan 1991 - Dec 1995	Jan 1996 - Dec 1998	Jan 1999 - Dec 2000	Jan 2001 - Dec 2005	Jan 2006 - Dec 2010	Jan 2011 - Dec 2015
US Dollar	42%	42%	40%	39%	39%	44%	44%	41.9%
Euro	NA	NA	NA	NA	32%	31%	34%	37.4%
Japanese Yen	13%	15%	17%	18%	18%	14%	11%	9.4%
British Pound	13%	12%	11%	11%	11%	11%	11%	11.3%
German Mark	19%	19%	21%	21%	NA	NA	NA	NA
French Franc	13%	12%	11%	11%	NA	NA	NA	NA

Source: Adapted from Pacific Exchange Rates Database, accessiable at: http://ex.sauder.abc.ca./SDR.html.

The use of the euro as a currency for the settlement or invoicing of international trade transactions has also shown a notable increase in recent years. There is concern that portfolio shifts from dollar-to euro-denominated assets, in particular, by central banks,could result in a sharp appreciation of the euro relative to the dollar. And a key question among politicians, academics, and the public is whether the euro will challenge or eventually displace the dollar as the leading international currency.

The prospects of big portfolio shifts from the dollar to the euro and the euro taking on some of the dollar's roles in the international financial system seemed unlikely a decade ago, when the first stages of European Monetary Union were designed. Some did argue that the euro could achieve the prerequisites for a major international currency and considered the consequences for international portfolio allocation and exchange rates. The dominant view, however, held that the euro's international impact would be small or that the expansion of its role would be very slow .

History also suggests that the primary considerations for the composition of reserves have been market liquidity (which in turn depends on central banks' willingness to ensure it, currency convertibility, financial stability, and the underlying development of financial markets) and a dominant position in international trade. Yet besides these economic reasons, geopolitical factors are also important. Sterling's internationalization occurred after the United Kingdom established itself as an imperial power, while the dollar ascended after the United States emerged as the dominant military power.

In terms of basket of currency as observed in SDR which might be treated as international liquidity or as international money when needed, the Euro is still confronting with Dollar as the dominant currency and when lender of the last resort would be applied by IMF,the question of unit of account would surely emerge and SDR might be win against Dollar as international money and the Euro would occupy the major share in the SDR basket and international liquidity problem would be a part of the demand for the Euro.

Chinn and Frankel (2005) use aggregate IMF data on the shares of seven main currencies in total identified official reserve holdings during the period of 1973-1998 to investigate determinants of the global composition of international reserves. Their main finding is that the shares of major currencies in global reserve holdings are very persistent (the coefficient on the lagged dependent variable is between 0.85 and 0.96). In addition, the lagged depreciation rate and inflation (or exchange rate volatility) enter with negative and significant coefficients, while income enters with a significantly positive coefficient. Chinn and Frankel also perform an out-of-sample forecast and compare it with the actual (reported) realized share of the euro. Their projections suggest that it will take at least 25 years for the euro to challenge the dominance of the dollar as a major reserve currency, unless there is a major deterioration in the stability of the dollar (depreciation, inflation).

More recently Eichengreen and Mathieson(2000) utilized confidential IMF data on shares of the major international currencies in reserve holdings in a large number of industrial and developing countries to investigate the high persistence. Although there are still data problems here, both studies find that currency pegs, the direction of trade, and the currency of foreign debt can explain the high inertia in reserve composition. Not only are these factors highly significant and robust determinants of the currency composition of reserve holdings, but their importance is very stable across time. The study of Dooley, Folkerts-Landau and Garber (2003, 2004) suggest that even if the East Asian countries increase their trade with the euro zone and issue euro-denominated securities, as long as they peg their currencies against the dollar, it is very unlikely that they will massively diversify away from the dollar.

References

BIS, 2010, BIS Annual Survey-2010

Chinn,Menzie and Jeffrey Frankel., 2005, Will the Euro Eventually surpass the Dollar as leading international reserve currency? *NBER, WP-*11510,August

Deutsche Bank, 2008, Deutsche Bank Annual Report-2008

Dooley, Michael P, David Folkerts-Landau, Peter Garber., 2003, An essay on the revised Bretton Woods system, *NBER, WP*-9971, September.

............, 2004, The revised Bretton Woods system: The effects of periphery intervention and reserve management on interest rates and exchange rates in center countries.*NBER,WP*-10332,March.

ECB, 2008, ECB Annual Report-2008

Eichengreen, Barry and Donald J. Mathieson., 2000, The currency composition of foreign exchange reserves:Retrospect and Prospect, *IMF,WP*-00/131, July

Helleiner, Eric., 2010, The 2007-2008 crisis and the future of global finance,*International Affairs,* 86:3:619-636

Peebles, Gustav., 2011, *The Euro and Its Rivals:Money and the Construction of a Transnational City*. Indiana University Press.

CHAPTER 14

FROM RECESSION TO RECOVERY IN EU: PROBLEMS AND PROSPECTS

Introduction

US financial crisis and the EU sovereign debt crisis which was termed as Euro crisis, were fundamentally turned the world economy into recession which was more severe than the great depression as opined by many spokesmen and economists and the monetarists because the high rates of unemployment and deepening output growth had greater spillover effects in present crisis than that of the great depression.Not only that its other economic and political effects were spread over longer period , but also it has reflected notoriously on international liquidity problems and international monetary System too. The euro area debt crisis of PIIGS countries had the spillover effects around the Europe and the world.The political integration of EU has been smashed by this crisis. Yet the period of recovery had started although the recovery of the great depression was more quicker than this recession. This chapter is an attempt to focus some important issues of recovery of the Euro Crisis from its recessionary trend.In this connection,we can quote from Joaquín Almunia, Commissioner for Economic and Monetary Affairs as"The EU economy is coming out of recession. This owes much to the ambitious measures taken by governments, central banks and the EU that have not only prevented a systemic meltdown but have kick-started the recovery. However, the road ahead is a challenging one. To maintain momentum and support the sustainability of the recovery, it is essential that we fully implement all announced measures and complete the repair of the banking sector. We must also begin to look more towards the medium-term, and consider how best to address the adverse effects that the crisis has had on labour markets, public finances and potential growth".

The trends of recovery

The world has experienced four global recessions since World War II—1975, 1982, 1991, and 2009. Since 2010, the global economy has been on a path of recovery, albeit a fragile one.

How different is the current global recovery from the earlier ones in the post-World war II?The slow path of economic recovery since 2010 has been quite similar to the path, on average, in the aftermath of the three other global recessions (Fig-14.1). In fact, if the projections of average global income—world per capita real GDP—are realized, recovery from the Great Recession, as it is often called, will have been faster than after the three previous global recessions. But the path of global income masks a very critical difference between advanced economies and emerging economies.

The recovery in advanced economies has been very sluggish compared with past recoveries (Fig-14. 2, left panel).Average income in some of these economies has not yet rebounded to its pre-recession level and is not forecast to do so even by 2014. In sharp contrast to developments in advanced economies, average incomes in emerging economies are generally back on the fast track they were on before the Great Recession (Fig-14.2, right panel).Income growth in these economies has already outpaced the growth seen during previous global recoveries, and is projected to continue to do so in coming years. The robust growth is widely shared among emerging economies. Notable exceptions are the emerging European economies, which are on a recovery track similar to that in advanced economies. World trade collapsed dramatically during the global recession of 2009 and was one of the reasons the recession evoked fears of another Great Depression and a resort to protectionist measures by governments seeking to shield domestic industries from foreign competition. But world trade has rebounded, and again the pace is quicker in the emerging economies than in advanced ones (Fig-14. 3).

Fig-14.1: On Track

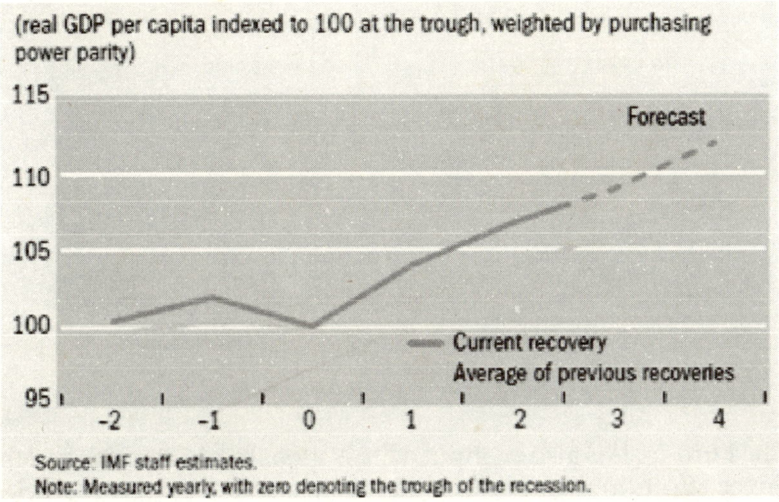

Fig-14.2:Two-speed rebound

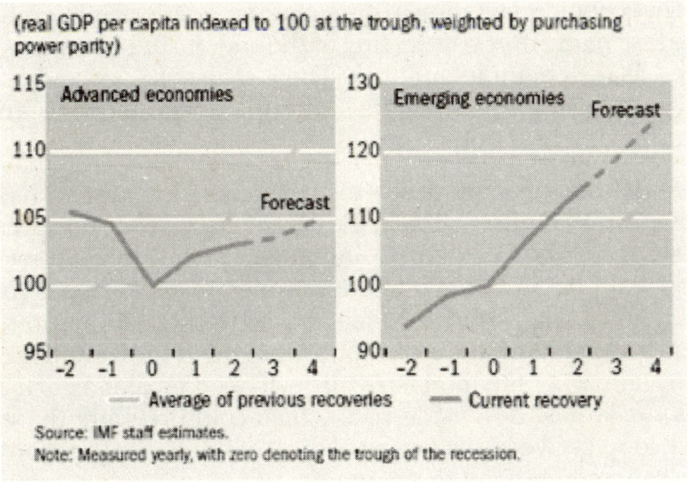

Fig-14.3:Trade Returns

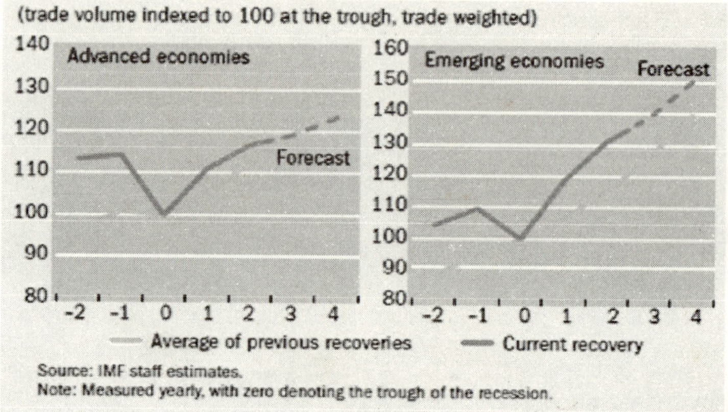

The Euro crisis is also an input of 2009 global recession and had the spillover effects in the developing as well as in developed countries, although the ill-effects have been found in intra-Euro Area and in EU.There are many important causes and barriers of revival from the recession arising out of the crisis.The important prospects and problems of recovery have been specified in brief.

[A] The economic situation in the euro area deteriorated significantly over the last year. After contracting at the end of 2011 , euro area GDP stabilised at the beginning of 2012. The loss of confidence due to the intensifying sovereign debt crisis, the oil price increases and the decelerating of world output growth have been weighing on growth.

While the risk of acute problems in the banking system has been eased by prompt policy action at the end of 2011, economic prospects remain sluggish. The European Commissions pricing forecast sees GDP as almost flat (-0.3%) in 2012, while a moderate expansion is forecast for 2013 (1.0%). This subdued recovery is predicated on a return of confidence and thus on the assumption that the crisis is contained and the financial-market situation normalises. Indeed, escalation of the crisis remains the largest downside risk, which could reignite the vicious feedback loop between the financial sector and the real economy and significantly reduce growth prospects.

Growth differences among the euro area Member States are expected to persist. There have been visible growth differences among the euro area countries since the outbreak of the global economic and financial crisis. These are expected to continue in the forecast horizon as Member States suffering from the legacy of internal and external imbalances are likely to register a much later and more protracted transition to a recovery than countries with lower structural impediments.

With the crisis deepening, the low growth was observed in EU. After averaging 1.5percent in 2011, euro area GDP growth is expected to be -0.3 and 0.7 percent in 2012 and 2013. Recent economic indicators continue to paint a bleak picture for Europe. They are confirming the view that the region is entering a new period of recession, after three quarters of negative or flat growth since the final quarter of 2010. But prospects continue to vary from country to country. In particular, the indicators forecast another year of very weak growth in 2013 in France and the U.K., and further declines in output in Italy and Spain. According to their latest forecast, it expects Euro zone GDP to contract by -0.8% this year (compared with -0.7% in our July forecast) and to be flat in 2013 (compared with 0.3% in July). Among the most meaningful revisions, the GDP forecast is estimated for Spain in 2013 to -1.4% from -0.6% in July .

The possible factors are:

[i] Private domestic demand is expected to remain subdued as banks and households continue to repair balance sheets and consumers and investors act cautiously amidst heightened uncertainty. With many of these headwinds significantly stronger in the periphery, grow this expected to be much lower there than in the core. Germany and France are expected to post weak-but-positive growth in 2012.(Fig-14.4)

Fig-14.4: GDP Growth Contribution,2012

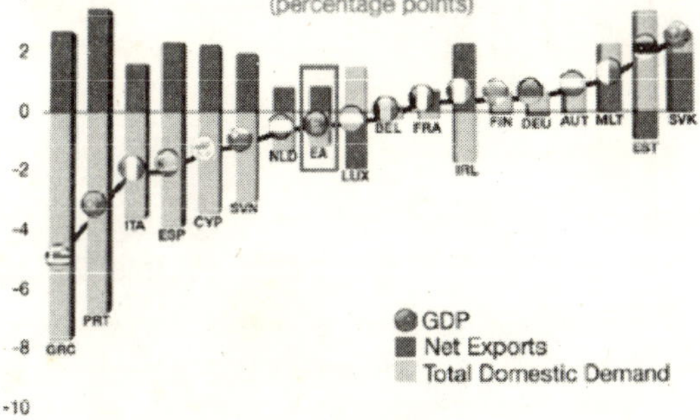

Source-IMF,WEO

[ii] Substantial and frontloaded fiscal consolidation will weigh on growth. In the aggregate, on current policies, the euro area structural deficit is projected to narrow by about 0.5% of GDP in 2012, 0.5% of GDP in 2013, and an additional 0.5% of GDP over 2014-17. The pace of fiscal adjustment is particularly accelerated in the hard-hit periphery countries: the projected consolidation over this and next year ranges from around 3.5 percentage points or more of GDP in Portugal, Greece, Italy, and Spain, compared with 0.5% or less in Germany, Austria, and Finland .

[iii] At the same time, the global outlook has deteriorated, reducing export demand despite the recent depreciation of the euro. External imbalances within the euro area will narrow, but the decline in periphery deficits will materialize largely as a consequence of weak activity and import compression.

[iv] Trend growth remains low. Even abstracting from current factors, euro area medium-term growth is set to disappoint in the absence of policy action. Reflecting well-known area-wide structural weaknesses, staff sees trend growth at only about 0.76% over the medium term.(Fig-14.5)

Fig-14.5:Annual Change in EA17 Structural Balance(% of GDP)

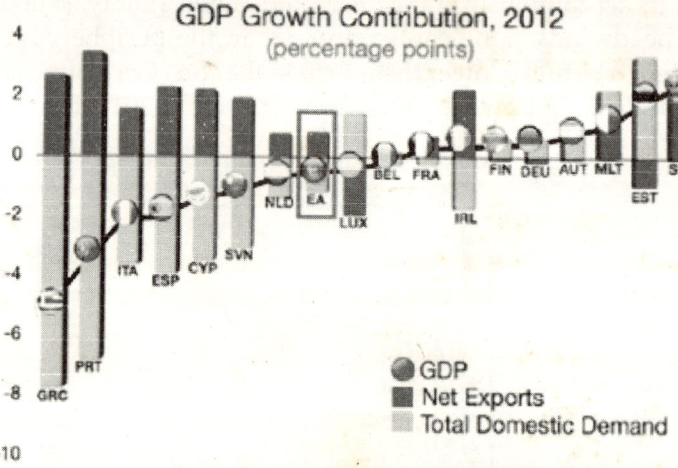

Source-IMF,WEO

Unemployment will remain high because of weak growth. In 2012, unemployment rates are expected to span a wide range, from about 5 .5% in Germany to 24 % in Spain. Staff projections also indicate that these differences will persist, as growth in countries under pressure (Portugal, Greece, Ireland, and Spain) will not be sufficient to return unemployment to pre-crisis levels. The unemployment rate of Euro Area was 9.6% in 2009 which increased to 10.2% in 2011 that ultimately projected to grow at 11.3% and 11.1% in 2013 and 2014 respectively.(Table-4A.1).

Fig-14.6: Returning to Pre-Crisis Unemployment Rates

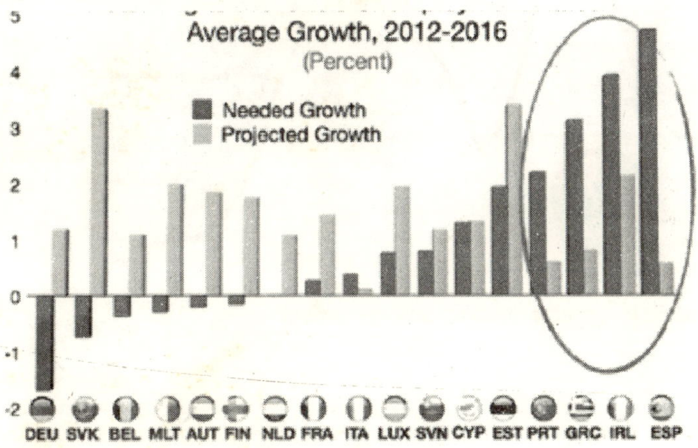

Source-IMF,WEO

Inflation is set to decline significantly and could even become negative. Headline inflation is expected to fall well below 2 % in 2013 and remain there through 2014. Although survey-based inflation expectations are still broadly anchored, market-based indicators are clearly pointing downward and core inflation (stripping out the most volatile components, such as energy and food prices) signals very low underlying inflation pressures (Fig-14.7). Moreover, given the subdued growth outlook, there is a sizable risk that inflation could even turn negative in the medium run. Specifically, the IMF's GPM projections indicate about a 25 % probability of below-zero inflation by early 2014. This risk of deflation is relatively low in the faster-growing economies but significant in the periphery, where administrative price and tax increases are masking more severe downward price pressures from still substantial output gaps. For example, staff estimates suggest that fiscal factors contribute over 1 percentage point to inflation in Italy in 2012.This disinflationary environment in much of the periphery will make it difficult for many countries to reduce the burden of debt.

Fig-14.7:Euro Area :Headline Inflation(%)

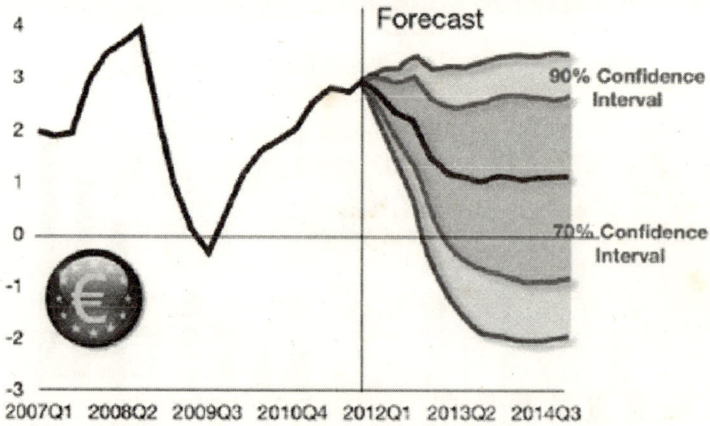

Source-IMF

Private consumption, the largest GDP component, had been one of the key drivers in the initial phases of the 2009-11 recovery in the EU and the euro area. In 2010, the annual rate of growth stood at around 1% in both areas, but in 2011 this growth almost came to a standstill (0.2%). With a contraction in the second half of the year, it was mainly the carry-over from 2010 (0.5% in both areas) that kept the annual growth rate in positive territory (Fig-14.8). A key reason for weak consumption growth has been the large squeeze on real gross disposable incomes, attributable to muted growth in compensations alongside high inflation.

Fig-14.8: Private Consumption and Consumer Confidence, Euro Area

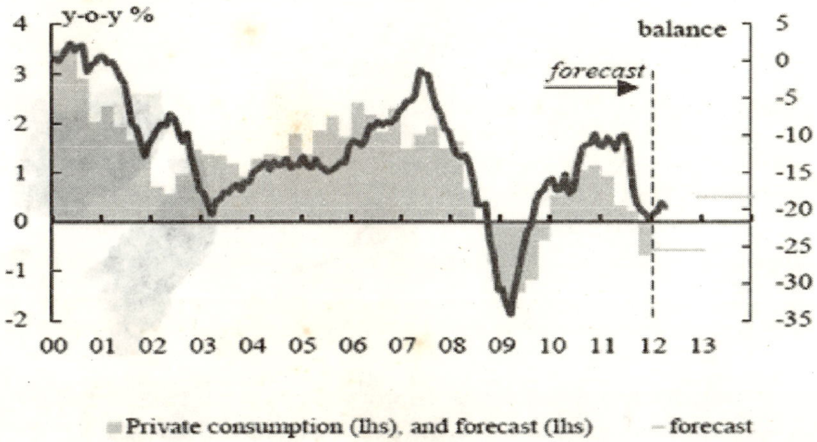

Source-Commission services

The Purchasing Managers' Indices (PMIs) for the month of August reveal that, overall, activity has stabilized at a low level in the manufacturing sector in the eurozone (European Economic and Monetary Union) and bounced back somewhat in the U.K. (Fig-14.9). However, a look at PMIs for individual countries in Europe has some brighter spots: Growth in the smaller open economies of Europe such as Switzerland, Sweden, or Belgium continues to show some resilience. On the other hand, the recession in Italy and Spain is deepening. The PMI employment index, standing below the 50-point threshold in the first three months of 2012, confirms this picture for the EU and the euro area. What further weighs on prospects for employment is the limited scope for the kind of supportive policy measures that upheld the EU labour market during the previous downturn. In addition, public sector employment may be reduced in some Member States.

Fig-14.9: Purchasing Managers' Indices for UK,Germany, France, Italy and Spain

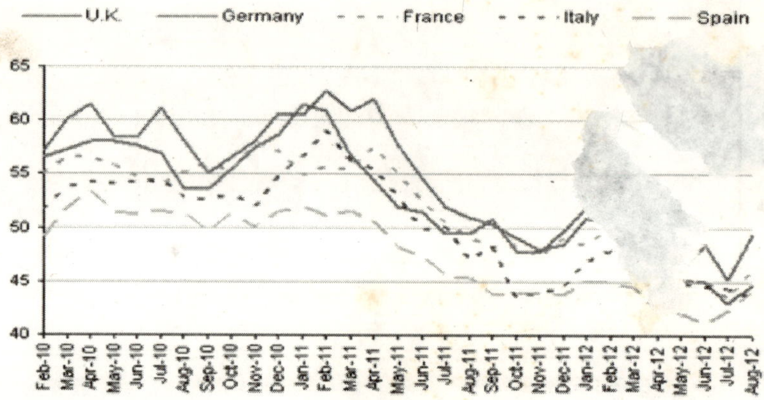

Source: Bloomberg.

© Standard & Poor's 2012.

[**B**] Policy measures introduced in the second half of 2011 and at the beginning of 2012 helped to rebuild market confidence in the early months of 2012, but the improvement proved temporary. In particular, the 3-year Very Long Term Refinancing Operations(VLTRO) carried out by the ECB filled acute refinancing gaps for euro area banks by guaranteeing banks access to medium-term funding at low cost. Also, to reassure markets about the banks' ability to withstand shocks and maintain adequate capital, the October 2011European Council agreed on an EU-wide recapitalisation plan coordinated by the European Banking Authority (EBA). The overall positive implementation of EU/IMF financial assistance programmes for Portugal and Ireland also contributed to improved market sentiment as did the ambitious reform programmes in other vulnerable countries. Other policy actions, such as the agreement on the second Greek adjustment programme, further strengthening of the firewalls and the reinforcement of fiscal governance also improved the sentiment towards euro area economies. Unfortunately, the improvement in sentiment proved only temporary and investors' confidence deteriorated again, which shows how fragile financial markets remain and that a failure to continue implementing appropriate policies can quickly turn market sentiment.

[C] Since the outbreak of the crisis public debt has increased substantially in the euro area. Government debt levels across the euro-area have increased by more than 20 percentage points and reached 88% of GDP in 2011, with large differences across Member States while euro area Member States have to restore sustainability in their public finances, there are short-term growth effects of fiscal consolidation. The main challenge for fiscal policy is to pursue fiscal consolidation in a growth friendly manner. (Fig-14.9)

The following are the dimensions of growth-friendly nature of consolidation:

(i) Differentiation of the pace across countries, (ii) strong attention to the composition of consolidation, including a clear focus on curbing age-related spending, and (iii)accompanying reform of budgetary institutions.

(i) Firstly,the size of fiscal challenge differs among the euro area Member States and calls for differentiated speed of consolidation.The Stability and Growth Pact provides a flexible and rule-based framework to guide the differentiated pace of consolidation.The strategy of fiscal exit from the extraordinary measures adopted to cushion the effect of the crisis reflects the flexibility embedded in EU fiscal rules.

(ii) Secondly, the composition of fiscal consolidation is critical to minimise the negative effects on growth. However, as the size of the required fiscal adjustment is significant, part of it might have to come from the revenue side in many Member States.The composition of consolidation has not always been growth-friendly. Tackling the budgetary implications of ageing population is key for public finance sustainability. Progress has been made with respect to pension reforms, but health care reforms are lagging behind.

(iii) Thirdly, reforms of national budgetary frameworks can make an important contribution to consolidation and alleviate growth-consolidation trade-offs. Improving national budget processes by drawing on identified best practices would improve fiscal policy-making on a lasting basis. Budgetary discipline and solidarity in the euro area could also be fostered by the common issuance of sovereign debt instruments. Appropriate policies can quickly turn market sentiment.

[D] One of the salient features of the first decade of the euro area's existence was the gradual accumulation of macroeconomic imbalances. The mounting current account deficits and surpluses were a counterpart to large capital flows across the euro area countries. The onset of the crisis triggered a reversal in the previous trends and current account imbalances in the euro area have been significantly reduced since. On the way forward, a key issue is whether the recorded narrowing of imbalances is structural or will be reversed once cyclical conditions improve. Even if the adjustment on the deficit side has been large, there are indications that it has not been complete in those countries which had the highest current account deficit. The required improvement in current accounts to stabilise or reduce external indebtedness often implies even more ambitious improvements in trade balances. Unlike current account deficits, large and sustained current account surpluses do not raise concerns about the sustainability of external debt or financing capacity for the countries concerned. Moreover, a closer look at the surplus economies reveals significant heterogeneity of the sector composition of their external positions and hence the potential for external rebalancing.

[E] Entrenched growth divergences, in particular if linked to a high debt burden, creates problems in the context of a monetary union. The growth weakness caused by deleveraging only adds to long-standing problems of low potential growth in the euro area. Therefore, the euro area as a whole faces a double challenge of rebalancing and strengthening growth in the medium and long term.

[F] Structural reforms that increase contestability and flexibility of markets can enhance growth and facilitate adjustment. In the current context of low growth, fiscal challenges and social tensions there is a need to sustain the reform momentum. Common monetary policy and strong cross-border spillovers give a case for stronger coordination of structural reforms in the euro area. Over the last 12 months, progress with structural reforms in the euro area has been correlated with the intensity of market pressure.

[G] The crisis highlighted weaknesses in euro area governance. Economic flexibility has long been recognised as a crucial adjustment channel in EMU. Markets failed to induce sufficient discipline during the first ten years of EMU. The crisis has slowed the financial integration process and ambitious steps to accelerate and deepen financial integration may be needed. Since the crisis erupted, the EU and the euro area have engaged in a comprehensive strengthening of its economic governance during the reform of economic governance in the euro area.The dynamics of switching from a 'good' equilibrium to a 'bad' one during the crisis gained further strength due to the cross-country spillovers.The establishment of robust euro-area financial stability mechanisms has also implied an important step forward in euro-area governance. Effective decision making arrangements are crucial for an efficient implementation of the strengthened surveillance framework for the euro area. In the future, additional reforms to economic governance may be considered to complete the institutional structure of EMU.

[H] Weaknesses in macroeconomic surveillance and enforcement at both the Member State and the EU level meant that the misallocation of resources and consequent macro financial imbalances were not detected early enough and adequately addressed by Policy makers.The surveillance and coordination of fiscal policies have been radically strengthened. The "six-pack" of legislation on economic governance has reinforced both the preventive and the corrective arm of the SGP. It defines quantitatively the meaning of a "significant deviation" from the MTO or the adjustment path towards it and operationalises the debt criterion of the Excessive Deficit Procedure through a numerical benchmark. A central innovation is the use of reverse-qualified-majority voting in Council decisions on most sanctions. Finally, the six pack also sets minimum requirements for all main aspects of fiscal frameworks at national level. The Macroeconomic Imbalances Procedure has introduced systematic economic surveillance in all areas that could potentially lead to harmful imbalances. The in-depth reviews confirmed that seven euro area Member States face macro-economic imbalances which call for policy action.The European Semester integrates the surveillance of the economic policies covered by the Europe 2020 strategy, as well as the preventive parts of the Stability and Growth Pact and the Macroeconomic Imbalances Procedure, and provides policy guidance to Member States before they finalise their budgets and economic reform plans.

Prospects of recovery through Banking Union

Deleveraging in the banking sector is necessary to restore investor confidence in the free flow of credit to the economy. The run-down of problematic assets, accumulated before the crisis, is essential to restore the flow of credit to the economy. The continuing low interest-rate environment coupled with banks' reluctance to recognise losses or foreclose properties could increase the propensity of banks to forebear on loans or other problematic assets.Delaying loss recognition, could constrain lending to more creditworthy borrowers, reduce potentially productive investment and exert negative effect on growth. Therefore correct and transparent risk recognition and timely restructuring is necessary to ensure the health of both the banking system and the economy.

A euro area banking union could combine three main elements:[1]A pan-European deposit guarantee scheme. [2]A pan-European bank resolution mechanism. [3]Common supervision by which reform of the banking system could be done and the council should decide it quickly to implement it.

Although the banking union should be consistent with European Union directives, it is particularly urgent for the euro area. This is because deposits move more easily within a currency area, and a deposit guarantee scheme covering all euro area depository institutions would help reassure retail depositors that their savings are safe and avoid sudden depositor flight. In the same way, a euro area bank resolution authority would weaken the bank-sovereign feedback loops operating within the currency union. At the same time, to align supervisory incentives within the euro area, the ECB could play the role of common supervisor. And to further strengthen its financial markets role, the ECB could also be given explicit responsibility for financial stability and full lender-of-last-resort functions, thereby eliminating bank sovereign linkages present in the current Emergency Liquidity Assistance (ELA) scheme.

The provision of common backstops for deposit insurance and bank resolution is a form of fiscal risk sharing. And unified regulatory and supervisory frameworks provide an important element of governance in the form of delegation of national sovereignty to the center.

Besides,several intermediate steps can pave the way for—and add to the credibility of—a banking union, namely,

[a]The recently proposed EU framework for harmonized national bank resolution processes and deposit insurance could become a helpful building block toward a banking union if fully implemented on an accelerated schedule. The new framework can reduce the cost

to taxpayers from future bank failures by providing strong powers to resolution authorities, including the power to bail-in unsecured creditors, thus reducing the 'too-big to-fail' subsidy.

[b]The existing EFSF/ESM framework could provide immediate financing for the common deposit insurance and resolution frameworks before industry contributions are available. In this regard, the use of EFSF/ESM resources for these purposes could be linked to advances in area-wide supervision, similar to the recent decision to consider direct bank recapitalization by the ESM.

[c]Strong coordination of macro prudential policies would also mark progress in the right direction. In this regard, the recent compromise draft of the CRDIV, which provides greater flexibility at the national level by allowing countries to impose stricter capital buffers, offers a helpful balance between the needs of the single rule book and financial stability concerns of national authorities. A common approach to capital and liquidity requirements is essential, with a strong role for pan-European institutions such as the ESRB and EBA.

Fig-14.10:Government deficit(% of GDP),2011

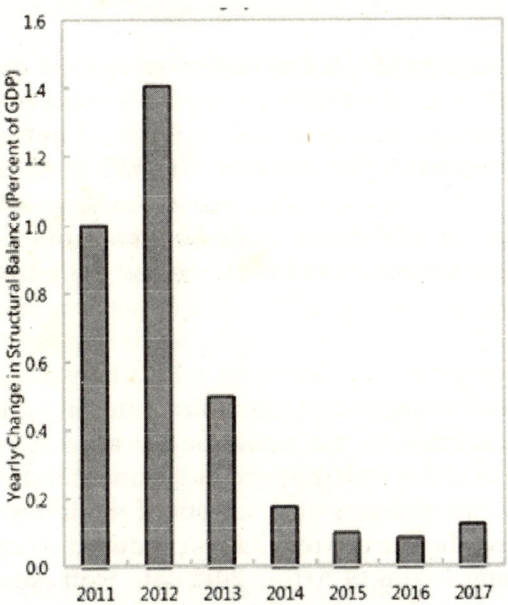

Source-IMF,WEO

Fig -14.11:Structural Balance(%GDP), 2011

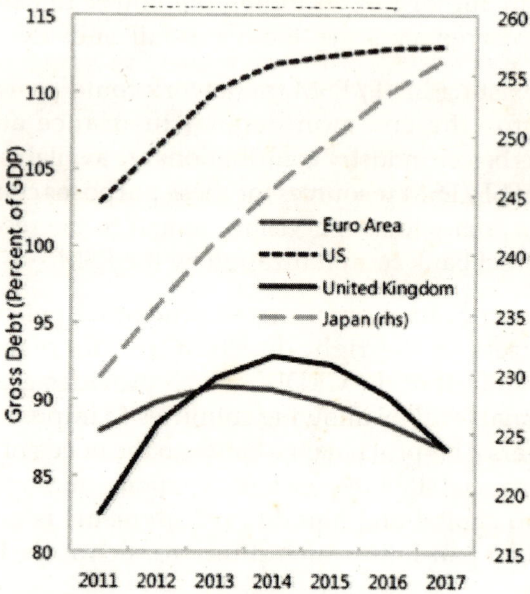

Source-IMF,WEO

The ECB can provide further defenses against an escalation of the crisis. These could include policies to support demand in the short run and fend off downside risks to inflation, as well as measures to ensure that monetary transmission, currently impaired by financial stress in some countries, operates well again across the euro area.It is stated more explicitly that since the beginning of the crisis,lending conditions have varied considerably across the EuroArea because financial corporate lending rate have risen sharply but have fallen in core countries.Pass through of policy lending rates has weakened especially in the periphery.Before the crisis intensified, lending rates broadly tracked changes in ECB policy rate but since 2010,retail lending rates started to rise while policy rates remain low.Staff analysis confirmed that both the policy adjustment and long run impact of ECB policy rate changes on a variety of retail interest rate have declined across the Euro Area. Also it induced to domestic bond yield to declining.Taking $Q_1$2007-$Q_1$2012 data, Staff estimates revealed that[i] bank's quarterly bank lending growth was significantly higher for higher,more profitable,more liquid capitalized banks,[ii]banks with higher loan/deposit ratio mismatch and higher CDS spread lent significantly less,[iii]bank lending were substantially higher in countries with higher GDP growth with higher prices.The study supports that a higher ECB-EONIA interest rate spread was associated with lower bank lending.

The other specific observations are as follows,

[i] Interest rate reductions- Economic weakness and downside risks to inflation in the euro area warrant further reductions in the main policy rates. Although the room for such reductions is limited, they would deliver a strong signaling effect and, in addition, provide some direct near-term support to weaker banks by reducing indexed borrowing costs under existing LTROs.

[ii] Quantitative easing (QE)- The ECB could achieve further monetary easing through a transparent QE program encompassing sizable sovereign bond purchases, possibly preannounced over a given period of time. Buying a representative portfolio of long-term government bonds—e.g., defined equitably across the euro area by GDP weights—would also provide a measure of added stability to stressed sovereign markets. However, QE would likely also contribute to lower yields in already "low yield" countries, including Germany.

[iii] More SMP purchases- Additional and clearly communicated SMP purchases could ensure the transmission of monetary easing where sovereign bond markets are subject to increase tress. With the possible exception of Greece, SMP purchases have been relatively small compared with the outstanding debt stock, in principle increasing the scope for additional intervention. And a well-communicated re-activation of SMP purchases would likely carry strong signaling effects which might mitigate the need for very large purchases. The benefits from lower yields would also ease collateral constraints on official and interbank lending facilities.

[iv] Further liquidity provision- This could encompass additional multi-year LTRO facilities, coupled with adjusted collateral requirements, if needed—including a broadened collateral base and/ or a lowering of haircuts—to address localized shortages. The associated credit risk to the ECB would be manageable in view of its strong balance sheet and high levels of capital provisioning.

Nevertheless, one of the disadvantages of the LTRO facility is that it tends to strengthen sovereign-bank links. Broadly speaking, through two three -year LTROs and a further relaxation in its collateral rules, the ECB allotted 1 trillion euro to euro area banks with a net increase in liquidity of 5000billion euro but further ECB liquidity support may be necessary if bank's funding conditions continue to deteriorate.Total wholesale debt roll over need of euro area banks is estimated at 630 billion euro in 2012 some of which has been pre-financed via three-year LTRO and some will be financed in the market.LTRO borrowing is around1.1 trillion euro(end May) but marketable collateral eligible for euro system operations is about 13 trillion euro and 3 trillion euro pre pledged collateral may be found,thus 2.4 trillion euro is needed for borrowing. However some individual banks of the periphery countries could be short of collateral.A further relaxation of collateral rules as well as a rethinking of collateral pricing and haircut policies may be necessary to ensure liquidity support to banks and prevent liquidity risks from escalating into insolvency risks. However, additional steps may be needed to cover liquidity risk of the collateral it accept.

Concluding remarks

Although late the recovery from recession in Euro Area has been started similarly with global recovery but it is too late. Newly built in policies in EU had been working slowly in spite of divergences in political integration. Franco-German leadership in Euro Area to bail out Euro crisis is rather illusion since convergence criteria is still not under control and the Cyprus debt crisis is added to fell EU in great distress in curbing recession. EMU is also in trouble for intervention policies of non-euro area having spillover effects. Above all, unemployment rate is beyond managed for mismatching growth unsustainability with economic potentiality. Monetary policy and introduction of banking union showed good impact in which ECB has a special role to play to keep in touch with IMF ,World Bank and BIS in close connection with EC. The recommendations for PIIGS are still due because bail out packages could not alone revive them from debt crisis until and unless macroeconomic imbalances are corrected.

Since this crisis is not just an economic crisis but also a social and political crisis. It calls for the implementation of new framework conditions, which would reward entrepreneurial activities on all levels more than finance alchemy. The European Monetary Fund is one core component of such a "New Deal for Europe".The European Financial Stability Facility (EFSF) set up in May 2010 could be transformed into the European Monetary Fund. The first politician who coined the term "European Monetary Fund" was the German finance minister *Wolfgang Schäuble* in spring 2010.

Its scope are fourfold

[i] The EMF provides euro governments with financial means by selling Eurobonds in the capital markets. These bonds are guaranteed by all euro countries to an unlimited extent. In addition, the EMF has full backing by the ECB (if necessary, the ECB buys Eurobonds from the EMF).

[ii] The EMF stabilizes Eurobond interest rates at a level slightly below the level of medium term economic growth (in nominal terms). Investors hold the Eurobonds at the EMF, they are not tradable but can be liquidated at any time. In these two respects, the present proposal differs most from Eurobond concepts already put forward.

[iii] The EMF helps to restore sound public finances in euro countries according to a systemic approach and, hence, in close cooperation with the ECB, the European Commission and national governments. To this end, the EMF provides funds for the euro states according to clear criteria ("conditionality") which are not exclusively restrictive.

[iv] The EMF overcomes the split between euro countries caused by widening interest rate differentials and strengthens thereby the cohesion and credibility of the EMU and of the EU as a whole.

Moreover, the EMF stabilizes the interest rate on Eurobonds, i.e., it determines the long-term interest level in a similar way as the ECB determines the level of the short-term interest rate. Investors hold the Eurobonds at the EMF, these instruments can always be liquidated but they are not traded in capital markets (like savings accounts).

Second, controlling the long-term interest rate enables the EMF in cooperation with the ECB and the EC to set the interest rate close to the level enjoyed by the "good countries" like Germany.

It should be generalized at the level of the EMU through the foundation of the EMF. Eurobonds can therefore also be conceived as fully liquid savings deposits of financial investors held with the EMF. The ECB serves as lender of last resort, however, to the EMF as intermediary which substitutes private banks.

On the issues of governance, all euro countries are members of the EMF. The contribution to the fund's equity as well as the voting rights could be allocated according to the economic strength of the members or the population (or some combination). This issue is left open to the political decision process. The finance ministers of the member states govern the EMF, they decide together on the amount of Eurobond sales and their distribution among its members. The latter is strictly bound to several criteria. This conditionality ensures that no member country can act as free rider. In contrast to most Eurobond proposals , there should be no general limit for Eurobond financing, it should become the normal way to fund euro states as they are members of a monetary union. If a country does not comply with the criteria for EMF funding, it will not get funds and, hence, has to rely on selling their national bonds for which they would have to pay unsustainably high interest. Knowing this in advance, highly indebted governments will stick to the consolidation measures accorded with the EMF and the EC.

APPENDIX

Table-14A.1:Standard and Poor's European Economic Forecast

	Germany	France	Italy	Spain	Netherlands	Belgium	Eurozone	U.K.	Switzerland
Real GDP (% change)									
2010	3.7	1.7	1.8	(0.1)	1.7	2.2	2.0	1.8	3.0
2011	3.0	1.7	0.4	0.7	1.2	2.0	1.5	0.8	2.1
2012f	0.6	0.1	(2.4)	(1.8)	(1.1)	0.0	(0.8)	(0.3)	0.8
2013(f)	1.2	0.4	(0.6)	(1.4)	(0.2)	0.5	(0.0)	1.0	1.1
2014(f)	1.7	1.3	0.9	0.7	1.4	0.9	1.2	1.6	1.3
CPI inflation (%)									
2010	1.2	1.7	1.6	2.0	0.9	2.3	1.6	3.3	0.6
2011	2.5	2.3	2.9	3.1	2.5	3.5	2.7	4.5	0.1
2012f	1.9	2.0	3.0	2.0	2.5	2.6	2.3	2.6	(0.5)
2013(f)	2.0	1.4	2.0	2.0	2.0	1.5	1.9	1.8	0.0
2014(f)	2.2	1.5	0.5	1.5	1.5	1.8	1.6	1.8	0.5
Unemployment rate (%)									
2010	7.1	9.8	8.4	20.1	4.5	8.3	10.1	7.8	4.5
2011	6.0	9.7	8.4	21.7	5.3	7.2	10.2	8.0	4.0
2012f	5.5	10.5	10.7	25.5	6.8	7.2	11.7	8.2	4.2
2013(f)	5.0	10.5	11.0	26.0	7.0	7.0	11.8	8.0	4.0
2014(f)	5.0	9.9	10.0	23.0	5.5	7.0	10.7	7.0	3.1
				--Alternative scenario: severe recession--					
Real GDP (% change)									
2012f	0.6	(0.2)	(2.6)	(2.2)	(1.2)	(0.3)	(1.0)	(0.4)	(0.2)
2013(f)	(1.2)	(1.3)	(2.1)	(2.5)	(2.2)	(1.7)	(1.9)	(0.6)	(1.5)
2014(f)	1.8	1.2	1.3	1.0	1.4	1.0	1.3	1.7	2.1

f--Standard & Poor's forecast.

Table-14A.2: Impact of fiscal measures 2012-16,deviations from baseline

EU27	2012	2013	2014	2015	2016
GDP (%)	-0.3	-0.6	-0.6	-0.7	-0.8
Employment (%)	-0.3	-0.5	-0.5	-0.5	-0.6
Consumption (%)	-0.3	-0.5	-0.7	-0.8	-0.9
Investment (%)	0.3	0.7	0.8	0.9	1.0
Exports (%)	0.8	0.9	0.8	0.7	0.5
Imports (%)	-1.1	-1.5	-1.5	-1.5	-1.4
Terms of trade (%)	-0.8	-0.8	-0.7	-0.6	-0.5
Gov. debt/GDP (pp.)	-0.5	-1.8	-3.5	-5.2	-6.9
Gov. balance/GDP (pp.)	1.2	1.8	1.9	2.0	2.1

Euro area	2012	2013	2014	2015	2016
GDP (%)	-0.3	-0.5	-0.5	-0.6	-0.6
Employment (%)	-0.2	-0.4	-0.4	-0.4	-0.4
Consumption (%)	-0.2	-0.5	-0.6	-0.7	-0.8
Investment (%)	0.3	0.6	0.8	1.0	1.1
Exports (%)	0.8	0.9	0.9	0.8	0.7
Imports (%)	-1.1	-1.5	-1.5	-1.5	-1.4
Terms of trade (%)	-0.8	-0.9	-0.8	-0.7	-0.6
Gov. debt/GDP (pp.)	-0.5	-1.8	-3.5	-5.2	-7.0
Gov. balance/GDP (pp.)	1.1	1.8	1.9	2.0	2.1

Source-Commission services

Table-14A.3:Euro Area debt dynamics

	average 2004-08	2009	2010	2011	2012	2013
Gross debt ratio[1] (% of GDP)	69.0	79.9	85.6	88.0	91.8	92.6
Change in the ratio	0.2	9.8	5.7	2.4	3.8	0.9
Contributions to the change in the ratio:						
1. Primary balance	**-1.1**	**3.5**	**3.4**	**1.1**	**0.0**	**-0.3**
2. "Snow-ball" effect[2]	**0.3**	**5.4**	**0.7**	**0.7**	**2.1**	**0.8**
Of which:						
Interest expenditure	3.0	2.9	2.8	3.1	3.2	3.2
Growth effect	-1.4	3.1	-1.5	-1.2	0.3	-0.9
Inflation effect	-1.3	-0.6	-0.6	-1.1	-1.4	-1.5
3. Stock-flow adjustment	**1.0**	**0.8**	**1.5**	**0.6**	**1.7**	**0.4**

[1] *End of period.*

Source-Commission services

References

Bhowmik, Debesh., 2013, Emerging Asian Monetary Fund: Progress or Pitfall?,forthcoming

European Commission,2012,Commission Staff Working Documents:Assessment of the 2011 national reform programme and stability programme for the Euro Area,Brussels,30-5-2012.

.................,2012,*European Economic Forecast*,Spring 2012

IMF,2012,Euro Area Policies,*IMF Country Report* No-12/181,July.

Kose, M. Ayhan., Prakash Loungani and Macro E.Terrones., 2012, Trackling the Global Recovery,*Finance and Development*, June,10-13.

Schulmeister, Stephan.,2012,The European Monetary Fund-A Systematic Problem Needs a Systematic Solution., *WIFO Working Paper No-414.* June, 2012

Standard and Poor's Rating Service,2012,The Eurozone's New Recession-Confirmed,*Ratings Direct*,September 25,1-14

.........................., 2013, Europe's Recession is Still Dragging down House Prices in Most Markets,*Ratings Direct*,January 17,1-20.

World Economic Forum, 2012, Euro, Dollar,Yuan uncertainties, Scenerios on the future of the International Monetary System, *World Economic Series*, June.

CHAPTER 15

CONCLUSION

This book containing 15 chapters tried to search the inherent causes and evolving roots of the Euro Area debt crisis which finally turned into financial crisis, as well as it showed some policy issues to revive the Stability of Euro, to increase the international liquidity for Euro, and to find out the policies to solve the debt crisis of the debt ridden countries. The Euro crisis had been related with the international monetary system and political economy concept of Euro zone which ultimately would able to clarify the genuine solution and revival process of the Euro crisis. Besides, there are important micro economic problems which bound with the nations during long years such as maintaining national sovereignty, ethical norms, customs, mobility, the stages of inequality, conflicting ideas of integration, democratic divergences, market differences, competitiveness etc which were not analysed in any section of the book. Even, there is a sharp differences of economic outcomes of Euro Area and EU-27 after the enlargement of the EU. The East European countries which were formerly belonged to the USSR, joined in EU incidentally and could not maintain the Maastricht criteria and even unable to follow common policies of EU which made great divergence among the members of the bloc. Even international trade pattern between Euro Area and non Euro Area created imbalances and unequal international trading partners. Eurozone common currency played differential values from international trade between Euro and non-euro areas. The unavailability of data made this idea was untouched in this book. The historical relation among the countries of EU-11 through the innumerable treaties and the hegemonic role of individual nation was quite clear and the prevailing of two speed Europe has been identified through the policy implications for Euro crisis when Britain left from the common currency-Euro, and a new EU-17 for Euro zone was forced to set up by the leadership of Germany and France which implied an anticlimax among the debt ridden countries and create political disintegration in EU-27 and the crisis-ridden EU comes closer to IMF, World Bank and G-8 for rescue packages. The political economy concept had cleared this phenomenon, yet the capitalist crisis including inabilities of corporate finance globalised the Euro Area and EU-27 in a diversified manner.

It is no doubt that the spillover effects from banking, financial, and money market both national and international spread in most of the OECD and developing countries which have been cleared that banking and financial integration including common monetary policy are urgent for maintaining the Maastricht criteria which have been analysed with great care where every nations should be more careful for better co-ordinations so that spillover effects of the crisis might be minimized.

Presently, Euro is not only the key currency of EU regional bloc but also is an international currency because international payments are met through Euro. Therefore, the European debt crisis emerges a critical situation of having the existence of Euro if Greece, Portugal and Spain left from the common currency or from zone if the bailout program of euro crisis failed. It is related fully with the present international monetary system where the euro dollar exchange rate became more volatile and went against the Euro where ECB's role is less important than the role of IMF in international payment mechanism. The evolution of the international monetary system showed that the hegemonic role of Pound Sterling, US Dollar and Euro were prevalent strongly in the international trade and payment. But, under the multilateral trading regime, the regional trading blocs and their common currency have been competing in international money game in trade and finance the shares of and thus the role of international monetary system has changed too and instability began where the Euro became the real substitute against the US Dollar in the international payment mechanism. In this circumstance, it is not legitimate to expect that only European debt crisis can collapse the Euro which is identical to the collapse of the Euro Area. It is not supposed to think that Euro will not remain in the SDR basket which might be the international money if any numeraire is cancelled and when the reform of the international monetary system would be realized. If so, the international monetary system would also collapse. Therefore, the democratization of the debt crisis solution in EU under the European commission is the urgent need in maintaining the existence of the EU regional bloc and its common currency Euro.

Lastly, we cannot safely assume that only the Maastricht treaty can solve the Euro crisis without properly required macroeconomic fundamentals because low saving-investment rates, low GDP growth rate with high unemployment rate including unusual credit rating with high current account imbalances could not be sound conditions of solution process and conversely,the instability of the Euro would surely begin. Therefore, proper macro-economic indicators maintaining convergence criteria would be the idal conditions for solutions of the euro crisis abiding by the rules and terms of the international monetary system in transacting international payments.

Moreover, we cannot deny that the U.S. and Euro zone economies command 40% of world GDP, 25% of world trade, 60% of world foreign direct investment flows, and 60%-70% of world banking assets and financial services. They also remain each other's most important market for exports of goods and services, and are each other's primary source for foreign direct investment.

U.S. companies operating in Europe and European companies operating in the United States employ up to 15 million workers on both sides of the Atlantic. Given these strong economic linkages, it is not surprising that the U.S. economy can be negatively impacted by the Eurozone crisis via both financial and trade linkages. Already there have been instances where concerns that the crisis is deepening have precipitated extreme volatility in U.S. stock prices ,for example, reportedly contributed to a 5% drop in European stock markets and a decline of more than 2% in major U.S. stock indices. If the Eurozone economy stagnates this year or slips into recession, demand for U.S.

exports and the sales and profits of U.S. multinationals operating in Europe will be depressed. If the euro begins to depreciate more steeply against the dollar due to slower growth and loss of confidence in the euro, these adverse impacts on the U.S. economy could be amplified. A stronger dollar/weaker euro would also likely have some effects on U.S.-Eurozone foreign direct investment flows. Currently, Eurozone countries account for 26% of all U.S. direct investment abroad and for 44% of all foreign direct investment in the United States. Based on slower growth in Europe, U.S. investors may look towards emerging markets for additional investments, particularly since profits generated in euros would translate into fewer dollars, hurting the bottom line of U.S. parent companies. An offsetting factor could be that European stocks and assets with a weaker euro would look cheaper and more attractive, attracting U.S. capital to Europe. Economists tend to be divided on the magnitude of any impacts on the U.S. economy. If the Eurozone economy contracts only modestly in 2012 (some forecasts are predicting a 0.2% drop in Eurozone GDP followed by a rebound to 1.0% growth in 2013) the impact on the U.S. economy is likely to be minimal. However, the economic impact could be much more substantial if the Eurozone were to plunge into a deep and prolonged recession or even break-up due to a deepening sovereign debt crisis. By one estimate, a complete break-up of the Eurozone could lead to a 10% cumulative loss of output over the first two years. Combined with a likely adverse impact on the functioning of the EU's single market, U.S. exports of goods and services to Europe (which totaled over $300 billion in 2011) could be significantly reduced.

Therefore, we cannot infer immediately that capitalist integration fails or the process of capitalist integration has been confronting with severe capitalist crisis rather the co-operation of G8, IMF and ECB seem to be apparently favourable for survival of regional blocs in multilateral trade and world financial integration where key currency domination principle became less prior in curing euro crisis.

BIBLIOGRAPHY

Asland,Anders., 2010, The Last Shall be the first:The East European Financial Crisis, Peterson Institute for International Economics, New York

Aubrey,Henry. C., 2007, Behind the veil of international money, *Essays in International Finance*, no-71,Princeton University, New Jersy.

Bagchi, J.K., 2008, *Regional Integration*, Mittal Publications, New Delhi.

Bergsten,C.F., 2000, The coming rise of Euro. Speech delivered on 28th January,www.ecb.net

................, 2002, The Euro versus the Dollar: Will there be a struggle for Dominance? Speech delivered on 4th January,www.ecb.net.

Bhaumik, Suman Kumar., 1999, The Euro: A brief overview , *Money and Finance*, No-8 ,Jan-Mar,78-88

Bhowmik, Debesh., 2003, *Essays on International Money*, Deep and Deep, New Delhi

...., 2003, The convergence criteria towards the Euro: An Analysis., *Vision*, Vol-XXII, No:3-4, Jan-June, 36-54

............, 2012, Analytical Framework of Euro Crisis, *International Journal of Business, Management and Social Sciences*,Vol-1,Issue 7 (III), March, 111-116

...., 2006, New Horizon in International Financial Institutions and Stability in The International Monetary System ,*Political Economy Journal Of India* ,Vol-15,Issues 3,4 ,July-December ,18-27.

........., 2003, International Financial Institutions, European Central Bank and International Monetary System, 86th *IEA Conference Volume*,Kolhapur,997-1006. published in V. Shanmugasundaram edt "*The New Institutional Economics*". Deep and Deep, NewDelhi, 2011, 288-301

....,1998, Regional Trading Blocs and International Money.-*81st Annual Conference Volume of IEA*,Bangalore, 372-384

............................,1995, Problems and prospects of Maastricht Treaty: Its impact on Indian and LIEs.(1995*) International Journal of Development Planning Literature.*Volume-10, No-3&4, July &December,93-106. And also in Raj Kumar Sen, Kartik c.Roy and Clement A. Tisdell (Ed) *World Trade and Development*(Atlantic Publishers & distributors,Delhi,1997), 114- 128

Cihak,Martin. ,Emil Stavrev,Thomas Harjes., 2009, Euro Area Monetary Policy in Uncharted Waters:Issues 2009-2185., *IMF, WP-09/185*,August

Cline,William R.,and Guntram Wolf.,2012,Resolving the European Debt Crisis, Peterson Institute for International Economics, NewYork

De Grauwe, Paul.,2000,*The Economics of Monetary Union*, OUP

Enders,Walter., 1995, *Applied Econometric Time Series*, John Wiley and Sons, USA.

Eichengreen,Barry.,1994,*International Monetary Arrangements for 21st Century*, Brooking Institution.

.........,2008, *Globalishing capital*, Princeton University Press.

.........,2011,*The Rise and Fall of the Dollar and the future of the International Monetary System*, Cambridge.

European Commission,2012, Communication from the Commission to the European Parliament and the Council :Roadmap towards a Banking Union,Brussels,12-9-2012

Fischer,Stanley.,2000,On the need for an International Lender of Last Resort, *Essays in International Economics*, No-220, November, Princeton University, New York.

Frankel, J.A.and M.Goldstein.,ed,1996, *Functioning of International Monetary System*, Vol-I and II, IMF

Grahl, John.,2012, Politics and the Euro Crisis. *Discussion Paper No-147*, Middlesex University, March.

Habermas,Jurgen.,2012,*The crisis of the European Union :A Response*,Polity Press, UK.

Hankel,Wilhelm,and Robert Isaak.,2011,*Brave New World Economy: Global Finance Threatens our Future*, John Wiley and Sons, New Jersy.

Henning,C.Randall.,1998,Europe's Monetary Union, the US and International Cooperation .Institute for International Economics. Speech delivered on 18th April,www.ecb.net.

http//europa.eu:Eurostat-*Statistical Yearbook.*

IMF,1996,*Direction of Trade Statistics*-1996

………,2007,*Direction of Trade Statistics*,2007

………,2011,*Financial Stability Report*-2011

………,1998,*International Financial Statistics*,1998

………2007,*International Financial Statistics*,2007

………,2012,*World Economic Outlook*-2012

Jackson,James K.,2010,*Financial crisis:Impact on and response by the European Union*,Diane Publishing Co.,UK

Jomo K.S.ed, 2006,*Globalisation under hegemony: The changing world economy*, OUP

Kenen,P.B.,1995,*Economic and Monetary Union in Europe:Money Beyond Maastricht*, Cambridge, UK.

Knight, Julian., 2012, *The Euro crises for Dummies*,John Wiley and Sons, UK.

Krugmam, Paul R., 2000, Currency Crises, *NBER*, University of Chicago Press.

Maddison, Angus., 2007, *Contours of the World Economy 1-2030AD:Essays in Macro-economic history*, OUP.

Marsh, David., 2011, *The Euro*,Yale University Press.

Mercier, Paul., and Francesco Papadia., 2011,*The Concrete Euro:Implementing Monetary Policy in the Euro Area*.OUP

Mundel, Robert, 1961, A Theory of Optimum Currency Areas, *American Economic Review*, 51,105-146

Langley ,Paul., 2002, *World Financial Orders: An Historical International Political Economy*, Routledge

Lynn,Mathew., 2010, *Bust Greece,the Euro and the Sovereign Debt crisis*,John Wiley and Sons, NewJersey.

Osterholt,Katharino., 2012, *Is the EU fiscal impact enough to avoid another Euro crisis*? Druck and Bindung ,Germany.

Perez-Quiros, Gabriel and Jorge Sicilia, 2002, Is the ECB predictable? *ECB,WP/192*,November

Rani,Saroj.,2009,*Regional Economic Integration: A Comparative Study of Central Asian and South Asian Regions*, Kalpaz Publications,NewDelhi.

Ross,Kelvin,2002,Market predictability of ECB policy decisions: A comparative examination, IMF, *WP/02/233*, December

Sarker, Siddhartha, ed., 2007, *Global Economic Integration and Inequality*, Serial Publications, New Delhi

Steinherr, Alfred., ed, 1994, *30 years of European Monetary Integration*, Longman, London and NewYork.

Susino-Lorca, Maria., *2010,The Euro in the 21st century:Economic crisis and Financial uproar,* Ashgate Publishing Limited,UK.

UNCTAD, 2011, *UNCTAD Report-2011*

UNCTAD, 2011, *World Investment Report-2011*

World Bank, 2012, *World Development Report-2012.*